Perspectives in American History

No. 40

THE BRITISH REGIME IN MICHIGAN
AND THE OLD NORTHWEST
1760-1796

THE BRITISH RÉGIME IN MICHIGAN AND THE OLD NORTHWEST
1760-1796

By

NELSON VANCE RUSSELL, PH.D.

PORCUPINE PRESS

First edition 1939
(Northfield: Carleton College, 1939)

Reprinted 1978 by
PORCUPINE PRESS, INC.
Philadelphia, Pennsylvania 19107

Library of Congress Cataloging in Publication Data

Russell, Nelson Vance, 1895-1951.
    The British régime in Michigan and the Old Northwest,
1760-1796.

    (Perspectives in American history ; no. 40)
    Reprint of the 1939 ed. published by Carleton College,
Northfield, Minn.
    Bibliography: p.
    Includes index.
    1.   Michigan-History — To 1837.   2.   Northwest,
Old-History.   I.   Title.   II.   Series:
Perspectives in American history (Philadelphia) ; no. 40.
F566.R87   1978   977   78-10896
ISBN 0-87991-364-9

Manufactured in the United States of America

TO MY WIFE

PREFACE

THE PURPOSE of the following study is to describe the transition from the French régime to the British, and from the British to the American in that part of the Old Northwest known as Michigan. It is understood that the word "Michigan" does not exactly correspond in territorial limits to the present State of that name. An attempt has been made to describe the political, economic, and social conditions during the period from 1760 to 1796, and especially to trace the progress of events which resulted in the overthrow of British rule and the substitution for it of a government by the United States.

In Chapters I and II, both of which are in a sense introductory, and in Chapters VIII and IX no serious effort has been made at original investigation. Nevertheless, I have sought to verify sources and secondary material, and to harmonize conflicting statements. The printed sources of value covering the period are numerous. Such publications as the *Michigan Pioneer and Historical Collections, Collections of the Illinois State Historical Library, Collections of the State Historical Society of Wisconsin,* and the *Reports of the Canadian Archives* have been invaluable. The work, as a whole, has been based, however, on manuscript sources found in various libraries and archives of the United States, Canada, and Europe. A personal search was made in the local libraries of certain middlewestern and eastern cities, as well as the Canadian Archives at Ottawa and the Public Record Office and

British Museum in London. In these archival depositories the bulk of the material was located.

A régime is defined as a "mode or system of rule or management; character of government, or of the prevailing social system." This definition applies to Michigan during the English occupation from 1760 to 1796. The British army arrived in Detroit on November 29, 1760, and at Michilimackinac in the spring of 1761. Thereafter, until the Jay Treaty in 1796, what government, civil or military, that existed was British. The prevailing social and economic system was based on the fur trade. The large traders formed a hierarchy under this system by which the small traders were governed. This era was the heyday of the fur trade. Hundreds of *voyageurs* and *engagés* came into the western woods and waters of the Great Lakes region to trade with the Indians and gain a living thereby. Closely connected to the trade was the control of the Indians. French influence remained paramount with the red men, while the Spanish in Upper Louisiana were constantly bidding for their allegiance, and later the revolting Americans made energetic efforts to gain the good-will and the co-operation of the tribes. The whole history of Michigan for the period consists of the interplay of these factors and the use made of the Indians as allies in war.

When the American War of Independence came to a close, the area of the Old Northwest was ceded by the Treaty of Paris, 1783, to the United States, but the British régime did not end. Troops continued to occupy Detroit, Michilimackinac, and other posts until 1796, and the monopoly of the British traders increased throughout the area. This brought on a series of wars with the tribesmen, which culminated in General Anthony Wayne's victory at Fallen Timbers in 1794. Soon after, in 1796, the English forces were withdrawn, thus ending the British régime.

Life in the small villages, which had been established by the French, differed little during the English period. The French settler took the oath of allegiance to the King of

England, but changed little in his language or mode of life. In the train of the British army came Scotch, English, Irish, and American fur traders who re-enforced the village groups. These, however, were not assimilated and soon dominated the political, economic and social life. If these fur barons had had their way, Michigan would have remained forever a neutral Indian State, or in the words of John Quincy Adams, a "howling wilderness" given over to Indians, wild animals, and fur traders.

The author is deeply indebted to the late Professor Claude Van Tyne, in whose seminar in American History at the University of Michigan this study was begun. I also wish to record my gratitude for helpful criticisms by the late Professor U. B. Phillips. I desire to express my thanks to Doctors Morley S. Scott and Edwin Dike, who made many helpful suggestions. The author is particularly indebted to Doctors Louise Phelps Kellogg, James Alton James, and Milo M. Quaife for their scholarly publications on the Old Northwest. Acknowledgments are also due to the Directors and the Staffs of the William L. Clements Library, the Library of the University of Michigan, and the Library of Congress, the Canadian Archives, the Public Record Office, and the British Museum. To Professor Ralph L. Henry and Miss Beatrice Wardell of Carleton College, I am grateful for intelligent assistance in editing, proof-reading, and criticizing the manuscript more than any mere formal acknowledgment can compensate. To my wife, I am under a debt of gratitude of which she and I alone know the extent.

Most of the text was written some years ago, but has been revised to date. Chapter V in somewhat different form was published in the March, 1938, issue of the *Journal* of the Illinois State Historical Society, and is republished with its kind permission. Chapters VII and X were published by the University of Michigan and are reprinted with its consent.

NELSON VANCE RUSSELL

NORTHFIELD, MINNESOTA
JUNE 30, 1939

CONTENTS

CHAPTER I

BRITISH WESTERN POLICY IN EMBRYO

"THE TRIUMPH OF WOLFE," says John Fiske, "marks the greatest turning-point as yet discernible in modern history." [1] With that event passed the old régime of France, and there was added to the British Empire a vast area peopled with savages and aliens. The ministry was now confronted with the vexatious problem of imperial organization, the necessity of strengthening the ties between the old colonies and the Mother Country, and the organization of the vast western territory. The attempts to solve these problems led directly to the War of Independence and the disruption of the Empire. The ink was scarcely dry on the Treaty of Paris when Choiseul, in a prophetic mood, said, "So we are gone; it will be England's turn next." [2]

In the early part of the seventeenth century France occupied the predominant position in Europe. The aggrandizements of Louis XIV and his ministers had seriously threatened the balance of power on the continent, while in North America the pioneers of France discovered, explored, and settled the immeasurable areas of the St. Lawrence and the Mississippi basins. To keep the English settlements between the Appalachians and the sea was the plan of the French explorers like La Salle, Iberville, and Bienville. The strategy of the French empire-builders was to have a fort at New Orleans to control

[1] John Fiske, *American Political Ideas Viewed from the Standpoint of Universal History* (New York, 1885), p. 56.
[2] Elroy M. Avery, *History of the United States and Its People from their Earliest Records to the Present Time* (Cleveland, 1904–10), IV, 351.

the Mississippi, whereas Niagara, Fort Frontenac, Montreal, and Quebec were to protect Canada. The weak point for France was the Ohio Valley. There in the middle of the eighteenth century English settlers were seeping in gradually. The final struggle for the New World was to begin in this region.[3]

The Seven Years' War radically changed the political status of North America. The territories of Canada and all of Louisiana east of the Mississippi River, except the city of New Orleans, passed to the British Crown. England also received by the terms of the treaty, the free navigation of the Mississippi and the territory of Florida, ceding Havana back to Spain.[4] Just before the definitive treaty was signed, France in a secret agreement ceded to Spain the city of New Orleans and the territory of Louisiana stretching from the Mississippi toward the Pacific.[5] The long struggle for the domination of the New World was virtually ended. England had gained an Empire! Open now to settlement was the vast region lying south and west of the Great Lakes, since known as the Old Northwest, of which Michigan was an integral part.

With these large areas added to the British dominion by the war, there came the need of some settlement of the western problem, a problem as old as European civilization in America. This problem has been likened to a rope of many strands, now twisted in a regular pattern, but more often tangled with each other and with strands from other ropes, or tortured into Gordian knots which only war could sever.[6]

Before the Seven Years' War was over, William Pitt had the greatest battle in his political career to convince the ministry and Parliament that Canada would serve the interests of the empire to a far greater extent than Guadeloupe. " Some are for keeping Canada; some Guadeloupe; who will tell me for which

[3] Francis Parkman, *Montcalm and Wolfe* (Boston, 1903), I, 39–67.

[4] The Peace of Paris was signed February 10, 1763.

[5] Text of the treaty in Adam Shortt and Arthur G. Doughty, *Documents Relating to the Constitutional History of Canada, 1759–1791* (Ottawa, 1918, hereinafter cited as *Can. Const. Docs.*), pt. i, p. 113.

[6] Samuel E. Morison, *Sources and Documents illustrating the American Revolution 1764–1788 and the formation of the Federal Constitution* (Oxford, 1923), p. xvii.

I shall be hanged for not keeping? " [7] asked Pitt as he faced the House of Commons. Before him, anxiously waiting for some decision of the problem, were the conservatives and progressives, the men who represented the sugar and fur trading merchants, the promoters of land companies, the imperialists and anti-imperialists, whose personal beliefs and private interests were greatly aroused over the question of the retention of a tropical or of a northern territory. [8] The die-hards, the conservatives, and the advocates of that dominant economic theory known as Mercantilism, were finally defeated by Pitt, who argued that Canada would furnish not only the raw products for the manufacturing interests of England, but also a market for the finished goods. The dream of the Great Commoner was to plant New Englands and to strengthen the empire.

There were powerful interests which clashed over any attempted solution of the imperial problem.[9] Each faction had its henchmen at Court and in Parliament, and whenever any scheme was proposed, bitter dissensions broke loose. Altercation followed altercation and rendered any ministerial program almost hopeless.

The largest and wealthiest of these interests was that of the fur traders. It was greatly to their advantage to keep back all settlers and leave the Indians in undisturbed possession of the vast interior. Whether the trade should be regulated by imperial, federal, or local authority, or whether the Indians should be left to the mercy of the traders, were baffling problems.

Again, the land speculators were demanding some definite program for the disposal of the public lands. By what methods should the land be acquired and disposed, by the colonies or by the imperial government?

[7] Horace Walpole, *Memoirs of George the Third* (Philadelphia, 1845), I, 26. See especially William L. Grant, " Canada versus Guadeloupe, an Episode of the Seven Years' War," *American Historical Review*, XVII, 735–43, for the story of Pitt's battle with the mercantilists.

[8] Clarence W. Alvord, *The Mississippi Valley in British Politics* (Cleveland, 1917), I, 19.

[9] The following treatment is largely based on the excellent and exhaustive study of Professor Alvord, *loc. cit.*

Also there were the "friends of the redmen," those who demanded that the Indian hunting grounds should be "reserved for them in the interests of Humanity." Should the white frontier be regulated and the backwoodsman be held within bounds? Should these vastnesses be kept, in the words of Theodore Roosevelt, "as a game preserve for squalid savages?" But English policy could not discourage English settlement.

Finally, there was in England an aggressive group called the Imperialists, who wished to spread British civilization over the world. This faction, which was powerful and well-organized, made an appeal to every patriotic Englishman of the day. No solution could possibly be reached without its approval.

The western problem of 1760 was peculiarly the problem of the region between the Alleghenies and the Mississippi, the Great Lakes and the Floridas.

Although this territory was included in several colonial charters of the seventeenth century it was not of great importance in British expansion until the second quarter of the eighteenth century. "From sea to sea, west and northwest," reads the Virginia charter of 1609.[10] The grant given to the Lords Proprietors of Carolina in 1662–1663, stated: "And to the west as far as the South Seas."[11] The Massachusetts charter of 1691 declared that that province should extend "towards the South Sea or Westward as far as our Collonyes of Rhode Island, Connecticutt and the Marragansett Countrey."[12] Other charters of an earlier date, and even as late as that of Georgia in 1732, contain similar provisions. Only vague and confused ideas of the geography of the North American continent existed in the seventeenth century.[13] The Stuarts had not the slightest conception concerning the huge grants of

[10] William MacDonald (ed.), *Documentary Source Book of American History, 1606–1898* (New York, 1911), p. 10.

[11] *Ibid.*, p. 64.

[12] *Ibid.*, p. 85.

[13] Almost as confused were the ideas of the geography of the Mississippi Valley in the eighteenth century. Bouquet to Gage, May 27, 1764, *Illinois State Historical Collections* (Springfield, 1915, hereinafter cited as *Ill. Hist. Colls.*), X, 252; George Croghan's "Journals, February 28, 1765–October 8, 1765," *ibid.*, XI, 34.

territory which the charters embraced. The " South Sea," so often spoken of, was supposed to lie very close to the Atlantic. This geographical ignorance explains the overlapping of many colonial grants and the subsequent friction entailed thereby.

Not until the eighteenth century did the English really become interested in exploring the trans-montane regions. An ephemeral attempt to cross the Appalachians was made in 1671. A small party of Virginians was sent to discover "the ebbing and flowing of the water on the other side of the mountains, in order to lead to the discovery of the South Sea." [14] Later, in the summer of 1686, Governor Thomas Dongan of New York began issuing licenses " for trading, hunting, and making discoveries to the southwest." [15] Somewhat apprehensive over the invasion of a territory belonging to a nation with which his own master was at peace, Dongan defended his act by stating that it was as fair for the English to trade with the interior Indian nations as it was for the French.[16] Some intrepid traders, accordingly, attempted to trade with the Ottawa on Lake Huron, but they fell into the hands of the French. English interest and activity in regions west of the Appalachians was largely dormant until the following century.

As long as the French remained in the Ohio Valley the English encouraged colonial expansion. The governors of Virginia as early as Governor Alexander Spotswood in 1718 wrote to the Board of Trade that if the encroachments of the French were not checked, they would soon engross the whole skin trade. The French sent out, according to Spotswood, whenever they desired, bodies of Indians to harass the back settlers. " Should they multiply their Settlements along these lakes," the Governor insisted, " they might possess themselves

---

[14] " A Journal from Virginia Beyond the Appalachian Mountains in Septr. 1671." Printed in Berthold Fernow, *The Ohio Valley in Colonial Days* (Albany, 1890), pp. 220 *et seq.*

[15] *Ibid.*, p. 66. Apparently English traders were found as far west as Michilimackinac in 1685. F. J. Turner, " The Character and Influence of the Fur Trade in Wisconsin," *Wisconsin Historical Society Proceedings* (Madison, 1889), 1889, p. 69; D. B. Martin, " The Fox River Valley in the Days of the Fur Trade," *ibid.*, (Madison, 1900), 1899, p. 120.

[16] Printed in Fernow, *The Ohio Valley in Colonial Days*, p. 66.

of any of these Plantations they pleased." [17] In order to cut off
the communication of the French between Canada and Louisiana, the Governor, after an expedition into the Ohio Valley in
1716, urged the establishment of a colony on the shores of
Lake Erie.[18] By 1720, the English realized that the French
encroachments were becoming a real menace. Governor
William Burnett of New York urgently pressed the Lords of
Trade to forestall their enemies, warning them that the English would lose the trade not only of the Mississippi Valley
but of the entire country.[19] The Marquis de la Galissonniere,
Governor of Canada, immediately after the treaty of Aix-la-
Chapelle, bent every effort to secure the trans-montane region
for his master, Louis XV.[20] The Lords of Trade, in connection
with a proposed grant to the Ohio Company in 1748, reported
that the great region lying to the west of the colony of Virginia
was distinctly of advantage in protecting the older settlements. They advocated settling the back regions in order to
check the encroachments of the French.[21] This, as well as the
cultivating of the Indian trade, was of course their major concern.[22] Governor Robert Dinwiddie made the most preposter-
ous claims for the colony of Virginia when in 1756 he wrote the
Lords of Trade that the colony of Virginia included all the
lands to the west of the Allegheny Mountains, from the northern boundary of Carolina to the southern limits of Canada.[23]
" I should gladly recommend," he wrote, " the Building of
Forts at the Extremes of the Lands that I think are indisputa-
bly the Right of the Crown of Britain." Governor Thomas
Pownall of New York also desired the establishment of western colonies as a barrier against the French.[24] No doubt this

[17] Collections of the Virginia Historical Society (N.S., Richmond, 1882–1892,
hereinafter cited as Va. Colls.), II, 296.
[18] Ibid., 297.
[19] E. B. O'Callaghan and Berthold Fernow (eds.), Documents Relating to the
Colonial History of the State of New York (Albany, 1856–1887, hereinafter cited
as N. Y. Col. Docs.), V, 576.
[20] Ibid., X, 229.
[21] Lords of Trade to the Privy Council. Printed in Fernow, Ohio Valley, pp.
245–46.
[22] Ibid.
[23] Va. Colls., IV, 339.
[24] N. Y. Col. Docs., VI, 893.

idea was in Benjamin Franklin's mind when he proposed the founding of western colonies at the Albany Congress of 1754. He saw, as in a vision, the West teeming with a flourishing population, " till they amount to perhaps a hundred millions of souls, invited to it by the pleasantness, fertility and plenty of the country." [25] Doctor John Mitchell, who had made a careful study of the American colonies, wrote in 1757: " If we consider the vast extent of those inland countries in North America and the number of natives in them with the still greater numbers of people they must maintain, the power they must necessarily give to any state possessed of them must appear to be very great." [26]

A barrier against the French was not the only motive in encouraging the extension of settlements. One of the primary considerations of all the colonial governors was the development of the fur trade. Reference has already been made to the licenses of Governor Dongan.[27] Sir William Gooch, Governor of Virginia, advised the Lords of Trade in 1747 to grant tracts of lands on the western side of the " Great Mountains," as the inhabitants could carry on an extensive skin trade with several nations of Indians who seemed willing to enter into commercial relations with them.[28] A few years later, in 1754, Dinwiddie strongly urged the British Government to establish settlements in the Ohio Valley, for the French were able through their forts to secure for themselves valuable trade in furs, which were so plentiful.[29] He believed that unless the British counteracted the depredations of the French, his countrymen might as well " bid farewell to the Furr and Skin Trade." [30]

At the conclusion of the Seven Years' War, four strategic areas in the West were still occupied by the French. There was

[25] A. H. Smyth (ed.), *Writings of Benjamin Franklin* (New York, 1905–1907), IV, 55.
[26] John Mitchell, *Contest in America Between Great Britain and France* (London, 1757), p. xvii.
[27] *Ante*, p. 7.
[28] Papers relating to the Ohio Company. Printed in Fernow, *Ohio Valley*, pp. 240 *et seq.*
[29] *Va. Colls.*, III, 95.
[30] *Ibid.*, 217.

first that emporium of the Old Northwest, Detroit, but then a village off the northwestern end of Lake Erie built by Cadillac in 1701. A second region of great importance centered around, opposite and below, the present city of St. Louis. Here a cluster of trading posts, forts, and missions, held the long line of communication between Canada and Louisiana. On the lower Wabash was still another post called Vincennes, which controlled both the Wabash and the lower Ohio trade routes. Far to the north, was the fourth strategic post of Michilimackinac at the juncture of Lakes Michigan and Huron, controlling the trade routes to the north and northwest.[31] Because of necessity or of the ingenuity of the pathfinders of New France, the sites of many of their posts are today marked by great and flourishing cities.

With the cessation of hostilities, it became necessary to take over the French posts in Michigan. Four days after the capitulation of the Marquis de Vaudreuil to Sir Jeffrey Amherst at Montreal,[32] Major Robert Rogers was dispatched by way of Niagara and Presqu' Isle to Detroit, thence to Michilimackinac and the entire Northwest, with orders to collect the arms of the inhabitants and to administer the oath of allegiance.[33] The command consisted of about two hundred Royal Rangers filling fifteen bateaux. The commander was a stalwart Ulster Scot from New Hampshire, who by his bravery had made himself the hero of the northern frontier, particularly in and around Crown Point and Ticonderoga. Major Rogers received

[31] There was also a small post on the Illinois River called Fort St. Louis, founded in 1682 approximately where Utica is today; also Ouiatanon on the upper Wabash, and St. Joseph on the St. Joseph River.

[32] Montreal surrendered September 8, 1760.

[33] W. L. Clements (ed.), *Journal of Major Robert Rogers* (Worcester, 1918), pp. 197–200. Caleb Stark, *Memoir and official correspondence of Gen. John Stark with notices of several other officers of the revolution. Also, a biography of Capt. Phinehas Stevens and of Col. Robert Rogers, with an account of his services in America during the "Seven Years' War"* (Concord, 1860), p. 468; *Michigan Pioneer and Historical Collections* (Lansing, 1877–, hereinafter cited as *Mich. Hist. Colls.*), XIX, 38–45; *Collections of the State Historical Society of Wisconsin* (Madison, 1855–, hereinafter cited as *Wis. Hist. Colls.*), XVIII, 223 *et passim; N. Y. Col. Docs.*, VII, 959; Francis Parkman, *The Conspiracy of Pontiac and the Indian War After the Conquest of Canada* (Boston, 1910), I, chap. VI; G. M. Wrong, *Canada and the American Revolution* (New York, 1935), pp. 80–86.

clothing, blankets, shoes, and other supplies at Niagara, and thence (in carrying out Amherst's orders) leaving most of his force at Presqu' Isle (now Erie), hastened with a few attendants, and visited Major General Robert Monckton at Pittsburgh, arriving October 17.[34] General Monckton reinforced him with a company of Royal Americans under the command of Captain Donald Campbell. Rejoining his forces at Presqu' Isle, he journeyed with the main body by water westward, whereas Captain Brewer went along the south shore of Lake Erie with a drove of one hundred cattle supplied by Colonel Henry Bouquet.[35] Captain Andrew Montour, with twenty Indians from the Six Nations, the Delawares, and the Shawnee, went along to protect him from the hostile tribes of the West.[36] The season was far advanced. All along the shore the woods were refulgent with autumn shades of bronze, scarlet, and gold. Rogers speaks of the dull rainy days, the chilly wind, and the stormswept lake. At last, on November 7, reaching the mouth of a river called Chogage,[37] Rogers ordered his men to make camp in the neighboring woods. Thus ventured into the vast and boundless West the first English military expedition with the distinct purpose of relieving the French of their possessions.

Not far from the site of the present city of Cleveland at noon on November 7, Rogers and his forces were met by about thirty Ottawa, carrying an English flag. After receiving a salute from the warriors, the two parties put ashore, where they shook hands, smoked, and drank. Later in the day George Croghan, the Indian agent, held a conference with the Indians, informing them of the reduction of Montreal, and the English plans for the occupation of the Northwest. Croghan assured them that they would enjoy a free trade and remain in possession of their country " as long as they adhered to his Majesty's

[34] Rogers, *Journal*, p. 209; *Mich. Hist. Colls.*, XIX, 38–49. See Monckton's orders to Rogers and Campbell, October 19, 1760, *ibid.*, 40–44.

[35] Robert Rogers, *A Concise Account of North America* (London, 1765), p. 241.

[36] Stark, *Memoir*, p. 474.

[37] Croghan calls this stream the "Onchuago." It is the Grand River whose Indian name was "Chaeaga." Croghan makes this the 5th.

interest." [38] The Indians expressed their pleasure in seeing the British and asked that they be forgiven for serving the French as they were obliged to get their supplies from them. " It was necessity and not choice that made them take part with the French," they explained. After furnishing the braves with guns, ammunition, and some flour, which Rogers supplied Croghan " for the good of his Majestys Indian Interest," the expedition continued on its way to Detroit. [39]

Rogers gives a different account of these conferences and of his first meeting with the Pontiac. [40] He relates that not far from the present city of Cleveland he was met by a body of Ottawa, who informed him that he was in the territory of their great chief Pontiac, who was " lord of the country," and advised him to halt until their great leader arrived. When Pontiac appeared he demanded to know the object of the journey and how the English dared to enter the country without his consent. [41] Rogers replied that the French " who had been an obstacle to our way to mutual peace and commerce " had surrendered Canada to the English, and that he had come to take possession of the country with no hostile intent toward the Indians. [42] Belts of wampum were exchanged, and Pontiac advised the English to go no farther without leave. Before withdrawing to his own camp, he asked the English whether there was anything they needed that he might supply. The Major replied that any provisions they bought would be paid for gladly. On the following morning several bags of parched corn, venison, and wild turkeys were received as an evidence of the great chief's friendship. [43]

Rogers further relates in his *Journal* that at the second meeting:

[38] Croghan, " Journal," November 5, 1760.

[39] Rogers in his *Journal* makes this meeting the seventh of November. This is the traditional meeting with Pontiac which Parkman so graphically described. Possibly Croghan's simple account is truer to the actual facts.

[40] Rogers, *Concise Account;* Rogers, *Journal;* Parkman, *Conspiracy of Pontiac,* I, 165; II, appendix B.

[41] Rogers, *Journal*, pp. 214–15.

[42] Rogers, *A Concise Account*, p. 241.

[43] *Ibid.*, p. 241.

He gave me the pipe of peace, and both of us by turns smoked it; and he assured me he had made peace with me and my detachment; that I might pass thro' his country unmolested, and relieve the French garrison; and that he would protect me and my party from any insults that might be offered or intended by the Indians; and as an earnest of his friendship, he sent 100 warriors to protect and assist us in driving 100 fat cattle, which he had brought for the use of the detachment from Pittsburg, by the way of Presque Isle. He likewise sent to the several Indian towns on the south-side and west-end of Lake Erie, to inform them that I had his consent to come into the country. He attended me constantly after this interview till I arrived at Detroit, and while I remained in the country, and was the means of preserving the detachment from the fury of the Indians, who had assembled at the mouth of the strait with an intent to cut us off.[44]

During the journey from the Grand River to Detroit, Rogers had several conferences with Pontiac, who showed a thirst for knowledge and great strength of judgment.[45]

The " lord of the west " was greatly interested in the English methods of manufacturing iron, cloth, etc., and was hopeful some day to visit England. He even offered Rogers a part of his vast dominion if he would conduct him there.[46]

He assured me that he was inclined to live peaceably with the English while they used him as he deserved, and to encourage their settling in his country; but intimated, that, if they treated him with neglect, he would shut up the way, and exclude them from it; in short, his whole conversation sufficiently indicated that he was far from considering himself as a conquered Prince, and that he expected to be treated with the respect and honor due to a King or Emperor, by all who came into his country, or treated with him.[47]

Thus Rogers explains Pontiac's offer of peace. Just what motives did impel Pontiac, the former close ally of the French, to renounce his friends? Parkman explains this on the ground that Pontiac was shrewd, politic, and ambitious, and although ignorant of much that was passing in the world, yet he could clearly see that the French power was on the wane. By making friends of the English he hoped to gain powerful allies, who

[44] *Ibid.*, pp. 241–42.
[45] *Ibid.*, p. 242.
[46] *Ibid.*
[47] *Ibid.*, p. 243.

would aid his ambitious projects. In this he was doomed to disappointment.[48] Another explanation was made to Major Henry Gladwin in Detroit by a close friend of Pontiac's. This Frenchman said that Pontiac had gone to Fort Pitt sometime before Rogers' journey and asked the commander what treatment the Indians would receive if the English won. They were told that:

All the Rivers would flow with Rum—that Presents from the Great King were to be unlimited—that all sorts of Goods were to be in the Utmost Plenty and so cheap, as a Blanket for two Beavers—four Raccoons, for a Beaver, with many other fair Promises, which they told in the Settlement on their Return with much Joy: in consequence of which, they allowed Rogers with a handful of Men to take Possession of the Fort and Colony, receiving them with Joy and using Monsieur Bellistre with much disrespect.[49]

Rogers was now entering uncertain territory. Sieur de Bellestre,[50] the French commandant at Detroit, was a capable officer and felt that his post was secure against any force. All during the war most of the fighting had occurred in the East, and none of the western posts had been molested. Far away from the stirring scenes of carnage, the French soldier and officer out on the frontier were aware only of the general course of events, and were largely ignorant of the more recent happenings. The various Indian tribes of the upper lake region, such as the Ottawa, Hurons, Potawatomi, and Wyandot were strongly attached to the French. " Those untutored children of the forest " were not familiar with the chess games the crowned heads of Europe played in which vast areas changed hands because of the failure of an inefficient leader or a royal mistress. " They did not wear their allegiance like a cloak to be changed with the fashion of the day." The very name English was repugnant to these Indians, for they associated them with

[48] Parkman, *Conspiracy of Pontiac*, I, 174.

[49] Tadeau to Gladwin, December 24, 1763, Canadian Archives, Indian Papers, IX, 26. " In about a year after Pontiac in particular had been heard to Complain, and say the English were Liars, which Opinion then became general." He felt the English made promises only to blindfold and delude the Indians. *Ibid.*

[50] Also, spelled Bellettre, Belestre, Belester. Belêtre. John Porteous, Diary of Siege of Detroit in 1763 (MS. in Detroit Public Library), gives an interesting account of Bellestre's actions.

the Iroquois, who had relentlessly made war upon the western Indians, carrying off their women and children, destroying their habitations, and plundering their crops. To allow this hated race to have control of their lands was far from welcome.

Upon reaching the mouth of the Detroit River, Major Rogers sent Lieutenant Dietrich Brehm with a message for the French commandant, informing him of the surrender of Canada, and that the English were approaching his post.[51] Bellestre asked for time, and in high dudgeon tried to rouse the fury of the Indians. Among other devices, he had a pole erected with the effigy of a man's head on the top. Upon this was a crow that was supposed to be scratching the brains out of the man's head. He then explained to the assembled tribes that this was indicative of the way he would treat the English if they continued their journey. The Indians were quite dubious and felt that the English would be more apt to reverse the act and scratch out the brains of the French.[52]

Major Rogers, continuing slowly up the river, sent Captain Campbell with a copy of the capitulation of Canada, and a letter from de Vaudreuil, directing that Detroit be given up. Bellestre, seeing his allies were failing him, was forced to yield, and in a very ill humor, asked for the terms of de Vaudreuil's capitulation and for his instructions. Rogers replied that the conditions of the capitulation were:

Particularly advantageous to Detroit, that all persons, even soldiers, were to retain their property, real and personal, including their peltries; that the soldiers were to be allowed to delegate to some resident the care of their property or to sell it to either the French or English, or they might take with them their portable property. They were to lay down their arms and agree not to serve again during the war.[53]

The English moved up the river to within a half mile of the fort, and encamped in a field on the opposite shore. There had

[51] Rogers, *Journal*, p. 215.
[52] *Ibid.*, p. 216.
[53] *Ibid.*, pp. 217, 222–26. The correspondence between Bellestre and Rogers is printed in J. H. Lanman, *The History of Michigan, Civil and Topographical* (New York, 1839), pp. 40–42; Canadian Archives, C. O. 5, LXI, *passim;* Rogers, *Journal*, pp. 217 ff.

been a rumor (no doubt begun by Bellestre) that the Indians following the English were bent upon plunder, and so the French and Indians were armed for self-protection. Soon after their landing, Bellestre, realizing the futility of holding out longer, sent a messenger to Rogers announcing the surrender of the fort. The French soldiery, much to their commander's chagrin and to the great amazement of the Indians, were marched out of the fort. Their arms were stacked, and they themselves were sent off as prisoners under the charge of Ensign Robert Holmes (with twenty rangers) to Pittsburgh, then New York and finally France.[54] The Canadian militia was also disarmed and disbanded, after taking the oath of allegiance.[55] With military honors the *Fleur-de-lis,* which for fifty-nine years had waved over the fort, was lowered with a "burst of triumphant yells," and the Cross of St. George, the symbol of a new régime, rose aloft in the breeze. This occurred on November 29, 1760, the beginning of Great Britain's domination over the Old Northwest.[56]

Major Rogers, after making a treaty with the neighboring tribes, and dispatching twenty men to escort the French units at the posts of Miami and Ouiatanon to Detroit, set out for Michilimackinac. The ice in Lake Huron completely obstructed his passage; and learning from the Indians that he could not reach the post by land without snowshoes, he returned to Detroit, where he replaced the ammunition and stores he had taken with him.[57] On December 23, 1760, he turned over the command of the fort to Captain Campbell and set out for Fort Pitt.[58] The posts of St. Joseph, Sault Ste. Marie, Michilimackinac, and Green Bay remained in the

[54] *Ibid.,* p. 229. Bellestre served notably in the British army during the War of Independence, particularly in opposing the American invasion at St. Jean, for which he received public thanks from the commanding general.

[55] This oath is found in the Canadian Archives, C.O. 5, LXI, pt. i, 292, and is published in *Mich. Hist. Colls.,* XIX, 42–43. Amherst wrote Sir William Johnson, February 14, 1761, of Rogers' work and said, "The Indians had come in and behaved remarkably well." Five hundred French took the oath. Canadian Archives, C. O. 5, LXI, pt. i, 291.

[56] The Indians were amazed that so many men would surrender to so few. *Ibid.*

[57] *Ibid.,* 230.

[58] *Ibid.,* 231.

hands of the French throughout the winter. Early in 1761, a unit of Royal Americans took possession of them; and thus passed the last vestige of French political control in Michigan.[59]

Now that the war was successfully ended, and the posts of Michigan occupied, the British ministry was confronted with the most important economic problem for Michigan: the regulation of the fur trade. We have described how Pitt convinced the Commons that the possession of Canada would be an asset of more distinct value than would Guadeloupe. Now the choice had to be justified![60] An illimitable waste country was a valuable acquisition only because of its trade. England must " render these acquisitions as beneficial in traffic as they were extensive in territory."[61] The sole source of immediate wealth was the fur trade. Indeed, many of the colonists believed that Great Britain had deliberately caused the Seven Years' War because " France had got the ascendant over the natives, and commanded the Fur Trade." " This," said Silas Deane, " is well known to have been the real ground of the last war."[62] According to the trade acts, furs were in the class of " enumerated articles," which could be exported only to a British port. The dominant economic theory of the eighteenth century was that colonies were of value only if they produced something that the Mother Country could not produce. This theory, known as Mercantilism, was based on the assumption that gold was the basis of a nation's wealth. Thus if the colony furnished those products which the mother country did not grow, that would leave more gold in the home coffers. This mercantilist policy would be frustrated if the Indians refused to sell their furs to the English and instead exported them to foreign ports. The English manufacturers, the exchequer, the

[59] *Ibid.* See especially Parkman, *Conspiracy of Pontiac*, I, chap. VI, for the story of Rogers' expedition; and C. P. Lucas, *A History of Canada, 1763–1812* (Oxford, 1909), pp. 11–13.
[60] *Ante*, p. 4; *Annual Register for 1763* (London, sixth edition, 1810), pp. 19 ff.
[61] *Ibid.*, p. 18.
[62] Memoir of Silas Deane to the French Foreign Office. Printed in *Collections of New York Historical Society for 1886* (New York, 1887, hereinafter cited as *N. Y. Hist. Colls.*), p. 272.

shipping interests, and the public would thus secure no value. Even the possession of the West would be of little benefit and the war would have been fought in vain.

The French had won the affections of the Indians by their " pliability and temperance," and had cemented this influence by religious instruction. They seldom appeared to the Indians as rulers and masters, but rather as companions and friends. The French traders were successful because of their consideration for the Indians but not the English. The French had always been liberal in their gifts to the red men, who in turn looked upon the gifts as tokens of friendship. General Amherst, as soon as victory seemed secure, cut off the usual gifts, or ordered the costly practice reduced to the smallest possible amount.[63] The parsimony of the English caused great hardships among the Indians, who never thought of the morrow, but, when plentifully supplied, lived riotously. When there was nothing to eat or wear, they suffered from hunger and cold in a land of plenty. Even the English officers sold the articles necessary for the Indians' welfare at exorbitant prices.[64]

Another grievance of the Indians was the bad character of many of the English traders.[65] Some of the English traders and some who were in their employ were villains of the worst kind " who vied with each other in rapacity, violence, and profligacy. They cheated, cursed, and plundered the Indians, and outraged their families." [66] It has been altogether too " fre-

[63] Amherst to Bouquet, January 16, 1762. *Mich. Hist. Colls.*, XIX, 127–28, Canadian Archives, *Report for 1889*, pp. 16, 18; *N. Y. Col. Docs.*, VII, 547, 569. Bouquet informed Amherst in January of 1763 that discontent was created among the Indians by the suppression of presents. Amherst replied that he was unwilling to give any presents, " by way of Bribes, for if they do not behave properly they are to be punished." Later he wrote: " You will of course order Capt. Ecuyer . . . not to give those who are able to provide for their Families, any encouragement to Loiter away their time in Idleness about the Fort." Amherst to Bouquet, February 16, 1763, *Mich. Hist. Colls.*, XIX, 178; Parkman, *Conspiracy of Pontiac*, I, 181; William Kingsford, *The History of Canada* (Toronto, 1887), V, 5–8.

[64] In a Conference at Johnson Hall on July 7, 1765, the Shawnee, Mingo, and Delaware Indians claimed that the English took six raccoons for one beaver, while the French took only four. Canadian Archives. Indian Papers, IX, 36.

[65] On the other hand some of the most estimable characters of Canadian and Michigan history were traders: such as James McGill, Isaac Todd, Alexander Henry, George Croghan, John Duncan, John Askin, Alexander Mackenzie, and many others.

[66] Parkman, *Conspiracy of Pontiac*, I, 182.

quent heretofore for the Traders to impose upon the Indians in the Price of their Goods," wrote Governor Spotswood as early as 1716.[67] Governor Dinwiddie attributed the Indians' lack of faith in the English to the traders whom he describes in no uncertain terms as " the most abandoned Wretches in the World, and in respect to Society, as uncivilized as the Indians themselves, and less to be trusted in regard to Truth and Probity." [68] Governor Cadwallader Colden called the traders " men of low or bad character " and urged some definite Indian policy.[69] General James Murray in his report to the Lords of Trade referred to the traders as men who "have failed in other countries. All have their fortune to make, and little solicitous about the means, provided the end is obtained."[70] Henry Hamilton, after considerable experience in handling Indian affairs, described the traders as " the Most Worthless vagabonds imaginable, they are fugitives (in general) from lower Canada, or the colonies who fly from their Debtors, or the law, and being proficients in all sorts of vice and debauchery corrupt the morals of the savage." [71] General Thomas Gage was very bitter in his denunciation of them. He described them to Lord Shelburne as a set of people, for the most part, as wild as the country they go in, or the people they deal with, and often far more vicious and wicked.[72] Such men naturally " could not fail of impressing the Indians with very bad Sentiments of all white People in general, of whom they took these Traders to be true Samples," as they have been " in general the most worthless and abandoned fellows in the Provinces." [73] Indeed the traders may be described as hard, cruel, and stern men, " who

[67] *Va. Colls.*, II, 145.
[68] *Ibid.*, IV, 340.
[69] *N. Y. Hist. Colls.* for 1876, p. 383.
[70] Canadian Archives, Q, II, 378.
[71] *Ibid.*, XII, 212. Major Robert Mathews in 1787 described the traders at Detroit as, " the lowest of all the profession resort to these obscure places, they are without education or sentiment many of them without common honesty." See Mathews to Frederick Haldimand, August 3, 1787, *Mich. Hist. Colls.*, XX, 288.
[72] Gage to Shelburne, February 22, 1767. C. E. Carter, *Correspondence of Thomas Gage with the Secretaries of State, 1763–1765* (New Haven, 1931), I, 124; Canadian Archives, Dartmouth Transcripts, 1765–1775, p. 66.
[73] This was the keen observation of Shelburne. Shelburne Papers, LX, 135. These papers are in the W. L. Clements Library of the University of Michigan.

had no compunction in obtaining money." On the other hand they were courageous, resolute, determined, and undaunted in the greatest danger, with a keen love for adventure. They never " shrunk from any alternative by which their ends would be gained." [74] They cheated the Indians right and left. Deceiving in the weight of their merchandise, doubling the price of goods to be sold, selling water for rum, using false weights, getting the Indians intoxicated, and then having them subscribe their names to land deeds, were only a few of the methods used.[75]

Chief among the many abuses committed by the unscrupulous traders was their gaining an advantage over the " children of the forest " with an excessive use of liquor. Incredible quantities of spirits were consumed, amounts inconceivable in this age of sobriety and temperance. With only slight exaggeration did Major Rogers picture this abominable practice in his tragedy *Ponteach*, with the following trenchant verses:

A thousand opportunities present
To take advantage of their ignorance;
But the great engine I employ is rum,
More pow'rful made by certain strengthening drugs
This I distribute with a lib'ral hand
Urge them to drink till they grow mad and valiant;
Which makes them think me generous and just,
And gives full scope to practice all my art.
I then begin my trade with water's dum,
The cooling draught well suits their scorching throats.
Their fur and peltry come in quick return;
My scales are honest, but so well contriv'd
That one small slip will turn three pounds to one;
Which they, poor silly souls! ignorant of weights
And rules of balancing, do not perceive.[76]

The Indian superintendent, the military officers, the colonials,

[74] *N. Y. Col. Docs.*, VII, 689, 836, 929, 955, 960, 964, 987; Thomas Pownall, *The Administration of the British Colonies* (London, 1765), II, 187–90; *Mich. Hist. Colls.*, XIX, 297; XX, 288; " Journal of Henry Hay," in *Wisconsin Historical Society Proceedings* (Madison, 1874 *et seq.*, hereinafter cited as *Wis. Hist. Soc. Proc.*), 1914, p. 244; Kingsford, *History of Canada*, V, 121; G. L. Beer, *British Colonial Policy, 1754–1765* (New York, 1907), chap. XII.

[75] *N. Y. Col. Docs.*, VII, 955, *et seq.*

[76] Rogers, *Ponteach, or The Savages of America* (Chicago, 1914), Act I, scene i, pp. 180–81; Parkman, *Conspiracy of Pontiac*, II, appendix B, 345.

and the ministries knew that such practices existed. Major Gladwin realized full well the awful toll that rum took among the Indians. After the Pontiac uprising, he wrote Amherst that if he intended punishing the Indians for their barbarities, " it may easier be done without any expense to the crown, by permitting a free sale of rum, which will destroy them more effectively than fire and sword." [77] This total failure to care for the rights of the natives could have no other result than the breeding of the deepest rancor, ready to burst into actual flames.

Not only were the traders hated by the Indians because of their arrogant, insolent, cheating methods, but equal opprobrium was directed against the officers and soldiers at the posts. During the French régime, whenever native warriors of distinction came to the forts they were welcomed and given every attention and respect. The subtlety and suavity of the French were large factors in promoting cordial relations.[78] British soldiers were often very brutal and uncivil. With oaths, menaces, and sometimes blows, the Indians were kept at a safe distance. The officers with cold demeanor and harsh words, never overlooking any inconvenience the presence of the " child of the forest " occasioned, made no attempt to learn their language and customs. There is no doubt that the French traders through misrepresentation of the English had long before the Seven Years' War created a genuine distrust amounting to hate.[79] Traders, *habitants, coureurs de bois,* all classes of the French population, in fact, dispersed themselves among

[77] Gladwin MSS., *Mich. Hist. Colls.,* XXVII, 675. This only shows the great havoc wrought by the huge consumption of rum. It was not Gladwin's idea to destroy the Indians by this method as the full quotation will show. Such an impression is left by Parkman.

[78] One must keep in mind that only the methods of the French differed from those of the English, for as a class the French merchants were probably just as dishonest or more so. New France was honeycombed with corruption and the trader was not immune. See Francis Parkman, *The Old Régime in Canada* (Boston, 1874), *passim.*

[79] Canadian Archives, C.O. 5, LXXXVI, 125; *N. Y. Col. Docs.,* VII, 525, 575, 689, 961; VIII, 85; E. B. O'Callaghan, *Documentary History of the State of New York* (Albany, 1849–1851, hereinafter cited as *Doc. Hist. of N. Y.*), II, 419; Lucas, *History of Canada, 1763 to 1812,* p. 10; Canadian Archives, C. O. 5, LXIII, pt. i, 310.

the Indians, holding secret councils with them, urging them to take arms against the English. The Indians listened attentively to the tales of the French *voyageurs,* and contrasted the French kindliness and friendliness with the British " grasping rudeness " and hauteur. The Englishmen were pictured in the worst light — falsehoods, calumnies, misrepresentations, nothing was omitted.[80] The excited Indians feared their race was to be uprooted, and they were to be hemmed in by forts and destroyed.[81] The fabrication which gained the widest credence was that the French king had been asleep, and during his slumbers the English had seized Canada, but now having awakened he was sending his ships and armies up the St. Lawrence and Mississippi to drive out " the red-coated dogs." [82] Arms, ammunition, provisions, and large quantities of rum were freely distributed. This again was in contrast with General Amherst's penurious policy. [83] Sir Guy Carleton well described the French methods of treating the Indians in a letter to Shelburne, March 2, 1768:

The System pursued by the French Government in Indian Affairs, was mostly according to the Discretion of Their Officers, who learned the language of the Natives, acted as Magistrates, compelled the Traders to deal equitably and distributed the King's presents; by this Conduct they avoided giving Jealousy and gained the affections of an ignorant, credulous, and brave People, whose ruling Passions are Independence, Gratitude, and Revenge, with an unconquerable Love of strong Drink, which must prove destructive to them and the Fur Trade, if permitted to be sent among them. Thus managing them by Address, where Force could not avail,

[80] " Journal of Thomas Morris," in R. G. Thwaites, *Early Western Travels* (Cleveland, 1904–1906), I, 30 ff.; " Journal of George Croghan," *ibid.,* 144 ff.

[81] Canadian Archives, C. O. 5, LXXXIII, pt. i, p. 53.

[82] Johnson to Amherst, July 11, 1763, *N. Y. Col. Docs.,* VIII, 532; Pownall, *Administration of the Colonies,* I, 187–90; John Rutherford's " Journal," Canadian Archives, M, 97; Canadian Archives, C. O. 5, LXXXIII, pt. i, p. 52.

[83] *N. Y. Col. Docs.,* VII, 547, 787, 929, 953 ff.; " Journal of Lieut. James Gorrell," *Wis. Hist. Colls.,* I, 25; *N. Y. Hist. Colls. 1876,* p. 269; *Ill. Hist. Colls.,* X, 50; *Mich. Hist. Colls.,* XVII, 653; Parkman, *Conspiracy of Pontiac,* I, 185; Alvord, *Mississippi Valley,* I, 186–87. Sir William Johnson considered Amherst's economy measures far more expensive in the long run. He wrote: " If we conquer their [Indians] prejudices by our generosity they will lay aside their Jealousys & we may rest in security. This is much cheaper than any other plan & certain of success." Johnson to Lords of Trade, August 30, 1764, *N. Y. Col. Docs.,* VII, 648; *Ill. Hist. Colls.,* X, 307.

they reconciled them to their Troops, and by Degrees strengthened the Posts of Niagara, Detroit, and Michilimackinac, without giving offense.[84]

The Indians were no doubt very troublesome and annoying because of their intrusive nature, but whenever they were found " lounging . . . about the fort or lazily reclining in the shadow of the walls, they were met with muttered ejaculations of impatience, or abrupt orders to be gone, enforced, perhaps, by a touch from the butt of a sentinel's musket. These marks of contempt were unspeakably galling to their haughty spirit." [85]

The cause most conducive to the growing discontent of the Indians was the ever-constant intrusion of settlers upon their lands. The colonial, feeling himself destined to march from ocean to ocean, with his face toward the setting sun, hungry for land, never tolerated any opposition to his desires. This movement was only prophetic of the nineteenth century westward march, which almost annihilated the red man. Many colonials felt crowded if they had neighbors within twenty miles. The Indians were greatly concerned over the steady movement of the white men, who by 1763 had extended their settlements beyond the Susquehanna, and were rapidly crossing the Alleghenies, " eating away the forest like a spreading canker." [86]

The Indians beheld in every garrison the germ of a future colony. When they " saw the French power, as it were, annihilated in North America, they began to imagine that they ought to have made greater and earlier efforts in their favour. . . . The French seemed more intent on trade than settlement," wrote the editor of the *Annual Register*. " Finding themselves infinitely weaker than the English, they supplied, as well as they could, the place of strength by policy, and paid a much more flattering and systematic attention to the Indians than we had ever done. Our superiority in this war rendered our

[84] Canadian Archives, Q, V, pt. i, p. 383
[85] Parkman. *Conspiracy of Pontiac*, I, 182–83.
[86] *Ibid.*; Theodore Roosevelt, *Winning of the West* (New York, 1889), I, *passim*.

regard to this people still less, which had always been too little." [87]

Sir William Johnson wrote as early as 1756 to the Board of Trade that " scattered settlements beginning to crowd upon the Indians had been a long eye-sore to them, infected them with a jealousy and disgust towards the English." [88] His attitude was ever watchful over Indian affairs, and the maltreatment of his wards by the frontiersmen greatly aroused his ire. " The Frontier Inhabitants, who seem regardless of the Laws and not only perpetrate murders whenever opportunity offers," wrote Sir William, " but think themselves at liberty to make settlements where they please ... bid defiance to Authority ..., for neither presents, fair speeches, and promises can reconcile the Indians to bear such encroachments and insults." [89] " It does appear to us," reads a report of the Board of Trade, in 1768, " that the extension of the fur trade depends entirely on the Indians being undisturbed in the possession of their hunting grounds; that all colonizing does in its nature, and must in its consequences operate to the prejudice of that branch of commerce." [90] At the close of the Seven Years' War, the Lords of Trade proposed that the King should issue a proclamation that no grants of land or any settlement could be made within certain fixed bounds, leaving all the territory free hunting grounds for the Indian Nations, and for the trade of all English subjects. [91] Thus it would seem that the British point of view was to restrict settlements, and definitely regulate the fur trade. But the Indians were ripe for revolt, and unsubdued, as their countrymen farther east had been; finding a strong man of their own race to lead them, they tried conclusions with the dominant white race in North America. [92] It

[87] *Annual Register for 1763*, p. 22.
[88] O'Callaghan, *Doc. Hist. of N. Y.*, II, 419.
[89] *N. Y. Col. Docs.*, VII, 836, 956, 987.
[90] Canadian Archives, C. O. 5, LXIX, 169; *N. Y. Col. Docs.*, VIII, 30; Morison, *Sources and Documents*, p. 73.
[91] Lords of Trade to Johnson, August 5, 1763, *N. Y. Col. Docs.*, VII, 535; *Ill. Hist. Colls.*, X, 18.
[92] Lucas, *History of Canada*, p. 11.

seemed to them that designs had been formed to drive them from their lands. If they remained, slavery would ensue; if they resisted, they would be exterminated.[93]

The British government had turned its attentions to the western problem early in the Seven Years' War. General Edward Braddock, "that ill-starred soldier," had laid the foundations of an imperialistic program by appointing two colonials of rare acumen in Indian affairs, Sir William Johnson and Edmund Atkin,[94] as superintendents of the northern and southern Indians, with the Ohio River dividing, in a general way, their spheres of jurisdiction. The excellent work of these men was largely undone by the parsimony of Amherst, the land-hungry frontiersmen, and the arrogant, cruel traders. To Amherst the Indians were " pernicious vermin " and an " execrable race " who might best be put out of the way by presents of blankets inoculated with smallpox, or might be hunted with dogs, with a view to annihilation.[95] Johnson and John Stuart (the successor of Atkin) were greatly handicapped because they lacked sufficient power to carry out any effective program. They were expected to protect the rights of the Indians, and also to give the imperial government all necessary information of western affairs. In 1761, because, to a large extent, of Johnson's influence, the sale and control of Indian lands, the red man's greatest grievance, was taken out of the

[93] Canadian Archives, C. O. 5, LXXXIII, pt. i, p. 53.
[94] Soon replaced by John Stuart.
[95] Amherst to Bouquet, quoted in Edward Channing, *A History of the United States* (New York, 1905), III, 27–28. Amherst wrote: " Could it not be contrived to send the Small Pox among those disaffected tribes of Indians? We must on this occasion use every strategem in our power to reduce them." To this Bouquet replied: " I will try to inoculate th— with some blankets that may fall in their hands, and take care not to get the disease myself. As it is a pity to expose good men against them, I wish we could make use of the Spanish method, to hunt them with English dogs, supported by rangers and some light horse, who would, I think, effectually extirpate or remove that vermin." Amherst rejoined: " You will do well to try to inoculate the Indians by means of blankets, as well as to try every other method that can serve to extirpate this execrable race. I should be very glad your scheme for hunting them down by dogs would take effect, but England is at too great a distance to think of that at the present." British Museum, Additional MSS., Bouquet and Haldimand Papers, 21,634. Also quoted in Parkman, *Conspiracy of Pontiac*, II, 44–5. There is no direct evidence that Bouquet put such a disgraceful plan into effect.

hands of the colonial executives, and placed under imperial control.[96] Thus some constructive work was really accomplished before the treaty of Paris was signed.

Another outstanding decision was reached during the winter of the epochal years of 1762–1763. A British army of twenty battalions, under the control of General Amherst, was to remain in America to protect the West against foreign and Indian enemies, and also to hold the new French and Spanish subjects under control.[97] Amherst determined to scatter the units in rather small detachments. The largest consisted of seven hundred and fifty men stationed at Quebec. Other forces were located at Montreal, Niagara, Pensacola, St. Augustine, Detroit, and in Nova Scotia, South Carolina, and the Lower Mississippi. Again these detachments were split up into many units to protect several posts within a district; for instance, the soldiers in the Detroit area were also to garrison the posts of Michilimackinac, of Miami, and a fort at the mouth of the Illinois River.[98] It thus appears that the ministry had reversed their former policy, and now hoped to develop the West rapidly by colonization: to colonize from the west eastward, since the boundaries would in this way be more easily protected from attack.

This decision to maintain a standing army in America brought forth issues " concealed in the womb of time " that were largely responsible for the War of Independence. It was humanly impossible for any ministry, so far removed from the scenes of conflict, to foretell what radical ideas would spring from the attempt to raise funds to maintain an army in the West. Michigan, so far removed from ministerial conflicts, indirectly played a notable part in the taxation problem, which led directly to the War for American Independence.

[96] Shortt and Doughty, *Can. Const. Docs.*, pt. i, p. 94. England also had in mind the protection of the trade interests, and maintaining the older colonies in a state of constitutional dependence upon the mother country. The idea of using the army to maintain the supremacy over the colonies became general, however, only at a later date, when it was readily seen that the distribution of troops in small units would not serve that purpose. Beer, *British Colonial Policy 1754–1765*, p. 266.

[97] Shelburne Papers, LXIX, 645; *Ill. Hist. Colls.*, X, 5–11.

[98] *Ibid.*, 6–8.

The solution of these many complex problems for Michigan and the West was well-nigh impossible. In England, ministry followed ministry so rapidly after 1760 that no constructive program could be worked out. Perhaps the only official who seemed to grasp the magnitude of the imperial problem was Lord Shelburne, who on April the twenty-third, 1763, became president of the Board of Trade in the Grenville Ministry. This "ablest and most accomplished minister of the eighteenth century," upon assuming office, gathered together with meticulous care all the available information on the West.[99] With great acumen and sagacity he arrived at a judicious decision of vital importance in Michigan history, which, if carried out, might have changed the whole course of American history.

The Lords of Trade found that there were three main issues to solve. First, the difficulty growing out of the presence of the army in the colonies. Just where was it to be stationed, and who should pay for its maintenance? [100] Next was the organization of the Indian Department, which had been rather well developed by Sir William Johnson. Last (and this proved to be the hardest nut to crack), was the establishment of a white frontier. This was of great concern to Michigan for if a line were drawn far to the east her future development would be greatly jeopardized. Everyone was agreed on the vital necessity of such a boundary, but as to the location of the line, there were many conflicting views. Should it be the natural boundary of the Appalachian watershed, or lie much farther to the west? Was a boundary once established unalterable? Did it create a perpetual Indian reservation? All these problems and many more of great concern to the West faced the young president of the Board of Trade.[101]

[99] This was Disraeli's opinion and is quoted in Alvord's *Mississippi Valley in British Politics*, p. 141. Quite a different opinion of Shelburne is given by R. A. Humphreys, in "Lord Shelburne and the Proclamation of 1763," *English Historical Review* (London, 1934), April, 1934.
[100] Alvord, *Mississippi Valley*, I, 162–63. For a thorough and scholarly account of Shelburne's work, see Lord Edward Fitzmaurice, *Life of William, Earl of Shelburne* (London, 1912), especially I, chap. IV.
[101] Shelburne was only twenty-six when he assumed this very responsible position. *Ibid.*, I, 173 ff.

Lord Egremont, Secretary of State, brought the attention of the Lords of Trade to the American problem, in a letter of May 5, 1763, in which he asked for information as to what new governments should be established in the West, what military forces would be deemed necessary, and what methods should be used to get the colonies to help contribute to the support of the troops. While at the same time to preserve peace it was necessary to reconcile the Indians; their territories were to be purchased at an honest price.[102]

At once Lord Shelburne, who dominated the Lords of Trade, concentrated all of his energy upon these questions, spending a month in further investigation. On all issues, he seemed to follow intelligent American opinion. He was an ardent expansionist and fully realized the futility of holding in check the white frontier. The pushing of the frontier westward, he realized, was only a natural operation which would come in due season from the " womb of time." He was opposed to centralization of Indian affairs, preferring to leave the questions which arose out of the white man's contact with the redman to the colonials. A British army was necessary for the protection of the West, he felt, but its maintenance should at first be provided for by the mother country.

In accordance with Shelburne's ideas and following Egremont's suggestions closely, the Lords of Trade formulated their report in June, and sent it to the ministry.[103] A careful analysis of this work shows a definite knowledge of colonial affairs, certainly an appreciation for the need of reconciling the westward expansion of the colonies with Indian protection. The Lords of Trade proposed a boundary line to be drawn from the northeast to the southwest along the crest of the Appalachian highlands but to zig-zag east and west so as to include all the white settlements beyond the mountains. It

---

[102] Shortt and Doughty, *Can. Const. Docs.,* pt. i, pp. 127–28. Egremont enclosed a paper of " Hints relative to the Division and Government of the conquered and newly acquired Countries in America." This document was discovered, identified, and printed by V. W. Crane, *Mississippi Valley Historical Review* (Cedar Rapids, 1922), VIII, 367 ff.

[103] Shortt and Doughty, *Can. Const. Docs.,* pt. i, pp. 132 ff.

was to be drawn in such a way as to protect the whites from Indian attacks and the latter from illegal encroachments.[104] Shelburne saw the futility of a boundary which did not include the area around the forks of the Ohio River, and farther south in Tennessee, an area already owned by land companies made up of Englishmen and Americans.[105] The immediate need of this boundary line was to pacify the Indians, for already the ministry was aware of the growing Indian dissatisfaction. Beyond this line, no settlement was to be made until a legitimate title to the land had been purchased by an imperial official. This would mean that Michigan and all of the Old Northwest would be left as a temporary Indian reservation, and such was Shelburne's plan.[106] This may be explained by the great ignorance among all officials concerning the geography of the West.[107] Shelburne must have known that troops had been dispatched to Detroit, Michilimackinac, and other western posts in 1760, but many did not know just where these posts were located.

Before Shelburne could carry out his plans, news arrived concerning the outbreak of the great Indian war known in history as the Conspiracy of Pontiac. At once he planned a more decisive policy, and on August 5, 1763, recommended that his ideas outlined above be put into an immediate proclamation.[108] Nothing was done until late in September, when Shelburne had withdrawn from a government with which he was not in sympathy, while new and untried men made the final draft of his proposals.

Certain basic conditions which greatly affected the formation and development of a British western policy for Michigan and the entire West became apparent at this stage. Clashing

104 For a recent scholarly analysis of the work of Shelburne and the Proclamation of 1763, see Humphreys, "Lord Shelburne and the Proclamation of 1763." A. L. Burt, *The Old Province of Quebec* (Toronto, 1933), chap. V, gives a very readable account of the Proclamation.
105 *Ill. Hist. Colls.*, X, 19 ff. Washington, Franklin, Laurens, and the Lees were some of the Americans prominently identified with the Land Companies.
106 Shortt and Doughty, *Can. Const. Docs.*, pt. i, 132 ff.
107 Peter Force, *American Archives* (Ser. 4, Washington, 1837–1853), I, 190.
108 Shortt and Doughty, *Can. Const. Docs.*, pt. i, 152.

political and economic interests between colonial aspiration and English desires, the problems of the French settler, the Indian and the fur trader, all presented difficulties almost insurmountable. Ministry rapidly followed ministry, bringing further chaos and confusion, so that nothing really constructive was accomplished. The frontier was not regulated; the vastnesses were not kept; and all was resolved by pushing the Indians toward the setting sun; while Michigan was left a temporary Indian hunting ground during this first phase of the British régime.

CHAPTER II

THE INDIAN UPRISING OF 1763

THE ILLIMITABLE WASTE into which the British came as con-
querors was a wilderness of forest, broken here by bodies of
water or prairies, there by tiny cleared areas for Indian corn.
Only small, widely-scattered posts, with a few men dependent
upon the Indians for supplies, guarded the boundless forest.[1]
But feeble as were these forces, they alarmed the Indians. No
longer could their canoes glide silently over the open waters
of the Great Lakes and down the Illinois, or the Ohio, without
passing the symbol of English authority: the Cross of St.
George. The cause of the red men could only be saved by their
own strength. By united action they hoped to drive the much
detested Redcoat into the sea.

It was a part of the British program from the beginning of
their occupation of Michigan and the West to hold conferences
with the Indians in an attempt to win their friendship, and
through it the fur trade. Major Rogers had scarcely received
the surrender of Detroit, before Croghan called a meeting of
the Wyandot, Potawatomi, and Ottawa in the council house.
The Indians professed a great desire to be friendly, to return
all English prisoners, and asked for cheap goods and freedom
from the oppression of the traders.[2] Croghan agreed to reopen
the trade, requested deputies to accompany Rogers to Michilimackinac, presented Captain Campbell as commandant of

[1] The smaller garrisons consisted of an ensign, a sergeant, and usually fourteen
men.

[2] Croghan, "Journals 1760–1761," in Thwaites, *Early Western Travels*, I,
114–22. The speculation and corruption of some of the French officers in the
West were notorious. Bellestre was not free from suspicion. Silas Farmer,
History of Detroit and Michigan (Detroit, 1884), p. 766.

Detroit, and advised the warriors if they wanted diversion for their martial spirits to find it among their natural enemies the Cherokees, " as all nations else are become the subjects of Great Britain." [3] The conference continued for four days before the council fire was covered up. Great quantities of gifts were lavished upon the chiefs, and more left for Captain Campbell to use at a later date. Croghan presented a bill to Johnson for £ 586/10/6 for his expenses with Rogers.[4] He explained that the enormous amount was due to the fact that he could not purchase provisions — particularly livestock — from the inhabitants of Detroit, for the French troops and Indians by their rendezvous of 1759 had left the people destitute of everything.[5] When Sir William [6] presented this bill to General Amherst, the latter was somewhat disturbed and wrote:

In looking over your Disbursements on account of the presents etc. for the Indians at the Detroit meeting, I confess the greatness of the Sum Surprises me, since it is almost Double what you at first demanded. Altho I have no doubts of your having used your utmost Endeavors to be as Economical as you judged best for the good of the Service yet I am of the opinion that we must deal more sparingly for the future; for from the now Tranquil State of the Country, and the good regulation you have put the trade under, I can see very little reason for bribing the Indians, or buying their good behavior, since they have no Enemy to molest them; but on the contrary every encouragement and protection they can desire for their trade.[7]

General Gage was also of the impression that Croghan had been " very bountifull." He felt it was necessary to pay the Indians for their services, " but," he wrote, " as to purchasing the good behavior, either of Indians, or any others, is what I do not understand, when men of what races soever behave ill, they must be punished but not bribed." [8] This seemed to be

[3] Croghan, " Journals 1760–1761." A scholarly account of Croghan's work is found in A. T. Volwiler, *George Croghan and the Westward Movement* (Cleveland, 1926).

[4] Canadian Archives, C. O. 5, LXI, pt. i, p. 298.

[5] *Ibid.*, Indian Papers, VIII, 42.

[6] Arthur Pound and R. E. Day, *Johnson of the Mohawks* (New York, 1930), is the most readable account of this great Indian superintendent.

[7] Amherst to Johnson, December 26, 1761, Canadian Archives, Indian Records, VIII, 141.

[8] *Ibid.*, C. O. 5, LXI, pt. i, pp. 312–13.

the policy of the British high command, with very far-reaching results.

With the capitulation of Canada, the death of George II, and the displacement of William Pitt by Lord Bute, Amherst was instructed, by the new ministry, to curtail expenditures.[9] He immediately instructed Johnson to retrench by cutting salaries forty percent in 1762. All presents were refused until the Indians released all captives. " As to appropriating a particular sum to be laid out yearly to the warriors in presents, etc. that I can by no means agree to," wrote Amherst, " nor can I think it necessary to give them any presents by way of *Bribes,* for if they do not behave properly they are to be punished." This new policy was one of the main factors in stirring up the western tribes.

Mutterings of discontent during the spring of 1761, and discovery of Indian plots against the English garrisons, caused Campbell, in July, to attend a council which the Ottawa, Chippewa, Potawatomi, and Wyandot held with some delegates of the Six Nations near Detroit. The Iroquois urged the western Indians to war because the English " treat us with much Disrespect, their Behaviour toward us gives us the greatest Reason to believe they intend to Cutt us off entirely." [10] Campbell reprimanded the Indians severely and forced a promise from the delegates of the Six Nations to go home and be good.[11]

But the discontent continued. A plot was discovered to attack Detroit, Niagara, and Pittsburgh simultaneously. This, and the desire to gain first-hand information, caused Johnson to decide to visit Detroit with a large Iroquois delegation.[12] General Amherst approved of Johnson's plans, and ordered

[9] See Volwiler, *George Croghan,* pp. 160–61; Wrong, *Canada and the American Revolution,* p. 74.
[10] Indian Council near Detroit, July 3, 1761, James Sterling's Letter Book (copy in Detroit Public Library). Most of the Six Nations were loyal to the English. These were Senecas who had always been friendly with the French.
[11] James Sullivan (ed.), *The Papers of Sir William Johnson* (Albany, 1921–), III, 450–53; W. L. Stone, *The Life and Times of Sir William Johnson* (Albany, 1865), II, 143.
[12] *Ibid.,* 145, 441–68; *Mich. Hist. Colls.,* XIX, 85; *Johnson Papers,* III, 524 ff.

Croghan to get cattle from General Monckton at Pittsburgh, in order to provide fresh provisions for the journey and for the conferences.[13] Johnson then sent Croghan ahead with a delegation of Shawnee and Delaware Indians, with the cattle and a large quantity of presents. After a long and trying journey of fifteen days on Lake Erie, Johnson arrived at Detroit on September 3, 1761.[14] In spite of finding Major Gladwin very ill with a fever, the lateness of the season, the loss of provisions and ammunition on the way, Sir William was in great hopes of accomplishing all he had planned.[15]

Hectic days followed, filled with numerous conferences and festive occasions. The Potawatomi, Wyandot, Delaware, Chippewa, Shawnee, Ottawa, Hurons, and the tribes around Lake Superior were all represented. So great was the assemblage that Johnson, Croghan, and Campbell were forced to hold the meetings in the open.[16] The Baronet spoke of the recent conspiracy, of the desire of the English to cultivate amicable relations with the tribes, and the hopes of building up the fur trade.

Altercations broke out between the Hurons and some Ohio Indians which would have ended in blows, had not Sir William adjourned the meeting, and promised to distribute presents to all on the following day. Several days were spent in holding informal conferences, with long ceremonies to impress the naïve Indians. These pow-wows were accompanied by long speeches, wampum belts, glasses of rum, roasting of oxen, and more and more presents; and at last friendly relations were established and better trading facilities were planned. The evenings were occupied with other pleasures, ball following ball, giving a delightful touch to the life of the post. Johnson, in pursuance of Amherst's orders, sent to Michilimackinac an officer and thirty men; to St. Joseph an officer and fifteen

---

[13] Canadian Archives, Indian Papers, VIII, 43.
[14] *Johnson Papers*, III, 524.
[15] *Ibid.*, Stone, *Life of Johnson*, II, 150 ff.
[16] *Ibid.*, 151 ff., gives an excellent account of these conferences. The complete account of the proceedings is found in *Johnson Papers*, III, 474–501. See *ibid.*, 503, for the expenses.

men; and to Miami and other posts the same number. By 1762, British garrisons were well established in all the Great Lakes region.[17] This was an expensive policy, but necessary to hold the new French and Indian subjects, to secure the fur trade, and to encourage colonization in the West.

The scattered posts, almost hidden by the primeval forests, were practically at the mercy of the Indians. Communication was uncertain and expensive, while life was most monotonous in these isolated places. Johnson made an effort to keep in touch with the garrisons and sent agents constantly throughout the West to transact such business as was necessary.

The year 1762 was full of ominous signs. Thomas Hutchins, a deputy Indian agent, held parleys early in 1762, with the Indians around Detroit, St. Joseph, and Michilimackinac.[18] He found much dissatisfaction everywhere, because of Amherst's failure to distribute presents and ammunition as bountifully as the French had done. Major Gladwin at Detroit found the braves sullen and restless.[19] Croghan informed Amherst that secret councils were being held near Detroit by the Potawatomi, Chippewa, Wyandot, and Ottawa. Two Frenchmen were present and deputies were sent to the western nations to arouse them.[20] As the year came to a close, Ensign Holmes at Fort Miami found a bloody belt, and warned Major Gladwin, who in turn informed Amherst.[21] Gladwin found that agents of the Ohio and Iroquois Indians were again among the western tribes, tampering with them. " They are ill disposed," he wrote, " and claim

we mean to make slaves of them by taking so many posts in their Country, and that they had better attempt something now to recover their liberty, than wait till we are better Established."[22]

[17] Sir William, while at Detroit, drew up instructions for the post commanders relative to their conduct with the Indians. *Johnson Papers,* III, 473.
[18] Canadian Archives, Indian Papers, VIII, 326.
[19] *Ibid.,* 172–76. Gladwin wrote Amherst on February 4, 24, 25, and March 5, emphasizing the hostility of the Indians.
[20] Croghan to Amherst, September 28, 1762; *ibid.,* 1761–1772 (no pagination).
[21] Holmes to Gladwin, March 30, 1763, *ibid.,* VIII, 389.
[22] Gladwin to Amherst, April 20, 1763, *ibid.,* 390; *ibid.,* C. O. 5, LXIII, pt. i, p. 79.

In spite of repeated warnings and ominous signs just a few weeks before the outbreak of the Pontiac Uprising, Amherst wrote Johnson opposing the distribution of presents.[23] " I cannot see any reason," he fumed, " for supplying the Indians with Provisions for I am convinced they will never think of providing for their families by Hunting, if they can support themselves by begging Provisions from us."

On the other hand, Johnson and his agents were anxious to win the confidence and friendship of the Indians, and they advocated a policy suitable to the conditions which they so well knew. If an ox, a keg of rum, or many presents would prevent Indian wars and build up the fur trade, the expense would be insignificant, they insisted. Nevertheless, Amherst refused to modify his policy; so he must share the responsibility for the great loss of life and goods which the Indian uprising cost. Amherst sat in a fool's paradise, " sunning himself in the smiles of the crowd." A letter to Sir William as late as May 29, 1763, shows a total lack of appreciation of western conditions.[24] After mentioning a letter from Major Gladwin speaking of a bloody belt, Amherst says:

Although I cannot think the Indians have it in their Power to Execute anything serious against us, whilst we continue to be on our guard, yet I judge it necessary to send you the Belt, which you will Receive herewith, as also Copys of what Major Gladwin has transmitted to me regarding this Affair; and I desire you will make such use thereof as may appear most proper for putting a stop to such treacherous Behavior for the future, and for showing the Indians the Contemptible Figure they must make in our eyes by violating the most solemn Promises of Friendship, without the least Provocation on our side. I mention the *contemptible Figure*, as it certainly is not in their Power to Effect anything of Consequence against us: but if they are so Rash as to make an Attempt, the Mischief they intend, will certainly Recoil on themselves.

[23] Amherst to Johnson, April 3, 1763, *ibid.*, Indian Papers, VIII, 401. Volwiler, *George Croghan*, p. 158. Page 164 gives an excellent account of Amherst's " zeal for economy."

[24] Amherst to Johnson, May 29, 1763, Canadian Archives, Indian Papers, VIII, 427. Nevertheless Amherst warned Gladwin to be always on his guard. He wrote, " In my opinion they [Indians] never can Hurt us, unless we are weak enough to Put Ourselves in their Powers." Amherst to Gladwin, May 29, 1763, *ibid.*, C. O. 5, LXIII, pt. i, p. 83.

Even while Amherst was writing, many of the western posts lay in ruins.

Early in the Spring of 1763, the stillness of the forest was broken. Yells of excited braves filled the air. Dusky warriors chanted the war songs, and danced the war dance around the dimly glowing fires. For months the call to war had been carefully passed from tribe to tribe, awakening the post officials to their great responsibilities. Stealthily passing the wampum belts and tomahawks, the symbols of war, messengers went throughout the whole western country arousing the natives. It was not at all surprising that religion played a part in stirring up the Indians, for in 1761 there appeared a chief of the Abenakis, who, as a prophet, called upon his people to purge themselves of all foreign influences and drive out the much-despised Englishman. In a vision, he told his people, the Great Spirit had appeared unto him and said:

I am the master of life. It is I who have made all men; consequently I ought to watch over their preservation. That is why I inform you that if you suffer the English among you, you are dead men. Sickness, smallpox, and their poison will destroy you entirely. It is necessary to pray to me and do nothing contrary to my wishes. I will sustain you; but you must abandon your altar mats and your manitoes. Plurality of wives is contrary to my law.[25]

A return to the simple life, with only its bare necessities, was the preaching of this Gandhi of 1761. Under the prophet's teachings an attempt was made to destroy all of the frontier posts. Some members of the garrison at Michilimackinac were surprised and massacred, and a similar fate would have overtaken the garrison at Sault Ste. Marie, but for a timely warning. Major Gladwin, the commandant at Detroit, realizing that the Indian discontent was growing, warned various garrisons, and also sent word to General Amherst asking for reinforcements. By this fortunate discovery the plans were frustrated.[26]

[25] *Ill. Hist. Colls.*, X, 51; Parkman, *Conspiracy of Pontiac*, I, chap. VII; Journal of Pontiac's Conspiracy, 1763 (Burton, ed.), pp. 20 *et seq.*

[26] Canadian Archives, A, XVI, 252; *ibid.*, *Report for 1889*, pp. 13–14; *Johnson's Papers*, III, 405; *Mich. Hist. Colls.*, XIX, 76, 79, 81, 88, 94.

Below the surface was great dissatisfaction. The Indians were very excitable, and the teaching of the prophet produced the spark necessary to set fire to the tinder. Their hatred of the white men who had invaded their country, and who were by all appearances going to stay, was daily increasing. The outbreaks of '61 and '62 afforded ominous signs of the seething discontent.

At the psychological moment, Pontiac, the astute Chieftain of the Ottawa, appeared upon the scene. This " Napoleon of the Indians " was largely the tool of French plotters.[27] Pontiac had capacity for organization which enabled him to use all the various discontented elements for his own purposes. It has already been noted how he professed a friendship for the English, hoping that he would be allowed to rule over his own people as a prince and perhaps over a confederacy of the tribes. After he discovered that the British had no special need for him, he was in high dudgeon, and then devoted all of his savage acumen and sagacity to founding a confederacy of the western Indians, to make a general war upon the white settlements. His program called for a simultaneous attack upon all the western posts during the change of the moon, in the month of May, 1763.[28]

The British were ill-prepared for the sudden blow. During May and June, post after post was attacked. Mostly by treachery, St. Joseph, Miami, Sandusky, Ouiatanon, Michilimackinac,[29] and several others fell to the Indians. Only Detroit

---

[27] The distinguished Canadian historian, Kingsford, in his *History of Canada,* V, 5–12, places all the blame on the French. Gladwin was of like opinion. See Gladwin's letters in Gage MSS. (in William L. Clements Library, hereinafter cited as Clements Library). Parkman was of the same impression. The most recent detailed account of the Indian uprising is found in Wrong, *Canada and the American Revolution,* chap. IV.

[28] Parkman, *Conspiracy of Pontiac,* I, 196.

[29] Captain Etherington was warned several times by Charles Langlade. After a " final warning," Etherington replied: " Mr. Langlade, I am weary of hearing the stories you so often bring me; they are the foolish twaddle of old women, and unworthy of belief; the Indians have nothing against the English, and cherish no evil designs; I hope, therefore, you will not trouble me with any more such stuff." " Capt. Etherington," said Langlade: " I will not trouble you any more with these old women's stories, as you call them, but I beg you will remember my faithful warnings." *Mich. Hist. Colls.,* XIII, 501; " Grignon's Recollections," *Wis. Hist. Colls.,* III, 224–25.

and Fort Pitt were saved. Thus in a few weeks the whole West was lost.[30]

All along the borders terror was supreme. Indian scalping parties spread throughout the valleys of Pennsylvania, Maryland, and Virginia, laying settlements in smoking ruins, murdering women and children, destroying the crops, wreaking death and destruction with indescribable fury. Tales of unbelievable horror were related by the pioneers who flocked into the larger settlements. To the north in New York, due largely to Johnson's influence, the Six Nations, to a large extent, remained peaceful.

General Amherst received word of the conspiracy on June 6, but procrastinated until June 12, when additional dispatches revealed the seriousness of the war. Two expeditions were forthwith dispatched; one under Colonel Bouquet with about five hundred regulars for the relief of Fort Pitt, and thence into the heart of modern Ohio; the other under the command of Captain James Dalyell, one of General Amherst's aides-de-camp, along Lake Erie and thence to Detroit.[31] When news of disaster after disaster reached Amherst, he believed all Indians were friends. He offered a reward of £100 New York currency " to whoever kills Pontiac," whom he described as the " chief Ringleader of the mischief," and a like sum for the murderer of Captain Campbell.[32] He ordered that all prisoners who were

[30] Helen F. Humphrey, " The Identity of Gladwin's Informant," *Miss. Valley Hist. Rev.*, XXI, September, 1934, pp. 147–62, gives an excellent account of the many myths written about Gladwin's informant.

[31] *Annual Register for 1763*, pp. 24–32; Canadian Archives, *Report for 1889*, pp. 59–71; *Mich. Hist. Colls.*, XIX, 219–22; Parkman, *Conspiracy of Pontiac*, II, chaps. XIX–XXII; " Bouquet's Journal," printed in *ibid.*, App. D, and also in S. P. Hildreth, *Memoirs of the early Pioneer Settlers of Ohio with Narratives of Incidents and Occurrences of 1775* (Cincinnati, 1834), chap. iii. The best sources for the study of the Pontiac Uprising are the " Gladwin Manuscripts," *Mich. Hist. Colls.*, XXVII; " Pontiac Manuscripts," *ibid.*, VIII; *Wis. Hist. Colls.*, XVIII; *Ill. Hist. Colls.*, X; *Annual Register for 1763*, chap. VI; Rogers, *Journal of the Siege of Detroit*; *N. Y. Col. Docs.*, VII; *Johnson's Papers*, III, F. B. Hough, *Diary of the Siege of Detroit in the War with Pontiac* (Albany, 1860); Canadian Archives, *Report for 1889*; Nelson Vance Russell, " The Battle of Bloody Run," *Canadian Historical Review* (Toronto, 1930), XII, 183–88; " Journal of John Montresor's Expedition to Detroit in 1763," *Transactions of the Royal Society of Canada, Third Series* (Toronto, 1928), XXII.

[32] Amherst to Gladwin, July 20, 1763; Canadian Archives, C. O. 5, LXIII, pt. i, 232; same to same, August 20, 1763, *ibid.*, 336.

in any way responsible for depredations be put to death.[33] The Senecas he characterized as " the Vilest Race of Beings that ever Infested the Earth and whose Riddance from it, must be Esteemed a Meritorious Act for the good of Mankind." [34] Finally, the mighty Pontiac, " Lord of the West," was defeated, and his territories became the spoils of his most hated enemies.[35] Many months ensued before the complete submission of the red man. Great councils were held at Niagara, Detroit, and Presqu' Isle, which brought about the temporary pacification of the Indians.[36] Pontiac expected aid from the French, but Pierre Joseph Neyon, the French commandant at Fort Chartres, under pressure from General Amherst, sent word to the great chief that "the great day had come at last wherein it had pleased the Master of Life to command the Great King of France and his of England to make peace between them, sorry to see the blood of men spilled so long.... Forget then, my dear children, all evil talks. Leave off from spilling the blood of your brethren, the English. Our hearts are now but one; you cannot, at present, strike one without having the other for an enemy also." [37] The failure to

[33]Amherst to Gladwin, August 10, 1763, *ibid.,* 341.

[34] Same to same, *ibid.*

[35] Pontiac sent a letter on November 1, 1763, to Major Gladwin asking for peace, and desiring that all that had passed might be forgotten on both sides. Gage to Halifax, December 23, 1763, Canadian Archives, C. O. 5, LXXXIII, pt. i, pp. 7–8. Published in Carter, *Gage's Correspondence,* I, 5. Gladwin said the enemy had sued for peace on October 12, " in a very Submissive manner." Gage advised Gladwin to make peace, provided the Indians could convince him " of the Sincerity of their Overtures." Gage to Halifax, January 7, 1764, *ibid.,* 7–8. Gage also ordered Gladwin to acquaint the Indians to repair to Niagara by the end of June, 1764, and to meet Sir William Johnson. Gage to Gladwin, March 23, 1764, in Gage MSS.

[36] *Johnson Papers,* IV, 466–81, 485–88, 526–33, 547–49; Shelburne Papers, XLVIII, 147; L, 273; *N. Y. Col. Docs.,* VII, 648, 686–88; Alexander Henry, *Travels and Adventures in Canada and the Indian Territories* (New York, 1809), p. 171.

[37] Gladwin MS., p. 628; Hough, *Diary of the Siege of Detroit,* p. 117; *Ill. Hist. Colls.,* X, 50, 256–57; XI, 53; Henry, *Travels and Adventures.* The best secondary accounts are Parkman's admirable work, *The Conspiracy of Pontiac;* Stone, *Life of Johnson;* Burt, *The Old Province of Quebec,* pp. 61–73; Charles Moore, *The Northwest Under Three Flags, 1635–1796* (New York, 1900). " Nine forts were captured, 2,000 soldiers, traders and settlers captured or killed, thousands of settlers driven to beggary, and goods valued at nearly £100,000 plundered," is Mr. Moore's summary of the disaster.

receive the much needed and expected aid from France brought about the collapse of the uprising.

On the other hand it was the help of the French in the West and the encouragement they gave which aided the savages against the British. Major Gladwin wrote Amherst that one-half the inhabitants of Detroit merited a gibbet and the remaining half ought to be decimated.[38] Yet he did find some honest men who furnished him with provisions at the utmost peril of their lives, " and I question without their Assistance," he added, " whether I should have been able to maintain my Post." [39] Gage noted that many of the disloyal inhabitants of Detroit were of the common people, but he understood they all fled to the Illinois " when the Indians made overtures of Peace." [40] Amherst, greatly irritated and surprised that the French were so treacherous, advised Gladwin to banish them at once or send them all down to Gage at Montreal.[41] Johnson said that the French traders had retired amongst the Indians upon the surrender of Canada and instilled them with the idea that the English had designs against their liberties.[42] And John Rutherford, a prisoner in Pontiac's camp during the early days of the siege of Detroit, wrote in his " Journal ":

The Canadians could never bring themselves to believe that the "Grand Monarque" could ever cede their country to Great Britain, and still flattered themselves that if they could excite the Indians for a little while that a reinforcement would arrive from France and they would drive the English out of the country. They had there-fore always assured the Indians that Major Gladwin had declared there was peace only to prevent them from attacking him.[43]

[38] Canadian Archives, C. O. 5, LXIII, pt. i, 308.
[39] He especially mentions Monsieur Navarre, the two Babys, and the two interpreters, St. Martin and La Bute. *Ibid.* Gage wrote Gladwin that Baby and St. Martin should be rewarded, " and you will let me know in what shape it can be best done," he asked. Gage to Gladwin, January 9, 1764, Gage MSS.
[40] Gage to Halifax, January 7, 1764, Canadian Archives, C. O. 5, LXXXIII, pt. i, 8. Published in Carter, *Gage's Correspondence,* I, 10.
[41] Amherst to Gladwin, August 10, 1763, Canadian Archives, C. O. 5, LXII, pt. i, 334.
[42] Johnson to Lords of Trade, November 18, 1763, *ibid.,* Indian Papers, IX, 41.
[43] " Journal of John Rutherford." Gladwin wrote Amherst, July 8, 1763: " I Conclude that the French are at the Bottom of this Affair, in order to Ruin the British Merchants and Engross the Trade to themselves, as many of them are stupid Enough to Believe that they will be permitted to Supply the Indians

There is a large measure of truth in all these statements, but many of the French were loyal and, as Gladwin observed, were really responsible for provisioning the garrison during the hectic summer days of 1763.

The greatest attempt the Indians ever made to drive out the white man was over, but new and perplexing problems remained to be solved. Gladwin found the "lying treacherous Brutes" quiet, though not to be trusted. He felt they remained "proud and undaunted," few making any overtures to peace in spite of being reduced to great misery.[44] Intrigues and plots continued at Michilimackinac and elsewhere so the officers had to be constantly on their guard.[45]

In September of 1764, Colonel John Bradstreet, who had been sent by Gage to succor Gladwin, held a great congress with members of the Ottawa, Chippewa, Miami, Huron, and Potawatomi tribes. The English and Indians agreed to the followings terms:

1. To acknowledge George III as their sovereign.
2. To make war upon any tribe violating the peace.
3. To deliver voluntarily and immediately any Indian plundering or killing any of His Majesty's subjects to the officers of the nearest garrison.
4. To deliver up all prisoners and deserters.
5. To move all persons settled upon the Indian lands immediately as a "testimony of our good intentions."
6. To pardon and forgive Pontiac, who was to be allowed to meet them in a conference later at Sandusky.[46]

with Everything they want before an Accommodation takes place." Canadian Archives, C. O. 5, LXIII, pt. i, 390. General Gage in a letter to Lord Egremont, August 28, 1763, said he believed the French were in collusion with the Indians, at Michilimackinac, as they were not molested at the time of the attack. He refused to allow any trade there until a new garrison was established. Gage to Egremont, August 28, 1763, Canadian Archives, Q, I, 211-12. Rogers as late as 1767 advised the removal of the French as a "public service." Rogers to Gage, February 12, 1767, Gage MSS. Gage held similar ideas in 1765. Gage to Halifax, August 10, 1765, Carter, *Gage's Correspondence*, I, 63.

[44] Gladwin to Johnson, May 11, 1764, Canadian Archives, Indian Papers, IX, 114.

[45] Gage to Halifax, August 10, 1765, *ibid.*, Dartmouth Transcripts, 1765–1775, pp. 6–7. Published in Carter, *loc. cit.*, I, 63.

[46] Canadian Archives, Indian Papers, IX, 215–16.

Sir William Johnson, from his great experience in handling Indian affairs, drew up a number of instructions for the officers, at the western posts. Through them he hoped to placate the Indians. Among other warnings he urged:

1. That kindness be especially shown toward the warriors.
2. That they be addressed affably.
3. That they be properly clothed, armed, and plentifully victualled, with a dram alike morning and evening.
4. That they be urged if they show desire to speak with the commanding officer.
5. That they be informed of any sudden change or movement, since the French had treated them so, and since the red man was suspicious in character.[47]

In 1766, Pontiac gave pledges of friendship upon a visit to Johnson,[48] who held a great council at Oswego, with the chiefs of the Ottawa, Hurons, Chippewa, and Potawatomi. The object of this meeting was to confirm the work of Bradstreet's council held at Detroit in 1764, with the chiefs throughout the West. Pontiac promised that in the future he and the western nations would live peaceably, forgetting all the enmity of the past.[49] A few years later, in 1769, he was killed in an Indian brawl. "Thus basely perished the champion of a ruined race," [50] and the red man's vision of independence or sovereignty in his native land faded away. Pontiac's body was buried with military honors near the new fort St. Louis. Today, for a mausoleum, a great city has risen above the grave of the " forest hero," and the people he despised, unheeding, unceasing, trample over his forgotten resting place.[51]

---

[47] Johnson to Bradstreet (MS. in the Huntington Library, San Marino, California).

[48] *N. Y. Col. Docs.*, VII, 854.

[49] *Ibid.*, 854, 867.

[50] Parkman, *Conspiracy of Pontiac*, II, 329. See page 329 notes, for other accounts of the cause of Pontiac's death. Parkman's account is the most reliable. Tradition claims that after Pontiac's murder his followers began a crusade to avenge his death. Tribes were rooted out, remnants alone remaining, and once again the forest resounded with the infernal yells of his followers.

[51] The St. Louis chapter of the D. A. R. have erected a tablet in the Southern Hotel to mark the burial place of " Pontiac, the friend of Saint Ange, killed at Cahokia, Illinois, in April, 1769."

By the Seven Years' War the two leading branches of the white race in North America, French and English, had determined which was to dominate; then followed the great attempt of the Indians against the victors; and already distant rumblings could be heard of the inevitable struggle between the Mother Country and her colonies, who, set free from the French and Indian menace, were to win their independence.

The collapse of Pontiac's Conspiracy marks the end of one era, and the beginning of another in the British control of Michigan. Never again did the red man attempt to challenge that power. After much unnecessary blundering, the English arms had brought victory, and once again the officials could turn their attention to the problem of the administration of the West, which the war had held in abeyance.

CHAPTER III

THE ADMINISTRATION OF MICHIGAN, 1763-1775

THE PRELIMINARIES of the Treaty of Paris had scarcely been signed when Great Britain took a very important step in the solution of the western problem. The Pontiac Uprising proved that something had to be done and done at once to quiet the fears of the Indians. The proposals of the Lords of Trade had not been acted upon and meanwhile more discomforting information had been received in England.

In August Lord Hillsborough succeeded Shelburne on the Board of Trade and Lord Halifax took the Earl of Egremont's place in the Cabinet.[1] The ministry had decided to follow the plans outlined by the Lords of Trade under Shelburne's direction, but with some minor changes. Egremont proposed the union of all the territory around the Great Lakes with the province of Quebec.[2] To this proposal, the Lords of Trade replied that Egremont's suggestion had been given serious consideration but they were of the opinion that this might lead " on some future Occasion " to questioning England's claim, whereas the title to the entire region was one of long standing and was not due to the exigencies of the late war. Other objections were given. For one, it might also confuse the Indian tribes, should they " be brought to consider themselves as under the Government of Canada." Again, there would be dangers arising to the fur trade if the whole of the country

[1] Alvord, *The Mississippi Valley*, I, 196; Fitzmaurice, *Shelburne,* I, chap. V.
[2] Egremont to the Lords of Trade, July 14, 1763, in Shortt and Doughty, *Can. Const. Docs.,* pt. i, p. 147. The Earl of Egremont died suddenly on August 21, 1763, and the Earl of Halifax temporarily took over the duties of the Department.

should " become subject to the Laws of a particular Government or Province"; also, that there would be the " constant and inextricable Disputes " which naturally would occur between the governor of Canada and the commanding officer of the troops, because of the large area under their control.[3] Halifax also ignored Egremont's suggestions and in a communication to the Lords of Trade on September 19, 1763, said the King approved their issuing " immediately a Proclamation, to prohibit for the present, any Grant or Settlement within the Bounds of the Countries intended to be reserved for the Use of the Indians." Among other provisions the Proclamation was to provide for the " speedy Settlement of the new colonies . . . the Friendship of the Indians more speedily and effectually reconciled, and Provision be made for preventing Inconveniences, which might otherwise arise from the Want of Civil Jurisdiction in the interior." [4]

Between September 28 and October 4, the Lords of Trade accomplished their task. Hillsborough had found the proposals of Shelburne on his desk, and he used these, with modifications, as a nucleus to which other clauses were added.[5] In the Proclamation as outlined, some hopes were held out to the future immigrants that an assembly would be established in due season.[6] This would no doubt have greatly encouraged migration, and should be remembered as the most liberal of all the plans proposed.

A very important change was made from the original plans concerning the Indian boundary — a change which meant that Michigan, and all of the Northwest, would not be open to settlement for some time, if at all. The first proposal had been to run a surveyor's chain through the forests and mountains in

[3] The Lords of Trade to the King, August 5, 1763, *ibid.*, pp. 151–52. For Alvord's opinion concerning the Proclamation of 1763, see *Mich. Hist. Colls.*, XXXVI, 21 ff. For his later ideas see *The Mississippi Valley in British Politics*, I, 183 ff. See Clarence E. Carter, *Great Britain and the Illinois Country, 1763–1774* (Washington, 1910), chap. II, for the results of this decision.

[4] Halifax to the Lords of Trade, September 19, 1763. Shortt and Doughty, *Can. Const. Docs.*, pt. i, p. 154.

[5] *Mich. Hist. Colls.*, XXXVI, 49.

[6] Shortt and Doughty, *Can. Const. Docs.*, pt. i, p. 165.

such a way as to include all lands which had been settled. By September of 1763, the ministry knew that Michigan was fairly teeming with warriors " drunk with blood," that settlers had been mercilessly butchered, and that the whole white frontier was threatened with extinction. Something had to be done, and done without delay to satisfy the Indians. Only a tangible definite line would be successful and satisfactory to the Indians. Such a line, the Appalachian watershed, had been used,[7] and so the Proclamation was issued following this boundary. Any Indian lands lying to the east of the boundary were to be sold, but only by properly qualified imperial officials.

This line need not have kept Michigan " outside the pale " forever. It was only a tentative boundary in the minds of the King's ministers and the colonial leaders, but to the Indians it must seem fixed and unchangeable. The colonial attitude was well expressed by Washington, who wrote to Colonel William Crawford, his western land agent, in September, 1767: " I can never look upon that Proclamation in any other light (but this I say between ourselves), than as a temporary expedient to quiet the minds of the Indians, and must fail, of course, in a few years, especially when those Indians are consenting to our occupying the lands." [8] Washington was undoubtedly correct, for in the report of the Commissioners for Trade, on Indian Affairs in 1769, the boundary line is defined as " mere provisional Arrangements adapted to the Exigence of the time." [9] Grenville had expressed himself that the " design of it was totally accomplished as soon as the country was purchased from the natives." [10] Franklin held similar ideas,[11] and surely no one was more conversant with both American and English western problems. Dr. Alvord has proved that the line of

---

[7] Canadian Archives, *Report for 1889*, p. 73.
[8] W. C. Ford, *The Writings of George Washington* (New York, 1889), II, 220–21.
[9] *Pennsylvania Archives*, IV, 315. Livingston held similar ideas. Jared Sparks (ed.), *Writings of Franklin* (Boston, 1837), IX, 130.
[10] *Pennsylvania Archives*, V, 37.
[11] *Ibid.*, III, 48.

demarcation was not intended to be a permanent barrier to westward expansion.[12] The colonists apparently understood this at the time, although later, when the Proclamation had been deliberately distorted by the Grafton Ministry into a permanent barrier,[13] it helped to promote colonial hatred against the British. The Proclamation was now hurriedly put into final form, and on October 4, the Lords of Trade transmitted the draft to Halifax.

The Proclamation issued by the King on October 7, 1763, provided for four new colonies, viz., Quebec, East Florida, West Florida, and Grenada.[14] Civil government was inaugurated in Quebec in 1764, and this document served as the basis of its constitution until the Quebec Act went into effect in 1775.[15] The populations within the newly established colonies were guaranteed that as " soon as the state and circumstances of the said Colonies will admit," legislative assemblies would be granted them.

The large area, which includes Michigan and was roughly bounded by the Hudson Bay territory, the Alleghenies, the Floridas, and the Mississippi, curiously was not included within the limits of any of the newly established colonies. It was reserved temporarily as a vast hunting ground for the Indian nations. There was also no provision made for the several French settlements, such as Detroit, Michilimackinac,

[12] Alvord, " Genesis of the Proclamation of 1763," *Mich. Hist. Colls.*, XXXVI, 21; Max Farrand, " The Indian Boundary Line," *American Historical Review* (New York, 1895–), X, 482 ff. Most historians have held the opinion that the ministry did intend to make a definite unchangeable boundary. Justin Winsor, *The Mississippi Basin* (Boston, 1895), p. 431. " There was doubtless in all this a number of objects to be gained. One was to limit the old colonies by the mountains." G. E. Howard, *Preliminaries of the Revolution* (New York, 1905), p. 233–34. " The King's Proclamation had entirely ignored the shadowy title of several of the colonies to the western territory." G. H. Alden, *New Governments West of the Alleghanies before 1780* (Madison, 1897), p. 38; Victor Coffin, *The Province of Quebec and the Early American Revolution* (Madison, 1896), p. 412 ff.; W. F. Poole, in Justin Winsor, *Narrative and Critical History of America* (Boston, 1888), VI, 687.

[13] *N. Y. Col. Docs.*, VIII, 27; Coffin, *The Province of Quebec*, p. 432.

[14] The Proclamation has many times been reprinted. Shortt and Doughty, *Can. Const. Docs.*, pt. i, pp. 163–68; *American Historical Leaflets*, No. 5. A map of the British dominions as fixed by the Proclamation is at the end of the *Annual Register for 1763*.

[15] Coffin, *The Province of Quebec*, p. 328.

or St. Joseph, within the area; and surely no ministry was ignorant of these villages.[16] The number and size of these places were underestimated, and absurd as it may seem, it is probable that the ministry expected that all the French would move across the Mississippi, and that all the Spanish of Florida would migrate into some other Spanish colony.[17] As the Proclamation shows, this omission was not due to any regard for colonial charters. No " loving subject " might purchase land or settle in the territory without special license; present residents should " forthwith to remove themselves " the Proclamation reads. The governors of the eastern colonies were ordered not to grant warrants of survey, or pass patents for lands beyond the sources of the rivers which empty into the Atlantic. There was to be no extension of settlements beyond the limits of the newly established colonies, for the absolute need of some panacea for the Indian ills was felt. The English newspapers were of the opinion that the Pontiac Uprising was " occasioned by the Indians being cheated out of their lands by the English in America." [18] Thus no attempt was made to institute civil government in Michigan, or in any part of the vast West, for this would have stirred up the Indians to a renewed resistance. Measures of conciliation were in order, if there were to be any returns from the fur trade. The *Annual Register for 1763* gives other reasons for the failure to make any provisions for the West. It states the necessity of quieting the Indians, and then shows it was imperial interests which demanded some abridgment of the many intangible and conflicting colonial claims to the West.[19]

Many more explanations are given why the French villages of Michigan and of Illinois were left without any civil government by the Proclamation. The *Annual Register* claims that,

[16] Military expeditions had been sent to occupy some of the western posts as early as 1760. It was not until May, 1767, that the cabinet concerned itself with the problem of providing some government for the western posts. " Minutes of American Business," *Ill. Hist. Colls.*, XI, 467.

[17] *Ibid.*, X, 492; XI, 112, 125, 130, 469.

[18] *N. Y. Hist. Colls. for 1876*, p. 270.

[19] *Annual Register for 1763*, p. 20.

because of ignorance of the new country and because the area of it was of little value, the old colonies were without definite boundaries. The early charters were given when the western limits were the limits of America itself, and prodigality was shown by the kings in what they considered of no importance. The same was true of the royal colonies, which led to much embarrassment. The unraveling of this difficulty could be solved, according to the *Register,* only by the mediation of Parliament.[20]

Hillsborough also offered his explanations. In the report of the Lords of Trade in 1772, he stated that the main objects of the Proclamation were to confine the settlements so that they should lie within reach of the trade and the commerce of the realm, and also to keep the colonies near the coast so that they might more easily be kept in due subordination. He believed that the main purpose of colonizing upon the continent of North America was to improve and extend the commerce, navigation, and manufactures of Great Britain. " Let the savages enjoy their deserts in quiet," he concluded. " Were they driven from their forests the peltry trade would decrease; and it is not impossible that worse savages would take refuge in them." [21] This was no doubt the mercantilist idea. It is probable that Hillsborough knew nothing about Michigan or the West, as he was extremely ignorant concerning the geography of the new regions. But the government did not follow this policy. The King and his advisers did not contemplate keeping the territory as a perpetual forest preserve. Tracts were to be purchased from the Indians from time to time as the need arose. The Proclamation line did temporarily restrict settlements but did not establish an ultimate boundary that would keep the West, in the word of Burke, " a lair of wild beasts."

[20] *Ibid.,* p. 21.
[21] Sparks (ed.), *Writings of Franklin,* IV, 303 ff. This was Hillsborough's answer to the petition of the Ohio Company. Franklin made a vigorous reply, and when the matter came up before the Privy Council the Ohio Company's petition was granted. Hillsborough was so much chagrined that he resigned immediately from the ministry. Alvord, *Mississippi Valley,* II, 134 ff.

The Proclamation did have a clause of great concern to Michigan. It attempted to place certain restrictions upon the unregulated fur trade. Traffic in furs was to be open in the future to all traders but only upon procuring a license. They were also required to give security that they would observe any regulations that the Crown or its commissioners might make.

There was immediate opposition to the Proclamation. The fur traders whom one contemporary called " base, cowardly and abandoned wretches," and the land speculators, who Johnson said preferred " a Bull feast at Albany and a little Rum," naturally opposed any restrictions.[22] They hoped the Indians might " consume like a March snow and no enquiry be made concerning lands patented." [23] Because of the disastrous results which occurred from leaving the Indian question to the various colonies, and the immensity of the additional burdens, the English policy was indeed the best one ever proposed by any colonizing nation up to this time. But aside from the traders and speculators, there were now great numbers in the colonies anxious to swarm into the new lands. No steps whatsoever were taken to settle this very difficult problem, which failure is in a large degree attributable to the sudden changes in the government at home. The effect on the colonial attitude was little less than a calamity. A prohibition which had been intended to be temporary seemed to have become permanent. Thus the decree, which was worked out with good intentions, and was of great significance for Michigan and all of the West, made quite a different impression on colonial minds. It seemed to them that a deliberate effort was under way to keep them out of the fertile lands of the West. At this same time new restrictions were placed upon their trade at sea, and this, along with many other limitations, made it appear to them that " they were being squeezed by the British Govern-

[22] Johnson to the Lords of Trade, May 24, 1765. *N. Y. Col. Docs.*, VII, 713; *Ill. Hist. Colls.*, X, 505.
[23] *N. Y. Col. Docs.*, VII, 714.

ment like nuts in a cracker." It is clear that the government had not intended to be tyrannical, yet this does not lessen its responsibility for the outcome.

In view of the Proclamation, Michigan was without any provisions for the arrest of offenders against the law within that region. This was one of the most serious blunders made, because the whole area suffered greatly from unscrupulous traders until 1775, when civil government was partially established. It had been seen, as Egremont pointed out, that just such a situation would arise, if there was no definite jurisdiction over the West, and Shelburne had proposed placing it under the control of the army chief.[24] In 1765 General Gage, aware of the situation, called it to the attention of Lord Halifax, who remedied the condition by a clause in the Mutiny Act of that year, whereby all persons were authorized to make arrests of criminals, and the military officers were empowered to bring them to the nearest colony for trial.[25]

The most serious error was perhaps the wording of the Proclamation so that Quebec received the same treatment as the other provinces. This directly affected the western areas as the post commanders of Michigan were responsible to the Brigadier General at Quebec. Shelburne had proposed to secure for the French inhabitants of the ceded territory all of the privileges guaranteed by the Treaty of Paris.[26] The object had been to increase the Protestant settlers, and ultimately to allow them a representative assembly. Neither Shelburne nor anyone else had any fears concerning the wisdom of this procedure, for this would make settlement more attractive. Had this occurred the laws of Canada would have been considerably changed. Indeed it was only reasonable to expect that Canada would at some future time have the same form of government as the other provinces.

[24] Lords of Trade to the King, August 5, 1763, Shortt and Doughty, *Can. Const. Docs.*, pt. i, p. 152. It is probable that the Board of Trade planned to place the Indian reservation under the jurisdiction of the Indian Department.
[25] Alvord, *Mississippi Valley in British Politics*, I, 206.
[26] Shortt and Doughty, *Can. Const. Docs.*, pt. i, p. 142.

What then was to be the law of the West? It would largely depend upon the procedure in Canada. The judicial system, according to the Proclamation, was to be established consisting of civil and criminal courts governed by law and equity " as near as may be agreeable to the laws of England," with the right to appeal, in civil cases, to the British Privy Council. The formal establishment of civil government was brought about by Governor Murray whose régime was marked by a real desire to conciliate the French. In practice English law was not introduced to the exclusion of French, but abuses in its administration, the conflict of law and of opinion, and the failure to define the exact legal status of the inhabitants brought about great uncertainty and some injustice.[27]

There were many other blunders made, but none which directly affected Michigan. Naturally very severe censure was soon directed toward those responsible for the Proclamation. No one was willing to admit himself the author of the document. On the supposition that English law had replaced French it is of interest to see what was the attitude of judicial England. " If it is to be considered as importing English laws, I take it to be an act of the grossest and absurdest and cruelest tyranny, that a conquering nation ever practiced over a conquered country," was the rhetorical flourish of Attorney General Thurlow in 1774.[28] Lord Mansfield, the greatest jurist of the day, broke forth in great invective when he heard of the act. " Is it possible," he said, " that we have abolished their laws, and customs, and forms of judicature all at once? a thing never to be attempted or wished. The history of the world

[27] Burt, *Old Province of Quebec*, chaps. V, VI are excellent accounts of Governor Murray; Humphreys, " Lord Shelburne and the Proclamation of 1763 "; R. A. Humphreys and S. M. Scott, " Lord Northington and the Laws of Canada," *Canadian Historical Review*, XIV, 42 ff. For an excellent, though brief, account of the beginnings of British rule in Canada, see Duncan McArthur, "The New Régime," in *Canada and Its Provinces*, III, 21-49. An excellent account is given in Burt, *loc. cit.*, chaps. II-VII. The Proclamation and the work of Murray and Carleton is ably presented by W. P. M. Kennedy, *The Constitution of Canada* (London, 1922), pp. 32-47.

[28] Sir Henry Cavendish, *Debates of the House of Commons in 1774* (London, 1839), p. 29.

don't furnish an instance of so rash and unjust an act by any conqueror whatsoever; much less by the Crown of England, which has always left to the conquered their own laws and usages, with a change only so far as sovereignty was concerned." [29]

Explanations offered for the blunder were many. The one most common was that the English law was intended to apply only to the new settlers who entered the territory.[30] Hillsborough placed all the blame upon the " weak, ignorant, and interested Men " who carried the Proclamation into effect, and " who expounded it in the most absurd Manner, oppressive and cruel to the last Degree to the Subjects, and entirely contrary to the Royal Intention." [31] He claimed as a member of the Board of Trade that it was never their intention to overturn the laws of Canada. In his letter to Carleton he asserted, " it never entered into Our idea to overturn the Laws and Customs of Canada, with regard to Property, but that Justice should be administered agreably to them, according to the Modes of administering Justice in the Courts of Judicature in this Kingdom." [32]

These excuses did not right the blunders made in regard to Canada and the West. The question of correcting them entered into the western policy of every succeeding British ministry.

The Proclamation line would have prohibited any settlers coming from the older colonies into Michigan to take up lands; but there were large unsettled areas to the east of that line, from whence gradually they might have spread as far as Michigan. To many the Proclamation seemed to deprive them of any share in the lands for which they had fought and bled.[33] No arbitrary line of demarcation would keep the frontiersmen

[29] Alvord, *Mississippi Valley in British Politics*, I, 208–209.
[30] A summary of various interpretations in Shortt and Doughty, *Can. Const. Docs.*, pt. i, p. 440–41.
[31] Hillsborough to Carleton, March 6, 1768. *Ibid.*, 297; Canadian Archives, Q, V, pt. i, pp. 347–48.
[32] Shortt and Doughty, *Can. Const. Docs.*, pt. i, p. 297.
[33] *N. Y. Hist. Colls. for 1886*, p. 270.

forever from pouring over the mountains into the inviting lands of the Ohio Valley.[34] Not even the Pontiac Uprising with its attendant horrors sufficed to keep back the tide of migration.[35] There was no real machinery to enforce the Proclamation, although Sir William Sharpe, Governor of Maryland, did suggest to Shelburne that the army be " directed to destroy such Houses and otherwise to punish such Offenders " [36] as attempted to settle beyond the boundary line. The detachments of troops, widely scattered, were quite inadequate to patrol the vast West. Some of the more conscientious provincial governors did attempt to prevent all illegal settlements; [37] but on the other hand, most were very inattentive in the premises.[38]

Very soon after the Proclamation was issued the Lords of Trade framed an elaborate plan as a result of correspondence with the Indian superintendents, for the future control of Indian relations and white settlements.[39] This plan was submitted to the King on July 10, 1764.[40] It proposed a well organized Indian Department, with two Indian superintendents; fixed revenues from the trade; licenses, definite regulations for all traders, and the repeal of all conflicting colonial laws. It remedied an old abuse by permitting the acquiring of the Indian lands only through an imperial agent, where formerly the colonial authorities had promiscuously purchased the lands.

For various reasons this plan, which would have solved the fur traders' problems for Michigan and the interior, was never put into execution. Sir William Johnson maintained that it was because of " the late disturbances in the Colonies that

[34] Ford (ed.), *Writings of Washington*, II, 221 note; *Archives of Maryland* (Baltimore, 1883–), XIV, 468.

[35] *Ibid.*, 211.

[36] *Ibid.*, 362.

[37] *Ibid.*, 199, 362.

[38] Sparks (ed.), *Franklin's Works*, IX, 130. Robert R. Livingston writing to Franklin said: " Virginia even after the Proclamation of 1763 patented considerable tracts upon the Ohio far beyond the Appalachian Mountains." *Ibid.*

[39] These letters are printed in the *N. Y. Col. Docs.*, VII, 535–72. See Alvord, *Mississippi Valley*, I, chap. VIII for a full discussion of this plan.

[40] *N. Y. Col. Docs.*, VII, 637; *Ill. Hist. Colls.*, X, 273.

required so much of the attention of His Majesty's Ministers."[41] The Board of Trade asserted that they were far too
busy with "other pressing business"[42] to work out any satisfactory instructions and plans for the Indian Department. No
doubt there is much truth in the statement of Colonel Guy
Johnson that the main cause for the failure of the scheme was
the influences of "some Indian Traders" whose business
might suffer if a more efficient administration in the West were
put into operation.[43] Perhaps the main stumbling block to the
inauguration of the new system was the expense involved,
which was expected to be £20,000 annually. The Bedford-
Grenville Ministry was pledged to economy, and to meet the
additional expense of the Indian Department it planned to
place a tax upon the fur trade. This would have necessitated
an act of Parliament; but the ministry never dared bring the
plan to such an issue.

In the meantime Johnson, expecting that his recommendations would be enacted, began carrying out the plan of 1764 in
his department. In spite of inadequate funds, treaties were
made with the Indians in order to establish a definite boundary line between them and the whites.[44] Licenses were issued
to the traders; rules for the various posts were drawn up; peace
negotiations were undertaken with Pontiac and his followers;
new posts were planned; commissaries were arranged for;
smiths and interpreters were appointed. All was to be regularly
supervised by deputies. The western area was divided into several districts. One of these, placed in charge of Guy Johnson,
was the Illinois which included the region of Michilimackinac,
Green Bay, and Niagara. Stringent instructions were drawn
up, which were intended to control all of the details of the
trade, in order to put an end to cheating the Indians. The
deputies were especially ordered to supervise carefully the
inspection of the trade.[45]

[41] *N. Y. Col. Docs.*, VII, 836.
[42] *Ibid.*, 842.
[43] *Ibid.*, 718–41, 1004.
[44] *Ibid.*
[45] *Ibid.*, VIII, 655.

Johnson, in carrying out the plans of 1764, sent Croghan to hold conferences with the tribes about Detroit in August of 1765.

To invitations sent by Colonel Bradstreet, thirty chiefs, and about five hundred braves of the Ottawa, Potawatomi, Ojibway, Wyandot, and neighboring tribes assembled. Le Grand Sauteur, better known as Minavavana, who had successfully led the assault on Michilimackinac in 1763, was among those present. Colonel Campbell and representatives of the Six Nations were present to aid Croghan. Pontiac was the most important member present and took an active part in the congresses. The warriors agreed to give up all prisoners, to permit the occupation of the western posts, and to recognize the sovereignty of the English. The King's agents promised that the trade would be reopened on favorable terms, and presents would be freely distributed.[46]

It was now definitely the task of the English ministry to accept or reject the achievements of the Indian superintendent. There was considerable opposition to the work of Johnson. At every turn he was handicapped by the colonial governors who issued licenses at random, which greatly increased the number of small traders throughout the fur regions.[47] The ministry also was opposed to the new plan because it would increase expenses. Shelburne was at heart a free trader.[48] He sincerely felt that it was the very " nature of Trade to regulate itself," and he hoped that the fur trade would do so, and thus eliminate the very heavy expenses connected with it.[49] He wrote to the Southern Indian Superintendent, and advised him to attend to the minutest detail of every expense connected with his department, for he complained " the expenses of your dis-

[46] Croghan's " Journals, 1765 "; N. Y. Col. Docs., VII, 734; Shelburne Papers, L, 273.
[47] I. A. Johnson, Michigan Fur Trade (Lansing, 1919), chap. IV.
[48] Shelburne had not as yet advocated the principles of free trade but had come under the influence of Adam Smith. J. Rae, Life of Adam Smith (London, 1895), pp. 153–54.
[49] Shelburne to Carleton, June 2, 1767. Canadian Archives, Q, IV, 131; Humphreys, " Lord Shelburne and British Colonial Policy, 1766–1768," gives an excellent account of Shelburne's policy.

trict run so much above all expectation and proportion." [50]

Perhaps the very center of the opposition was the fur traders themselves. Soon after the British occupation, there came into the country a large number of Scotchmen, who, by their business acumen and thrift, were soon able to gain control of the fur trade, and thus began that brilliant line of Scotch fur barons which is still in existence.[51] Under the French system, the *coureurs de bois* had been accustomed to go among the Indians in their villages, and accompany them on their hunting expeditions in order to exchange their merchandise for furs. This system made it unnecessary for the red men to make long journeys in order to sell their pelts.[52] The English plan of 1764, which proposed bringing the furs to specified posts, ran contrary to an age-old custom. Naturally it failed. If the proposed scheme was to have worked at all, it would have meant such an increased number of posts and soldiers as to render the cost prohibitive.

No rules and regulations drawn up in far-away London were going to stop the unscrupulous traders. Indeed, little or no attention was ever given to them. All the post officials found it a practical impossibility to enforce the trading laws, while dishonest traders always found ready accomplices in the French *habitants*. Major Bassett, while commandant at Detroit, wrote Haldimand that he had no possible means of controlling unscrupulous traders.[53] Sir William constantly complained to Shelburne that the traders roamed at will, without passes, contrary to former practice. In absolute defiance of the government, he said, many of these traders lived in the Indian country where they were under no inspection whatsoever. It was unnecessary for them to come to the posts for fresh supplies, because they might have the supplies sent up country by

[50] Shelburne to Stuart, December 11, 1766. *Ill. Hist. Colls.*, XI, 454.

[51] Johnson, *Michigan Fur Trade*, chap. V, *passim*. The best account of the fur traders is in Wayne Stevens, *The Northwest Fur Trade, 1763–1800* (Urbana, 1928).

[52] Carleton to Shelburne, March 2, 1768, Canadian Archives, Q, V, pt. i, p. 383.

[53] Bassett to Haldimand, April 29, 1773, *Mich. Hist. Colls.*, XIX, 297.

the great merchant houses. He felt that this was very injurious to the fur traders. The only solution he could offer was to allow the traders to go where they pleased and operate at their own discretion, or to confine them totally to the posts.[54] In 1765, the traders of Detroit and Michilimackinac, through their merchants at Montreal, memorialized Governor Murray and his council on the conditions of the fur trade.[55] The many obnoxious restrictions on their trade, they said, "discourage the traders from engaging therein to the total ruin of that Valuable Branch of Commerce, the lessening of his Majesty's Revenue and the Consumption of British Manufactures more especially the Woollen; besides depriving the Merchants of the necessary Remittances." They argued that when the Indian trade was free and open, not only did the trade increase, but the Indians were kept in good humor, and thus were attached to the interests of Great Britain.[56] They also pointed out that many Indians like the Sioux, Fox, and Sacs, had to travel a considerable distance to purchase their supplies, and that many traders made no pretense of obeying the various regulations, thus giving them a decided advantage over those who did.[57] To add to all of these difficulties, the French traders were intruding in every direction.[58]

The traders were unable to get any satisfactory redress from Governor Murray, who considered some of the commercial element as "Licentious Fanaticks," and characterized three of them, one as a "Turbulent Man" and a "notorious smuggler," and another as a "weak Man of Little Character," and the third a "conceited Boy."[59] Friction became general, and

---

[54] Johnson to Shelburne, May 30, 1767, *N. Y. Col. Docs.*, VII, 929.
[55] There are many of these memorials. Canadian Archives, Q, VIII, 133 ff.; C. O. 42, II, pt. ii, p. 362.
[56] *Ibid.*, I, pt. i, p. 113.
[57] *Ibid.*, Q, XLVIII, pt. ii, p. 363.
[58] Shelburne Papers, XLVIII, 91. They penetrated to the sources of the Mississippi, into Lakes Superior and Michigan, and far into surrounding regions. There were no restrictions placed upon them by the home government, and they also had had the great advantage of a long and friendly intercourse with the natives. *Ibid.*, LI, 205.
[59] Governor Murray to the Lords of Trade, October 29, 1764, Shortt and Doughty, *Can. Const. Docs.*, pt. i, pp. 231-32.

finally trader and merchant petitioned the King for the recall of the Governor.[60] The London merchants also urged the establishment of civil government in Canada hoping to bring about peace in the colony, and to reap additional results from the trade.[61]

In 1766, Murray was succeeded by Sir Guy Carleton. At once, he was petitioned by the traders, with whom he was more sympathetic than Murray had been. He soon realized that many of the new British regulations were inapplicable to the fur trade, and concluded that the best plan for its conduct was to follow the old established course. To this effect he wrote the Lords of Trade in March, 1767, requesting that the Canadians conduct the fur trade under the old system. He said that if the present restraints were continued, there would be a great diminution in the trade, and perhaps it might be thrown again into the hands of the French, " over whom," he claimed, " the English have many advantages if they are properly pursued." [62] Due mainly to Carleton's influence, as well as that of Johnson, Shelburne in 1767 ordered the superintendent to allow traders to roam at will over all the region north of Lake Superior and the Ottawa River.[63] This was a great help to the Michilimackinac traders.

The general policy of Great Britain toward Michigan and the West was determined by the fur trade and the Indians.[64] General Gage considered the peltry trade the principal benefit to be derived from North America.[65] He thought that it should be developed at the least expense possible, with all emphasis laid upon due regulations to stamp out the illegal or unlicensed trading and smuggling. There was no effective force at his

---

[60] Petition of the Quebec Traders to the King, *ibid.*, pp. 232–34.

[61] Petition of the London Merchants to the King, *ibid.*, pp. 235–36.

[62] Carleton to the Lords of Trade, March 28, 1767, Canadian Archives, Q, IV, 198; Carleton to Johnson, March 27, 1767, *Mich. Hist. Colls.*, X, 222–24. See especially the excellent article by Marjorie G. Reid, " The Quebec Fur Traders and Western Policy, 1763–1774," *Canadian Historical Review*, VI, 15–33.

[63] Canadian Archives, Q, V, pt. i, p. 383.

[64] *Ante*, pp. 50–51.

[65] Gage to Hillsborough, November 10, 1770, printed in Carter, *The Illinois Country*, p. 78.

disposal to do this, for the number of the troops was so small, and they were so widely scattered, that the exercising of police power would be an impossibility.

Illicit trading went on throughout the Old Northwest. The traders whom Major Bassett well described as " the outcasts of all Nations, and the refuse of Mankind," [66] would charge the members of the garrisons exorbitant prices. They smuggled in their goods with the aid of the French, and were a constant source of friction. The defeat of the Indians in 1763 did not make them any more inclined to trade with the English than before. The English officials were aware of the fact that the French had a great hold on the peltry trade.[67] The fur imports to England fell off instead of increasing after the conquest of Canada,[68] a fact which would ruin the very aims of the mercantilist policy. Many Britishers had expected that by placing garrisons in the western posts, the French control of the fur trade would be broken up. There is no doubt that the fur exports from Michigan were greatly diminished because the English traded as a rule around the established posts, while the French and the Spanish carried on a trade in all directions by land and by water.[69] There was especially keen competition among the rival traders, where the French carried on an unlicensed trade, as they had the advantage of the good will of the Indians, and freely mingled among them. This the English traders were legally not allowed to do.[70] The French

[66] Bassett to Haldimand, April 29, 1773. *Mich. Hist. Colls.*, XIX, 297. On August 3, 1787, Bassett wrote Haldimand: " In Trade the lowest of all the profession resort to these obscure places, they are without education or sentiment & many of them without common honesty." *Ibid.*, XX, 288.

[67] O'Callaghan, *Documentary History of New York*, II, 476–503.

[68] The value of the skins exported from America in 1764–68 was as follows:

1764	£28,067/18
1765	£27,801/11
1766	£24,657/ 0
1767	£20,262/ 2
1768	£18,923/18

Printed in Carter, *Illinois Country*, p. 94 n. The total value of beaver skins exported from Canada in 1764 was £ 17,259 sterling, and in 1768 it was £ 13,168 sterling. *Ibid.* Croghan estimated the fur trade in the Illinois country amounted to £ 80,000 sterling per year, mostly going to the French via New Orleans. Croghan to Gage, January 16, 1767, Shelburne Papers, XLVIII, 153.

[69] O'Callaghan, *Documentary History of New York*, II, 476.

[70] *Ibid.*, 531.

ascended the Ohio, the Wabash, and the Illinois Rivers, and crossed the Mississippi River above the Illinois, even coming within twenty leagues of Detroit,[71] plying their traffic as far to the northward as Lake Superior, thus into the most productive area in fur-bearing animals of the Mississippi Valley.[72] Through intrigues, false representations, and presents, the French planned to checkmate every move of the English, and were unusually successful.[73] The redmen were shown how they would suffer from the penurious policy of the English.[74]

The very geography of the Upper Mississippi Valley was also a large factor in losing the peltry trade of Michigan. Only small portages at the Fox, St. Joseph, or Miami Rivers were necessary for an easy passage down to the Mississippi and thence to New Orleans. It was perfectly natural to follow the path of least resistance, and float the goods down stream to New Orleans, the natural emporium of the basin.[75] This was a keen disappointment to the English government. General Gage thought as long as furs sold at a higher price in the New Orleans market than at London, some English manufactures might reach the West, but none of the peltry exchanged for them would ever reach Great Britain.[76] He felt that the trade would naturally " always go with the stream . . . either down the Mississippi or the St. Lawrence." [77] Johnson was of the same opinion.[78] Unless the fur trade could be diverted from its natural course, or New Orleans and Louisiana annexed to the West, few of the pelts would find their way into Great Britain again frustrating the purposes of Mercantilism.

[71] Johnson to Lords of Trade, November 16, 1767, *N. Y. Col. Docs.*, VII, 775; Johnson's Report, 1767, *ibid.*, 965; Carleton to Johnson, March 27, 1767, Canadian Archives, Q, IV, 125; *Mich. Hist. Colls.*, X, 222–24.

[72] Gage's report on the state of government of Montreal, printed in Shortt and Doughty, *Can. Const. Docs.*, pt. i, p. 96. Frobisher found French traders in the Lake Superior region in 1766. " Observations on the Indian Trade." November 10, 1766, Shelburne Papers, L, 351.

[73] *N. Y. Col. Docs.*, VIII, 105, 263.

[74] Johnson to Carleton, January 27, 1767, Canadian Archives, Q, IV, 115.

[75] Carleton to Johnson, March 27, 1767, *Mich. Hist. Colls.*, X, 222–24.

[76] Gage to Shelburne, February 22, 1767, Carter, *Gage's Correspondence*, I, 121–22; Canadian Archives, Dartmouth Transcripts, 1765–1775, pp. 61–62; O'Callaghan, *Documentary History of New York*, II, 485.

[77] *Ibid.*, 486.

[78] *Ibid.*, 488.

The English officials in America were not at all lukewarm to these problems, and their minds were far from being stagnant. Officers far and wide tried to find some panacea for the situation. As early as 1764, Lieutenant Governor Colden outlined to the Lords of Trade an effective plan for the prevention of smuggling, and for the payment of the various duties. According to it, the duties on the furs were to be paid, in kind, at a definite rate, at the posts where the pelts were procured. A certificate of the duty paid was to be sent with every pack of furs to the customs houses where they were exported. All furs, paid in kind at the post, were to be sent once a year to the customs houses, where they would be sold at public auction.[79]

The merchants at Detroit argued that the only remedy for the situation was to remove all the cumbersome restraints which had been placed on the trade.[80] They maintained that the only possible means of preventing the evils in the future, and removing the discontents of the Indians, was to permit them (the traders) to roam at will among the red men, and thus they could check the French menace by underselling them.[81] This was the program, they claimed, that was used by the French so successfully.[82]

General Gage placed great confidence in the army as a means of restraining illicit traders. He believed that if the officers at the respective posts were given judicial power, the various regulations could be rigidly enforced. He advised increasing the garrisons in Michigan, and the erection of posts at the mouths of the Ohio, the Illinois, and other rivers which would prevent bateaux from descending to New Orleans.[83] This would involve such great expense that Gage reluctantly gave up the plan.[84]

Sir William Johnson wanted to confine the northern trade

[79] N. Y. Hist. Colls., IX, 380–86.

[80] Memorial of Detroit Traders to Jehu Hay, September 4, 1767; Memorial of Detroit Traders to Johnson, November 26, 1767, Canadian Archives, Q, IV, 125 ff.

[81] Ibid., 126.

[82] Quite the contrary was the case. Johnson, Michigan Fur Trade, chaps. II, III.

[83] Gage to Amherst, March 20, 1762, Mich. Hist. Colls., XIX, 17 ff.

[84] Ibid.

strictly to the posts in communication with the Great Lakes. Thus all furs would go down the St. Lawrence, putting an end to the illicit traffic from Michigan and other parts of the Northwest through New Orleans. He hoped that the trade of the Mississippi might be diverted from West Florida where French traders were plentifully supplied. This would be a difficult task, Sir William thought, because each province had its own peculiar interests which often interfered with the good of the whole.[85]

The possible solution to this problem lay in the seizure of Louisiana from Spain. The ministry had such a plan in mind, and much correspondence passed between Generals Gage and Haldimand who was stationed in West Florida, as to the best method for an attack upon New Orleans.[86] When controversy with Spain over the Falkland Islands broke out in 1771, Hillsborough instructed Gage to prepare an army to attack New Orleans by way of the Ohio and the Mississippi Rivers.[87] This no doubt would have solved the western trade problem, for it never could be settled in its international aspect until the whole Mississippi Valley was controlled by one nation. War was averted and New Orleans was not disturbed. It is worth while to notice at this time that the West had never been of great profit to any European nation.[88]

In December, 1767, the Lords of Trade made a favorable report to the ministry upon a final determination of the western boundary line. They attributed the many complaints of the Indians to the continual encroachments upon their lands. The report recited that the superintendents of Indian affairs had long urged the necessity of establishing a boundary line between the Indian country and the settlements of the white people, and urged the ministry to send orders at once to Johnson to make a final settlement of this boundary line in a congress for that purpose, and to make such " gratification to the

<hr />

[85] O'Callaghan, *Documentary History of New York*, II, 488.
[86] Carter, *Illinois Country*, p. 143.
[87] Hillsborough to Gage, January 2, 1771, *ibid.*, appendix III, pp. 182–84.
[88] *Ibid.*, chap. V, gives an exhaustive account of trade conditions from 1765–1775.

said Indians, as the nature and extent of the concessions on their part shall appear to require." [89]

The ministry advised Sir William of their desires, and as a result the treaty of Fort Stanwix was negotiated in 1768, with the Six Nations.[90] It was of small importance for Michigan. Although the imperial government was going to allow settlements beyond the line of 1763, still no settlers could migrate as far west as the present Wolverine state. A similar agreement was made with the Indians by the Treaty of Lochabar in 1770, which opened another small area to white settlement.[91]

There can be no question concerning the wisdom of these treaties, although they may have retarded the growth of Michigan's population. No doubt further illegal encroachments upon the redman's lands would have plunged the western people into another Indian war.

But in vain was the hope of those who thought by a paper boundary to keep back the hardy American pioneers. The pleasing valleys of the Ohio, the rolling prairies of Illinois, and the rich fur regions about Michigan, were far too great a temptation to be resisted. The pioneers came first as fur traders or hunters, then as prospectors, and lastly as settlers. They hunted the big game, set up claims to the lands, cleared the forests, built rude dwellings, and began to populate the great and potential West. Already the wide wedge of the future western migration was set, which, as the decades rolled by, was to open wider and wider the breach.

There was much talk of planting new colonies in the West, and perhaps schemes might have matured had it not been for the American War of Independence. Croghan, when in London in 1764, reported to Johnson that Lord Halifax was greatly interested in the establishment of a colony on the Ohio, and desired to have all the necessary information concerning that region.[92] Bradstreet, in 1764, asked permission to plant

---

[89] *N. Y. Col. Docs.*, VII, 1004-5.
[90] *Ibid.*, VIII, 111 ff.
[91] The *Annual Register* and the *Gentlemen's Magazine* give clear indications of widespread interest in western lands.
[92] Croghan to Johnson, March 10, 1764, *Ill. Hist. Colls.*, X, 223.

a colony at Detroit for the purpose of keeping the control of the fur trade in the hands of the English.[93] It was not until 1768, that the British ministry gave any serious attention to the problem of western colonies. Previous to that time, Michigan with its posts was looked upon as of value only for keeping control of the fur trade. In 1768, Shelburne proposed to establish and maintain three English settlements in the West, one at Detroit, one on the Upper Ohio, and the third in the Illinois region.[94] The Lords of Trade, while not opposing this, suggested that " The proposition of forming inland colonies in America is, we humbly conceive, entirely new; it adopts principles in respect to American settlements different from what has hitherto been the policy of this kingdom, and leads to a system which, if pursued through all its consequences, is in the present state of this country of great importance." [95] Nothing definite came of Shelburne's idea, and the government made no effort to encourage settlements in the West. Thus the population of Michigan showed only a normal increase during the British régime.

There was never as much interest in establishing settlements along the " Straits " as in the Ohio and Illinois Valleys. In 1764, Governor Colden, in his report to the Board of Trade, suggested that Indian lands be purchased at the various posts sufficient only for a few farmers to raise provisions for the garrison.[96] This seemed to be Haldimand's plan during the war.[97] Under the freedom finally given by England to the fur traders, the peltry trade became so profitable that most of the farms were neglected. This made it necessary to carry provisions to the villages of Detroit and Michilimackinac from the

---

[93] Shelburne Papers, L. 276.
[94] N. Y. Col. Docs., VII, 982; VIII, 27.
[95] Ibid. Shelburne was of the opinion such settlements would keep the Indians under control, furnish the army posts with food, secure the fur trade, check the intrigues of the Spanish and French, and protect the old colonies as an " exterior line of defense," Shelburne Papers, L, 178–81.
[96] N. Y. Hist. Colls. for 1876, p. 381.
[97] Haldimand to Hamilton, October 7, 1778. Mich. Hist. Colls., IX, 405; X, 302; same to De Peyster, July 13, 1780, ibid., 412.

East, making the support of the garrisons a heavy burden.[98] Colden stated that there were four hundred new subjects at Detroit who were familiar with farming and had raised wheat.[99] He therefore advised the Crown that " in order to make them more industrious in farming," they should be prohibited from trading with the Indians and from keeping goods and spirituous liquors in their houses for trade.[100]

Colden's suggestions were not carried out, nor were the plans of Shelburne given careful consideration. It seemed to be the policy of the government to oppose any schemes of colonization, because the settlement of the West would be harmful to the fur trade.[101] Perhaps the general attitude of the government may be discerned by its action toward the Vandalia project.[102] By this action it may be understood why no successful colonization plans were carried out in Michigan.

This proposed colony faced considerable opposition. The attitude of Lord Hillsborough has already been described.[103] He opposed the gradual expansion of the colonies because he felt that sound policy required the people to be kept together " in as narrow a compass as the nature of the lands and the state of things will admit." [104] Lord Dunmore likewise was opposed to any land projects on the ground that the establishment of colonies across the Appalachians would be of no value to England or the seaboard colonies; while immigration to a new colony would seriously reduce the value of land in the tidewater regions.[105] In spite of all the opposition, the Board of Trade approved the Vandalia scheme,[106] but by reason of

98 Stevens, *Northwest Fur Trade*, chaps. V, VI; Johnson, *The Michigan Fur Trade*.

99 *N. Y. Hist. Colls. for 1876* p. 381.

100 *Ibid.*

101 For the British estimate of the fur trade see Hansard, *Parliament Debates*, XXIII, 382, 409.

102 For the action of the Board of Trade on the Vandalia project, see Alvord, *The Mississippi Valley in British Politics*, II, 150 *et seq.*

103 *Ante*, p. 50.

104 Hillsborough's report of April 15, 1772, printed in Sparks (ed.), *Franklin's Works*, IV, 322.

105 *N. Y. Col. Docs.*, VIII, 253.

106 O'Callaghan, *Documentary History of New York*, II, 578.

the unsettled conditions in the colonies the charter for the company never passed the seals. It is quite unlikely that the government would have sanctioned new settlements which would possibly have diminished the fur trade. This would apply particularly to the territory north of the Ohio, though south of that river the government seemed to favor expansion.[107] This was probably due to the fact that the southern fur trade was considered of little importance. As to Michigan, the government clearly intended to leave it as a permanent Indian reservation.

The plan to keep the lake region for an Indian reserve did not go unchallenged. There were many Englishmen who held that the only solution to the western problem was, as Hillsborough said, " to let the savages enjoy their deserts in quiet . . . were they driven from their forests the peltry trade would decrease." [108] There were many others who made attempts to found colonies in the West,[109] and one of these concerned Michigan because part of her territory was included in the grant. Citizens of Connecticut were interested in the West because of their colony's claim to the large area directly to the south and west of Lake Erie. The largest part of this came under the jurisdiction of Detroit. Silas Deane showed an interest in the value of this region after Pelatiah Webster made known its potential greatness. He said that the West in the very near future would be very thickly populated and was

[107] Coffin, The Province of Quebec, p. 428.
[108] Sparks (ed.), Franklin's Works, IV, 318. Other opposition was expressed as shown in an anonymous letter to Dartmouth. The writer said that new settlements would:
    1. Take many people away from the older colonies by the novelty of the good soil and climate.
    2. Make the carriage of manufactures over the mountains prohibitive.
    3. Cause settlers of necessity to live on game and the use of pasture for their animals, and instead of being useful subjects they would become the " scurge of the Maritime colonies."
    4. Direct trade down the Mississippi to the French and Spanish. " Can a British Minister countenance the Loss of so many of our People to British Mfgs.," the writer exclaimed. " Possibly he is a politician who wants the West to increase and multiply and when numerous may become what the Tartars are in China, as he sees we now have no sufficient curb on our colonies," he further added. Canadian Archives, Dartmouth Transcripts, 1765–1775, pp. 305–308.
[109] Alden, New Governments West of the Alleghanies before 1780, passim.

destined to control the whole continent.[110] Deane suggested
to Samuel Parsons of Philadelphia that they form along with
the aid of Ebenezer Hazard of New York a company to make
a settlement near the southwest corner of Lake Erie or if
necessary on the Mississippi.[111] In 1774, an association was
formed with definite regulations formulated by Hazard. A
release of all the rights of Connecticut to the lands between
the western boundary of Pennsylvania and the Mississippi
was to be purchased by the money which each member was
to pay when admitted to the association. Every member in
good standing was to be entitled to one two-thousandth part
of all the lands granted by the Connecticut Assembly.[112] Hazard presented himself at Hartford in 1774 with a petition to
the General Assembly to procure a quitclaim; but it was rejected and the whole scheme was abandoned.[113] Deane did
not lose sight of this scheme entirely, for while in Paris in 1776,
he recommended to the Second Continental Congress that a
tract of land along the southern shore of Lake Erie be opened
for sale to settlers, and that the proceeds be used for the reduction of the public debt, or the payment of expenses.[114] At
this time the War of Independence consumed the entire energy
and thoughts of the members of Congress, so no attention
was paid to Deane's suggestions. Had the Americans failed
to win their freedom, Deane was of the opinion this region was
far enough away from the coast and might serve as a haven
for the patriots.

If Michigan had been open to settlement it would have
precipitated another Indian war. Johnson feared as much,
and he warned General Gage that in spite of the government's
policy illegal settlements were constantly being made beyond
the boundary line.[115] As time passed, things went from bad

[110] R. R. Hinman, *A Historical Collection from Official Records* (Hartford, 1842), p. 536.
[111] *Collections of the Connecticut Historical Society* (Hartford, 1860–), II, 131–35.
[112] *Ibid.*, 134.
[113] *Ibid.*, 133 n.
[114] *N. Y. Hist. Colls. for 1886*, p. 383.
[115] O'Callaghan, *Doc. Hist. of New York*, II, 503.

to worse for the Indians. The pioneers, in order to reach the West, were solving the problem their own way. Settlers began to crowd the wilderness trails. The Indians, much exasperated, could not be restrained from occasional scalping parties.[116] These were followed on the part of the frontiersmen by bloody outrages and reprisals. Often the eastern conservatives would leave the frontiersmen to the mercy of the Indians.[117] The cowardly revenge of the " Paxton boys " in December, 1763, against the peaceful Conestoga Indians was the outcome of just this lack of protection,[118] while Lord Dunmore's War is another case of this friction at a later date.

[116] Roosevelt, *Winning of the West,* I, *passim;* Nelson Vance Russell, " The Indian Policy of Henry Hamilton," *Canadian Historical Review* (Toronto, 1930), XI, 20 ff.
[117] This was particularly true in Pennsylvania.
[118] *Colonial Records of Pennsylvania,* IX, 138–42. The backwoodsman's viewpoint is well represented in the " Remonstrance from the Pennsylvania Frontier, 13 February, 1764."

CHAPTER IV

THE PROBLEMS OF PROVINCIAL ADMINISTRATION

THE EXPRESSION " Michigan " is used here to designate a small part of the western territory ceded by France to England in 1763. During the French period of control and under the English rule, Michigan, as a political unit, consisted of all the area within the boundaries of the present state, most of Wisconsin, and parts of northern Indiana and Ohio, as well as settlements on the left bank of the Detroit River. Because of the great importance of Detroit, the governor residing there was the most important official in the West, and Detroit was usually considered as the capital. During the French régime, Michigan was governed as a part of New France, and under British control it was considered a part of the province of Quebec.

The very year that marked the unsuccessful attempt of Connecticut to colonize in the West saw the passage by Parliament of the Quebec Act. Conditions in the trans-montane were approaching anarchy. Crime and disorder had become so widespread that it was impossible to expect any improvement until a civil government was established which could be expected to regulate the fur trade and the western posts. One of the definite purposes for the enactment of the Quebec Act was the desire to relieve this state of affairs and to provide for the creation of some legal power in the western areas. The British government had long recognized that the Proclamation of 1763 had been quite unsatisfactory for solving the many vexatious problems of the former French territory. Also in Quebec the many restrictions placed upon the free and unhindered worship of the Roman Catholics caused friction, while the status and privileges of the church needed more careful definition.[1] Certain evils and abuses in the administration of justice could be corrected only by clarifying which system of civil and criminal law was to prevail. But most important for Michigan were the regulations needed for the fur trade, the supervision of the Indians, and the need of some kind of civil government. To remedy these errors the ministry in 1773 summoned General Gage home, ordering him to bring together all available material relating to the West which would "explain as well the causes as the effects" of the many abuses and disorders in the West.[2] As a result of Gage's recommendations and those of Governor Carleton, Chief Justice Hey, and Lieutenant Governor Cramahé, and the careful investigation of the ministry, the Quebec Act, "the Magna Charta of the French Canadian race," received the royal assent on May 2, 1774.[3]

From the point of view of Michigan one of the major provisions of the Quebec Act was the annexation of all the area of the Old Northwest to the province of Quebec.[4] Because of the unsettled conditions in the old colonies it was deemed inexpedient to join the West with the East. It seemed most natural from economic, religious, social, and geographical reasons, to annex the region north of the Ohio to Quebec, as had been done by the French. "This," explained Lord North, "was the motive of the Lords in passing the Quebec Bill."[5]

This enlargement of the boundaries was of vital significance for Michigan and its fur trade. The traders were concerned over the establishment of a government which not only

[1] For a concise account of the restrictions placed on the Roman Catholics see Kennedy, *The Constitution of Canada*, pp. 35, 39–42; Coffin, *The Province of Quebec*, pp. 432–43; R. Coupland, *The Quebec Act* (Oxford, 1925), pp. 52–54.

[2] Canadian Archives, Q, VII, 7; B, X, 165, 178.

[3] The text of the act is found in Shortt and Doughty, *Can. Const. Docs.*, pt. i, 570–76. The most recent scholarly discussions of the Quebec Act are R. Coupland, *The Quebec Act*; Kennedy, *The Constitution of Canada*, chap. VII; Chester Martin, *Empire and Commonwealth* (Oxford, 1929), chap. III; Lucas, *A History of Canada, 1763–1812*, pp. 79–89; Burt, *The Old Province of Quebec*, chap. IX.

[4] Canadian Archives, *Report for 1884*, pp. 59, 61, 232.

[5] *Annual Register for 1774*, p. 76.

would secure their lives and property in the Great Lakes' area, but also would put an end to the constant encroachment by the white people on the Indian lands. It was William Knox's [6] contention, and surely he was well informed, that the western lands were included in the province of Quebec " with the avowed purpose of excluding all further settlement therein, and for the establishment of uniform regulations for the Indian trade." [7]

Politically Michigan as the result of the new legislation became an integral part of the province of Quebec, a crown colony, with a governor and a legislative council appointed by the King.[8] But, as there were so very few English inhabitants, and the French were unfamiliar with representative institutions, no provision was made for an assembly. General Carleton, who had been acting as governor, was retained. In the instructions issued to him dated January 3, 1775,[9] provision was made for the government of Michigan. It was to be governed from Quebec, and lieutenant governors or superintendents were to reside at Detroit and Michilimackinac. These instructions also provided for the establishment of inferior courts of criminal and civil jurisdiction in Detroit and Michilimackinac, which would co-operate with the superior courts at Montreal and Quebec.[10] These courts, together with the lieutenant governors, were to compose the civil government.[11] Carrying out these instructions, Governor Carleton appointed Henry Hamilton, the first lieutenant governor of Detroit, but the confusion attending the outbreak of the War of Independence prevented the establishment of the courts. Carleton wrote Hamilton: " The Legislative Council is met, but the times will not at present admit of any regulations being made for distant or remote situations while the commotions con-

---

[6] One of the Under-Secretaries of State for America.
[7] Printed in Alvord, *Mississippi Valley*, II, 242.
[8] Coffin, *Province of Quebec*, p. 278; *Parliamentary History of England from the Earliest Period to the Year 1803* (London, 1806-), XVII, 1358.
[9] Shortt and Doughty, *Can. Const. Docs.*, pt. ii, pp. 600 *et seq.*
[10] *Ibid.*, 600.
[11] *Ibid.*, 600, 607.

tinue, the power of the sword is chiefly and indeed only to be trusted to." [12] Hamilton was given a commission as a justice of the peace, with the right to issue warrants " for apprehending and sending down any Persons guilty of Criminal offenses " in his district, at least such as were " of consequence enough to deserve, taking that journey." [13] This seems to have been the extent of civil government during the war and the years immediately after in the Michigan area. The supreme power over the Indian country was to all intents and purposes vested in the governor-general at Quebec, while the lieutenant governors in the West were expected to carry out his orders in their respective posts. During the governorships of Carleton and Haldimand, the governor-general was also commander-in-chief of the army in the province. Thus a semi-military régime was the real government for all the upper country for a number of years. Undoubtedly this was the best which could have been worked out during the disorders of the Revolutionary period and the chaotic years immediately following.

Following Carleton's instructions Hamilton set out for Detroit where he arrived in November, 1775, after a long and perilous journey.[14] The American invasion of Canada late in 1775 and the subsequent events so completely absorbed the energy of Carleton that in spite of his efforts to keep well informed on affairs in the Old Northwest, especially with regard to military conditions, the lieutenant governors, the people, and the posts of the region were left largely to their own resources and devices.[15]

Prior to the attempted establishment of civil government under Hamilton, the commandants were the King's representatives in Michigan. They were confronted with most trying problems which, however, they attempted to solve to the best of their ability.

[12] Carleton to Hamilton, February 2, 1777, Mich. Hist. Colls., IX, 345.
[13] Ibid., 346. See especially the instructions to Lieutenant Governor Sinclair, article 2, ibid., 517.
[14] Hamilton passed through General Montgomery's lines disguised as a peasant. Canadian Archives, Q, XIII, 275.
[15] Mich. Hist. Colls., IX, 343–407; X, 261 et seq.

No sooner had English settlers entered Michigan than they began to agitate for the establishment of a civil government, an activity Murray and Carleton found common throughout the whole region under their jurisdiction.[16] The French inhabitants of Michigan had no spontaneous prompting toward things political. Theirs was to obey. From time immemorial they had been used to despotic rule, and were wholly untaught in any of the matters of self-government. The commandant had absolute dominion over them, and the priest, their most venerated man, had all power over their spiritual life. They considered they had been abandoned by their King at the close of the Seven Years' War, but still their affection for him continued. For the English government they felt no special regard, and considered it a " foreign yoke." [17] Although hope never entirely faded that in some way they might be restored to France, their habits of obedience were so well ingrained that they never organized a revolt. But they did cause much uneasiness to the post commanders during the War of Independence.[18] In general, one may think of them as rather indifferent during the struggle.[19]

Captain Donald Campbell, a " canny Scot " and a man of rare diplomacy, had two very delicate problems to solve as the first post commander at Detroit.[20] He and Major Rogers had been ordered to disarm the French inhabitants,[21] but as these settlers were so dependent on their guns for subsistence, Campbell was allowed to " leave some few " to those whose loyalty was unquestioned.[22] The Captain was also instructed to reconcile the Indians, and he succeeded admirably in this

[16] Canadian Archives, Q, I, pt. i, 372; Coupland, *The Quebec Act*, pp. 44–47; Kennedy, *Constitution of Canada*, p. 43 *et seq.*; Martin, *Empire and Commonwealth*, pp. 100–102.

[17] Canadian Archives, Q, XIV, 80.

[18] *Ibid.*, B, XCIX, 29. Carleton wrote Germain, September 28, 1776: " There is nothing to fear from the Canadians, so long as things are in a state of prosperity; nothing to hope for from them when in distress." *Ibid.*, Q, XII, 188.

[19] Hamilton to Haldimand, September 22, 1778. *Mich. Hist. Colls.*, IX, 478.

[20] Captain Campbell, later Major Campbell, assumed his duties in December, 1760. He was treacherously murdered by the Indians in July, 1763. Christie to Bouquet, July 10, 1763, *ibid.*, XIX, 211; Parkman, *Pontiac Conspiracy*, chap. XIV.

[21] *Mich. Hist. Colls.*, XIX, 43.

[22] *Ibid.*, 41–42.

task by a lavish distribution of presents.[23] The tremendous expense he incurred by so doing was a constant source of worry to him.[24] He found the people " in great want of everything," [25] as he expressed it, and upon his informing Colonel Bouquet of this condition, the latter sent two Dutch traders to Detroit in 1761 who brought thither the first stock of goods after the beginning of English rule.[26] The French respected Campbell, and during his period of control (December, 1760, to July, 1762), the small settlement prospered. He wrote Bouquet that the people seemed very happy at the change of government,[27] and later, " they have granted everything I have desired, . . . and I have not had one complaint against our soldiers," which condition he attributed to the fact the soldiers had not had any rum.[28] The women were beyond the commandant's fondest expectations, but the men he found very independent " like the rest of America." [29] His major difficulties seemed to be in getting supplies and ammunition.[30]

Before 1775, when civil government was proposed by the Quebec Act, the British inhabitants at Detroit were exceedingly pestiferous in their demands for an assembly, or at least for a civil government.[31] Colonel Bradstreet was of the opinion that a civil government would greatly encourage settlement in the region about Detroit, and he urged the ministry to take some action. He felt that such a government would be of great value for the following reasons:

(1) The Indians could better be controlled if the settlement grew;

[23] Monckton to Campbell, October 19, 1760, ibid., 44; Campbell to ———, May 21, 1761, ibid., 67–68.
[24] Campbell to Bouquet, December 23, 1760, ibid., 50; same to same, June 8, 1762, ibid., 151; same to same, September 23, 1762, ibid., 164.
[25] Same to same, November 2, 1760, ibid., 45.
[26] Ibid., 50, 99. Croghan claimed the French and Indians by their rendezvous of 1759 plundered the inhabitants, leaving them destitute of everything. See ante, p. 31.
[27] Campbell to Bouquet, November 2, 1760, Mich. Hist. Colls., XIX, 45.
[28] Same to same, undated, ibid., 48.
[29] Same to same, March 10, 1761, ibid., 63.
[30] Ibid., pp. 50, 116, 120, 129, 138, 153.
[31] Abbott to Dartmouth, 1770, Canadian Archives, Dartmouth Transcripts, M, Vol. 650, p. 323.

(2) More inhabitants would increase the food supply and thus furnish the garrison with provisions;

(3) Civil government was much better suited to regulate the fur trade than military control;

(4) There was need of more knowledge concerning the lakes and the military had no men to send on such a mission;

(5) More people at Detroit would certainly secure the communications with the St. Lawrence;

(6) They also would be a check on the machinations of the French and the Spanish in the West.[32]

Bradstreet was fearful lest the ministry might think that people so far removed from England would throw off their dependence upon the mother country, so he argued that the settlers never could supply themselves with manufactured goods, nor sell their furs elsewhere than in England.[33]

The merchants of London were also greatly concerned over the military establishment in Canada. In a memorial to the Lords of Trade in 1765, they claimed that their business at the western posts was greatly handicapped by the " impractical regulations of traders " that the military imposed.[34] They further declared that a military government was incompatible with the spirit of commerce and asked that an assembly be granted.[35] It was the opinion of many colonial officials that the military entertained great contempt for the mercantile people.[36] Much of this trouble would have been settled by the Quebec Act, had not the War of Independence made it quite impossible.

Many of the western officials had unusual success in pleasing all the conflicting peoples at the posts: the traders, the Indians, the merchants, and the *habitants*. Certainly one of the most successful was Patrick Sinclair. When he was recalled from the naval service on Lake Huron in 1768, a public

---

32 Shelburne Papers, L, 277.
33 *Ibid.*
34 " Memorial " of April 18, 1765, Canadian Archives, Q, II, 345 ff.
35 *Ibid.*
36 *Ibid.*, 378.

dinner was given in his honor by his friends as a testimony of their regard.[37]

The Indians, particularly the Chippewas, who had adopted Sinclair as a father, were so enraged at his removal that they threatened Detroit.[38] Thereupon Captain George Turnbull built some small outer forts, and had the old and new militia parade to show the Indians they had both the French and English to deal with. The Chief of the Chippewas demanded that Sinclair be returned, saying, " things may not go well if he does not come." By his " indefatigable assiduity in learning and suiting himself to their manners, customs and language," as well as by his generosity in supplying their wards and the care he gave the old men, women, and children, he had endeared himself to them as a demigod.[39]

Not all post officials were so popular. The people were very hard to please, and the problems were baffling and complex. Alexander Henry tells of being at Detroit in 1784 when Governor John Hay arrived. He was " received with much ceremony," he wrote, " but I expect he will be a *tight* lad for the Detroit Gentry." [40] The public were much dissatisfied with

[37] Letter from Detroit, August 15, 1768, published in the Quebec *Gazette*, November 3, 1768. Sinclair was presented with a fine piece of plate on this occasion.

[38] *Ibid.*, July 27. 1769. Letter from Detroit of April 29, 1769.

[39] *Ibid.* Turnbull told the Chippewas of Sinclair's safe arrival in New York, and said he would soon hear of his arrival in England. He expressed a hope that Sinclair would return to Detroit, and further advised the Indians that their new official, Captain Robinson, was not as rich as Sinclair, so they should not expect as much of him. *Ibid.*, August 3, 1769. In 1768, when Major Rogers was sent to Detroit and thence to Montreal for trial, Gage wrote Hillsborough, [August 17, 1768] that a " disorderly Tribe of Chippewas went there [Michilimackinac] with their Arms, and threw their English Belts into the Lake and invited other Nations to join them in releasing the Major from his Confinement. The Officer Commanding tryed to pacify them by various Methods but at length put the Garrison under Arms, and by the help of two Armed Boats conveyed Major Rogers on Board a Vessel, and sent him to Detroit." Canadian Archives, Dartmouth Transcripts, 1765–1775, p. 147. Printed in Carter, *Gage's Correspondence*, I, 184.

[40] Henry to William Edgar, August 11, 1784. Edgar MSS. Hay's health was very bad. He died in 1785 leaving a widow and six children, all under age. The oldest boy served under Sir William Johnson. Henry Hamilton, when governor of Canada, asked the ministry for a pension of £ 100 yearly for the mother and three girls. He explained that by a chain of events Hay had been unable to save anything, though he had served the crown faithfully twenty-nine years. Hay found the necessities of life at Detroit double what they were in England,

Hay, but they especially disliked Major William Ancrum, the post commandant, for he was found to be " very unsteady " and of a " violent temper."

Abuses of all kinds were bound to exist in such far-away posts, and generally there was no remedy. Some officials were summarily discharged and usually found no recourse. As late as 1794, the commandant at Michilimackinac dismissed Thomas Lusby, the blacksmith for the Indian Department.[41] The Indians complained of Lusby's beating and otherwise mistreating them if they did not make him presents for the work he was ordered to do. Charles Gautier, the interpreter and storekeeper at the same post, was later charged with embezzling an " enormous amount of the king's goods."[42] At Michilimackinac seemed to center much of the misgovernment and corruption. Many complaints were made against John Dease, the Indian deputy, for disposing to private traders large quantities of merchandise provided by the government for the Indians.[43] Lord Grenville found this justifiable, for the funds were used by Dease to repair the storehouse.

Every post commander always had to be alert to the Indian problem. Too many of the officials adopted the very unfortunate attitude of General Amherst, who said the savages were " the Vilest Race of Beings that ever Infested the Earth and whose Riddance from it, must be Esteemed a Meritorious Act for the good of Mankind."[44] Firm methods were always necessary, but Captains Campbell and Turnbull, Major Arent De Peyster, and others found the problem not insoluble if

Hamilton said, and he well knew. Unless the pension were granted. Hamilton felt the mother and girls would be reduced to beggary. Canadian Archives, Q, XXV. 149-50. Not all the problems arose among civil authorities. John Campbell had trouble with the grenadiers who refused to cut wood. Campbell to Gage. February 25, 1765. Gage MSS.

[41] Doyle to Chew. June 9. 1794. Canadian Archives. C. CCXLVII, 174.

[42] Doyle to England, February 2, 1793, *ibid.*, Q. LXVII, 171-74. The deficiency was valued at £ 481/6/6. This charge was later dismissed.

[43] Grenville to Dorchester, October 20, 1789, *ibid.*, Q, XLII, 145. Grenville was a " trifle " suspicious and he asked Lord Dorchester to investigate the charges, which the latter did. but did not condemn Dease. Dorchester to Grenville, June 21, 1790, *ibid.*, XLV, pt. ii, pp. 497-503. A similar case arose with Capt. Hopkins. Letter to Gage, Detroit, November 12, 1763. Gage MSS. This letter is signed by Rogers, Brehm, Cuvlor, McDougall, and several others.

[44] Canadian Archives, C. O. 5, LXIII, pt. i, p. 341.

the red men were properly treated.[45] Much responsibility must be laid to the French who stirred up the Indians. Gladwin wrote to Amherst in great wrath after the trying experiences of the Pontiac Conspiracy that the French people for the most part were traitors.[46] He did find some honest men among them.[47] The records show that the French stirred up the Indians to murder the English traders. Gage wrote Hillsborough in May, 1768, that two English peltry merchants were murdered by the Indians at St. Joseph and that " the vagabond French who have sheltered themselves in the Indian Villages, are suspected to have excited the savages to these Acts of cruelty." [48] Campbell was clever enough to see that the red men could be easily handled if they received little or no rum.[49] While he was in control at Detroit, every effort was made to place reasonable restrictions upon the amount shipped to the post.[50]

The unscrupulous traders used excessive amounts of liquor to cheat the Indians.[51] The British officials were most anxious to stamp out this iniquitous practice. McKee urged John Johnson to forbid licenses to traders with rum, for " it ruins the trade," he claimed.[52] The Indians even parted with their clothing for a small drink.[53] Daniel Claus was insistent that the pernicious traffic caused the loss of many of the red men.[54] It provoked murder and stealing, it left whole families destitute, and it lost to the Indians their hunting grounds,[55] most of the Indian agents thought. Governor Bassett of Detroit

[45] *Ibid.*, p. 291.
[46] Gladwin to Amherst, July 8, 1763, *ibid.*, 308.
[47] *Ibid.*, Monsieur Navarre, the two Babys, St. Martin, and La Bute. " They furnished me with Provisions at the utmost Peril of their lives, and I question without their Assistance, Whether I should have been able to Maintain my Post," he wrote. *Ante*, p. 41.
[48] Canadian Archives, LXXXVI, 125. Printed in Carter, *Gage's Correspondence*, I, 173.
[49] Campbell to Bouquet, December 11, 1760, *Mich. Hist. Colls.*, XIX, 48.
[50] *Ibid.*, 99, 128.
[51] *Ante*, p. 20.
[52] McKee to Johnson, June 20, 1791, *Mich. Hist. Colls.*, XXIV, 264.
[53] *Ibid.*
[54] Claus to Cramahé, July 25, 1772, Canadian Archives, Claus Papers, I, 137.
[55] *Ibid.*, 133.

observed that drinking kept the Indians from hunting,[56] and the chiefs declared it killed more of the young men than did war.[57] Amherst issued strict regulations to the officers at the posts not to permit any rum whatsoever to pass by.[58] He was determined to put an end to a trade so destructive to the Indians and so heavy and useless an expense to the Crown.[59] It did appear for a time as if only a small quantity of liquor was consumed.[60] Carleton followed Amherst's plan, and earnestly attempted to put an end to the practice which he spoke of as " so pernicious to the natural Commerce of this Country and so destructive of the Savage Race." [61]

In spite of all these attempts, during the War of Independence the consumption of rum increased to unheard of amounts.[62] General Haldimand reported that the expenditure for rum at Detroit was beyond his comprehension,[63] and since it brought poverty and disease to the Indian families, he placed definite limitations upon the sale of the liquor.[64] None of these restrictions could be enforced, for the post commanders had to have Indian support during the War, and this could only be maintained by freely distributing rum. In 1779 it was computed that 17,502 gallons were consumed at Detroit alone.[65] Because of the effect of the Governor's warning, the following year showed a consumption of only 10,254 gallons.[66] At Michilimackinac in 1780, over 1,800 gallons were used for the Indians.[67] There were several other posts supplied from the government's store, so naturally it was of great concern to limit the amounts. The evil was never stamped out. In 1793 Jacob Lindley was deeply distressed over the degradation of

[56] Bassett to Haldimand, April 29, 1773, *Mich. Hist. Colls.*, XIX, 296.
[57] *Ibid.*
[58] Amherst to Bouquet, January 16, 1762, *ibid.*, 128.
[59] *Ibid.*
[60] Amherst to Bouquet, June 7, 1762, *ibid.*, 148.
[61] Carleton to Claus, October 22, 1767, Canadian Archives, Claus Papers, I, 111.
[62] *Mich. Hist. Colls.*, IX, 408, 418; X, 345; XIX, 440.
[63] Haldimand to Bolton, July 23, 1779, *ibid.*, 451–52.
[64] Same to De Peyster, June 24, 1781, *ibid.*, X, 492.
[65] *Ibid.*, IX, 408.
[66] *Ibid.*, XIX, 644.
[67] *Ibid.*

the savages caused by their love of strong drink.[68] He considered the trade in spirits as " the great engine, and mainspring, which has prepared the way and led to thousands of acts of hostility, and murders without number." [69] It appeared to him as the greatest obstacle in the way of civilization and happiness of the Indians.[70]

The many attempts to solve the traders' problems have already been noted. The traders were one of the greatest vexations with which the post officers had to deal. Major Bassett at Detroit described them as the " outcasts of all Nations, and the refuse of Mankind." [71] Major Mathews was not less harsh in his attitude toward them after the war. He pictured them as without education, sentiment, or honesty,[72] saying that the very lowest in the profession resorted to Detroit and the obscure western posts, where they knew the law was too distant for any immediate effects.[73] All contemporary observers are united in like sentiments.[74] The trader used every method conceivable to cheat with his rum the " child of the forest." [75] The governors at Detroit and at all the other western posts were especially admonished to placate the Indians. Shelburne was well acquainted with the character of the traders. He indignantly called them " the most worthless and abandoned Fellows in the Provinces," [76] and observed

[68] Jacob Lindley. " Journal on Expedition to Detroit in 1793," entry of June 14. Printed in Mich. Hist. Colls., XVII, 589.
[69] Ibid., 595–96.
[70] Ibid. See also Joseph Moore, " Journal of Expedition to Detroit," June 29. 1793. Printed in ibid.. 632–66.
[71] Bassett to Haldimand. April 29. 1773. ibid.. XIX, 297. This is a very one-sided picture of the traders. Evidently the officials were speaking largely of the worst ones. forgetting such able men as Sterling, Askin, Edgar, Robertson. and many others.
[72] Mathews to Haldimand, August 3, 1787, ibid., XX, 288.
[73] Ibid.
[74] Ante, pp. 18–20. " The number of traders not being limited, allows of many engaging in it, who have no principle of Honesty, and who impose on these poor people in a thousand ways to the detriment of honesty and to the disgrace of the name of trader among the Savages, which usually means with them an artful cheat. the distrust and disgust conceived for these traders occasions many disputes which frequently end in murder." Hamilton to Dartmouth, August 29, 1776. Canadian Archives, Q, XII, 212 ff.
[75] Ante, pp. 20–21.
[76] " Shelburne's Observations," undated. Shelburne Papers, LX, 135.

how the Indians were impressed with them, and how they came to distrust and hate all the British.[77] He accordingly instructed the post officials to regulate the trade strictly, especially near the frontier, hoping thus to prevent all prospect of impunity and of refuge among the back settlements and to forestall Indian hostility and revenge.[78] The solution of this most trying problem came through the forming of the great fur trading companies at the close of the American War.[79]

While England was attempting to conquer her recalcitrant colonies, De Peyster, Hamilton, Richard Lernoult, and other post officials were having serious difficulties with the French who were under their control. Hamilton was of the opinion that the country was filled with " ignorant Bigots and busy Rebels"; [80] and Lernoult felt that all the Canadians, as the French were called, were " Rebels to a man." [81] De Peyster handled the French more diplomatically, because he found that many of them had great influence with the Indians;[82] but in spite of his finesse, he found the inhabitants helping the rebels whenever opportunities were offered.[83] Haldimand said the French in the Upper Country had lost all sense of their duty and were inclined to favor the enemy.[84] Hamilton found " no British spirit in Detroit," [85] and complained to

[77] Shelburne to Carleton, June 2, 1767, Canadian Archives, Q, IV, 131.

[78] *Ibid.* Governor Murray, who had excellent opportunities to observe the traders, said that they were chiefly adventurers of mean education such as have failed in other countries. " All have their fortune to make and are little solicitous how they make it," he exclaimed. Murray to Lords of Trade, March 3, 1765, *ibid.*, II, 378. Gage called the traders: " A Set of People, who for the most part, are near as wild as the Country they go in, the People they deal with, and by far more vicious and wicked." Gage to Shelburne, February 22, 1767, *ibid.*, Dartmouth Transcripts, 1765–1775, p. 66. Printed in Carter, *Gage's Correspondence*, I, 124.

[79] *Post*, p. 122.

[80] Hamilton to Germain, June 23, 1777, Canadian Archives, Q, XIV, 87. Hamilton claimed that not one in twenty of the French would be bound by their oath of allegiance. Hamilton to Haldimand, undated, *Mich. Hist. Colls.*, IX, 465.

[81] Lernoult to ———, March 26, 1779, *ibid.*, X, 328.

[82] De Peyster to Carleton, June 13, 1777, Canadian Archives, Q, XIII, 327.

[83] De Peyster to Haldimand, November 16, 1780; *Mich. Hist. Colls.*, X, 448; same to same, May 27, 1781, *ibid.*, 482.

[84] Haldimand to ———, December 3, 1780, *ibid.*, 450.

[85] Hamilton to Carleton, June 23, 1777, Canadian Archives, Q, XIV, 80.

Carleton that loyalty was but a name.[86] He found that all of his labors were undermined by the secret intrigues of the rebels.[87] The Americans were well aware that the French at Detroit were ill-disposed toward protecting the post for the English.[88]

There were many disaffected people in Michigan, aside from the French, especially at Detroit [89] and Michilimackinac.[90] James Cassidy of Grosse Pointe [91] and many others were arrested because they were suspected of favoring the Americans.[92] There were as many as five hundred prisoners in Detroit in 1779,[93] almost one-fourth of the population, so it was natural that the post officials would be greatly concerned over the disloyalty of the people. Carleton directed that all suspicious persons should be arrested and sent down to Montreal.[94] Haldimand issued orders that any individual who in any way aided, abetted, or indirectly helped the enemy should be sent to Niagara.[95] John Leith who was a prisoner at Detroit in 1778 wrote to Colonel George Morgan that the Canadian volunteers were lukewarm, and would not assist the English if an American army appeared.[96] He thought that the Governor alienated the merchants by treating them harshly, especially if they seemed at all to lean toward the States.[97] In his opinion many of the merchants were " warm friends of the colonials," [98] but there were also many who were bitter enemies.[99] Other information was received by the Americans to the effect that the French desired to be neutral because

[86] *Ibid.*
[87] MS., State of Garrison at Detroit, October, 1776, in Clements Library.
[88] Hamilton to Carleton, July 3, 1777, Canadian Archives, Q, XIV, 42.
[89] *Mich. Hist. Colls.*, IX, 408, 432, 462, 465, 480; X, 448, 450, 482.
[90] De Peyster to Carleton, June 6, 1777, Canadian Archives, Q, XIII, 273; same to same, June 17, 1777, *ibid.*, 324.
[91] *Mich. Hist. Colls.*, X, 343–45, 346, 356.
[92] Canadian Archives, *Report for 1887*, p. 221.
[93] *Mich. Hist. Colls.*, X, 326.
[94] *Ibid.*, IX, 345.
[95] Haldimand to Lernoult, June 13, 1779, *ibid.*, X, 338.
[96] Leith to Morgan, August 19, 1778, *Wis. Hist. Colls.*, XXIII, 130.
[97] *Ibid.*
[98] Among these were Obadiah Robins, James Forsyth, Philip Bayle, Jerry and James Cockran, etc. *Ibid.*
[99] Hayes, Desyoung, Thomson, McCrygar, etc. *Ibid.*

they had no members of the upper class to arouse them.[100] This perhaps was the real situation, for the natural inclination of the *habitant* was to remain neutral.[101]

The fickleness of the Indians made the life of the officials most uneasy. No amount of presents given in the most lavish manner could hold them loyal.[102] It has been noted what great quantities of rum were freely distributed.[103] Councils were held by the dozens and the braves were admonished and cajoled, all to no avail.[104] After much experience, De Peyster summed up in a letter to General Haldimand the causes for the officers' failure to hold them:

I have wrought hard to endeavor to bring them to it, [better discipline] but, I find it impossible altogether to change their natures. I assemble them, get fair promises, and send them out, but once out of sight the turning of a Straw may divert them from the original plan. If too severe with them, upon such occasions they tell us we are well off that there are no Virginians in this Quarter, but such as they bring here against their inclinations.[105]

He well realized that the expenses of the Indian Department were tremendous, but that they were not altogether thrown away; for if the red men were " delicately managed," they would not favor the rebels, and surely would prevent the inroads of the Virginians into Michigan.[106] Nevertheless, costs continued to mount, and the post officials found it almost impossible to carry out their superiors' directions. Aside from De Peyster and Sinclair, Hay, who was sent to Detroit as governor in July, 1784, had a prolonged controversy with the Quebec authorities over Indian expenses. Finally in high dudgeon Haldimand wrote that his commands governing

[100] Draper MSS., III, U, 580. Printed in R. G. Thwaites and L. P. Kellogg, *The Revolution on the Upper Ohio, 1775–1777* (Madison, 1912), p. 147.

[101] Canadian Archives, Q, XII, 188. See *ante*, p. 75.

[102] Brehm to Sinclair, April 17, 1780, *Mich. Hist. Colls.*, IX, 536; Haldimand to De Peyster, February 12, 1780, *ibid.*, 634; same to same, July 6, 1780, X, 408; same to same, July 13, 1780, *ibid.*, 412; " Return of Indian Presents," *ibid.*, VIII, 472–74; XI, 356; XIX, 517, 658–61.

[103] *Ante*, p. 20.

[104] *Mich. Hist. Colls.*, XX, *passim*. Russell, " The Indian Policy of Henry Hamilton."

[105] De Peyster to Haldimand, January 26, 1782, *Mich. Hist. Colls.*, X, 548.

[106] *Ibid.*

Indian costs should be "strictly observed" and from which there should be no deviation. "These *Regulations* were not hastily put together," the Governor said, "but were founded upon Conviction and the best information I could obtain." Haldimand was well aware his orders would not be relished by the western officials, "but they were not calculated to gratify vanity nor any other propensity, but entirely to prevent abuses which had so glaringly displaid themselves," he maintained.[107]

It seemed to be the consensus of opinion among all British officials that the Indians were being stirred up constantly by the Spanish and the French.[108] Some tribes refused to fight at all,[109] and were very haughty in making demands upon the English.[110] Lieutenant Thomas Bennett discovered only one young Ottawa chief who was really zealous for the good of the service, and this leader was much chagrined by the unsteady conduct of the rest.[111] Hamilton learned that Spanish agents were tampering with the savages early in the spring of 1778,[112] but thought them unsuccessful.[113] The year before he wrote Lord Germain that every fresh account confirmed the news of the hostilities committed by the Spaniards.[114] It seemed that the English hated the latter because of their

---

[107] Haldimand to Hay, September 3, 1784, Canadian Archives, B, LXIV, 259–60.

[108] Croghan to Gage, January 16, 1767, Shelburne Papers, XLVIII, 142; Hillsborough to Carleton, November 4, 1769, *ibid.*, Q, VI, 122; De Peyster to ————, June 6, 1777, *Mich. Hist. Colls.*, X, 275; Hamilton to Carleton, August 6, 1778, Canadian Archives, *Report for 1887*, p. 209; C. M. Burton, (ed.), *Journal of John Lees* (Detroit, 1911), pp. 40–41; Gage to Halifax, August 10, 1765, Canadian Archives, Dartmouth Transcripts, 1765–1775, p. 6. Printed in Carter, *Gage's Correspondence*, I, 63; Gage to Haldimand, April 26, 1768, Canadian Archives, B, III, 242. As late as 1794 conditions were just as bad. "There is a few Frenchmen at Detroit who are continually preaching up a dangerous doctrine to the Indians. I don't wish to name them . . . some rigorous measures must immediately be taken with those people who endeavors to poison every well disposed mind." Smith to McKee, October 24, 1794, *ibid.*, Claus Papers, VI, 249.

[109] Bennett to De Peyster, September 1, 1779, *Mich. Hist. Colls.*, IX, 396.

[110] *Ibid.*

[111] *Ibid.*, 397.

[112] Hamilton to Carleton, August 6, 1778, Canadian Archives, *Report for 1887*, p. 209.

[113] *Ibid.*

[114] Hamilton to Germain, September 5, 1777, *ibid.*, Q, XIV, 225.

machinations with the Indians, and they also found the French as fickle as the savages, often interfering in favor of the rebels.[115] It was commonly known by some merchants that the Indians were supplied secretly by the French traders from Detroit, who stole out of the post in the stillness of the night without the knowledge of the commanding officer.[116] John Lees reported that the Spaniards were lavishing presents upon all the Indians to gain their friendship,[117] and also believed that the savages around St. Joseph were under French control.[118] In spite of generous presents, the English could never depend upon the aborigines during the entire war.

Time never went slowly for the post commandants, for whether in peace or war, there were always baffling economic problems to solve.

The *habitants*, like all other frontier peoples from the beginning of time, were opposed to taxation. During the French régime the people paid as a rent to the Crown, an annual tax of from one to two sols per front foot if they lived within the fort;[119] while the farmers paid two-eighths of a sol and one-half bushel of wheat per acre of frontage.[120] Donald Campbell required the farmers in 1760 to pay a tax of a cord of wood per acre of frontage. This was increased to two cords the following year.[121] The proprietors of the fort had to pay a tax for the support of the garrison, which under the first year of Colonel Gladwin amounted to 2,770 livres or £ 184/13/4, New York currency.[122] Colonel Bradstreet, who was in command for only a short time in 1764, reduced taxes much to the satisfaction of the inhabitants.[123] Their joy was of short dura-

[115] *Ibid., Report for 1887*, p. 213.
[116] *Journal of John Lees*, p. 40.
[117] *Ibid.*, p. 41.
[118] *Ibid.*, p. 40.
[119] Taxes before 1764 were usually paid in kind, furs or produce. In 1764 the first money known as N. Y. C. began to circulate in Detroit. A sol equals 2 shillings.
[120] MS., "A protest against excessive taxation." MS. in Burton Hist. Colls. Published in M. M. Quaife, "Some Glimpses of Life in Ancient Detroit," *Burton Historical Collection Leaflet*, III, no. 1.
[121] *Ibid.*
[122] *Ibid.*
[123] MS., "A protest against repairing Fort Detroit," *ibid.*

tion, for under Colonel John Campbell, Bradstreet's successor, the taxes were greatly increased.[124] The people protested, and presented the commandant with a memorial against his policy.[125] Nothing came of the protest, for Campbell soon afterwards left Detroit and was succeeded by Captain Turnbull. The taxation difficulties came to an end during this administration, for Gage ordered that no taxes whatsoever should be laid upon the inhabitants.[126]

There were two other major conflicts between the post commanders and the inhabitants. One was the struggle of the people with Major Bassett to keep the commons free from the encroachments of the military;[127] and the other was the demand to keep Ile aux Cochons as a public commons, for the pasturing of their cattle and hogs.[128] Presumably the French government had granted the Island to the people in 1730.[129] In 1768, General Gage gave Lieutenant George McDougall the right to a temporary occupation of the Island. It was thought that the land could be cultivated and be of some support to the Detroit garrison.[130] Accordingly McDougall purchased the Island from the Indians for the sum of " Five Barrels of Rum three Roles of Tobacco three Pounds of Vermillion and a Belt of Wampum, and three Barrels of Rum and three Pounds of Paint." [131] Immediately the people protested to Turnbull, claiming that from time immemorial they had held the sole

[124] *Ibid.* Increased to 1 shilling per foot for lots within the fort and 10 shillings for the farmers.

[125] These protests are printed in *Mich. Hist. Colls.*, VIII, 462–66.

[126] Canadian Archives, B, XXVII, 105. Major Robert Bayard was commandant for a short time in 1766 before the arrival of Captain Turnbull.

[127] Bassett to Haldimand, April 29, 1773, *Mich. Hist. Colls.*, XIX, 297.

[128] *Ibid.*, II, 585. The inhabitants claimed the Island was absolutely necessary for their use, " to receive their cattle in summer, to avoid their running wild in the Woods or the Indians destroying them in any of their drunken Foolicks." Carleton to Hillsborough, June 18, 1769, Canadian Archives, Q, VI, 73.

[129] *Mich. Hist. Colls.*, II, 585. John Campbell protested the granting of the island to Gage. He felt the people needed it for their stock, etc. Campbell to Gage, October 3, 1764. Gage MSS.

[130] Carleton to Hillsborough, June 18, 1769, Canadian Archives, Q, VII, 196; Gage to Turnbull, August 29, 1768, *Mich. Hist. Colls.*, X, 234.

[131] *Ibid.*, 235 (about £194/10 N. Y. C.). This was done according to the King's orders.

right to the Island, a right that was inalienable.[132] Turnbull did not heed the protest; so the people outlined their grievances and sent them to the " Gentlemen of Trade " at Montreal, and also to Carleton and Gage. Nothing came of these petitions, except that on October 13, 1769, the authorities at Detroit held a meeting with the citizens in which the whole question was debated.[133] The government was not at all favorable to the people's protests and finally gave McDougall full possession of the Island in the spring of 1771.[134]

Because of the remoteness of the post commanders from the central authority, they did not hesitate sometimes to rule arbitrarily, and several officials were known to have exploited their positions to reap great advantages.[135] General Conway, in 1766, gave explicit orders to the governors at Detroit and Michilimackinac to be extremely careful of their conduct and of all the officers under them lest suspicion arise.[136] He felt that some of the commandants, " taking advantage of their powers," had turned traders and insisted upon a preference for themselves of all the furs that were brought to the market, greatly to the discouragement and injury of the Indian trade.[137] Lord Shelburne was of the opinion that most of the disorders and troubles of the back regions were due to the fraudulent grants and purchases of lands which the governors countenanced, and were actuated by shameful motives of

---

[132] " Petition of Sundry Inhabitants of Detroit," May 16, 1769, *ibid.*, 237–38.

[133] *Ibid.*, 239–41.

[134] *Ibid.*, II, 585. General Gage requested McDougall to arbitrate the question, but McDougall refused and asked Hillsborough's support. McDougall to Hillsborough, May 29, 1770, Canadian Archives, Q, VII, 110. Hillsborough thought McDougall should arbitrate as a " just and equitable " way of settling, but finally the matter went to his Majesty in Council. Hillsborough to McDougall, October 30, 1770, *ibid.*, 196; also VI, 73. In 1769 McDougall had sold the north half of the Island for £900 to be paid in nine years. Register of Notaries, p. 132. During the war General Haldimand ordered De Peyster to reclaim Belle Isle and cultivate it, in order to cut down expenses. Haldimand to De Peyster, July 13, 1780, *Mich. Hist. Colls.*, IX, 638. Later De Peyster wrote of two families settled with an appraisal of the buildings made. De Peyster to Haldimand, September 9, 1780, and October 10, 1780, *ibid.*, X, 427, 440.

[135] Canadian Archives, Q, IV, 131.

[136] Conway to the governors of Michilimackinac and Detroit, March 27, 1766, *ibid.*, Q, III, 9.

[137] *Ibid.*

self-interest.[138] The merchants, especially at Michilimackinac, claimed that the officers placed their own interpretations on the fur regulations and added many others which tended " to the greatest oppression or almost entire ruin of several individuals," and to the general detriment of the peltry business.[139] They also complained that the exclusive right to trade in " an immense tract of land . . . to the westward of Michigan " had been given to certain friends by the post commander, which alarmed and greatly discouraged the merchants and traders in that region.[140] Trade was gradually becoming a monopoly in the hands of a few particular friends of the commandant. "It happened by degrees," William Robertson told Governor Simcoe's council, " to be discovered that none but those who bought their goods of them [the commandants' friends] were perfectly loyal or good subjects." [141] These complaints reached London and every attempt was made to put an end to such practices.[142]

There were many personal difficulties which made life irksome for the western officials. The officers at Detroit constantly protested against paying the very heavy charges for transporting their stores across the Niagara Portage.[143] In 1768 General Gage ordered that all officers' stores be transported " In like manner as the provisions for the posts." [144] Hamilton found the council room at Detroit entirely inade-

[138] Shelburne to Carleton, June 2, 1767, *ibid.*, Q, IV, 130.
[139] *Ibid.*, C. O. 42, V, 158.
[140] *Ibid.*
[141] *Ibid.*, C, XLI, pt. i, p. 97; *Mich. Hist. Colls.*, XI, 639. One of the leading merchants of Michigan was John Askin. See M. M. Quaife (ed.), *The John Askin Papers, 1747–1795* (Detroit, 1928).
[142] Canadian Archives, Q, III, 9 ff.; IV, 130 ff. The suspected attempt of Rogers in 1766 to turn the post of Michilimackinac over to the French because of the government's curbing his extravagance is well known. Rogers, *Journal at Michilimackinac in 1766* (W. L. Clements, ed.); Rogers, *Ponteach* (Nevins), pp. 115 ff. Rogers' guilt was never established and it is wholly uncertain whether he ever contemplated the treasonable designs charged against him. The whole plot may have been the invention of his enemies. Carleton to Shelburne, October 9. 1767. Canadian Archives, Q, IV, 304–306. See especially Louise Phelps Kellogg. *The British Régime in Wisconsin and the Northwest* (Madison, 1935), chaps. IV–VI.
[143] Gage to Brown, February 22, 1768, *ibid.*, B, XVIII, 92.
[144] Hamilton to Germain, June 17, 1777, *ibid.*

quate and felt it absolutely necessary to build a new one.[145] He wrote Lord Germain describing his quarters " as open to the incursions of the Natives; and I can scarce boast the mildness of a Savage Chief, who goes far beyond me in bearing all sorts of inconveniences with apparent indifference"; and later he said, "I am having a variety of distractions, the Savages holding their Councils in the Very room where I now write." [146]

The problem of salaries usually caused considerable friction. De Peyster refused to pay one of his men, because he made lampoons upon the King.[147] He later certified the account to avoid prosecution. Hamilton's salary as lieutenant governor and superintendent at Detroit was £ 200 sterling, and in addition lods, ventes, and the king's rents.[148] When he left Detroit on his disastrous Vincennes campaign, never to come back, Major De Peyster assumed many of his duties. Hamilton memorialized the Lords of the Treasury, for the arrears in pay for the years 1781 and 1782,[149] which De Peyster refused to pay. This amounted to £ 1,021/9/11¼, New York Currency. No record has come to light as to the outcome of this controversy.

Patrick Sinclair had a very prolonged altercation with Governor Haldimand over his salary and expenses while governor at Michilimackinac. Sinclair's expenditures from October 20, 1781, to October 24, 1782, amounted to the enormous sum of £ 63,912/13/5.[150] Haldimand was outraged, claiming these expenses were incurred in direct opposition to his orders,[151] and offered to settle only for such articles as appeared reasonable, leaving the remainder to a minute investigation.[152]

[145] *Ibid.*, Q, XIV, 83.
[146] *Ibid.*, 91.
[147] Mathews to De Peyster, May 15, 1784, *ibid.*, B, LXIII, 296.
[148] Hamilton to the Lords of the Treasury, July 30, 1784, *ibid.*, C. O. 42, XVI, 42. See *Askin Papers,* I, 27–30, for an explanation of feudal grants. Also *ibid.*, 46–50.
[149] For 1781, £ 416/15/3. For 1782, £ 614/14/11. There is a difference here of £ 10/0/2¾ for which the record leaves no explanation.
[150] Haldimand to Burke, October 25, 1782, Canadian Archives, B, LV, 222.
[151] Same to Sinclair, March 18, 1785, *ibid.*, LXIV, 436.
[152] *Ibid.*, LV, 222.

Nothing was done until 1785, when Haldimand was informed by his solicitor that an action for £ 50,000 was brought against him by the holders of the bills.[153] The Governor was of the opinion that his cause was that of the public, so the whole affair should be taken care of by the Crown.[154] Sinclair asserted that Haldimand had expressed a wish for a court-martial, which Haldimand denied for he could not see what good one would do.[155] This altercation dragged on until 1799, when the Treasury ordered Sinclair's salary paid to the time of the surrender of his post at the rate of £ 200 per year.[156] Nevertheless, the vacant official positions in the western posts were not without applicants, and even considerable pressure was brought to bear upon high government officers to reward personal friends with the rich political plums.[157]

There was considerable bickering by the post governors over their commissions. They usually insisted upon having charge of all civil and military matters. Sinclair, who was sent to Michilimackinac in 1779, insisted upon having full control.[158] Hamilton and especially Hay did the same at Detroit.[159] Finally Haldimand, realizing how detrimental to the service this condition was, laid down some definite regulations for the civil and military officials.[160]

The post commanders had many serious altercations with their inferior officers. Major Rogers greatly hampered the work of the Indian agent, Benjamin Roberts, who tried to carry out Sir William Johnson's embargo on the sale of rum to

---

[153] Same to Sydney, April 10, 1785, *ibid.*, Q, XXIV, pt. i, pp. 73–75.

[154] *Ibid.*

[155] Same to Sinclair, March 19, 1785, *ibid.*, B, LXIV, 437. Sinclair's commission was dated April 1, 1780.

[156] *Ibid.*, G, CCCLIX, 50.

[157] Bassett in 1772 urged a friend to influence Hillsborough to appoint him governor at Detroit, where he said, " The people seem anxious to have him, as some of the principal merchants have signified that he would be very pleasing to them." Bassett to ———, September 10, 1772, Canadian Archives, Dartmouth Transcripts, 1765–1775, pp. 295–96.

[158] Sinclair to Haldimand, July 27, 1779, *Mich. Hist. Colls.*, IX, 518; Haldimand to Sinclair, August 17, 1779, *ibid.*, 519. Other correspondence follows.

[159] Hay to Haldimand, November 4, 1783, *ibid.*, XI, 399; Haldimand to Hay, November 5, 1783, *ibid.*, 400.

[160] " Instructions for Governor Sinclair," October, 1779, *ibid.*, IX, 516–18; Haldimand to De Peyster, October 30, 1783, *ibid.*, XI, 397.

the Indians.[161] Heated quarrels followed until Rogers, flying into a passion, had Roberts put in irons.[162] Rogers also quarreled with his secretary, Nathaniel Potter, and the climax of their troubles was the revealing by the latter of the scheme of Rogers to turn the post over to the French.[163] Sinclair and John Mompesson quarreled about their rank [164] until General Haldimand had to interfere and settle the dispute.[165] This doughty Irishman seemed to live on quarrelling. He had continual trouble with De Peyster at Detroit over supplies,[166] and also with Lieutenant Alexander Harrow at his own post.[167] The soldiers, finally much grieved over their arrears in pay and the high-handed methods of Sinclair, did a most unusual thing for privates of that day in sending a petition to their former commander, De Peyster, requesting his aid.[168] De Peyster was very sympathetic, and wrote the petitioners that he would forward their grievances to Colonel Mason Bolton,[169] for which he was sharply censured.[170] Captain Joseph Schlosser at St. Joseph had his troubles, mainly because of his lack of judgment and good temper, in handling the Indians and French.[171]

[161] Roberts to Johnson, August 20, 1767, *ibid.*, X, 225. Rogers, *Michilimackinac Journal* (Clements, ed.). Roberts complained of Rogers taking rum from the Indian stores. Canadian Archives, Indian Papers, IX, 447.

[162] Rogers, *Ponteach* (Nevins, ed.), p. 136; Kellogg, *British Régime*, pp. 78–81.

[163] *Ibid.*, 79–81; *Mich. Hist. Colls.*, X, 225 ff. Gage ordered Rogers to Montreal for trial where he arrived after suffering severe punishment on July 17, 1767. Canadian Archives, C. O. 5, LXXXVI, 33–34; Quebec *Gazette*, July 28, 1768. The trial did not end until October 29. *Ibid.*, January 12, 1769. Rogers was acquitted. Carleton was of the impression the whole difficulty was actuated by jealousy and motives of revenge. *Ibid.*, Q, IV, 304–306.

[164] Mompesson to Haldimand, August 22, 1780, *Mich. Hist. Colls.*, IX, 589.

[165] Haldimand to Bolton, September 12, 1780, *ibid.*, XIX, 570–72.

[166] *Ibid.*, IX, 565, 578, 598, 615, 618, 628, 639.

[167] Powell to Haldimand, May 20, 1781, *ibid.*, IX, 633.

[168] "Petition to Major De Peyster," July 30, 1780, *ibid.*, 587–88. Gladwin and Colonel John Campbell had great difficulty with Captain Joseph Hopkins. Gage wrote Gladwin that Hopkins was "reduced" and sent home and then he censured Gladwin for not keeping proper authority in his command. Gage to Gladwin, April 26, 1764. Gage MSS. Gladwin replied that he was lenient with Hopkins as he "did not choose to ruin him." Gladwin to Gage, June 7, 1764, *ibid.*; Campbell to Gage, August 27, 1765, *ibid.*

[169] *Mich. Hist. Colls.*, IX, 588.

[170] Haldimand to Bolton, September 12, 1780, *ibid.*, XIX, 571.

[171] Campbell to Bouquet, April 26, 1762, *ibid.*, 139; same to same, June 8, 1762, *ibid.*, 151. For other quarrels see *ibid.*, IX, 589–604.

Perhaps the most outstanding altercation was between Governor Hamilton and Captain Mompesson. A certain jeweler who was tried for a petty crime and acquitted had been ordered by Hamilton to be drummed out of town. When the drummers entered the citadel, Mompesson ordered them to be silent, declaring that Hamilton might be as oppressive as he pleased in the town, but he would not suffer it in the citadel.[172] This led to more serious matters until the town was in a turmoil.[173] Finally in September, 1777, General Carleton ordered Captain Lernoult, who had been at Detroit previously in charge of the troops, to return and take Mompesson's command.[174] This ended the troubles at Detroit, and until the close of the English period no more serious disputes arose.

The western officials were human, and with an inadequate salary [175] were easily influenced by the merchants to favor their trade. Rogers was accused of favoritism while at Michilimackinac,[176] while his predecessor, Captain William Howard, was open to serious charges of allowing only his own friends to trade with the savages.[177] Facing ruin, his enemies, to whom he refused passes, went trading without official sanction. Howard unroofed their homes, pulled down some, and confiscated and sold their goods.[178] When the officials favored the merchants, the latter were loud in their praise, but when things did not go well, they dipped their pens in the gall of the dragon to abuse them.

Soon after Detroit was taken over by the British, companies of merchants at Montreal, Albany, and New York organized

[172] Canadian Archives, Q, XIV, 87.
[173] Hamilton to Germain, June 23, 1777. ibid., 89.
[174] Carleton to Bolton, September 24, 1777, Mich. Hist. Colls., X, 280.
[175] Canadian Archives, Q, XXV, 149–50
[176] Carleton to Shelburne, October 9. 1767. ibid., Q, IV. 304–306.
[177] Johnson to Gage, December 21, 1765. ibid., C. O. 5. LXXXIV, 305–307.
[178] " Merchants' Petition " to Rogers, August 22, 1766. ibid., Baby Collection, I. Of course many traders never called at the forts for passes. This was very detrimental to the king's service. Ibid., S. 1771–1776, June 12, 1771. Traders found it no difficult matter to pass the posts unobserved in the night, or by collusion with the Indians, got by unmolested at all times. The officials did not want to quarrel with the Indians if it could be avoided. Gage to Shelburne, February 22. 1767, ibid., Dartmouth Transcripts, 1765–1775, pp. 61–62. Printed in Carter, Gage's Correspondence, I, 122.

to develop the trade of the West. They sent one or more representatives to the western posts to look after the business. These men used every known means to influence the post officials, and usually succeeded. James Sterling, Detroit partner of a group of associates,[179] has left posterity many interesting descriptions of the means employed to curry favor with the officials.[180]

In a letter to John Duncan, July 20, 1761, Sterling asks for "some good wines, which gentlemen of the army need." He found Donald Campbell very kind and obliging, using his influence to promote his [Sterling's] interest among the French.[181] Later, fearing a change in the commandant, he repeatedly urged the agent at Niagara to send on his goods by the first vessel. When his goods were placed in the King's store during the siege of 1763, Sterling appealed for a release to Gage, but before the order had arrived he had been able to get his goods through the influence of Campbell. He writes of this affair to his partners:

> To tell you the Truth the most of them (goods) was sold long before, (the order came) never the less I carried home the Trunks and Barrels with as great formality as if they had been full. Whist! hold your tongue and so will I.[182]

During the Indian uprising of 1763, Sterling found no trouble in getting his goods transported in the King's ships. He wrote a long letter to his brother John desiring him to keep the greatest secrecy in the affair. For he said:

> the Major [Gladwin] was unwilling that it should be known he has done so much for me least the other merchants should grumble and Complain thinking themselves entitled to the same Indulgence.[183]

[179] Captain Walter Rutherford of New York, Lieutenant John Duncan, Lieutenant George Coventry, and James Syme, all of Schenectady, were the other partners.

[180] Information from Sterling Letter Book. Copy in Burton Hist. Coll.

[181] Sterling won the confidence of the French, and during the Pontiac Uprising of 1763, they chose him to be commander of the local militia. He married Angelique Cuillerier (niece of Bellestre) who is thought to have disclosed the plot of Pontiac to the British. Askin Papers, I, 47, note 29. Humphrey. "Identity of Gladwin's Informants."

[182] Sterling to Duncan, April 26, 1765. Sterling Letter Book.

[183] Sterling to John Sterling, April 18, 1763. Ibid.

Affairs did not always go so well for this clever Ulster Scotch-
man, for during the War of Independence, Hamilton, suspect-
ing Sterling of sympathizing with the rebels, arrested him and
sent him to Lower Canada.[184]

Great Britain was more fortunate as a whole in her choice of
governors for the Michigan posts than for those of most of the
older colonies. It was the opinion of travelers that these governors were deservedly esteemed and respected both by the
inhabitants and traders for their fairness, tolerance, and propriety of conduct.[185] They seemed to have insurmountable
difficulties.

Michigan was governed by the post commanders until July
of 1788 when, by the proclamation of Lord Dorchester, four
new districts were created in Quebec, and liberal and popular
changes were brought about.[186] Detroit and the surrounding
region were thereafter known as the District of Hesse.[187] The
boundaries of Hesse according to the proclamation were very
vague,[188] because of the fact that Great Britain did not presume openly to assert ownership to territory which had been
ceded to the United States by the Treaty of Paris of 1783.[189]
Following closely upon the proclamation of July, 1788, came
the proposal to divide Canada into two provinces.[190] Each
province was to have a legislature composed of a council, appointed by the Crown for life, and an assembly chosen by the

[184] Apparently he never returned to Detroit. *Askin Papers,* I, 47, note 29.
Sterling was early incensed at the number of merchants who kept crowding into
the West. "There is such a damn'd sett of Claus, Hans, and Derricks arrived
here from Albany and Schenectady that I begin to fear a famine," he wrote to
Duncan, August 4, 1762. Sterling was a friend of the Jewish trader, Chapman
Abrahams. He wrote him, February 19, 1763: "Damned Jew I thought you
should act like a Christian since Sir Robert Baptised you, but I find you are a
Jew still by your mistrusting your best friends, do you think because you have
been absent a little while that Sterling has forgot you or is unwilling to serve
you." Sterling Letter Book.
[185] J. Carver, *Travels through the Interior Parts of North America* (London,
1778), p. 152; Captain Brehm especially praised Major Lernoult's work at
Detroit. Brehm to Haldimand, May 28, 1779. *Mich. Hist. Colls.,* IX, 412.
[186] Shortt and Doughty, *Can. Const. Docs.,* pt. ii, 953–54.
[187] *Ibid.*
[188] *Ibid.*
[189] MacDonald, *Documents,* p. 204.
[190] Shortt and Doughty, *loc. cit.,* pt. ii, p. 1031 ff.

land owners or rent payers.[191] The division took place in December, 1791,[192] but no election was held until the following year,[193] when D. W. Smith and William Macomb were chosen to represent the district about Detroit.[194]

Governor Simcoe assembled the first provincial Parliament of Upper Canada at Newark (Niagara) September 17, 1792,[195] and a few days later a petition from the citizens of Detroit was laid before the assembly, requesting that some law be passed to prevent accidents by fire.[196] This was done and seven other acts were passed at the first session of the Parliament. This first legislature renamed the districts, and the Detroit area fell into the Western District, in the County of Kent. Several of the laws passed were applicable to Detroit as well as the rest of Upper Canada, and the difficulty arose to word the law so that it would apply to Detroit without mentioning the place by name. This was done by wording the legislation so as to use the County of Kent instead of Detroit.[197]

In 1792 there was a rumor that the Americans were going to attack Niagara and Detroit; so Governor Simcoe was induced to make a visit to the latter post in order to determine the best means of assuring communication between the two posts.[198] He arrived at Detroit in April, 1793, and after spending three days reviewing the troops, examining the fortifications, and planning some effective means to combat General Anthony Wayne at Miami, he returned to Niagara.[199] His journey was productive of much good, for the settlers of Western Upper Canada had been greatly disturbed by the movements of the

[191] *Ibid.*, p. 1032.
[192] *Ibid.*
[193] *Ibid.*, p. 55.
[194] *Mich. Hist. Colls.*, XXXVIII, 338. Alexander Grant, Commodore of the King's Navy, was appointed to the Council. Grant resided at Grosse Pointe. No provision was made for Michilimackinac. See especially M. M. Quaife, "Detroit's First Election," Burton Historical Collection *Leaflet*, November, 1926.
[195] Kingsford, *History of Canada*, VII, 346.
[196] Ontario Archives, *Report for 1909*, pp. 1 ff.
[197] *Ibid.*, p. 17; Smith to Askin, October 2, 1792, *Askin Papers*, I, 437; the boundaries of Kent are given in *ibid.*, 417.
[198] E. A. Cruikshank (ed.), *The Correspondence of Lieutenant Governor John Graves Simcoe* (Toronto, 1923–), II, 193.
[199] *Ibid.*, 213.

American forces, and the apparent indifference of the Governor.

At the second session of the First Parliament, which began in May, 1793,[200] thirteen acts were passed, one being of more than usual significance. It provided for the popular election on the first Monday of March in every year of two town assessors, one collector, a town clerk, six overseers of highways, a pound keeper, and two wardens, and thus looked clearly toward popular self-government. Another act prohibiting the further importation of slaves will be discussed hereafter. Still more important was the bill validating marriages of Protestants at Detroit. Seldom was there a chaplain attached to the garrison, and many marriages had been solemnized by the commandant or by the lieutenant governor which were of doubtful legality. This law made legal all marriages performed " before any magistrate, or commanding officer of a fort, . . . or any person in any public office." Justices of the Peace were allowed to perform the ceremony provided there were no Protestant ministers within eighteen miles of the residence of the persons to be married.[201]

In June, 1794, Parliament met for the third time and passed twelve acts;[202] and in August, 1795, the fourth session was held at which five acts were passed.[203] The two sittings made provisions for the various courts for the province, for juries, and for expatriated Americans.[204] This was the last legislation passed by a Canadian Parliament applying to the Michigan area, for in 1796, when Second Parliament met, the members already were aware of the Jay-Hamilton Treaty and thus passed no laws which were applicable to Michigan.

[200] Ontario Archives, *Report for 1909*, pp. 21 ff., 30, 151.
[201] *Ibid.*
[202] *Ibid.*, pp. 47 ff.
[203] *Ibid.*, pp. 55 ff.
[204] *Ibid.*

CHAPTER V

ECONOMIC AND SOCIAL BEGINNINGS

THE ECONOMIC and social history of Michigan and the Old Northwest during the period under survey, though somewhat complex in its effects, nevertheless has its picturesque aspects. From 1760 on it represents a story of an irrepressible movement onward — a story of steady growth. But this development was complicated by various problems of population — number and distribution, defense, trade and trading posts, servants, social classes, education and illiteracy, religion and morals.

Perhaps the most flattering description of Detroit and the surrounding country at this time was given by Lieutenant Thomas Mante, who came to Michigan as a member of Colonel Bradstreet's army in 1764. Mante wrote:

In purity and wholesomeness of air, and richness of soil, it may be said to equal, if not excel any, even the best parts of America. Every European grain flourishes here in the utmost perfection; and hemp and flax, in particular, might be raised to the greatest advantage. The woods are everywhere filled with vines of spontaneous growth; and their grape yields a juice equal in flavour to the most excellent burgundy. The country around it appears like a great park stocked with buffaloes, deer, pheasants, wild turkies, and partridges. Domestic animals and fowls are here in the utmost perfection. Aquatic birds of every species are in the greatest plenty, and of the highest flavour; and the rivers afford an astonishing variety of the most delicious fish. The soil and climate are so favorable to vegetation, that every vegetable is to be procured with the smallest trouble. In short, a man that can shoot and fish, and understands the art of making wine, may enjoy every luxury of the most sumptuous table, at the sole expense of his own labour. The inhabitants of Detroit are not numerous; and, notwithstanding the allurements which plenty holds forth to people to settle here, the want of a sufficient force to secure them against the caprice of the neighboring Indians, and of authority to secure good order amongst themselves, has hitherto deterred such as have any settlements elsewhere, from endeavoring to partake of the abundant produce of nature, at the expense of the property they already enjoy, and perhaps their lives. But should Detroit be ever formed into a regular government, we will venture to prophecy, that it will greatly extend itself; and from the plenty, variety, and richness of its produce, prove a beneficial settlement to the mother-country.[1]

Jonathan Carver, who visited the district along the Detroit River in 1766, 1767, and 1768, became eloquent over the country's potential wealth. He characterized the soil as exceedingly fruitful and suitable for the cultivation of wheat, corn, oats, and peas. The poor agricultural methods of the French disgusted him.[2] There is abundant evidence to show that the present Wolverine state never failed to impress with its beauty and its possibilities the government official, the priest, and the traveler.[3] In 1787, the new English commandant at Detroit, Major Mathews, wrote to General Haldimand that had Mr. Oswald or Lord Lansdowne seen the delightful settlement of Detroit, " they surely never could have signed away the right of the nation to it — In point of climate, soil, situation & the beauties of nature, nothing can exceed it." [4] Isaac Weld, an Irish traveler, visited the Lakes region in 1795 and 1796. Because of his keen power of observation, his descriptions are quite reliable. The climate of Detroit did not impress him as satisfactory, but like other witnesses he became enthusiastic over the scenery and the future possibilities of the region.[5] Likewise, Robert Rogers gives an alluring picture of Eastern Michigan. He reported that the soil along the Detroit River was of the very best, and the surrounding area timbered with

---

[1] Thomas Mante, " Description of Detroit," *Wis. Hist. Colls.*, XVIII, 272–73.
[2] Carver, *Travels*, p. 151.
[3] Hamilton to Dartmouth, September, 1776, Canadian Archives, Q, XII, 212; *Mich. Hist. Colls.*, XVII, 638 ff. " Detroit is Situated in the Northeast and finest climate for all N. America, the Lieut. Gov.'s House and gardens may serve for an Eastern Monarch." Dobie to Claus, December 18, 1785, Canadian Archives, Claus Papers, IV, 88.
[4] Mathews to Haldimand, August 3, 1787, *ibid.*, B, LXXVI, 288; Additional MSS., 21,736, f. 321; *Mich. Hist. Colls.*, XX, 287.
[5] Isaac Weld, *Travels through the States of North America During the Years of 1795, 1796, 1797* (London, 1799), II, 183–91.

"white and black oaks, hickerie, locusts, and maple."[6] He found wild apples of a pleasing taste growing in abundance, and treeless savannahs, miles in extent, with grass many feet high, which rotted each year adding greatly to the fertility of the soil.[7]

In spite of all these attractive descriptions, settlers did not come into the region in large numbers until after the War of 1812. As compared with almost any other American frontier region before 1800, Michigan was slow to develop.

There are several explanations given for this condition. It has already been seen that the English Government under certain ministries was opposed to any westward expansion.[8] Almost unlimited areas of land had been claimed by many persons by virtue of Indian concessions.[9] Claims of from three thousand to eight thousand acres were quite common.[10] It was found by the deputy surveyors in 1791 that whenever settlers did come into the Lakes region they were told that the King had no available lands in that area. Naturally many had to return or purchase grants at exorbitant prices. Many persons at Fort Pitt who were inimical to the best interests of the government spread reports that there was no available land at the King's disposal. It was [they said] claimed by a very few individuals.[11] The method of survey along the navigable waters no doubt impeded settlement. This survey from 1790 on was made in three concessions beginning along the river.

[6] Rogers, *Journal*, p. 231.
[7] *Ibid.* Colonel Bradstreet wrote Shelburne that Detroit was situated in the finest climate in all America, with extremely rich soil capable of producing all sorts of European grain, and the woods were filled with vines which produced grapes of a delicious flavor. Bradstreet to Shelburne, September 7, 1764, Canadian Archives, Shelburne Papers, L, 145. James Abbott describes the soil as rich and easily cultivated, and the climate as mild. *Ibid.*, Dartmouth Transcripts, 1765–1775, pp. 323–24. John Lees also noted that the land was "uncommonly fertile, which makes the settlers very indolent." *Journal of John Lees*, p. 38. Amherst wrote Pitt that "from all accounts It [Detroit] is a very fine country." Amherst to Pitt, February 27, 1761, Canadian Archives, C. O. 5, LXI, pt. i, p. 221. The Quakers who visited Detroit in 1793 gave a similar description. *Mich. Hist. Colls.*, XVII, 640.
[8] *Ante*, pp. 50 ff.
[9] McNiff to Finlay, May 3, 1791, *Mich. Hist. Colls.*, XXIV, 85.
[10] *Ibid.; American State Papers, Public Lands* (Washington, 1832), I, 265.
[11] McNiff to Finlay, May 3, 1791, *Mich. Hist. Colls.*, XXIV, 85.

Only two farm lots could be granted in the front, two in the second, and twelve in the third concession. The settlers could not leave a large quantity of wooded land in their front, and the very heavy cost of roads made it prohibitive to settle the third concession. Governor Hamilton complained to Carleton that the population decreased because of the vexatious restrictions on land.[12] A Quaker who visited Detroit in 1793, one Jacob Lindley, was of the same impression. In his " Journal " he states that the increase of population of the country was restrained " not only by the wet, unhealthy state of the country," as by the landholding conditions. He observed that one-seventh of all lands was reserved for the Crown, and another equal share to the Anglican clergy. He pointed to an old law of Canada, which provided that all real estate, " though sold seven times in seven years, must be sold at the chapel door, mostly on the first-day afternoon," one-ninth of which went to the Roman church.[13] All of these restrictions, which proved to be a severe hindrance in Michigan's growth, may best be understood by tracing the population increase during the period of British control.

When Major Rogers arrived at Detroit in the fall of 1760, he found the settlement contained about five hundred men who could bear arms.[14] The total population at this time on both sides of the river was estimated at about two thousand five hundred, living in about three hundred dwellings.[15] The settlement was considerably spread out on both banks of the river, up and down, for some distance. George Croghan, who visited Detroit in 1764, estimated that there were three or four hundred families there.[16] Colonel Bradstreet, in the same year, estimated the number at about six hundred, mostly French.[17]

[12] Hamilton to Carleton, undated, *ibid.*, IX, 433.
[13] " Expeditions to Detroit, 1793," Jacob Lindley's Account, *Mich. Hist. Colls.*, XVII, 609.
[14] Amherst to Johnson, February 14, 1761, Canadian Archives, C. O. 5, LXI, pt. i, p. 291.
[15] Rogers, *A Concise Account*, p. 168.
[16] Croghan's " Journal," February 28, 1765, to October 8, 1765; *Ill. Hist. Colls.*, XI, 37; *Pennsylvania Colonial Records*, IX, 250 ff.
[17] Shelburne Papers, L, 275.

This discrepancy may easily be explained by the fact that the figures were often grossly exaggerated. It may also be seen from these figures that few, if any, of the people left the country after the surrender of the French to the British.[18] According to the treaty stipulations the inhabitants of the ceded territory were to be given eighteen months in which to retire, the time to be computed from the date of the exchange of the ratifications.[19]

In the year following the collapse of Pontiac's rebellion, the first real census of Detroit was taken.[20] It reveals 243 farmers able to bear arms, 164 women, and 294 children: a total of 701. This census stated that there were thirty-three French families living in the fort with forty-one children and sixty slaves, while the inhabitants owned 281 horses, 136 colts, 196 bullocks, 235 cows, and 224 calves.

How Detroit grew from these meager beginnings possibly is shown best by the following chronological table:

Year	Detroit
1765	868
1768	572 [21]
1770	2,000 [22]
1773	1,282 [23]
1779	2,653 [24]
1782	2,191 [25]
1788	4,000 [26]

[18] In the Illinois Country there was a large migration of the French across the Mississippi. *Ill. Hist. Colls.*, XI, 125. Another account places the total population for the area at 2,000 souls. Canadian Archives, Dartmouth Transcripts, 1765–1775, pp. 223–24.

[19] Shortt and Doughty, *Can. Const. Docs.*, pt. i, p. 116.

[20] Census of Detroit, 1765. MS. in the Library of Congress.

[21] Canadian Archives, C. O. 5, LXXXVI, 130. The total for 1765 is only an estimate and probably includes only those individuals living in the fort.

[22] Governor Abbott's estimate to Lord Dartmouth. *Ibid.*, Dartmouth Transcripts, 1765–1775, p. 323.

[23] This is the population along the right bank of the river of whites only, soldiers not included. *Magazine of Western History*, III, 272.

[24] *Mich. Hist. Colls.*, X, 312–26. In 1780 the census showed 2,307 people. *Ibid.*, 446.

[25] *Ibid.*, 601–13.

[26] *Ibid.*, XI, 636. Only 3,000 is given in 1790. Canadian Archives, Q, XLIX, 300.

The fluctuations in population, the vicissitudes of the people, are to be accounted for variously. The earlier censuses are largely estimates, sometimes including the settlers on both sides of the river, and sometimes not. Seldom were the soldiers in the fort enumerated. During the War of Independence Detroit became a haven for the loyalists of the West, and the population shows a marked increase during the early years of the struggle.[27] The returns of 1782 indicate a decrease from 1779. This may readily be explained by the large absence of the soldiers, militia, Indians, etc., in the campaign of Hamilton against Clark.[28] After the war the population made a slow and steady increase. The inhabitants spread up and down the Detroit River for a distance of sixteen miles, and a small settlement was forming at the mouth of the Huron River near Lake Erie.[29] It was estimated that the village of Detroit contained fully 300 houses at the close of the British régime.[30]

The post at Michilimackinac did not experience growth equal to that of Detroit. The fur trade was the only business there. Even though this prospered highly in times of peace, the post never acquired a large population. It was reported that the village contained thirty families during most of the period.[31] At Sault Ste. Marie in 1762 there were only four houses, one used by the Governor, one by the interpreter, and the others for barracks.[32] The post was abandoned before the Pontiac Uprising, and never again during the English period did it assume any large importance.[33] St. Joseph also had a

[27] Apparently Hamilton expected nearly 5,000 " souls " dependent upon him in 1778. Haldimand to Hamilton, August 6, 1778, *ibid.*, B, LXII, 59–60.
[28] The census says " exclusive of them employ'd in the King's Service." *Ibid.*, X, 446.
[29] Canadian Archives, Q, XLIX, 637. This settlement was not far from the present city of Monroe.
[30] Weld, *Travels*, II, 183.
[31] Henry, *Travels*, p. 40; Carver, *Travels*, p. 18. Askin wrote in 1778 there were nearly 100 houses in " the Subarbs." Askin to McMurry, April 28, 1778, *Askin Papers*, I, 69.
[32] Henry, *Travels*, p. 58.
[33] John Long speaks of being at the Sault in 1768 and mentions a small fort built by the Indians, and about ten log houses used as residences for the traders, but he does not state whether these were occupied. Long, " Voyages and Travels," in Thwaites, *Western Travels*, II, 79; Henry, *loc. cit.*, p. 206.

small settlement consisting of a few French, slaves, and half-breeds.[34] In 1779 some of the inhabitants were removed to Michilimackinac,[35] although when the post was plundered and destroyed by the Spaniards in 1781, there were eight families comprising forty-one persons and "seven individuals, each one in his house."[36] It was never rebuilt. It is no wonder that these posts were never rapidly populated by the British. The French were quite hostile and it took a stout heart to venture so far into the hinterland where the Indians, never too friendly, were largely under French influence;[37] and furthermore, during a considerable portion of the British period, the fur trade also suffered from the many Indian wars and the American War of Independence.[38] Naturally the population did not increase greatly by birth or by immigration.

Little reliance can be placed on the figures given in the colonial reports concerning the population of Michigan between 1760 and 1796, because no care was used in assembling the data. Farmers, traders, slaves, Indians, soldiers, etc., were all thrown together. The traders resided in a place only a short

[34] *Mich. Hist. Colls.*, X, 406–7.

[35] *Ibid.*, 435.

[36] Francis Wharton (ed.), *The Revolutionary Diplomatic Correspondence of the United States* (Washington, 1889), V, 363. In 1767, there were forty Frenchmen at St. Joseph. "Traders from Montreal, traders from the other side of the Mississippi, and the Lord knows from where." Hambach to Edgar, March 23, 1767, Edgar MSS.; *Mich. Hist. Colls.*, XIII, 58–59.

[37] Canadian Archives, Q, IV, 115; *Journal of John Lees*, 40–41.

[38] Henry, *Travels and Adventures*, p. 155; *Wis. Hist. Colls.*, XVIII, 270; Simcoe to Dorchester, August 24, 1793, *Mich. Hist. Colls.*, XXIV, 600; Smith to Leith, February 14, 1792, *ibid.*, 375–76; *ibid.*, XI, 483–85; Stevens, *Northwest Fur Trade*, chap. ii. One trader wrote: "The Returns from the Indian Country are this year very bad, which with the great fall in prices at home, will go nigh to ruin every man concerned in the Trade. . . . May all the curses of Emaulphus fall upon these *Sans Culottes Villains of France!* The War injures this Country most seriously in every point of view." Richardson to Porteous, August 15, 1793, Canadian Archives, M, Vol. 852, p. 57. Another trader wrote: "The Indian Trade is much on the decline at Detroit, there is about 500 packs short of last years Quantity from that quarter." Forsyth to Porteous, *ibid.*, p. 3. "The Detroit trade is very bad," wrote Henry to Edgar, September 1, 1785, Edgar MSS. A letter in the Quebec *Gazette* for August 18, 1768, described the trade as "very dull" and said that the French and Spanish were underselling the English. See especially the report of the Montreal merchants in 1791, *Mich. Hist. Colls.*, XXIV, 306. It was admitted in 1792 that the trade was unsafe and unprofitable, *Wis. Hist. Colls.*, XIX, 272; and Simcoe in a report of September 1, 1794, describes the effects of the Indian war on the trade at Detroit, *Mich. Hist. Colls.*, XXV, 29.

period of the year, and sometimes in the census they were counted and sometimes not.

The garrison at Detroit in peace times contained about two hundred men.[39] During the Pontiac Uprising and the War of Independence this number was augmented to four or five hundred.[40] When the British surrendered Detroit to the Americans in 1796, the garrison consisted of only fifty-three men.[41]

The post at Michilimackinac was occupied by a large detachment from the Sixtieth and Eightieth regiments in September, 1761, under the command of Captain Henry Balfour.[42] Leaving Lieutenant William Leslye in command, Balfour proceeded to occupy Green Bay. When Michilimackinac was surprised by the Indians in 1763, the garrison numbered thirty-two.[43] The post had over one hundred men under Sinclair's command in 1781.[44] When the United States came into possession in 1796, there were only twenty-one men all told.[45] At St. Joseph only fourteen regulars were stationed when the English took control. These were captured and murdered or made prisoners in 1763.[46] After the Pontiac War the fort was not reoccupied by a regular garrison, although it was a strategic center of great importance. It was captured in December, 1780, by a Spanish force who plundered the post, and early in 1781 the village was destroyed and abandoned.[47]

The aboriginal population of Michigan consisted mainly of

[39] *Ibid.*, XIX, 38–45; Carver, *Travels*, p. 152; Rogers, *Journal*, pp. 197–200. Gladwin had 200 men in 1763. *Journal of John Lees*, p. 41. In 1791 militia returns showed 741 men. Canadian Archives, Q, LII, 197.

[40] *Mich. Hist. Colls.*, X, 291, 615; *Journal of John Lees*, p. 41. State of the Garrison at Detroit in 1776, MS. in Clements Library. The militia return of July 27, 1791, shows a total of 741 men. Canadian Archives, Q, LII, 197.

[41] *Mich. Hist. Colls.*, XXV, 120.

[42] Campbell to Bouquet, October 12, 1761, *ibid.*, XIX, 116; same to same, November 8, 1761, *ibid.*, 120. Henry, *Travels*, p. 51 mentions 300 men under Lt. Leslye at Michilimackinac. See Thwaites' statement in *Wis. Hist. Colls.*, VII, 151, 164.

[43] *Mich. Hist. Colls.*, XXVII, 624–25.

[44] *Ibid.*, X, 471. See letter of John Dodge to Washington, Letters of Washington (MSS. in Library of Congress), XVIII, November 21, 1778.

[45] At least this was Beckwith's orders of June 1, 1796. *Mich. Hist. Colls.*, XXV, 120.

[46] Gladwin MS., *ibid.*, XXVII, 636.

[47] *Ibid.*, X, 435; De Peyster to Haldimand, January 8, 1781, *ibid.*, 450; same to McKee, February 1, 1781, *ibid.*, 452.

the Potawatomi, Chippewa, Ottawa, and Huron tribes. These were all of the Algonquian stock. The Potawatomi lived along the western shore of Lake Huron and south along the western shore of Lake Michigan.[48] The Ottawa, during the English period, lived in the region bounded on the north by the Ottawa River, on the west by Georgian Bay, and on the south by Lake Simcoe. They often resorted to Michilimackinac to barter with the traders. Living along one of the great highways of commerce, they were skilled traders and canoeists.[49] The Chippewa were closely connected to the Ottawa and one branch of the tribe spent most of its time around the St. Mary's River, where fish, which was their main article of food, were abundant.[50] The Hurons, who were greatly scattered by the Iroquois between 1648 and 1650, settled mainly in the region south of Lake Simcoe, south and east of Georgian Bay, while a few small units settled near Detroit in 1736.[51]

The population of the posts consisted largely of French known as *habitants*. There were also large numbers of half-breeds, free negroes, panis, and negro slaves.[52] Immediately after the British regulars occupied the country, Colonial, English, and Scotch fur traders followed in their train.[53] Two Jews, according to the record, were also interested in the trade by 1763.[54] During the latter part of the British régime the population took on a somewhat cosmopolitan complexion. In 1793 the committee of Quakers who visited Detroit described the in-

[48] E. H. Blair, *The Indian Tribes of the Upper Mississippi Valley and the Region of the Great Lakes* (Cleveland, 1912), II, pp. 355–56; Hamburgh's Journal of 1763, MS. in Library of Congress; *Journal of John Lees*, p. 38.
[49] F. W. Hodge (ed.), *Handbook of the American Indians* (Washington, 1910), II, 167–171.
[50] Hamburgh's Journal of 1763. MS. in the Library of Congress.
[51] *Ibid.*, R. G. Thwaites (ed.), *Jesuit Relations and Allied Documents* (Cleveland, 1904), I, p. 26; XXXIV, 123; *Journal of John Lees*, p. 38.
[52] *Mich. Hist. Colls.*, X, 613.
[53] Stevens, *Northwest Fur Trade*, p. 21. Two of the most famous of these early traders were Alexander Henry and John Askin.
[54] Rogers, *Diary of the Siege of Detroit*, May 22, 1763. In 1777 there is again mention of a passport given to a Jew. Canadian Archives, B, XXXIX, 493; *Mich. Hist. Colls.*, X, 274; Chapman Abrahams [or Abrams] was one of the first traders in Detroit. In the Claus Papers, VI, 29, mention is made of Moses Davis "another cheap Shop Adventurer" arriving with a cargo. Sterling writes Abrahams, February 19, 1763, that he was willing to serve him. Edgar MSS.

habitants as consisting of many nationalities. "English, Scotch, Irish, Dutch, French, Americans from different states, with black and yellow," and Indians of different tribes made as great a mixture of peoples as one could find in any frontier community.[55]

Not one of the villages in Michigan during the British period presented a very attractive picture; surely not one that would allure many prospective settlers. Major Rogers found at Detroit a small fort surrounded by a wooden stockade about twenty-five feet high and 1,200 yards in circumference.[56] The stockade was usually made of long logs, sharpened at each end, one of which was pushed far into the earth while the other served to keep out marauders. Donald Campbell, who became commandant when Rogers returned East, had a better impression of Detroit. He wrote that the fort was very large and in good repair, " There are two Bastions toward the water, and a large fast Bastion towards the inland the point of the Bastion is a Cavalier of wood on which are mounted the three pounders and three small mortars, or cochons. The Palisadoes are in good order. There is a scaffolding around the whole which is only floored toward the Land for want of Plank, it is by the way of a Blanket." [57]

The post was enlarged after the Indian War of 1763 to hold about one hundred houses.[58] The streets were made more regular, and new and more pretentious barracks were built. A large parade ground was located on the south side of the fort, while to the west was the King's garden belonging to the commandant, who took care that it was laid out well and carefully cultivated.[59] A small bastion was erected on the stockade at each of the corners, in which were mounted several small cannon.[60] When Hamilton came to Detroit in 1776, he found the

[55] Mich. Hist. Colls., XVII, 639.
[56] Rogers, A Concise Account, p. 168.
[57] Campbell to Bouquet, December 11, 1760, Mich. Hist. Colls., XIX, 47–48.
[58] Carver, Travels, p. 151.
[59] This garden was described as worthy of an eastern monarch. Dobie to Claus, December 18, 1785, Canadian Archives, Claus Papers, IV, 88.
[60] Carver, Travels, p. 152. Some repairs were made in 1773. Haldimand ordered Bassett that they be conducted with the strictest economy. Haldimand to Bassett, August 12, 1773. Canadian Archives, B, XXXIII, 69; Mich. Hist. Colls., X, 254.

fort in a tolerable state of defense.[61] An enemy unprovided with cannon, he felt, would be unable to take the works. A stockade of twelve hundred paces, fortified with eleven block houses and batteries, was quite a formidable frontier fort. The palisades were fifteen feet high and mostly new.[62] The old and rotten block houses were torn down and new ones built. Because of the lack of equipment and the scarcity of labor, the repairs and improvements advanced too slowly to suit the governor.[63] Considerable damage was done in 1777 to the fort, and to the ditch surrounding the citadel,[64] by a terrific rain, the heaviest known in forty years. This was Hamilton's excuse to Germain, in explanation for the numerous delays and requests for additional aid.[65]

James May, a prominent merchant of the village of the Straits, gives in his diary a picture of the post during the Revolution.[66] He wrote that there were sixty houses, principally one story high, made of logs.[67] The inhabitants were mainly French, though he mentions thirty Scotch, fifteen Irish, and a few English. There were twenty retail stores. The inhabitants were spread out, up and down both banks of the river, and " there were no settlements nor improvements in any other part of the Territory than that in the immediate vicinity of Detroit." [68] This, no doubt, describes only that part which is now on the American side of the river.

During the War of Independence fears were entertained for

---

[61] Hamilton to Dartmouth, August 29 to September 2, 1776, *ibid.*, X, 265. Turnbull had built an additional guard house while he was at Detroit, for which Gage censured him for putting the crown to any expense unless absolutely necessary. " Must keep expenses down," Gage insisted. Gage to Turnbull, November 17, 1766, Canadian Archives, B, XXVI, 108–109.

[62] Hamilton to Dartmouth, *loc. cit.*; State of the Garrison at Detroit in 1776. MS. in Clements Library.

[63] Hamilton to Dartmouth, *loc. cit.*

[64] This citadel was built by Israel Putnam in 1764. C. M. Burton, *The Building of Detroit* (Detroit, 1912), p. 18.

[65] Hamilton to Germain, June 23 to July 3, Canadian Archives, Q, XIV, 83. In 1782 De Peyster wrote that the fort had almost undergone an inundation. " If this weather continued I fear it will level our works. The oldest people do not remember such a rainy season." De Peyster to Powell, June 12, 1782, *ibid.*, Q, XX, 145.

[66] " Diary of James May, Esq.," 1778.

[67] Croghan in his " Journal " gave eighty as the number of the houses within the stockade in 1764. Croghan's " Journal," in *Early Western Travels*, I, 152.

[68] " Diary of James May, Esq.," 1778.

the safety of Detroit. After Hamilton set out on his campaign against Vincennes, Captain Lernoult set to work to build a new fort. Work began early in November, 1778, and continued to February.[69] Engineers and masons were sent from Canada; a stone magazine was erected; new and larger bastions were built; all in all a formidable defense was erected against any invaders.[70] Rains played havoc with the exterior part of the citadel, washing away four to five feet of the surface into the ditch which surrounded the place. This was remedied by making the outer protection entirely of clay to a thickness of ten feet, well beaten and held together every three feet by layers of brush and cedar stakes. Over all this was placed a sod six inches thick.[71] The garrison now felt secure against any force which could be sent by the Americans to capture Detroit.

By the Treaty of Paris of 1783, Great Britain surrendered all her claims to the region south of the Great Lakes, but deemed it inexpedient at the time to surrender the Northwest posts.[72] In fact, she strengthened the posts considerably. In 1789, Captain Gother Mann made a careful survey of Fort Lernoult and advised that considerable repairs and enlargement of the fort be undertaken.[73] The following year he reported that all the work was completed and the fort in excellent condition.[74] While John Jay was in London negotiating with Lord Grenville for the surrender of the Northwest posts, Colonel Richard

[69] Brehm to Haldimand, May 28, 1779, *Mich. Hist. Colls.*, IX, 411; same to same, June 23, 1779, *ibid.*, 415. MacLeod to McKee, April 6, 1778, mentions work on a new fort nearly a year earlier, Canadian Archives, Claus Papers, II, 11. Bird gives a detailed account of the work in his letter to Powell, August 13, 1782, *Mich. Hist. Colls.*, X, 625–27.

[70] *Ibid.*

[71] *Ibid.*, 625.

[72] In 1782 De Peyster ordered the labor on all public works to cease. Hay found the town without pickets, etc., and said, " a discontented Indian could set fire to the town any night." Haldimand quotes this statement of Hay in a letter to De Peyster of September 4, 1784, *Mich. Hist. Colls.*, XX, 254–55. See De Peyster's answer of October 1, *ibid.*, 262–63. Haldimand refused to honor any additional expenses. Haldimand to Hay, September 3, 1784, *ibid.*, 251; same to De Peyster, September 4, 1784; *ibid.*, 254; Mathews to De Peyster, June 21, 1784; *ibid.*, 232.

[73] Canadian Archives, Q. XLVII, pt. i, pp. 112 ff.

[74] *Mich. Hist. Colls.*, XXIII, 373 ff. Oliver Spencer gives an interesting description of Detroit in 1793 in his narrative. Printed in *Burton Leaflet* III, no. 5.

England was spending many a " goodly " pound in keeping the fort at Detroit in first-class condition.[75] There seemed to be almost a forlorn hope that the possession of the posts might be continued.

Jacob Lindley, who visited Detroit in 1793, spoke of the excellent condition of the post. He found the way to the town carefully guarded, as watchmen were placed at all the entrances.[76] On the ramparts and bastions stood sentinels, who from nine A.M. until three A.M. called to each other — " All is well," and the last one, " All is very well." [77] Isaac Weld, who was in Detroit shortly after the English evacuation, felt that the fortifications were only of value against savages.[78] Thus in spite of continued repairing, the outlay of considerable sums, and constant care, the fort could not have withstood any American attack supported with artillery.[79]

Another feature of the post at Detroit was the large area extending from the south side around to the north known as the commons. All the wood and underbrush had been cleared from this space to prevent giving cover to any enemy. It was considered the property of the community and was not to be cultivated by any one person.[80] In 1773 the inhabitants were greatly incensed when Major Bassett fenced in a small area of forty-two acres, and they at once sent a memorial to General Haldimand, saying that the Major wanted to use the land for his own purposes.[81] The petition was favorably received and Bassett's plan was defeated.[82] The people had saved their commons.

Within the stockade, encircling the whole village, was a street called the "Chemin de Ronde." All the other streets bore

[75] *Mich. Hist. Colls.*, XXIII, 390–93.
[76] *Ibid.*, XVII, 596.
[77] *Ibid.*
[78] Weld, *Travels*, II, 183.
[79] Such had been Carver's observations as early as 1766. Carver, *Travels*, p. 152.
[80] Bassett to Haldimand, April 29, 1773, *Mich. Hist. Colls.*, XIX, 297–98. On June 15, 1773, advice was sent to Bassett from New York not to fence the " Domain," or to cause the Crown any expense. *Ibid.*, X, 252.
[81] Canadian Archives, B, LXX, 44.
[82] Haldimand to Bassett, June 15, 1773, *ibid.*, XXXIII, 5.

such French names as Ste. Anne, St. Louis, and St. Joseph. The principal traders' homes, places of business, the barracks for the members of the garrison, the commandant's dwelling of stone, the small parade ground, and the parish church were all on Ste. Anne's, which was the widest of all the streets. The streets were usually narrow,[83] and of course none was paved; so whenever it rained, they were very muddy. Along most of them, footways were made by using square logs, laid transversely close to each other.[84] The houses were built of wood after the style of Lower Canada,[85] crowded closely together because of lack of space within the palisade.[86] Nevertheless, visitors found that accommodations were quite comfortable.[87]

The next post in importance was Michilimackinac. When the English took possession, they found the fort sadly in need of repairs.[88] The fortification at this time was placed close to the upper point of the lower peninsula of Michigan. Alexander Henry described it as built on a sand bank, a strong stockade, within which were thirty houses and a church of fair proportions.[89] The place was greatly strengthened by Captain George Etherington, the second English commander, who arrived in September, 1762.[90] Carver found upon his visit in 1766 that the post had not grown since French rule was relinquished.[91] The people consisted, apart from the garrison, of traders who found the fort very conveniently situated for traffic with the Indians. Indeed Michilimackinac was the place of deposit and point of departure for the regions of Lakes Michigan and Superior, the Upper Mississippi River, and far to the northwest. From this point the furs were shipped by Lake Nipissing and the Ottawa River to Montreal, or by the Lakes past Detroit

[83] Weld, *Travels*, II, 182. Ste. Anne Street was from twenty to forty feet wide. Most of the other streets were about fifteen feet.
[84] *Ibid.*, II, 183.
[85] *Ibid.*, 182.
[86] *Mich. Hist. Colls.*, XVII, 596.
[87] *Ibid.*, 639.
[88] Hamburgh's Journal of 1763. Michilimackinac is the Chippewa name for tortoise and the place is supposed to have received its name from Mackinac Island lying about six or seven miles to the northeast, within sight of the fort, which had the appearance of a tortoise. Carver, *Travels*, p. 19.
[89] Henry, *Travels*, p. 40.
[90] Leslye to Bouquet, September 30, 1762, *Mich. Hist. Colls.*, XIX, 166.
[91] Carver, *Travels*, p. 19.

and Niagara.[92] The intrepid trader journeyed forth from this post far into the interior of North America. Michilimackinac was the entrepôt for the great fur traffic of the Northwest.[93] After the Indians captured the fort in 1763, it was reoccupied in the fall of 1764 by a detachment of English regulars under the command of Captain Howard, who at once made considerable repairs to the old fort.[94] Apparently soon after, a new fort was built on some sand dunes farther to the west about a mile from the present Mackinac City.[95] This fort was not as strong as the former, and not as commodious or prepossessing.[96] Located among uninteresting sand dunes which caused no end of trouble, it was bleak in winter and extremely hot in summer. It was surrounded by a heavy stockade, and nearby was a small cluster of log houses belonging to the traders.[97] Stretching back from the village was a small rectangular plot used by the *habitants* to raise some vegetables.[98]

While the War of Independence was in progress and George Rogers Clark's agents were negotiating with the Indian chiefs far to the north, Patrick Sinclair was commissioned in 1779 as lieutenant governor of Michilimackinac and its dependencies, and was charged with the enlarging and rebuilding of the King's fort.[99] Major De Peyster, who had been much perturbed by Clark's success in Illinois, had strengthened the post before he was sent to take charge of Detroit in 1779.[100] Upon his arrival, Sinclair readily saw that the old fort, battered to pieces by the fierce storms of the lakes, was beyond repair.[101] He determined to remove it from the mainland to an island

[92] Henry, *Travels*, chaps. II, III; Stevens, *Northwest Fur Trade*, chap. V.
[93] *Ibid.;* "Memorial" of the Merchants of Montreal, April 4, 1786, *Mich. Hist. Colls.*, XI, 483–85.
[94] *Wis. Hist. Colls.*, XVIII, 270; "Journal of Captain Montresor," *N. Y. Hist. Colls. for 1881*, pp. 287 ff.; Gage to Halifax, April 27, 1765, Carter, *Gage's Correspondence*, I, 57.
[95] R. G. Thwaites, *How Clark Won the Northwest and Other Essays in Western History* (Chicago, 1904), p. 218.
[96] Rogers, *Ponteach* (Nevins), p. 115.
[97] De Peyster to Brehm, June 20, 1779, *Mich. Hist. Colls.*, IX, 387.
[98] "Journal of Peter Pond," *Wis. Hist. Colls.*, XVIII, 330.
[99] *Mich. Hist. Colls.*, XXIV, 3. Sinclair's instructions are in *ibid.*, IX, 516–18.
[100] De Peyster to Haldimand, June 27, 1779, *ibid.*, IX, 388.
[101] Sinclair believed the old fort was defenseless. Sinclair to Brehm, undated, *ibid.*, IX, 528; same to Haldimand, undated, *ibid.*, 545.

seven miles northwest of the old village, called by the Canadians " La Grosse Isle." [102] Sinclair appropriated this uninhabited island. Later he paid £ 5,000 (New York Currency) for it to members of the Chippewa Tribe.[103] Very soon afterward he began to erect a durable fort on the Island, and having received General Haldimand's permission, he moved thither in the spring of 1781.[104] The traders, though reluctant to leave their homes,[105] realized the necessity of having the protection of the army; so they also moved over.

Haldimand was generous in sending masons, carpenters, and supplies.[106] Accordingly, all through the winter of 1779–1780 work on the wharf and stockade was pushed. Land to the amount of four acres was cleared around the fort, and plans were made for using the limestone which was so abundant.[107] There was a proposal made to name the new fort after General Haldimand, but he preferred to keep the old Indian name. " I have never known," he wrote, " any advantage resulting from changing the names of Places long inhabited by the same People." [108] The fort was never completed by the British and when Captain Mann made an elaborate survey in 1788, he felt that the greater part of the expense bestowed was a huge waste of money, time, and materials.[109] This apparently indicates that the suggestions for repairing the post made by Richard Hockings, the engineer who visited the place in 1782, had not been carried out.[110]

The English considered Michilimackinac of great strategic value for the control of the fur trade and the Indians, so at the close of the War of Independence, like Detroit and other northwestern posts, it was not surrendered. Trade again be-

[102] *Ibid.*, XIX, 633.
[103] *Ibid.*
[104] Haldimand to De Peyster, April 16, 1780, *ibid.*, X, 390; Brehm to Sinclair, April 17, 1780, *ibid.*, IX, 533–34.
[105] Sinclair to Haldimand, May 29, 1780, *ibid.*, IX, 553. " Opinions Regarding Removal of the Fort," *ibid.*, 556–57.
[106] Brehm to Sinclair, April 17, 1780, *ibid.*, 534.
[107] Sinclair to Brehm, February 15, 1780, *ibid.*, 540.
[108] Haldimand to Sinclair, August 21, 1780, *ibid.*, 574. For a more detailed account of the building of the new fort, see E. O. Wood, *Historic Mackinac* (New York, 1918), I, chap. V.
[109] *Mich. Hist. Colls.*, XII, 33–34.
[110] *Ibid.*, X, 641–45.

came prosperous after the Treaty of Paris, and the Island once more assumed its former importance. A very interesting picture of the Island before it was surrendered to the United States in 1796 as a result of the Jay Treaty is given in Major Caleb Swan's " Journal." He wrote:

On the south side of this Island, there is a small basin, of a segment of a circle, serving as an excellent harbor, for vessels of any burden, and for canoes. Around this basin the village is built, having two streets of nearly a quarter of a mile in length, a Roman chapel, and containing eight-nine houses and stores; some of them spacious and handsome, with white lime plastering in front, which shows to great advantage from the seas.[111]

The English had erected a government house of fair dimensions, which the various officials had fitted up in rather elaborate taste for a frontier post. The rooms were very large and well arranged. In front was a spacious garden, well planned, gently sloping to the water's edge. At the rear were two natural springs in the midst of a large grove of sugar trees. At a distance of twenty rods from the house the rocks rose suddenly and almost perpendicular to a distance of about one hundred feet. On this height stood the fort, built of stone and lime, with sufficient towers and bastions. Still farther in the rear, about a half mile, was another eminence rising fully two hundred and fifty feet from the water. From it one might see the fort, the neighboring islands, and the many channels lying prostrated at the foot of the hill, while on the southwest Lake Michigan lay in all its immensity, and to the north Lake Huron loomed, stretching to the bounds of the horizon.[112]

Under the French system in Illinois and Canada the farm lands outside the village were divided into two large fields — one the common field, and the other the commons. The common field was divided into long narrow strips, ten to forty perches [113] in width, extending back from the river,[114] which the inhabitants cultivated. The commons was the wood and

---

[111] " Journal of Major Caleb Swan," *Magazine of American History* (New York, 1888), XIX, 74.
[112] *Ibid.*, 75.
[113] Census of Detroit, 1763; MS. in Library of Congress. A perch = 16.5 feet. The common unit of measurement was the arpent = 192 feet. The narrower farms were usually an arpent. Practically all were two or more arpents wide.
[114] *Ibid.*

pasture land and it belonged to the community, being separated from the cultivated field by a fence. The time for plowing, sowing, and harvesting was regulated by the inhabitants in an assembly. These assemblies were usually held after mass outside the church door, and were attended by all males of military age.[115] This system did not prevail at Detroit because the farms stretched up and down the river several miles, and were held in individual ownership.

When the English assumed control, they disallowed all the French land grants unless they were registered.[116] The last French commander had made grants of large numbers of acres; these were considered fraudulent by the newcomers.[117] Orders were sent out by Gage to annul all grants which were not made directly by the governors representing the King.[118] Whenever any settlements had been made, the officials were ordered to " pull down as fast as any persons shall presume to build up " and seize and send the offenders who settle among the savages " down the Country." [119] This illustrates how careful the government was in placating the Indians. In spite of the government's restrictions, many people squatted on the inviting lands, especially around Detroit. The problem became so acute that Hamilton had to allow "necessitous persons with large families " to till the lands, but he informed Haldimand that he gave them to understand the temporary indulgence was not a grant.[120] The English government was very careful to purchase the lands from the Indians, at a fair price, and they were to be carefully surveyed.[121] After the War of Independence, the government planned to give lands which it actually owned to the officers, soldiers, Indian agents, and loyalists, but to the latter only after they had

[115] *Ill. Hist. Colls.*, II, xxiii.
[116] Gage to Stephenson, April 8, 1771, Canadian Archives, B, XXVII, 184; *Mich. Hist Colls.*, VIII, 468; X, 245; XX, 301.
[117] *Ibid.*
[118] *Ibid.*
[119] *Ibid.* See especially Shelburne's orders to Johnson as early as 1767. Shelburne to Johnson, June 20, 1767, *ibid.*, 301.
[120] Hamilton to Haldimand, September 9, 1778, *ibid.*, IX, 474.
[121] Haldimand to Hay, April 26, 1784, *ibid.*, XI, 410.

taken the oath of allegiance and made a special declaration. These orders were given a very liberal interpretation, and much confusion resulted, which the land board of the District of Hesse attempted to straighten out after the British evacuation of the posts.[122] General Haldimand was very much afraid that under the disguise of loyalists the rebels would claim lands at Detroit and thus act as spies. He warned Hamilton to be especially careful.[123] When the English officials became aware of the great confusion over land titles and the effect upon the population, they established a land board that sat at Newark for the distinct purpose of bringing order out of chaos.[124] Not very much was accomplished, for the flag of England soon ceased to wave over the territory of Michigan. When British power waned, land-thirsty pioneers bought millions of acres from the Indians for little more than a keg of rum [125] — a custom practiced everywhere as the white frontier was pushed westward.

There was some speculation in lands in and about Detroit during the British régime.[126] Farm lands frequently changed ownership; real estate was always sold at the door of Ste. Anne's; and the Justice of the Peace held a public auction of debtors' lands to foreclose mortgages.[127] This was done without legal sanction, but conditions demanded drastic action. Real estate within the post was active at times and prices soared while the redcoat held sway. Some small lots within the fort sold for as much as large farms in the nearby region. In 1767, Philip Dejean sold ground on St. Joseph Street for £ 6/10, which measured four feet by twelve and one-half feet deep; in the following year the same plot including a very

122 Haldimand to De Peyster, March 29, 1784, *ibid.*, XX, 217–19. See especially " Land Settlement in Upper Canada, 1783–1840," Ontario Archives, *Report for 1920* (Toronto, 1921).
123 Haldimand to Hamilton, August 6, 1778, *Mich. Hist. Colls.*, IX, 399.
124 Canadian Archives, *Report for 1881*, p. 16; " Land Settlement in Upper Canada," *loc. cit.*
125 *Mich. Hist. Colls.*, XXIV, 44–84, 174–76, 342–57; XXV, 142–53. Some lands were rented for cash and kind. *Askin Papers*, I, 46–47.
126 C. M. Burton, *City of Detroit* (Detroit, 1922), II, 200.
127 *Ibid.*

small house sold for £ 2,666/13/4; [128] but in 1776 this parcel was purchased for £ 300! [129] Thomas Williams bought a lot of forty-six feet front by sixty-three feet deep on the " street leading to the water gage," for £ 366/13/4. [130] Transfers show that property values increased rapidly as the years passed. [131] The early inhabitants of Michigan were not much concerned in agricultural pursuits. [132] They never exported grain as the people of Illinois did, [133] although all the travelers were glowing in their praise of the possibilities of growing every European grain. [134] The easy-going, pleasure-loving, adventuresome French followed the path of least resistance, but a path which never would lead to the development of an empire. There never seemed to be sufficient food at Michilimackinac, for most of the inhabitants were interested only in the fur trade. [135] Governor Hamilton complained to Dartmouth that agriculture did not interest the people because the bare necessities of life were so easily procured. [136] Wood was plentiful, the Strait was well stocked with fish, and the forests were well supplied with game. The Governor noted that the French were nearly as lazy as the savages. John Lees

[128] Ibid.

[129] Ibid.

[130] Williams Day Books, Burton Historical Collection.

[131] Ibid., also Moran Papers, passim. In 1774 George McDougall sold a house and lot in Detroit for £ 250 N. Y. C. to James Thompson. It had a 42 foot frontage. Canadian Archives, Askin Papers, XXV, September 1, 1774. In 1779 Pierre Drouillard sold King George III 1/2 arpent in front by one in depth for £ 1,050 N. Y. C., ibid., Register of Notaries, V, 344–45. A so-called tenement and lot 40 x 45 feet was sold in 1780 for £ 5,200, ibid., Askin Papers, XXV, July 13, 1780. In 1780 nine acres at entrance of St. Clair River sold for £ 1,200 N. Y. C., ibid., Register of Notaries, VI, 423–24. A lot 60 x 150 sold for £ 200 N. Y. C. in 1784. Ibid., 415–18. Askin sold Todd and McGill large areas of land freeing himself from debt in 1796. Some of this sold for £ 4,000. Ibid., Askin Papers, XXV, passim.

[132] The Curé, Father Hubert, to Haldimand, December 21, 1781, claimed that the people took to hunting instead of agriculture. Canadian Archives, Report for 1886, p. 544; Mich. Hist. Colls., XIX, 673.

[133] Winsor, Narrative and Critical History of America, V, 53.

[134] Ante, pp. 99 ff.

[135] Such were Frobisher's observations in 1776. " Michilimackinac & the Country around does not produce any Provisions; except Indian Corn and Fish, & there is seldom a Sufficiency for the Annual Consumption," he wrote. Shelburne Papers, L, 351 ff.

[136] Hamilton to Dartmouth, August 29 to September 2, 1776, Mich. Hist. Colls., X, 266, claimed the French did not even have a seine though fish were plentiful.

said that the settlers were so indolent because the land was uncommonly fertile.[137] The soil was so good that in spite of ignorance and indolence, wheat, corn, barley, oats, potatoes, onions, pease, and buckwheat yielded well.[138] Melons, peaches, plums, pears, apples, grapes, and mulberries, besides several sorts of smaller fruits, grew in abundance.[139] When the English came into possession, no sheep were raised, but in 1776 it was estimated there were about two thousand sheep and three thousand head of black cattle.[140] The Canadian officials continually urged the post commanders to concentrate on the production of food.[141] During the War of Independence, when communication by the lakes was precarious, the post officials bent every effort to raise sufficient provisions for the garrisons. Haldimand suggested to De Peyster to cultivate portions of Belle Isle,[142] and Sinclair at Michilimackinac proposed to use Canadians, refugees, and provincials to increase the food supply for his post.[143] Detroit could raise sufficient food during peace times, but during war the men were needed for pursuits not agricultural.[144] The Curé of Detroit, Father Hubert, said

[137] *Journal of John Lees,* p. 38.

[138] *Mich. Hist. Colls.,* X, 266. James Sterling sent Lt. Wynne at Fort Erie a barrel of 900 good onions in 1765, " enough," he wrote, " to spoil your kissing for one Winter." Promised to send potatoes when dug. Sterling Letter Book, September 18, 1765. Firewood came from a distance and gave John Campbell no end of trouble. He wasn't able to supply the garrison at 5/ per cord and found 7/2 was the cheapest he could purchase. Campbell to Gage, May 31 and October 31, 1765, Gage MSS.

[139] *Mich. Hist. Colls.,* X, 266. See the Diary of Askin at Michilimackinac in 1774 for the methods employed by a careful and enterprising farmer on the frontier. The original is in the Askin Papers at Ottawa. Published in *Askin Papers,* I, 50–58.

[140] *Mich. Hist. Colls.,* X, 266. In 1768 there were 600 " horned cattle " and 576 hogs in Detroit. Gage to Hillsborough, May 15, 1768, Canadian Archives, C. O. 5, LXXXVI, 130. In 1793, Askin sold McKee 30 head of " black cattle " weighing 21,898 pounds at the Rapids of Miamis for the use of the Indians. *Ibid.,* Claus Papers, V, 281.

[141] *Ibid.,* Q, V, pt. ii, p. 760. Haldimand urged Hamilton to discover some " effectual means " to raise food at Detroit even if a part of the garrison was employed. Haldimand to Hamilton, October 7, 1778. Haldimand wrote Germain that grain of all kinds should be raised at Detroit for supplying Niagara and Michilimackinac. Haldimand to Germain, September 25, 1779, *ibid.,* LIV, 190. Apparently Belle Isle was cultivated for in 1791 there were sowed 37 bushels of winter wheat, 25 bushels of spring wheat, 20 bushels of oats, 2 acres of potatoes, and 8 acres of Indian corn. *Ibid.,* Register of Notaries, IV, 71.

[142] Haldimand to De Peyster, July 13, 1780, *Mich. Hist. Colls.,* IX, 638.

[143] Sinclair to Brehm, October 7, 1779, *ibid.,* 525.

[144] Bolton to Haldimand, March 24, 1779, *ibid.,* 428.

that the people much preferred hunting to settling down to farming,[145] and noted that they even made lazy hunters.[146] In 1777 one hundred and fifty head of cattle were driven across country in thirty-two days from Illinois to the Detroit garrison.[147] In spite of all the well-planned attempts to raise supplies, prices were very high and often there was a scarcity. Hamilton in 1778 wrote to Haldimand that he was feeding five thousand souls,[148] and De Peyster spoke of the rangers as " walking spectres." [149] In 1778 attempts were made to regulate the price of wheat, flour, pease, and corn.[150] At this time flour was selling at 50s,[151] and two months later it rose to 60s.[152] Hamilton even attempted to keep a frugal table for the younger officers who were unable to support their new rank.[153] He wrote that " New England rum has been at the exorbitant price of 28s York per gallon, sold for 2s at the manufacturing place in time of peace. Beef is 2d the pound; salt 4d the pound, and other things in proportion." [154] Hamilton's expedition against Clark took so many oxen and men from Detroit that the beasts could not be purchased at one thousand livres per head, and the scarcity of men made it impossible to thresh the grain.[155] Prices soared higher and higher in spite of all at-

---

[145] Canadian Archives, *Report for 1886*, p. 544.
[146] Father Hubert to Haldimand, December 31, 1781, *Mich. Hist. Colls.*, XIX, 673.
[147] Hamilton to Germain, July 14, 1777, Canadian Archives, Q, XIV, 94.
[148] *Ibid.*, B, CXXI, 25. Mentioned also by Haldimand in his letter to Hamilton of August 6, 1778. *Mich. Hist. Colls.*, IX, 400. In 1794 there was a great scarcity of provisions and the season " so advanced " they could not be sent from Canada although there were 3,500 Indians and many more stragglers and soldiers to feed, dependent on Detroit. England to Le Maistre, October 28, 1794, *ibid.*, C, CCXLVII, 308–10.
[149] De Peyster to McKee, October 23, 1782, *ibid.*, Claus Papers, III, 181.
[150] *Ibid.*, *Report for 1887*, p. 206. For prices at Michilimackinac see *Askin Papers*, I, 74, 100.
[151] *Mich. Hist. Colls.*, IX, 439.
[152] *Ibid.*, See *Askin Papers*, I, 96, 164; and *ibid.*, 241, 259, 262, 263, for some problems of the farmer. Flour was 40 livres per cwt. in 1764, Quebec *Gazette*, July 12, 1764.
[153] Hamilton to Germain, June 23 to July 3, 1777, Canadian Archives, Q, XIV, 84.
[154] *Ibid.* In 1788 salt was 2/6 per bushel at Montreal, 15/ at Kingston, and 40/ at Detroit. Public Record Office, C. O. 42, vol. 316, p. 198.
[155] Bolton to Haldimand, March 24, 1779, *Mich. Hist. Colls.*, IX, 428.

tempts at regulation.[156] David Zeisberger found flour so scarce in 1784 that it sold for £ 7/13 per hundred pounds.[157] Distress was not unknown,[158] for weather, pests, and indifferent farmers played havoc with the food supply. The governors at Quebec were exasperated at the continual demands made upon them for money to purchase provisions. Economy was constantly urged. This state of affairs was not due to lack of attention on the part of the post officials, but because Haldimand, hundreds of leagues away, could not appreciate the problem.[159] After the war, conditions never became normal during the British régime. The continual Indian wars and the fur trade interests of the people retarded everything to a surprising degree.[160]

The fur trade was the chief occupation of the settlers and was practically the only inducement to draw the British col-

[156] Hamilton to Carleton, April 25, 1778, *ibid.*, 437. See *ibid.*, 439 for prices at Detroit in 1778.

[157] Zeisberger, "Diary," June, 1784. Even in 1764 flour was 40 livres per hundred, and beef 16 sols per pound. Quebec *Gazette,* July 12, 1764.

[158] *Ibid.*, July 17, 1789; De Peyster to Bolton, March 10, 1780, *Mich. Hist. Colls.*, XIX, 502.

[159] Haldimand was always urging economy as did the other officials in Canada. *Mich. Hist. Colls.*, IX, 355, 357, 359, 405; X, 302, 377, 409–10, 412. Haldimand asked De Peyster if the soldiers could not eat deer meat and fish. Haldimand to De Peyster, December 25, 1778, Canadian Archives, B, LXII, 347–48. De Peyster replied that the scheme was impracticable, as the taking of fish was "too precarious," and not five carcasses of Indian meat of any kind brought to the post in a year. De Peyster to Haldimand, June 1, 1779, *Mich. Hist. Colls.*, IX, 383. De Peyster claimed that provisions arrived in such a bad state that the soldier did not get half of his allowance. De Peyster to Haldimand, May 2, 1779, Canadian Archives, Q, XVI, pt. i, p. 252. Large amounts of supplies were ruined in the long journey to the Northwest, and some were stolen. Captain Howard found his goods "all damaged." Campbell to Gage, October 31, 1765, Gage MSS. In 1796 the deficiency in Indian stores was valued at £ 92/13/5½ and the damage was £ 82/9/9½. *Mich. Hist. Colls.*, XX, 455. Sterling had 41 barrels of rum sent to Detroit in 1761 but only 38 "full ones arrived." "I believe the Light Infantry made too free with them," he wrote. Sterling to ———, August 25, 1761, Sterling Letter Book. On September 1, 1760, Sterling found many things "soiled, bruised or broken." *Ibid.* This was likewise Askin's experience. Askin to Messrs. Todd and McGill, June 29, 1778, *Askin Papers*, I, 151–52.

[160] There was never any lack of sap for sugar. *Mich. Hist. Colls.*, XVII, 613, describes the Indian methods of manufacture. Rents for homes were rather high. Sterling paid 600 livres for rent in 1761. Sterling Letter Book, January 31, 1761. William Macomb received £ 48 for one year's house rent. Macomb Ledger, June 3, 1789. Rents were as high as £ 5/10 per month. Duggan to McKee, October 3, 1793, Canadian Archives, Claus Papers, VI, 29.

onists to Michigan. There was little or no land speculation like that which enticed many settlers to the Illinois country.[161] The fur trade during the British régime falls into two periods. The first was from 1760 to the War of Independence, when the trade was carried on by independent traders, although the great Scotch fur barons were tending to get control of the peltry. The second was from the War until the surrender of the posts in 1796, marked by the rise of the great fur companies. The Colonial struggle of 1775-1781 was a blessing in disguise to the Montreal merchants, for it eliminated the rivalry between them and the merchants of New York, Philadelphia, Albany, and Schenectady for the supremacy of the Northwest trade.[162] During the hostilities the English held the lines of communication and practically excluded the colonials from any share in the Northwest trade until 1796, and even to a large degree until the War of 1812. It is not the purpose of the writer to treat the fur trade in Michigan during the British régime — that has already been well done.[163] But since practically all of the energies of the people centered in this business, no real understanding of the era can be gained without some study of this great business.

In the first period the free policy of trade pursued brought in such an influx of traders that they nearly ruined the business by their attempts to undersell each other. It was a transitional age, changing from the French policy and influence to the English, during which time the latter gained a firm foothold in Michigan. The Indian was also subdued, and through presents enlisted on their side during the War of Independence. By 1779 merchants at Michilimackinac combined for protection, and this association was soon followed by the North West and Mackinac Companies, which gained a great hold on the peltry trade of Michigan. This was the main characteristic of the

---

[161] Alden, *New Governments West of the Alleghanies Before 1780*, p. 45.
[162] *Ill. Hist. Colls.*, II, xxix; Morgan Letter Book, *passim*.
[163] Johnson, *Michigan Fur Trade*, chaps. IV, V; W. F. Stevens, "The Organization of the British Fur Trade," *Mississippi Valley Historical Review*, September, 1916. The most scholarly and exhaustive account of the fur trade is Stevens, *The Northwest Fur Trade, 1763-1800*.

second period, a period in which thousands of pelts were taken out of the present state.[164]

There were two great water routes from the East to the West used by the traders.[165] One followed the Great Lakes by way of Niagara to Detroit, the other the Ottawa River, Lake Nipissing, and French River to Georgian Bay. Both led to the post at Michilimackinac and thence around the wild shores of Lake Superior to the Kaministikwia and the Grand Portage.[166] Broadly speaking, the Niagara route led to Detroit, to the Ohio, the Illinois country, and the Mississippi; while the Ottawa route was the great highway to the far west, although for a considerable time this was also the recognized route to the Illinois and the Mississippi.

Through the British period the French inhabitants, somewhat scattered, remained the largest element in the white population of Michigan. Most of them came originally from Canada, although some migrated directly from France and the Illinois country.[167] There existed among the French population two classes: the gentry and the *habitant*, the latter by far the larger in numbers. The *habitants* had belonged to the lower classes in Canada and possessed very few of the graces and tastes of the gentry. They spent most of their time in collecting furs or in carrying the goods from post to post, and thus came into closest contact with the Indians, with whom they associated in the most intimate way, even marrying the Indian girls.[168] They had small need for things of this world and the scant income that they procured from the fur trade or as boatmen [169] was very soon spent upon their returning to the posts. They cared little for agriculture as it was too settled a pursuit;

[164] Grant to Haldimand, April 24, 1780, *Mich. Hist. Colls.*, XIX, 509–11; XXV, 202–204; Stevens, *Northwest Fur Trade*, chaps. II, IV.

[165] *Proceedings and Transactions of the Royal Society of Canada*, VIII, 185. Stevens, *loc. cit.*, 150–53.

[166] An excellent account of the importance of the Portage is W. E. Stevens, "The Fur Trade in Minnesota during the British Régime," *Minnesota History Bulletin*, V, no. 1.

[167] M. Bossu, *Travels throughout that part of North America called Louisiana* (London, 1771), p. 126.

[168] *Ibid.*

[169] Lees, *Journal*, p. 43.

and during the whole period there was almost a total lack of any attempt to lead a settled life.[170] Even as late as 1793 it was observed that they raised scarcely enough corn or wheat for their own sustenance, so poorly were the fields tilled.[171] Governor Hamilton was greatly exasperated at the *habitants'* total indifference to farming. A soil, virgin and rich, they ignored; they scarcely scratched its surface. So improvident were they, though abundant crops could be grown with little labor, they left their cattle to starve in winter for lack of fodder.[172] In spite of all his conspicuous faults, the *habitant* presented a strong contrast to the American frontiersman. The frontiersman, as a rule, had very little use for law or any authority, while the *habitant* much preferred to be guided by law in all his affairs.[173] Quarrels were frequent but instead of the duel or a mere fight, recourse was had to arbitration.[174] Whenever possible, the assistance of a judge or notary was always sought in business dealings.[175]

Those *habitants* who spent their entire time hunting, trading, and living with the Indians were known as *coureurs de bois, voyageurs,* or bush lopers. They dressed like the Indians, wearing little else than the hunting skirt, leggings, and moccasins; in colder weather a buffalo robe was wrapped around the body. Priest and governor were loud in their complaints of the lawlessness of these people.[176] They were perhaps no better, perhaps no worse, than the people with whom they associated. They were a merry, patient, faithful, and hardy folk, warm in their friendships, but ever ready for revenge if

[170] Canadian Archives, *Report for 1886,* p. 544; Hamilton to Dartmouth, August 29 and September 2, 1776, *Mich. Hist. Colls.,* X, 266–68. The French and Indian War, and especially the Pontiac Uprising, had left these people "miserably poor." Campbell to Gage, October 31, 1765, April 10, May 3 and 9, 1766, in Gage MSS.

[171] *Mich. Hist. Colls.,* XVII, 595.

[172] Hamilton to Dartmouth, August 29 and September 2, 1776, *ibid.,* X, 266–68.

[173] *Ill. Hist. Colls.,* II, xviii.

[174] *Ibid.*

[175] *Ibid.,* xix.

[176] Parkman, *The Old Régime in Canada,* II, 102–105, 109–15; C. W. Alvord, *The Illinois Country, 1673–1818* (Springfield, 1920), p. 72; Canadian Archives, *Report for 1899,* p. 317.

they were wronged in the slightest degree. In spite of a life amid danger they never became brave, bold, resourceful men like the American frontier folk.[177] All the great fur trading companies who employed these *voyageurs* testify to this. Upon returning to the settlements they were careless, indolent, pleasure-seeking, spending their time and petty earnings in drinking and gambling.[178]

On the other hand, the picture of village life would be far from complete if only the *habitants* were considered. There was a small group who kept the social life on a higher plane, and these were the larger merchants and farmers known as the " gentry," who came from the better classes in Canada or France.[179] They surrounded themselves with such elegant and luxurious things as could be imported. Some were distantly related to the nobility, and many were wealthy and exerted powerful influence in the community. Sir William Johnson calls them gentlemen in character, manner, and dress, " men of abilities, influence, and address." [180] They kept slaves,[181] built large houses,[182] and were very hospitable to strangers. Thus among the French one may look in vain for the democracy of the American frontier. There was a refinement, an elegance, which, though simple, presents a striking contrast to American pioneer life. Among the more prominent families at Detroit were the Beaubien, Navarre, de Jean, Grant, Baptiste, Campion, Sterling, Askin, Barthe, as well as many others.[183]

The French settlement to a very large degree resembled, as far as external appearance was concerned, the villages of the

[177] H. M. Chittenden, *The American Fur Trade of the Far West* (New York, 1902), I, 55–57.
[178] *N. Y. Col. Docs.*, IX, 140–42, 152–54; Turner, " The Character and Influence of the Fur Trade in Wisconsin," pp. 66–67; J. Reynolds, *My Own Times* (Chicago, 1879), chap. xii.
[179] Parkman, *The Old Régime*, II, 51–61; Canadian Archives, Q, II, 233; B, VII, 1.
[180] *N. Y. Col. Docs.*, VII, 965.
[181] *Post*, pp. 127–132.
[182] For a typical house of this period, see *Ill. Hist. Colls.*, II, 282; and descriptions in C. F. Volney, *A View of the Soil and Climate of the United States of America* (Philadelphia, 1804), p. 368.
[183] Burton, *The Story of Detroit*, III, *passim*.

mother country. Like the English, the French transplanted to the new soil the village community in which they had had former experiences. Their homes were usually of one story with a large veranda on one side. The poor people built their homes of logs laid horizontally with the interstices filled with clay and finely cut straw or moss.[184] The wealthier ones constructed their dwellings of stone and had one or more fireplaces, of huge dimensions, placed in each room. Outside the house was a bake oven in the old French style.[185] There were also slave quarters, and a " pole stable " which could be easily removed when accumulation of manure made it necessary. Around each home was a yard inclosed by a small wooden fence, within which was perhaps an orchard and a garden.[186] The poorer houses were very badly kept, for the French women were careless, indolent, and gossipy. Yet Governor Hamilton found that on holy days the inhabitants were very fond of being clean, and he describes them as dressing far beyond their means.[187]

The smallest element, but the most powerful part of the population of Michigan, was the British who came into the region soon after the conquest of Canada. By their business acumen and initiative they soon supplanted the French gentry in their influence. Hamilton felt that it was only a short time before the French would be dependent on the newcomers, or bought out of the possession of their lands by them.[188] He found that the navigation of the lakes was entirely in the hands of the English by 1776.[189] The new settlers were also

184 *Mich. Hist. Colls.*, XVII, 594 ff. These were not very well built. Duggan in Michilimackinac in 1796 paid three dollars a month for two " miserable rooms " in the priest's house, and then had to put on some roofing, some plaster, and whitewash. Duggan to Selby, June 20, 1796, Canadian Archives, Claus Papers, VII, 259. John Campbell complained to Gage about his miserable lodgings. Campbell to Gage, October 3, 1764; August 27, 1765, October 31, 1765. Gage MSS.
185 Picture of an oven in *Harper's Magazine*, CXVI, 440.
186 A brief description is in Hamilton's letter to Dartmouth, August 29, September 2, 1776, *Mich. Hist. Colls.*, X, 267. The home of Jacques Baby still stands in Winsor, as do several others.
187 *Ibid.* Jacob Lindley writes in 1793: " The old French settlers in general are poor economists, and proud withal — live miserably at home, yet appear grand abroad." *Ibid.*, XVII, 594–95. For an experience of an American traveler among the French see Volney, *A View of the United States*, pp. 373 ff.
188 Hamilton to Dartmouth, *loc. cit.*
189 *Ibid.* Many of these new settlers were Scotch. *Askin Papers*, I, 303.

considered better farmers, as they could work the lands to better advantage.

Another element in the population was the slaves. There were a considerable number of both negro and Indian slaves at Detroit and Michilimackinac.[190] The Indian slaves were known by the name of panis, and were recognized by the French law.[191] Such persons were ordinarily obtained from neighboring tribes who had in turn secured them by barter or warfare from the weaker tribes of the south. Their economic and social status was like that of the negro slave in name only. Alexander Henry was saved by such a slave in 1763 when the Indians captured Michilimackinac.[192] It is rather hard to determine the exact numbers of the panis, but frequent mention is made of them in the documents of the time. One finds Sir Jeffrey Amherst issuing a warrant to Major Gladwin for the trial of two panis at Detroit for the murder of John Clapham.[193] No one Michigan family held as large a number as the Beauvois family in Illinois.[194] Jacob Burnet claimed that the panis were excellent servants, docile and well behaved.[195] In 1779 there were sixty male and seventy-eight female slaves in Detroit according to the census.[196] The next survey, made in 1780, noted an increase to one hundred and seventy-five,[197] while in 1782 the number had risen to only one hundred and seventy-nine.[198] It is safe to conclude that there were more than three hundred slaves in Detroit by 1796. At Michilimackinac no definite statistics are available. The Parish " Register " frequently reveals that

    [190] *Mich. Hist. Colls.*, X, 326, 446, 613; " Mackinac Parish Register," *passim;* Askin Letter Book for 1778, Canadian Archives, pp. 79, 113, 135.
    [191] *Documents of History Society of Montreal*, I, 5.
    [192] Henry, *Travels*, p. 80. The word panis, pawnees, or panise was applied to all Indians in slavery.
    [193] Gladwin MSS., 674. Campbell to Bouquet, August 4, 1762, *Mich. Hist. Colls.*, XIX, 160–61. Amherst writes Johnson, May 27, 1763, after learning that the male pani escaped: " I am only sorry the Chief Perpetrator did not meet with the same Punishment for then the Example would have been Compleat." Canadian Archives, Indian Records, 1761–1772.
    [194] Beauvois family at one time had 80 slaves. *Ill. Hist. Colls.*, II, xviii.
    [195] Jacob Burnet, *Notes on the Early Settlement of the Northwestern Territory* (Cincinnati, 1847), p. 823.
    [196] *Mich. Hist. Colls.*, X, 326.
    [197] *Ibid.*, 446.
    [198] *Ibid.*, 613.

there were Indian and negro slaves at this post.[199] The priests scrupulously recorded their baptism, marriage, and death. The word " esclave " often appears, and this may refer to either a red or a black slave.[200] There is an entry of April 16, 1760, of a seven-year-old slave given " out of gratitude " to the Mission by M. Le Chevalier, because of his safe return from the " extreme West." [201] There are frequent items recording marriages of the *voyageurs* to panis,[202] and even to negroes.[203] There is one account of the marriage of an Indian and a negro.[204] In the burial section of the " Register," one finds that a slave was " carefully laid to eternal rest beside her mistress." [205] During the period of British control more frequent references were made to negro slaves who were used by the officials as domestic servants.[206]

The price of negro and panis slaves varied considerably. Pomp, one of John Askin's negroes, was valued at £ 100 in 1776, at £ 116 in 1779, and at £ 150 in 1789.[207] The total value of Askin's six negroes, four males and two females, in 1776 was £ 390, in 1779 £ 400, and 1781 £ 680, a rather large increase in value considering the fact there was one less in 1781.[208] George Lyons of Detroit inventoried his estate in 1791 as consisting of " 2 men slaves, a negro man and Le Bay a Panise." [209] In 1777 Charles Langlade, interpreter for the King, sold two slaves, male and female, for two thousand livres.[210] A negro boy was valued at £ 75 in 1768.[211] John

---

[199] " Mackinac Register," May 25, 1760 *et passim;* Canadian Archives, Askin Letter Book for 1778, pp. 79, 113, 131, 135.

[200] " Mackinac Register," *passim.*

[201] *Ibid.,* April 6, 1760.

[202] *Ibid.,* April 7, 1794.

[203] *Ibid.,* October 9, 1760.

[204] *Ibid.,* January 27, 1762.

[205] *Ibid.,* January 24, 1748; other slaves on September 14, 1754, December 10, 1754, October 26, 28, 1757, March 8, 1762, and several more.

[206] Sterling was of the impression that the French were afraid to buy negro men without the wenches lest they run away. Sterling Letter Book, November 12, 1764; *Askin Papers,* I, 58, 98, 135, 320, 410; " Mackinac Register," *passim.*

[207] Canadian Archives, Askin Papers, miscellaneous. Askin purchased Pomp and another negro named Jupiter from Abraham Dow in 1775 for £ 190. *Askin Papers,* I, 58–59.

[208] Canadian Archives, Askin Papers, Miscellaneous.

[209] *Ibid.,* Notary of Registers, IV, 71.

[210] *Wis. Hist. Colls.,* VII, " Memoirs of Charles de Langlade." These slaves

Askin sold to George Jacobs for £ 100 N. Y. C. a panis wench named Susannah aged twenty-five years and also her child named Susannah about one year old.[212] A trader, William Maxwell by name, of Michilimackinac, sent a wench and child to William Edgar at Detroit in 1778.[213] He asked £ 120, but if this price was too high she was to be sent back or left temporarily with some friends.[214] Sometimes slaves were sold for their value in corn or flour,[215] for there was usually a dearth of food stuffs at the upper posts.

Slaves were procured in other ways than through purchase. The Chippewa offered the commandant at Michilimackinac [216] an Indian slave for killing another Indian in the fort. They were sorry for their deed, which was not intended as an insult to the English.[217] In 1777, Captain Lernoult sent a negro prisoner to Niagara who had been brought to Detroit by the Delaware Indians, for they found the negro " disturbing their village and discovering everything he could for the rebels." [218] Captain Henry Bird in 1784 gave " the wench Ester and her male child " to William Lee for " his having cleaned sixteen acres of Land." [219] But the most curious arrangement the records show was the selling of one-half a negro

were described many years later by Langlade's grandchild, A. Grignon. See " Grignon's Recollections," *ibid.*, III, 256; Burton, *Detroit*, II, 196. See Detroit Notarial Records, A. B. C. for other sales.

[211] Canadian Archives, Register of Notaries, V, 19.

[212] *Ibid.*, Askin Papers, XXV. McIntosh paid £ 100 for a negro wench in 1788, while Sterling sold two slaves to Mr. Bannerman in 1777 for £ 240. McIntosh Letters, March 21, 1777, July 3, 1788.

[213] Maxwell to Edgar, August 27, 1778, Edgar MSS.

[214] This was not unusual. In 1770 Maxwell sent a " fine young Pawneese " to Edgar to sell for " not less than £ 30 and as much more as you can get." But if Edgar could not sell her directly and had no use for her, he was to " give her some good woman for victuals." *Ibid.*, September 25, 1770.

[215] *Ibid.*, Frobisher to Edgar, June 17, 1769. Value was £ 40 N. Y. C. £ 40 was demanded for a " fine Pawnee girl who understood French and English." *Ibid.*, Isaac Todd to Edgar, August 21, 1769. The largest price paid in the records available was in 1777 when James Sterling sold Sam Thomas for £ 240 to McTavish and Bannerman. *Ibid.*, March 31, 1777; and Askin sold a panis for 750 livres in 1778. *Askin Papers*, I, 119.

[216] This was Captain Etherington.

[217] Canadian Archives, Indian Papers, July, 1761–October, 1763, p. 320.

[218] Lernoult to Carleton, June 16, 1777, *ibid.*, Q, XIII, 323.

[219] *Ibid.*, Register of Notaries, IV, 75. Bird had received Esther from the Indians who had gotten her at Martin's Fort, Kentucky, when the inhabitants had to surrender the fort to the Indians.

wench by Catherine Tucker of Detroit in 1791 to William Tucker for one-half of a " certain house and lot on St. Anthony's Street." [220]

There were free and freed negroes at all the posts.[221] Many of these were manumitted for some special deed, or often they were common law wives of the traders.[222] John Askin manumitted at Detroit Mannete [or Monette] a slave woman whom he had at Mackinac.[223]

Some of the slaves did not adapt themselves willingly to their conditions. Records show that they murdered their masters [224] and fled when occasion offered. At Montreal in 1768, a panis was tried for the murder of Ensign Schlosser, formerly stationed at St. Joseph, and his servant. He was found guilty and " sentenced to hang and the body was ordered given " to the surgeons for dissection.[225] Governor Hamilton in 1778 forbade the sale of a mulatto woman, whom he suspected of being a runaway, and sent her back to Kaskaskia.[226] Toward the close of the English régime in 1792, the government of Upper Canada forbade the further importation of slaves, but the order was not strictly enforced.[227] Finally the second session of Parliament which met at Newark (Niagara) May 31, 1793, passed a stringent act to prevent further introduction of slaves.[228] Slavery was not discontinued, but a law was passed which provided that children born of slave mothers

---

[220] *Ibid.*, VI, 268. There is the record of a female slave in 1779 (probably a cook) in the navy but none in the army. *Ibid.*, B, CXII, 329. John Askin writes to Charles Patterson of Montreal, June 17, 1778: " There is a Boy here who was sold to the Ottawas, that everybody but yourself says is yours, he suffered much poor child with them. I have at length been able to get him from them on the promise of giving an Indian Woman Slave in his Stead — he's at your service if you want him, if not I shall take good care of him until he is able to earn his Bread without Assistance." *Askin Papers,* I, 135.

[221] " Mackinac Register," *passim.*

[222] *Ibid.;* Moran Papers, June 14, 1794; Detroit Notarial Records, A, 33, *passim.*

[223] *Askin Papers,* I, 13; Canadian Archives, Register of Notaries, V, 20–21.

[224] *Mich. Hist. Colls.,* XIX, 160.

[225] Quebec *Gazette,* September 15, 1768.

[226] Detroit Notarial Records, B, 142.

[227] Article XI, sec. i, " Journals of Legislative Assembly of Canada,"

[228] *Ibid.,* July 9, 1793.

should abide with the masters of the mother until the child was twenty-five years of age, and then should be free.[229] These acts aroused the owners of the slaves and they organized for resistance. Simcoe wrote that the owners of the slaves argued that labor was dear, and very difficult to get.[230] The slave owners felt that any law was very unjust which would deprive them of so much property.[231] Parliament finally settled the problem by securing the property already held and by putting an end to importation as noted above. Thus slavery would gradually be extinguished. The Treaty of Paris, 1763, and the Jay Treaty, 1795, provided that inhabitants should be protected in their property.[232] In 1787 the famous Northwest Ordinance dedicated the region between the Ohio River and the Great Lakes to freedom.[233] When the United States came into possession of Michigan, many slaves crossed over from Canada hoping to gain their freedom, but by appealing to the Jay Treaty the owners were able to get their slaves returned.[234] Slavery existed in Michigan for many years after the British evacuation. In the War of 1812, slaves even accompanied their masters to the field of battle.[235] The Constitution of

[229] *Ibid.*

[230] Simcoe to Dundas, September 16, 1793. Cruikshank (ed.), *Correspondence of John Graves Simcoe*, II, 53.

[231] Canadian Archives, Askin Papers, January 1, 1781, Inventory of Estate.

Jupiter, a negro man	£ 120
Pomp, a negro man	150
Francois, a Panies Boy	150
Sam, A Pani, blacksmith	100
Susannah, a wench, and two children	160
	£ 680

Smith wrote Askin, June 25, 1793: "We have made no law to free the Slaves. all those who have been brought into the Province or purchased under any authority legally exercised, are Slaves to all intents & purposes, & are secured as property by a certain act of Parliament. they are determined however to have a bill about Slaves, part of which I think is well enough, part most iniquitous! I wash my hands of it. A free man who is married to a Slave, his heir is declared by this act to be a slave. fye, fye. The Laws of God & man cannot authorize it." *Askin Papers*, I, 476.

[232] MacDonald, *Documents*, pp. 204, 244.

[233] *Ibid.*, p. 208.

[234] Burton MSS., XIV, 145; XV, 28, 49; CCCCLIX, 115; XMLXVI, 177.

[235] Campbell Papers, pp. 81, 217.

Michigan in 1835 expressly prohibited slavery,[236] but economic factors had extinguished it some time before.

Another kind of labor used by the early inhabitants of Michigan was the indentured servant. Israel Ruland, sixteen years of age, in 1772 bound himself to Gerrit Graverat to serve until he became of age, at which time he was to receive forty pounds N. Y. C. and a suit of clothes, " fit for a servant of his station." [237] Also, in 1776, John Simon bound himself for one year to work for Obadiah Robins for the sum of twenty-four pounds. Simon was to behave himself, to obey every lawful command, and to go with Robins wherever he needed him.[238] In 1792 John Hardock, a sailor, bound himself to serve John Drake from November first " to the end of the Navigation next year," to do all kinds of work in the winter season, such as " Cutting, Squaring, Sawing and Carting Timbers." Hardock was to " serve obey and Execute faithfully and diligently " all orders as " an honest and faithful Servant ought." If he quit or absented himself, he lost his wages which were to be the sum of £ 5 N. Y. C.[239] John Askin indentured Robert Nichol for £ 50 N. Y. C. per year in 1795 to keep diligently and faithfully his books and accounts, without disclosing the secrets of the " business, or dealings, to any person." [240] Men were sometimes hired without any contract. On May 8, 1774, Askin hired a French canoe hand for £ 200 and a pair of trousers, a shirt, and a pair of leggings.[241] April 18, 1775, he employed a man on his farm for seven shillings per week " he to find himself in Everything," and six days later hired another for £ 3 per month,[242] while he gave a Mr. McDonald 1,170 livres to carry his goods, and McDonald's Indian assistant 900

[236] Article XI, Section 1.
[237] Detroit Notarial Records, A, 245; Askin Papers, I, 545.
[238] Ibid., B. A typical indenture is given in Askin Papers, I, 199.
[239] Ibid., 448; Detroit Notarial Records, B, 448.
[240] Askin Papers, I, 567–68.
[241] Ibid., 51. Often such goods were furnished. Askin to Barthe, May 29, 1778, ibid., 103.
[242] Ibid., 55. Askin paid £ 21 wages for three months labor plus a shirt, a pair of leggings, and a " brayet." Askin to Barthe, May 29, 1778, Askin Papers, I, 103.

livres plus provisions and a quarter of a pint of rum daily.[243] Thus wages were dependent, even in those early days, upon the law of supply and demand.

The religious life of the people, the Church as an institution, cannot be overlooked in any story of the early inhabitants of Michigan. The people were devoted to their religion and built substantial and often imposing edifices. The priest exercised tremendous influence over the French. No matter how debauched, how wayward the *habitant* became, he was invariably made to realize his utter dependence upon the Church. For baptism, for marriage, for interment, the *voyageurs* always sought the priest.[244]

There were two parishes within the present confines of the State of Michigan, one at Michilimackinac, which in spite of repeated requests, never had a resident priest during the English period,[245] and the other was located in Detroit, known as Ste. Anne's. These parishes, as well as all others in the Northwest, were in the diocese of the Bishop of Quebec.[246]

From the " Mackinac Register " one can picture the influence the priests had upon the spiritual life of the people. Not all baptisms or marriages were performed by the Jesuits. In 1781, Governor Sinclair baptized more than one child.[247] Military officials also performed marriages,[248] and more often at Michilimackinac than at Detroit, because no regular priest

243 Same to same, June 6, 1778, *ibid.*, 114. Other prices paid in 1788 to 1792 were £ 28 for a gardener, £ 36 and £ 48 for house rent; £ 1/4 for 2-2/3 days reaping; £ 3 for one month's " common " wages according to William Macomb's ledger. James McIntosh paid Thomas McCraw £ 2/6/6 for a tailoring bill in 1791, and 9s for a necktie. McIntosh Papers, *passim.*

244 " Mackinac Register " and Ste. Anne's Register of Detroit.

245 " Petition from the Merchants of Michilimackinac," July 23, 1778, *Mich. Hist. Colls.*, X, 286; Orillat to ————, March 13, 1779, *ibid.*, 308; " Request of the Merchants " to Haldimand, 1782, *ibid.*, 599. Whenever a priest visited Michilimackinac, he usually journeyed to St. Joseph. George Paré, " The St. Joseph Mission," *Mississippi Valley Historical Review*, June, 1930.

246 J. G. Shea, *Life and Times of the Most Reverend John Carroll* (New York, 1888), chap. III.

247 " Parish Register," August 13, 1781, *et passim.* De Peyster also performed some marriage ceremonies at Detroit. Canadian Archives, Register of Notaries, May 7, 1781, VI, 212. *Mich. Hist. Colls.*, X, 288–89, for subscription list of people for a priest of July 25, 1778, at Michilimackinac. The subscription list for Reverend George Mitchell at Detroit for 1787 is given in *Askin Papers*, I, 303.

248 " Parish Register," April 19, 1781, *et passim.*

was stationed at the former place. Whenever the missionary was expected at the post, the news was swiftly spread far and wide around the Great Lakes.[249] At once entire families would hasten to Michilimackinac in canoes to receive the sanction of the Church to their domestic relations. The " Register " shows that common law unions were frequent.[250] The Mother Church accepted this inevitable condition and made the best of it, hoping that in the course of events the marriage would be legitimatized. Sometimes the Church had long to wait. A comparison of the marriage and baptismal register shows the fact that children were baptized some years before the parental union had been blessed.[251] There are notes of offspring of unknown fathers, whose names the discreet priest did not record, or of fathers who belonged " in the woods." [252]

During the French régime a marriage to be valid had to be celebrated by a priest ordained by a Roman Catholic Bishop. The *habitants* from far and near came to Michilimackinac when a priest arrived, in order to have the Mother Church sanction their common law union. In Michigan after the cession to England the marriage ceremony performed by a priest continued to be valid.[253] According to British law, within the lines of the army, wherever serving, the soldiers and individuals accompanying the army were not subject to local law, but might marry according to English statutes.[254] In every part of Michigan which was not settled and therefore might be considered a heathen country, the English law allowed that in the case of a British subject the same rule applied as in the case of a member of the army.[255]

In the early days of the English occupation of Michigan, there was no Protestant clergyman stationed at Detroit, at St. Joseph, or at Michilimackinac. Some individuals who were

[249] Miss. Valley Hist. Assoc., *Proceedings*, VI, 207.
[250] "Parish Register," August 8, 1787, *et passim*.
[251] *Ibid., passim*.
[252] *Ibid.* See also Paré, " The St. Joseph Mission."
[253] W. R. Riddell, " Some Marriages in Old Detroit," *Michigan Historical Magazine*, VI, 114.
[254] *Ibid.*
[255] *Ibid.,* 115

reluctant about having a priest perform the ceremony as a matter of course contracted many illegal marriages. In Detroit a layman who had been appointed by the Protestants to read prayers to them on Sunday often performed the marriage ceremony.[256] After the War of Independence and the incoming of loyalists, Justices of the Peace usually performed the rites,[257] and after 1788, when a number of persons were appointed Justices of the Peace for the District of Hesse, this was the usual practice.[258]

From 1791 until July, 1796, Michigan was *de facto* part of the province of Upper Canada. In 1792 Governor Simcoe emphatically stated that the English laws prevailed in all the territory to the west. " Settlers at Detroit," he wrote, " & at the other posts are Subject to the Laws of the Province . . . so long as the Posts are in our Possession all Persons resident within the same must be considered to all intents and purposes as British Subjects." [259] According to the English law (since the reign of Elizabeth) the marriage ceremony had to be performed by a priest or deacon Episcopally ordained.[260] Thus after 1792 all marriages of French or English, Catholic or Protestant, were irregular unless performed by an Anglican clergyman. At Detroit there was no Anglican priest, and the situation became so grave that it demanded legislative action. Even members of the governor's council, as well as of the lower house, had contracted marriages which were irregular.[261]

In 1792 a bill was presented to Parliament, meeting at Newark, which failed to pass, but another in 1793 was successful.[262] This act validated all marriages heretofore " publicly contracted before any Magistrate or Commanding Officer of a

[256] Burton MSS., I, 277.
[257] Ontario Archives, *Report for 1906*, pp. 157–58. For the Justices of Peace, Canadian Archives. Q. XXXIX, 134. The names of the Justices in 1788 are in the *Mich. Hist Colls.*, XI, 622.
[258] Canadian Archives, Q, CCLXIX, pt. i, p. 169.
[259] *Simcoe Papers*, II. 80.
[260] Riddell, " Some Marriages in Old Detroit."
[261] Simcoe to Dundas, November 4, 1792, *Simcoe Papers*, I, 250. Simcoe wrote: " almost all the Province are in that predicament."
[262] Canadian Archives, Q. CCLXXIX, pt. i, p. 227. Riddell, " The Law of Marriage in Upper Canada," *Canadian Historical Review*, September, 1921.

Post, or Adjutant, or Surgeon of a Regiment acting as Chaplain, or any other person in any public office or employment." The bill also provided that all those who wished to preserve the testimony of their marriages must within three years of the passing of the act make affidavits of the ceremony and the issue from the marriage before a magistrate. Several very prominent citizens of Detroit took advantage of the act to preserve the evidence of their marriages.[263]

During the War of Independence the Moravian missionaries were removed from Ohio by the English and located near the present city of Mt. Clemens. This occasionally gave a Protestant minister's services to Detroit. David Zeisberger, one of the Moravian ministers, was very unfavorably impressed with the moral and religious life of Detroit. He called the place Sodom, and felt that no sin was left uncommitted. He notes that the English do not seem to care for a minister, although they could have one if they desired.[264] In 1786, at the request of Alexander McKee, the superintendent of the Indian Department, and "some of the principal Inhabitants" of Detroit, the Reverend George Mitchell came to Detroit and remained eighteen months as pastor of the Protestant people.[265] His salary was raised by popular subscription among the English-speaking people.[266] No other Protestant preached in Detroit during the British régime.

Most of the people of Michigan were more or less illiterate. One contemporary account speaks of them as " so illiterate that very few can read." [267] There was very little done by the French toward educating their children. The priests made

---

[263] Ibid. See also " Marriage in Early Upper Canada," Canadian Magazine, LI, 384.

[264] Mich. Hist. Colls., XXX, 63; Askin Papers, I, 217 ff., 245–47, 260, 262–63; E. F. Bliss (ed.), Diary of David Zeisberger (Cincinnati, 1885).

[265] Askin Papers, I, 301–303.

[266] Original paper in the Burton Library. For the subscription lists and the problems of raising the money, ibid., 302–15. The first clergyman at Detroit was apparently the Reverend Philip Toosey, who came prior to George Mitchell in 1787. These early priests were sent no doubt by the Society for the Propagation of the Gospel in Foreign Parts. Askin Papers, I, 313, note 52.

[267] Canadian Archives, Q, XII, 214. In October, 1788, Robertson claimed that most of the inhabitants of Detroit could not write. Mich. Hist. Colls., XI, 633.

some attempts, but those who could afford an education sent their offspring to Quebec or Montreal. There is very little indication of any schools until 1775, when James Sterling speaks of selling some goods to " Grouin, schoolmaster at Chapotons."²⁶⁸ In 1781 Daniel Garrit is mentioned as " schoolmaster to the children " of the soldiers.²⁶⁹ In the last decade and a half of the eighteenth century, more frequent mention is made of private schools. There were several of these, schools where the French Catholics were educated, and schools for the English. The boys and girls were not usually taught together and there were no school buildings. A room in the home of the teacher sufficed, for which the pupils helped to furnish the wood and candles for dark days. Books were not uniform, and, as these were scarce and expensive, the custom was to hand them down from generation to generation.²⁷⁰ The pupil paid tuition by the term. Mary Crofton in 1782 charged £ 1 per month,²⁷¹ while Hugh Holmes in 1790 charged only 6s, 6d per year.²⁷² Some of the slave owners believed in sending their negroes; for in John Askin's account book is an entry as follows: " paid Francois Houdos, French Schoolmaster, one year's account for teaching children and slaves, £ 15 10s."²⁷³ It would appear that some of the more wealthy members of the Detroit colony guaranteed to pay the expenses of a school, in order to get their children educated. John Askin and Commodore Grant paid one-third and two-thirds, respectively, of the expenses of Mrs. M. Pattinson's school in 1795.²⁷⁴ They perhaps charged tuition from the parents who sent children to this school. The total expense was £ 35/10, a rather large amount for the time. Salaries were rather high for teachers, especially when one

²⁶⁸ Sterling Letter Book, 1775. There was some attempt to build up a parochial school connected with Ste. Anne. Sister Mary Rosalita, *Education in Detroit Prior to 1850* (Lansing, 1928), pp. 17–24.
²⁶⁹ Sterling Letter Book, 1780.
²⁷⁰ Burton, *The City of Detroit*, I, 706. In 1795 John Askin paid 8s for two spelling books. William Macomb ledger.
²⁷¹ Canadian Archives, Askin Journal, 1790.
²⁷² *Ibid.*
²⁷³ *Ibid.*, Askin Account Book, September 30, 1794.
²⁷⁴ *Ibid.*, March 5, 1796.

compares them with the present scale. A number of prominent citizens subscribed £ 30 per annum, and tuition in addition, to pay Matthew Donovan in 1794.[275] The government never paid much attention to education in Michigan. After 1783 Great Britain had no legal right to the West, and only sought to keep up the military works. The education of the people was best described by Robertson in 1788 when he said that at Detroit the people were " wholly illiterate, and if we except five or six Canadian families I am justified to say ... that there will not be found twenty people nor perhaps half the number, who have the least pretensions to education, or can even write their name or know a Letter of a Book." [276]

[275] Burton MSS., I, 50. Apparently Donovan did not begin his work until 1797. Sister Mary Rosalita, *op. cit.*, p. 29.
[276] *Mich. Hist. Colls.*, XI, 642.

CHAPTER VI

THE FRENCH AND BRITISH AT PLAY

THE SETTLERS of Michigan and the Old Northwest during the British régime found considerable time for leisure, midst a busy life, although it is true that their energies were mainly devoted to the practical problems of clearing small areas of the forest for their villages, planting crops, building homes, trading in furs, and constantly struggling with the Indians. These people were the pioneers of a new civilization in the vast hinterland which now comprises the populous states of Michigan, Wisconsin, Illinois, Indiana, and Ohio. Theirs was to toil and fight, and yet a study finds that there were many leisure hours to be filled with games and sports of all kinds. Despite a large degree of isolation from the outside world, and the fact that distances were so great from village to village as to make common exchange of interests and ideas almost impossible, one discovers that the social activities were about the same in the various villages as they were in the East. Human nature did not vary greatly whether in the fur posts of Detroit and Michilimackinac, or in Puritan Boston and Quaker Philadelphia.

The leading citizens of the villages were made up of three different groups. First, and by far the most important group, was made up of the old and well-established French families, among whom there was to be found a considerable degree of refinement and culture. Gay they were, and lighthearted, yet pious; honest beyond comparison, generous to a fault, hospitable, free, and laughter-loving, with no cares from " ambition or science." They always seemed to enjoy life keenly, being gay even when times were at their worst. Possibly ignorant of books they were, but certainly neither boorish nor unintelli-

gent. Their easy-going ways were doubtless due to their placing no great value on time, of which they had an abundance.

The British fur traders and merchants who came into the
country at the close of the Seven Years' War made up another
social group. They were industrious and energetic, and it was
not long before success crowned their efforts, making them
clearly the leading force both economically and socially.

Again, there were the military officers at the fort, who found
time hanging heavily on their hands, with only the dull routine
of garrison duty to perform. They constituted a very important element in the social life, and found plenty of attractive,
vivacious young women for partners at the balls, which were
the principal convivial activities of the posts.

Below these groups was the large mass of people: *habitants,
coureurs de bois, voyageurs,* and slaves. These were pleasure-
loving, also, dissipating their energies for the most part in
" drinking, gambling and gossiping; and as irresponsible as
children, they were easily turned aside from the pursuit of their
real interests." C. F. Volney, the noted traveler who made a
tour of the Upper Mississippi Valley toward the close of the
eighteenth century, was not favorably impressed with these
people. He wrote:

They know nothing of civil or domestic affairs: their women
can neither sow, nor spin, nor make butter, but spend their time in
gossiping and tattle, while all at home is dirt and disorder. The
men take to nothing but hunting, fishing, roaming in the woods,
and loitering in the sun. They do not lay up, as we do for winter
or provide for a rainy day. They cannot cure pork or venison,
make sour kraut or spruce beer, or distill spirits from apples, or
rye, all needful arts to the farmer. If they trade, they try by exorbitant charges to make much out of a little; for *little* is generally
their *all,* and what they get they throw away upon the Indian girls,
in toys and bawbles. Their time is wasted too in trifling stories of
their insignificant adventures, and journies *to town* to see their
friends. (Thus they speak of New Orleans, as if it were a walk of
half an hour, instead of fifteen hundred miles down the river) . . .

The Frenchman, on the contrary, will be up betimes, for the
pleasure of viewing and talking over matters with his wife, whose
counsel he demands. Their constant agreement would be quite a
miracle: the wife dissents, argues, wrangles, and the husband has

his own way, or gives up to her, and is irritated or disheartened. Home, perhaps, grows irksome, so he takes his gun, goes a shooting or a journeying, or to chat with a neighbour. If he stays at home, he either whiles away the hour in good-humoured talk, or he scolds and quarrels. Neighbours interchange visits: for to visit and talk are so necessary to a Frenchman, from habit. . . . There is nowhere a settler of that nation to be found, but within sight or reach of some other. On asking how far off the remotest settler was, I have been told, He is in the woods, with the bears, a league from any house, and with nobody to talk to. . . .

The Frenchman's ideas evaporate in ceaseless chat; he exposes himself to bickering and contradiction; excites the garrulity of his wife and sisters; involves himself in quarrels with his neighbours; and finds in the end, that his life has been squandered away without use or benefit.[1]

Other travelers seemed to be more or less of the same impression. Victor Collot, after an extended journey through the interior of North America, described the settlers as follows:

These people are, for the most part, traffickers, adventurers, hunters, rowers, and warriors; ignorant, superstitious, and obstinate; accustomed to fatigue and privations, and stopped by no sense of danger in the undertakings they form, and which they usually accomplish.

In domestic life their characters and dispositions are similar to those of the Indians with whom they live; indolent, careless, and addicted to drunkenness, they cultivate little or no ground, speak a French jargon, and have forgotten the division of time and months. If they are asked at what time such an event took place, they answer, " in the time of the great waters, of the strawberries, of the maize, of potatoes:" if they are advised to change any practice which is evidently wrong, or if observations are made to them respecting the amelioration of agriculture, or the augmentation of any branch of commerce, the only answer they give is this: " It is the custom; our fathers did so: I have done well; my children will do the same." They love France, and speak of their country with pride.[2]

The French gentlemen, when entertaining guests and attending mass or balls, dressed " beyond their means " and loved to appear " grand abroad." [3] Travelers record that stores and shops were well furnished, with every kind of fine cloth,

---

[1] Volney, *A View of the Soil and Climate of the United States of America,* pp. 336–37, 346–47.
[2] Victor Collot, *A Journey in North America* (Paris, 1826), pp. 232–33.
[3] Hamilton to Dartmouth, August 29–September 2, 1776, *Mich. Hist. Colls.,* X, 267; Lindley's " Journal," *ibid.,* XVII, 595.

linen in fact, and every article of apparel for men and women.[4] These were sold on the frontier nearly as reasonably as they were in New York and Philadelphia. Descriptions of dances, especially the more elaborate balls, pictured the men as wearing "very fine fur caps" adorned with "Black Ostridge Feathers" and amazingly large "Cockades" of white tinsel ribbon, and again, dressed in "their best bibs & Tuckers."[5] The women at the posts, like many of their sex still, were said to pay too much attention to dressing their heads, and when making social calls decked themselves as though "their parents possessed the greatest dignities in the state."[6] As in every age and clime, the men complained of their improvident attention to the newest fashions, since, in spite of their isolation, the women were not unfamiliar with the best of the day's vogue. Relatives or friends who traveled advised the frontier women of all the changes of Dame Fashion. One, Archange Askin, second child of Mr. and Mrs. John Askin of Detroit, married Captain David Meredith and shortly after moved to England. Her charming and vivacious letters to her parents and sisters at home kept them well informed on the styles of dress in England.

Low crowned chip hats [she advised], with large bows of strip colored ribbon, is the prevailing system, with frilld calico jackets, and broad sashes, and nothing is now so vulgar for either gentleman, or lady, as to be seen with a silk stocking that appears the least blue.[7]

She was very observant, all which duly affected the styles in the far-away frontier posts.

I notice [she wrote her mother] that all ladies are wearing their skirts almost under the arms so as to raise the waist line. Sashes are about the width of a narrow collar and are fastened at the back with a buckle. Neckerchiefs are very open as formerly and the neckband

---

[4] Weld, *Travels*, II, 185–86.

[5] Henry Hay, "Journal from Detroit to the Miami River," M. M. Quaife (ed.), *Wis. Hist. Proc.*, January 19, 1790. Henry Hay was the son of Lieutenant Governor John (Jehu) Hay.

[6] *Ibid.*

[7] Mrs. Meredith to Askin, April 7, 1793, *Askin Papers*, I, 470–71. James MacDonald mentioned in a letter of March 10, 1761, the "handsome appearance" of the ladies who came to the commandant's quarters "every Sunday night . . . to play at Cards & Continues till twelve O'clock at night." Photostat in the Clements Library. The original is in the British Museum.

very narrow. The hair is curled, hanging at the back and arranged in small curls in front, with a piece of ribbon or a band of muslin around the head; even a thin lawn handkerchief arranged for a head-dress, with a white feather in it, is very fashionable in the best society, so there is no need of going to great expense about dressing the hair.[8]

A careful inspection of the contemporary records furnishes data which accord rather poorly with the popular conception of frontier habits and dress. The inventories of wardrobes found in these wilderness settlements show a profusion of rich attire. John Askwith, a clerk of John Askin, falling heavily into debt, had his wardrobe, which he brought from Montreal, sold at public auction.[9] One item, two pairs of leather breeches, was quite in keeping with the times.

" But what manner of life did this recently penniless Detroit clerk live that should account for the possession of thirty-six other pairs of breeches and trousers? A vest is a conventional article of male attire, but what social functions did Askwith attend which should necessitate the possession of thirty different vests? " For the most part these garments are not described, but included in the number was one satin vest (did it match the satin breeches?), one of cassimere, one of white cloth, and one " black vest princess stuff." Among other items of this pioneer Detroiter's wardrobe were a dozen shirts, ten cravats, and fifteen coats. There was a " camblet " coat, and a " camblet " cloak, a great coat, a white cloth coat, three black coats, and three flannel jackets.

A " parcel old hose and black tosels " was sold for nineteen shillings. Did the auctioneer arbitrarily lump these things together, or did a Detroit gentleman in those days wear tassels on his hose? If not, to what other use did Askwith put the tassels, and what did the purchaser expect to do with them? In the absence of more detailed information one can only speculate on these matters. But there is no need to speculate over the " parcel of ruffles and 2 black stocks," which were sold immediately after the hose and " tosels."

Then there were silk gloves, shoe-buckles, and other articles

[8] Mrs. Meredith to Mrs. Askin, February 3, 1795, *Askin Papers*, I, 534–35. Her letters are full of such descriptions. *Ibid.*, 517, 575–76. Some of the military men picked their wives from the frontier women, and found upon their removal to England some social difficulties. Captain Henry Bird found himself in such a predicament. He wrote: " The ladies have undertaken to drill Mrs. Bird and do not despair of her coming in and out of a room without being taken for an Indian Lady in less than a year." Bird to William Edgar, January 28, 1785, Edgar MSS.

[9] For this information and much which follows I am indebted to the valuable article by M. M. Quaife, " John Askwith," *Burton Historical Collection Leaflet*, VII, no. 4.

too numerous to mention. One finds no lack of clothes for every occasion.[10]

The women had other traits of Mother Eve, aside from their interest in clothes and styles. One traveler recorded:

One of the first questions they propose to a stranger is, whether he is married. The next, how he likes the ladies in the country, and whether he thinks them handsomer than those of his own country; and the third, whether he will take one of them home with him.[11]

In this game of love, some unusual events occurred. William Edgar with his " amorous Competitor, C. Barber " broke the heart of the " once admired Miss Gouin." [12] James Bannerman thought this passion contagious at Detroit, " where its operations " seemed " in general singular and sometimes whimsical." John Hay longed to be back at Detroit, for he detested New York. This, he admitted, was because of the rumor that: " fair Ellen [was] murdering people by dozens." He was not surprised, for he acknowledged she had " charmed enough to captivate many." [13]

But, as in all other phases of life, love was not without serious problems, for even the frontier had a code of morals. Captain Bird complained to Edgar of his serious loss when Mrs. Schieffelin left Detroit:

I was deprived of the happiness of her Society some months before her departure, some illiberal transactions of her very unworthy Partner, banished him from every Gentleman's company and I (from the arbitrary exactions of hard hearted custom) was reduced to the situation of Tantalus, and endured an intellectual famine in sight of a Rational banquet.[14]

[10] Askin wrote from Michilimackinac for a piece of silk with all the " trimmings." Askin to Todd and McGill, May 8, 1778, *Askin Papers*, I, 84; and later of his great need of waistcoats and breeches, and six or eight yards of fine cloth for trimmings. Same to same, June 23, 1778, *ibid.*, 143–44. In May, he ordered twelve pair of shoes for Mrs. Askin, and a wedding gown of " french fashion " for Kitty. Same to same, May 28, 1778, *ibid.*, 102; also, same to Richard Dobie, June 15, *ibid.*, 132, a request for a gold thimble. See Hay's descriptions of styles, etc. at Miamitown in his " Journal," pp. 216 ff.

[11] Peter Kalm, *Travels into North America* (London, 1770), pp. 691–92. This was typical of the frontier, it seems. Askin in 1778 congratulates Sampson Fleming upon the birth of a boy. " Perhaps," he wrote, " he may one Day become my Son in law, I have Girls worth looking at." Askin to Fleming, April 28, 1778, *Askin Papers*, I, 79.

[12] Bannerman to Edgar, October 14, 1779, Edgar MSS.

[13] Hay to Edgar, July 27, 1784, *ibid.*

[14] Bird to Edgar, July 8, 1784, *ibid.*

He asked Edgar to see his friend and tell her: " no man admires her more, that I even love her as much as I ought." [15] Neither did love go smoothly for William Maxwell, for his Sally " eloped from her bed and board " to live in a " house of her own." [16] But he seemed, after living with her a year, to be glad of the change. " She tired me heartily," he claimed, " I mean with her tongue and hands." To his friend he confided: " I believe on the whole Socrates need no more be quoted for his patience with his wife where my story is known." [17] Nevertheless, in spite of all difficulties, these people were jovial and light-hearted, ever seeking pleasure in racing, hunting, dancing, lavish entertaining, card playing, and the various winter sports.

The settler was especially fond of horses, and horse racing was one of his favorite pastimes.[18] With the coming of the English, more and more horses were introduced and efforts were put forth to improve the breed; in the last decade of the eighteenth century almost everyone had at least one horse, while the more prosperous merchants and traders possessed several.

During the winter months, pony racing on the ice was indulged in, with every young man of the village testing out a pony of uncertain speed.[19] An individual might challenge the whole village, or the whole village might challenge him, and then, things began to happen. When the ice was solid, these races would take place along the banks of a river or lake; at

[15] *Ibid.* He began: " Mrs. Schieffelin whose figure and genius you and I have so often admired."

[16] Maxwell to Edgar, May 25, 1767, *ibid.*

[17] *Ibid.* On August 4, 1768, he wrote that all is going well again. Fleming wrote Edgar: " kiss all the ladies for me that will let you and I'll do the same for you." *Ibid.,* September 9, 1782. Edgar must have been the Don Juan of Detroit. Apparently doctors advocated a change of clime when a youth suffered a " melancholy disorder " from love affairs. This was Campbell's impression. Campbell to Bouquet, April 20, 1763, *Mich. Hist. Colls.,* XIX, 182. Sterling sent Lieutenant John Wynne at Fort Erie a barrel of 900 onions, " Enough," he wrote, " to spoil your kissing for one Winter." Sterling Letter Book, September 18, 1765.

[18] *Mich. Hist. Colls.,* IV, 74–5. Lindley noted that the French after mass were seen " frolicking and horse racing in the road passing the worship house." *Ibid.,* XVII, 595.

[19] *Ibid.,* I, 54; IV, 75.

Detroit they were held most frequently upon the River Rouge, a small stream below the main settlement, which, having a sluggish current, furnished excellent ice in season. This made an ideal place for that kind of sport, especially on account of the circuitous channel which allowed spectators to spread out considerably and have an unobstructed view.

Every Sunday after mass the crowd gathered at the appointed place and the fun was on. The challenged and the challenger brought out their ponies and scored for a start, while the crowd sized up the animals and the betting was furious. There was no starter, no jockey, no bookmaker, no drawing for the pole. Each driver handled the reins over his own animal. He maneuvered for position and took his chances with his adversary. And when at last the ponies were off for the mile stretch down the river, the excitement among the multitude on the bank was something tremendous! If ever violence was done to the French language, it was upon such occasions, when individual opinions were struggling for utterance from hundreds of throats. Large sums of money changed hands, considering the financial resources of the town.

Races often ended in severe altercations, sometimes leading to blows, and disputes were commonly settled in court.[20]

No less popular in the winter were the sleighing and skating parties.[21] When the autumnal rains came, submerging the lowlands, the wintry frosts soon followed, converting the flooded areas into a miniature sea of glass. Detroit was especially fortunate in this respect, for about three or four miles above the fort was a large marsh called by the French *Le Grand Marais*. Here, when the winter weather was favorable, the inhabitants of the fort and village gave themselves unrestrainedly to the pleasure of dancing and other festivities. Early in the fall the young men of the town would build a long, narrow log hut with a fireplace at each end for their parties. Rough hewn tables, which were easily taken down, were placed here and there. Early on Saturdays, young and old would come in sleighs, and after a sumptuous meal of wild turkey, bear steak, and venison, washed down with quantities of wine, the rest of the day

[20] H. M. Utley and B. M. Cutcheon, *Michigan as a Province, Territory and State* (New York, 1906), I, 316.

[21] *Mich. Hist. Colls.*, I, 360–61; Madelaine Askin to her father, October 15, 1792, *Askin Papers*, I, 441.

was spent in games of various kinds, but principally in danc-ing. These activities continued until the booming of the eve-ning gun warned the merry party that:

> The evening shades might be but vantage ground
> for some fell foe.

Next day, Sunday, the gentlemen would go back after mass and spend the day in carousal, feasting on the remains of the preceding day's feast. Sleigh-riding on the ice, as there were no roads, and balls and parties in town filled the interim. " The summer's earnings scarce sufficed for the winter's waste." [22]

Descriptions of these parties are found in the poetry of the period, for even the frontier did not lack its poets. One of the best known of all the post officials was Colonel De Peyster, who settled at Dumfries, Scotland, after the War for American Independence. Here he became a close friend of his neighbor, Robert Burns. De Peyster was somewhat of a writer, and sev-eral of his short poems relate to his life at Mackinac, Detroit, and Niagara, where he was commandant during the stirring years of 1775-1783. In one of his poems he pictured the canoe-ing and the racing on the ice of the River Rouge. [23] He enumer-ated those who were present, described the festivities, the dancing, the races, and of course the drinking. All who had horses were present. The manager of the festivities for the occasion was Guillaume La Mothe, a Frenchman, who was an officer in the Indian Department. An elaborate frontier feast followed the race, which was greatly enjoyed by the officers of the post, their wives, and their guests. So much drinking was indulged in that the party became boisterous and hilarious. With unusual license, the poet had the wild bears and deer come from the nearby woods and watch the pleasure seekers in their hilarity.

The *habitant* was especially fond of a wedding, and kept up

[22] E. M. Sheldon, *Early History of Michigan from the First Settlements to 1815* (New York, 1856), pp. 371–72. Entertaining was very common, and there was a genuine hospitality.
[23] This is based on the poem " Red River " by Colonel De Peyster in J. W. De Peyster (ed.), *Miscellanies by an Officer, 1774–1813* (New York, 1888).

its festivities several days. The banns, announced at mass [24] on three preceding Sundays, formed the main subject of conversation in the ensuing days, for marriage was a life-long contract of serious import, divorce being unknown. At the betrothal, the marriage contract was signed by both parties, their relatives, and their friends.[25] The bride also furnished a dowry, the amount depending upon the position of her father.[26] The ceremony took place soon after the betrothal. After the signing of the certificate and church register, a great celebration followed, lasting for many hours, or until all were fatigued.[27] Sometimes the party took place at the *Grand Marais*, or with dancing and feasting at the home of the bride. The menu was in strange contrast with our modern feasts:

The *coup d'appetit* was passed around, brandy for the gentlemen, some mild cordial for the ladies; then followed the repast. Soup, *poissons blanc* [whitefish], *poisson doree* [pickerel], pike, roast pig, with its dressing of potatoes, blood pudding, partridges, wild turkey, ragouts, venison larded, pates of *pomes de terre* [potatoes], sagammite, a dish of porridge made of cracked corn, eaten with cream and maple sugar, . . . *praline* was dried corn, pounded fine and mixed with maple sugar; . . . *galettes au beurre*, *crocquecignole* [a sort of doughnut], *omelette soufflee*, floating islands, pears, apples, raspberries, grapes in summer. Coffee ended the feast.[28]

[24] Sometimes this could not be done as the "Mackinac Register" shows. The priest under unusual circumstances failed to announce the banns. *Ibid.*, XVIII, 471 ff.; XIX, 149.

[25] See *Mich. Hist. Colls.*, IV, 75, for a copy of a marriage contract; also *Burton Leaflet*, III, no. I, pp. 6–8.

[26] *Askin Papers*, I, 31–37. When James Sterling married Angelique Cuillerier, her father gave nearly a thousand pounds in dowry consisting of horses, money, and peltry. Sterling Letter Book, February 26, 1765.

[27] One can trace the relationship and social position of the parties in the church registers. "Mackinac Register," *passim.* R. G. Thwaites, "At the Meeting of the Trails," *Miss. Valley Hist. Assoc. Proc.*, VI, 210–14, gives a vivid picture of some marriages which occurred at Mackinac.

[28] *Mich. Hist. Colls.*, IV, 76–77. Vegetables, fruits, and meats of all kinds were found in abundance. See especially "Grignon's Recollections," *Wis. Hist. Colls.*, III, 255; *ibid.*, XVIII, 272–73; *Mich. Hist. Colls.*, XVII, 640 ff.; Canadian Archives, Claus Papers, IV, 88, and the accounts of officials such as Hamilton, Rogers, Bradstreet, Abbott, and Dobie, and various travelers such as Carver, Weld, Lees, Henry, and the Quakers who visited Detroit in 1793. Even delicacies from the outside world were not unknown. Captain Brehm sent a keg of olives to some friends in Detroit, and wrote: "They were extremely good when I got them and I hope will arrive sound and good to your place." Brehm to Edgar, April 29, 1772, Edgar MSS.

The festivities ended by drinking the health of the newly married couple in many a bumper.

Other diversions were shooting,[29] hunting, and fishing. Every man had his gun and knew how to use it. Indeed, his life very often depended upon his proficiency in the use of this instrument. The neighboring woods abounded in partridges (grouse), wild turkey, hares, deer and what not, while the waters were filled with fish, such as trout, whitefish, and sturgeon.[30] Record after record tells of fishing parties on the Great Lakes in the winter. Holes were cut in the ice, in which were set lines and bait. Nets were dexterously placed under the ice for whitefish weighing three to seven pounds, which were used as bait to catch trout weighing from ten to sixty pounds. Now and then this sport ended in stark tragedy, for many a fisherman never returned.[31] In summer, the weather was so hot and the air so filled with mosquitoes and black flies as to be a " counterpoise to the pleasure of hunting " and fishing. Nevertheless, Alexander Henry relates his pleasure that the wild pigeons at Sault Ste. Marie were plentiful and the shooting excellent.[32]

During the spring, summer, and early fall, boat races were very popular. Every male was trained early in the management of the canoe, for boats were objects of necessity on the frontier. Rivers and lakes were the only roads in summer and the only vehicle was the canoe.[33] The canoes used by the inhabitants were made of the bark of trees,[34] birch being preferred; for the longer boats, trunks of trees were dug out or burned by slow fire. Great care had to be taken in all cases

[29] Fleming described his pleasures in hunting on the *Grand Marais* at Detroit. When leaving Montreal for Ireland to shoot ducks, he requested a small bag of wild rice from *Grand Marais*, " cost what it will." Then he added a postscript: " Kiss all the ladies for me that will let you and I'll do the same for you." Fleming to Edgar, September 9, 1782, *ibid.* See also Henry, *Travels*, p. 53.

[30] *Mich. Hist. Colls.*, I, 361; Henry, *Travels*, pp. 53, 59, 62–3.

[31] " Mackinac Register," *passim.*

[32] Henry, *Travels*, p. 61.

[33] *Mich. Hist. Colls.*, I, 365–67.

[34] Henry, *Travels*, p. 14, gives a good description of a canoe. Other descriptions are found in Stevens, *The Northwest Fur Trade,* p. 151; Turner, " The Character and Influence of the Fur Trade in Wisconsin," p. 78.

to see that the wood was perfect, for a boat which leaked was a great annoyance. Besides races, on a warm summer evening, the rivers and lakes along the settlements were filled with canoes in which young men and women enjoyed each other's company.

Nowhere can one find a lovelier picture of hardy frontier folk whose livelihood depended upon the waterways, than in those descriptions of the boatmen or *engagés*, who were noted for their songs. As they pulled across the placid waters of lake and river, labor was lessened by the chorus of voices that kept time to the strokes of oar and of paddle.

> Faintly as tolls the evening chime,
> Our voices keep time, and our oars keep time,
> Soon as the woods on the shore look dim,
> We'll sing at St. Ann's our parting hymn,
> Row, brothers, row! the stream runs fast,
> The rapids are near, and the daylight is past.[35]

Thus one might hear a hundred voices, rising and falling in unison, as the picturesque boatmen passed over the waters of the Old Northwest.[36]

These *engagés* were picturesque, dressed in " gaudy turbans, or hats adorned with plumes and tinsel, their brilliant handkerchiefs tied sailor-fashion about swarthy necks, their calico shirts, and their flaming worsted belts " which circled their waists, holding their knives and tobacco pouches. Rough trousers, leggings, and cowhide shoes, or gay moccasins completed their outfits.[37] Whenever a burial cross appeared, or a stream was left or entered, these rough " sons of the woods " removed their hats, and made the sign of the cross while one of their number would utter a short prayer; and again they were off, their paddles beating time to a rollicking French song.

[35] *Mich. Hist. Colls.*, XXXVIII, 327.

[36] Other songs are found in *ibid.*, I, 366–67; James H. Lanman, " The American Fur Trade," *Hunt's Merchants' Magazine* (New York, 1840), III, 189; Mrs. John H. Kinzie, *Wau-Bun* (Chicago, 1932), pp. 47–49; Bella Hubbard, *Memorials of A Half-Century* (New York, 1888), pp. 152–54; Martin, " The Fox River Valley in the Fur Trade," pp. 122–23.

[37] This is the description given by Turner, *op. cit.*, pp. 77–78.

Dans mon chemin, j'ai recontré
Trois cavalières, bien montées;
L'on, lon, laridon daine,
Lon, ton, laridon dai,

Trois cavalières, bien montées,
L'un à cheval, et l'autre à pied;
L'on, lon, laridon daine
Lon, ton, laridon dai.[38]

In all social life French characteristics predominated even throughout the British régime. During the summer evenings, though they were given much to drinking and gambling, the dance was the favorite amusement, and to this frolic came the men and matrons, young men and maidens; even the parish priest graced these festive occasions. The careless, pleasure-loving *coureurs de bois* and *voyageurs* returning to the settlements, gave added color to these celebrations, at which all danced until the early morning hours or even daybreak, with little appearance of rowdyism or vulgarity to mar their simple festivities. There were no age restrictions at these parties. Alexander Grant, Commodore of the Royal Navy on the Upper Lakes, wrote to his friend, John Askin: " We hop and bob every Monday night in the Council House." [39] Later, at the age of seventy-one, he felt himself growing quite hearty again: " Danced fifteen couple down the other night," he wrote.[40] By this time, in addition to his strenuous life on the frontier, the Commodore had reared a family of twelve children (eleven of them were girls). His home, known as Grant's Castle, was always the scene of much gay life and hilarity.[41]

[38] *Ibid.*, p. 80.
[39] *Mich. Hist. Colls.*, III, 27.
[40] Grant to Askin, December 19, 1805, *Askin Papers*, II, 498.
[41] Quaife, " Commodore Alexander Grant," *Burton Hist. Coll. Leaflet*, VI, no. 5, 76. " We have endeavored to make the Winter pass as agreeably as we could, by having a Dance every week," wrote Askin to Grant, April 28, 1778, *Askin Papers*, I, 77. Also Askin to Charles Patterson, June 17, 1778, *ibid.*, 135. This seemed to be general. Richard Cartwright wrote: " I am glad you are so gaily and agreeably amused at Detroit, and tho we cannot pretend to vie with you in Brilliancy yet we have our little Entertainments for which we are entirely beholden to the Gentlemen of the Garrison. We drink tea at the Fort every Saturday Evening, after that have a Concert, and then dance till about 12 o'clock, when we go to Supper." Cartwright to Edgar, February 17, 1780,

One of the outstanding characteristics of frontier society was its open-handed hospitality. Isolation from the outside world caused the people to welcome visitors, even total strangers, to their homes. Traveler after traveler testifies to this trait, nowhere better pictured than in the warm reception and parties given Sir William Johnson when he visited Detroit in 1761.[42]

It was a glorious September day when Sir William arrived. "Acutely aware that he appeared better on a horse than off," Johnson sent George Croghan ahead to procure mounts. A few miles below the settlement he met his deputy and mounted for his entry. The Indian villagers ran out to salute him; in reply he had the Royal Americans return three volleys from their boats. The naïve delight of this great man in the warmth of his reception in the heart of New France speaks in these lines of his diary:

All along the road was met by Indians, and near the town, by inhabitants, traders, etc. When I came to the verge of the fort, the cannon thereof was fired, and the officers of garrison with those of Gage's Light Infantry received me, and brought me to see my quarters, which is the house of the late commandant Mr. Belestre, the best in the place.

The time available, when not in Indian Council, was spent in wining and dining, almost as feverishly as in modern Detroit. Sir William greatly enjoyed the sustained sociability, for he was never happier than when reveling in the table talk of men and the tea talk of ladies. Let Sir William tell of these delights:

Edgar MSS. In the early part of 1780 the following dancing bills were paid by:

Major De Peyster	£ 14/9/11
Captain Britton of the Navy	12/12/7
Captain Grant of the Navy	14/9/1
Captain Burnet	14/9/1
Mr. Forsyth	20/12/7

See Macomb Account Books in Burton Collection. In 1780, the dancing bills amounted to £ 566/6/2. *Ibid.* The records also mention "Country Dance Books," and fiddles. *Askin Papers,* I, 79, 87, 142. Henry Hay's Journal, *passim.* The amount of liquors consumed at these parties was startling. See especially, Charles I. Walker, "The Northwest during the Revolution," *Mich. Hist. Colls.,* III, 27.

[42] "Private Manuscript Diary, kept by Sir William Johnson, on his Journey to and from Detroit, 1761," printed in Stone, *The Life and Times of Sir William Johnson,* II, 457.

Sunday [September] 6th. — A very fine morning. This day I am to dine with Captain Campbell, who is also to give the ladies a ball that I may see them. They assembled at 8 o'clock at night to the number of about twenty. I opened the ball with Mademoiselle Curie — a fine girl. We danced until 5 o'clock the next morning.

Saturday, 12th. . . . This morning four of the principal ladies of the town came to wait on me. I treated them with rusk and cordial. After sitting an hour, they went away.

Sunday, 13th. — Very fine weather. . . . At 10 o'clock, Captain Campbell came to introduce some of the town ladies to me at my quarters, whom I received and treated with cakes, wine, and cordial. Dined at Campbell's. . . .

Monday, 14th. — Fine weather. This day I am to have all the principal inhabitants to dine with me; . . . I took a ride before dinner up toward the Lake Saint Clair. The road runs along the river side, which is thickly settled nine miles. . . . The French gentlemen and the two priests who dined with us go very merry. Invited them all to a ball to-morrow which I am to give the ladies.

Here again he met the beautiful young lady, evidently by appointment, for he wrote:

Tuesday, 15th. — This day settled all accounts. . . . In the evening, the ladies and the gentlemen all assembled at my quarters, danced the whole night until 7 o'clock in the morning, when all parted very much pleased and happy. [I] Promised to write Mademoiselle Curie as soon as possible my sentiments; there never was so brilliant an assembly here before.[43]

Mademoiselle appeared no more in the diary. Might one raise the query whether this short-lived gaiety, with folk of his own kind, seriously tempted Sir William to marry a woman of his class? We cannot answer; we only know from him of the " polite flutings of an elderly gallant a long way from home and enjoying what must, after all, be considered a butterfly flight in the fading sunlight." At least it was a strenuous life. But it would have been far more strenuous if his wife (his housekeeper, he called her), Molly Brant, had known of his doings at Detroit. It was well for her peace of mind, and possibly also well for Sir William's personal safety, that she was kept in ignorance, for there is little doubt that Molly's influ-

43 *Ibid.*, 457, 459, 461–63.

ence was very great with the Indians, and she was devoted to Sir William.[44]

The hospitality continued even through the departure. On Thursday, September 17, Sir William went down stream to a village of the Hurons, where he visited the priest. When the officers from the fort arrived, he treated them and the Indians, and was carried in a chair to Captain Jarvis' for breakfast; the good captain having three of these luxurious conveyances to prove the leadership of Detroit in transportation. " Officers prancing on horseback, Sir William and Captain and Mrs. Jarvis carried in their sedan chairs," the party went through three merry miles, stopping here and there to bid adieu to various citizens, who no doubt entertained them with the best their conditions afforded. " Dined with the company out of doors, parted [from] them at this place," he wrote. Probably there were " adieus, good-bys, godspeeds, much fluttering of handkerchiefs, perhaps a furtive tear. After all, it had been a splendid visit, both in solid accomplishment and the hospitality offered by a cultivated French society, the more remarkable because of the leagues of wilderness which hemmed it round." [45]

Another charming picture of life on the frontier is given by Henry Hay, who as a young fur trader, visited the post of Miamitown (now the teeming city of Fort Wayne) during the winter of 1790.[46] His " Journal " presents, as it were, a moving picture film, a cross section of life in the most romantic period in the history of the Old Northwest. Here one finds that many of the French settlers were slothful, vicious, indolent, yet with the characteristic vivacity and gaiety of their race. Hay particularly speaks of the hospitality of these simple folk. He relates that he had only been at the post a few days, when a Mrs. Adhamer showed him a mark of her politeness and attention by begging him to send his clothes and linen to her home

---

[44] Molly was Joseph Brant's sister, and she possessed great influence among the Six Nations, especially the Senecas. *Ibid.*, 382, 503.
[45] *Ibid.*, 464–65; Pound and Day, *Johnson of the Mohawks*, pp. 341–42.
[46] " Henry Hay's Journal from Detroit to the Miami River."

for her panis slave to launder, as it was most difficult to get clothes washed in such an out-of-the-way place.

From the " Journal " one might gather the impression that life was all play, feasts, and dances, for all kinds of ceremonies followed each other in almost kaleidoscopic succession. The ringing of three cowbells by three boys running through the village " making as much noise as twenty cows would," called the settlers to midnight mass, and also to morning and evening prayers on Sunday. Musicians played the flute and fiddle indifferently for drinking bout, dance, or mass, and sometimes went " reeling from the one to the other." On one occasion a joke was played on Mrs. Adhamer by stealing her pig, which was her " only support when the fresh meat " was killed; and the journalist added: " What hurt her more was, that she intended to kill it tomorrow." The excuse given for this fun was that she was a woman who was " amazingly fond of playing her jokes upon other people; . . . for which they were fully determined to play her this one, which we premeditated upwards of three weeks ago."

Temperance reform or an age of sobriety certainly had not made any appearance at the forks of the Maumee. On December 25, Hay and his companions became " infernally drunk"; so far gone were they that one of the traders gave our journalist " his daughter Betsy over the bottle." The morning following, they found themselves " damnation sick " and unable to eat any breakfast. Nevertheless, they " went to mass and played as usual," first partaking of a cup of coffee to settle their heads. This did not keep them sober long, for the following evening all except the author became " very drunk"; one, being too drunk to leave, had to stay at the home of his host all night. The very next evening, the celebrants are " damned drunk " and the writer added that upon visiting some ladies the following morning he found his companions there imbibing again, but he refused their invitations to partake " at so unseasonable an hour as 11 o'clock in the morning," however he promised to join them in the afternoon. This was the regular routine night after night, for on the occasion of one evening party it is deemed worthy of recording that none of the men became drunk, " which is mostly the case in this place when they collect together."

Interesting, too, was the custom on New Year's Day, when our journalist made the round of the " principal families " kissing all the " Ladies young and Old." Not even the flooding of the town sufficed to quench the gaiety, for before the flood had subsided the ladies were taken for a row on the river to the accompaniment of fiddle and flute.[47]

One does not find the same hospitality manifested toward the close of the century. The incoming horde of Americans was regarded by the old French stock much as the cultivated Romans regarded the invading Germanic barbarians. Nowhere is this situation better illustrated than in a letter which Frederick Bates, a young Virginian (and neighbor and friend of Thomas Jefferson), who had recently come to Detroit to seek his fortune, wrote to his sister. Bates may be regarded as a fair representative of the Virginia planter aristocracy of the time, and both in Detroit and in St. Louis (to which place he removed) he held numerous and important public offices. At the time of writing this letter, Bates was twenty-two years of age, and a comparatively recent arrival at Detroit. He wrote:

I make but little progress with the french girls. They are not very apt to think favorably of the Americans. They think them a rough unpolished, brutal set of people. The pleasure of walking on a Sunday evening, is almost counterbalanced by the trouble attendant on that parade & ceremony with which the salutations of the French must be returned. The Miss Grants daughters of the Commodore of the British Squadron on the upper Lakes, are the finest girls in this country. Their mother is a Canadian and they are Roman Catholics. Last Christmas I went early to the midnight mass, and seated myself in their Pew. They came, and with the most obliging good nature, requested me to make room, — I rose — apologized for my intrusion — & seated myself in the

---

[47] *Ibid.* Oliver Spencer had similar experiences when a captive of the Indians in 1792. He wrote of the pleasure he had in Detroit. Quaife, " Oliver Spencer's Narrative," *Burton Leaflet,* III, no. 5, p. 69.

Pew next to them, Determined to be diverted at my expence, they beckoned to me as many as three times to move, as I was in the seat of a lady who was coming in. After mass, I remonstrated with them on their cruelty in taking such pleasure in my embarrasment. They thought it a cruelty which they might very innocently exercise. Their father altho in the British service lives on this side the Strait, on one of the best Farms in the Country. Their mother (which is a singular circumstance among French Ladies) superintends the farm, the produce of which, supports the Family very decently. The old Gentleman's salaries as Commodore and privy Counsellor, are funded, as portions for the girls.[48]

Even an election day was a holiday for old and young, voter and voteless. They were occasions " to meet, to smoke to carouse and swagger " though the records leave one in doubt as to whether they ended in drunken brawls. A leading candidate for the provincial legislature of Upper Canada, in the election of 1792, was David W. Smith of Detroit, who has left considerable correspondence concerning this campaign.[49]

Perusal of these records leaves no doubt that neither human nature nor the methods of politicians have altered materially since 1792. Smith was willing to spend money freely, although, even as with candidates today, there could be no hope of ever securing its return unless by indirect means. The inducements to the voters took the form of free tavern entertainment, accompanied by lavish dispensing of liquors. " Should I be returned without an undue Election or the appearance of party or bribery, I shall be most happy," wrote Smith on July 26, " & in that case I beg an Ox may be roasted whole on the common, & a barrel of Rum be given to the mob, to work down the Beef."

With the passage of time the candidate's ideas concerning entertainment of the voters became more expansive, and in a letter to John Askin, August 14, he presented this captivating picture:

The french people can easily walk to the Hustings, but my gentry

[48] Quoted in Quaife, " Commodore Alexander Grant."
[49] For the information which follows I have drawn upon Dr. Quaife's excellent article " Detroit's First Election," *Burton Leaflet*, V, no. 2.

will require some conveyance; if boats are necessary you can hire them, & they must not want beef or Rum, let them have plenty, and in case of success I leave it to you, which you think best to give my friends a public dinner, & the ladies a dance, either now, or when I go up. if you think the moment the best time You will throw open Forsyths Tavern, & call for the best he can supply. I can trust you will feel very young on the occasion, in the dance, & I wish that Leith and you should push about the bottle, to the promotion of the Settlements on the Detroit. The more broken heads & bloody noses there is the more election like, and in case of Success (damn that If!) let the White Ribbon favors be plentifully distributed, to the old, the Young, the Gay, the lame, the cripple & the blind — half a score cord of wood piled hollow, with a tar barrel in the middle, on the Common, some powder, pour tirer, & plenty of Rum. I am sure that you will preside over & do ev[er]ything that is needful, as far as my circumstances will admit. there must be no want & I am sure you will have ev[er]ything handsome & plentiful.

Elliot I am sure will give you a large red flag to be hoisted on a pole near the Bon fire, and some blue colored tape may be sewn on in large letters E S S E X. . . . Have proper booths erected for my friends at the Hustings, employ Forsyth to make large plumb Cake, with plenty of fruit & ᶜᵃ & be sure let the Wine be good & plenty. Let the peasants have a fiddle, some beverage & Beef.[50]

It would be easy to add numerous descriptions of the many other sports which tempt one to linger, but one can only mention other phases of social activity which more than filled the hours of leisure. Running, wrestling, rowing, bowling on the narrow streets, arrow shooting, quoits, and especially card playing during inclement weather, are only a few of the many ways in which the inhabitants of the Old Northwest enjoyed life to the fullest.

So happy and carefree was life in the western wilderness that those who moved elsewhere were inclined to yearn for the pleasures of the posts. " I cannot but repeat again our Inclinations and wishes are to be with you . . . [My wife's] [51] mind is occupied with reflections of the many happy hours passed at Detroit, it is to be hoped that sometime or another we shall have a renewal of the like pleasures," wrote Lieuten-

[50] Smith to Askin, August 14, 1792, *Askin Papers*, I, 427–28.
[51] Refers to Phyllis Barthe, wife of Lieut. David Mercer.

ant Mercer to John Askin.[52] De Peyster was most happy during his stay in Michigan. " A sore heart it gave us to leave Detroit," he informed a friend, " had we but some of our relations there, I could have spent my life in its little society." [53] Richard Cartwright, Jr.,[54] described the people of Detroit being so " gaily and agreeably amused " and admitted that the social life at Niagara cannot pretend to vie with Detroit in its brilliancy.[55]

After the War of Independence with its ravages, and the continued uncertainty which prevailed concerning trade and the western posts, social life lost much of its thrill and charm. Some found the winters long and tedious, and hoped to move away.[56] " This place once the gaiest and most sociable known has undergone surprising changes," wrote George Anthon [57] to Edgar. " Numbers of people ruined," he continued, " old Acquaintances Dead and gone, a gloomy Aspect in all most every ones face, great demands and small remittances, seizures and Executions in Abundance, and I am afraid a Universal Bankruptcy will ensue among the Trading people here." [58] These conditions did not last long, however. The depression was temporary, and soon life was as gay and brilliant as ever, and with the return of normalcy, continued so to the close of the British régime.[59]

[52] Mercer to Askin, Reading (in Berkshire), April 29, 1790, *ibid.*, I, 365. Askin's daughter Madelaine wrote her father she was sure that she would not have as pleasant a winter at Queenstown as she had had at Springwells, " but I may have the pleasure of talking about them with the ladies of the 5th. I assure you they regret leaving Detroit." Madelaine Askin to John Askin, October 15, 1792, *ibid.*, 441. From Plymouth, England, John Burnet wrote Askin of his " many happy days " at Detroit. Burnet to Askin, March 6, 1787, *ibid.*, 283.

[53] De Peyster to Edgar, July 7, 1784, Edgar MSS.

[54] See *Askin Papers*, I, 188, for sketch.

[55] Cartwright to Edgar, February 17, 1780, Edgar MSS.

[56] Anthon to Edgar, September 26, 1785, *ibid.*

[57] See *Askin Papers*, I, 48, for sketch.

[58] Anthon to Edgar, September 26, 1785, Edgar MSS. He mentions Detroit people who put money in the Bank of North America as " broke and undone."

[59] Nevertheless, there was much isolation and people longed for outside news, well expressed by this bit: " For God's sake send me some of the latest papers." Duggan to Selby, January 10, 1796, Canadian Archives, Claus Papers, III, 145. Another view is expressed by Donald Campbell. He wrote: " For my own part I am heartily tired of Detroit, tho' the best frontier Garrison I begin

One is inclined to dwell longer and in much greater detail upon the social activities of these past romantic days. Life in the harsh conditions of the wilderness, when intercourse with the outside world was so uncertain, was not one of seclusion, or of toil only, but was interspersed with all the hilarity and joymaking that could be obtained in such a situation. Human nature was far from being suppressed, and the picture left is one of charm and gaiety, often of passion unrestrained. Those were happy days. It was a simple life with simple pleasures, possibly a life which cannot be found in the tumult and shouting of this ultra-modern age.

to know the People too well, I do not think they improve on a long acquaintance." Campbell to Bouquet, July 3, 1762, *Mich. Hist. Colls.,* XIX, 154. Also this comment: " Your talk of your place [Detroit] being duller than ever . . . believe me it cannot be put in competition with ours [Michilimackinac] for dulness jealousy & envy with all the etceteras mentioned in your's. Where society is thin, I agree with you, They should make the most of it." Duggan to Selby, June 3, 1796, *ibid.,* XII, 211.

CHAPTER VII

TRANSPORTATION AND NAVAL DEFENSE*

THE WORLD WAR established conclusively the thesis of the late Admiral Mahan that land power and sea power are complementary. From that day when General Wolfe sounded the knell of France's colonial empire, to that autumn day in 1813 when Commodore Oliver Perry administered a fatal blow to the English navy on Lake Erie, the British fleet was an important, if not the decisive, factor in the British control of Michigan and the Old Northwest. From 1760 to 1796 Britain had exclusive authority, and later, from 1796 to 1813, divided authority, over the large areas tributary to the Great Lakes and the Upper Mississippi. Throughout this period of British control, there was built and equipped a small navy which became the essential factor in transporting men, supplies, and equipment, as well as maintaining communication between the East and the western posts.[1] In spite of the significance of this development, and the fact that, since the scholarly work of Frederick Jackson Turner, historians have given increasing time and study to the trans-Allegheny West and its peculiar contribution to America's progress, no serious study, as far as I am aware, has been made of this important phase

* This chapter, in somewhat different form, was read at a joint session of the American Historical Association and the Mississippi Valley Historical Association at Toronto, December 27, 1932.

[1] This was well expressed by Joshua Loring who wrote: "They [the Indians] are greatly surprised at seeing Vessels on those Lakes and are thereby convinced of our power to distress them, their Villages and Settlements being generally on the Banks of the Lakes and at the mouths of Creeks and Rivers for the Convenience of Fishing etc. Thus when they do amiss by Pillage or Hostility they are subject to an immediate visit by the troops at the Posts." Shelburne Papers, LXVIII, 233.

of the history of the Old Northwest, a study obviously both interesting and valuable. The present inquiry is limited to the first period beginning with the arrival of Major Rogers into the lake regions in November of 1760, and ending with the evacuation of the post in the summer of 1796.

From the advent of the French into the interior regions, two well defined routes were established from Montreal leading into the Upper Country: one by the Grand or Ottawa River, across Lake Nipissing to the French River, and the other by the St. Lawrence to the Great Lakes. Most of the trade to and from Detroit and the immediate vicinity came by the latter route,[2] and that of Michilimackinac came through both channels, with the less bulky articles, such as furs and merchandise, including rum, firearms, and ammunition, going over the northern artery, and the goods of larger volume, such as corn, flour, pease, and other provisions, going via the Great Lakes.[3] Toward the end of the century, more and more goods were sent down to Montreal from the northern ports in sailing vessels.[4]

Transportation between the East and Michilimackinac was more rapid by the northern route than by the Great Lakes, for the distance was much shorter, as a view of the map shows. Nevertheless, this way was more hazardous, because of numerous falls and rapids, which constantly delayed navigation: there were over forty portages between the East and West where goods had to be unloaded and transferred, sometimes for miles, on the backs of the *voyageurs*. The Ottawa River, above the site of the present city of Ottawa, was impassable to navigation for anything excepting canoes. These boats could carry three or four tons, and were usually paddled by eight men; they carried, besides, one or two clerks, who in-

[2] There are exceptions to this, for in 1793, 1,979 packs of peltry were sent by the northern route. Canadian Archives, Q, LXXXIX, 169; *Askin Papers,* I, *passim.* For the difficulties on this route which the merchants faced during the War of Independence see *ibid.,* 101, 110.

[3] Sometimes furs were sent down by sailing vessels. Indian goods were sent up via the lakes if there was no particular hurry for them. Stevens, *The Northwest Fur Trade,* pp. 150–51.

[4] *Askin Papers,* I, *passim*; Edgar MSS.; Sterling Letter Book.

creased the load many pounds.[5] Birchbark canoes were about thirty-five feet long, four to five feet wide, and two and one-half feet in depth. The birch bark, which was a quarter of an inch in thickness, was lined with small splints of cedar-wood, and ribs of the same material were used to strengthen the boat, the two ends being fastened to the gunwales. " Several bars, rather than seals," according to Alexander Henry, " were laid across the canoe, from gunwale to gunwale." The small roots of the spruce tree afforded the *wattap,* with which the bark was sewed; and the gum of the pine tree supplied the place of tar and oakum. Bark, some spare *wattap,* and gum, were always carried in each canoe, for the repairs which frequently were necessary.

The canoes were navigated not with oars, but with paddles, and, occasionally, with a sail.[6] The average cargo of furs — for this was the largest and most important item in commerce — consisted of about thirty-six packs. Ordinarily the trip from Michilimackinac to Montreal required three to four weeks, though of course this varied considerably.[7] Cost of transportation, to and from the East, was always one of the greatest problems for the western settler.

Sailing vessels came more and more in usage with the advent of the British on the southern route. Goods were brought down the St. Lawrence to Carleton Island in bateaux, unloaded and placed aboard ship, again unloaded at Niagara,[8] and carried across by *voyageurs* to be reloaded at Chippewa;

[5] Henry, *Travels,* pp. 13–15.

[6] *Ibid.* To every three or four canoes there was a guide or conductor. Skilful men, at double wages, were placed at the bow and stern. These men received (according to Henry) three hundred livres each, and the others one hundred and fifty per trip. *Ibid.,* p. 14. See *The Journal of John Lees,* p. 43, for other wages paid.

[7] Stevens, *op. cit.,* p. 151. An excellent description of these birchbark canoes, their cargoes, the crews, wages paid, and yearly outfits is found in the admirable article by Turner, " The Character and Influence of the Fur Trade in Wisconsin," pp. 52–98.

[8] Ernest Green, " The Niagara Portage Road," *Ontario Historical Society Publications* (Toronto, 1926), XXIII, 260 ff.; Henry R. Howland, " The Niagara Portage," *Buffalo Historical Society Publications* (Buffalo, 1903), VI, 35 ff. Before 1775 large quantities of goods came via Schenectady and the lakes to Detroit and other posts.

thence on to Detroit and Michilimackinac by direct sailing vessels. Toward the close of the régime sailing vessels increased rapidly.

There were a number of well designated avenues of commerce with the interior regions through which passed the bulk of the trade of Detroit and Michilimackinac. Most of the traders resorting to the Upper Louisiana Country reached the Mississippi by way of Lake Superior and the St. Croix River. There were two main and well defined routes from Lake Michigan to the Mississippi: traders could go by way of the Fox and Wisconsin Rivers, or by the Illinois, the latter being reached through the Chicago River or by the St. Joseph and Kankakee Rivers. Those going from Detroit to the Vincennes area paddled up the Maumee, and made a portage to the Wabash, while numerous small streams and portages gave access to the Shawnee Country and the Upper Ohio Valley. Canoes were employed on these streams, and the goods were usually transported over the carrying places on the backs of the *voyageurs,* though occasionally horses and carts were used.[9]

Sometime before the advent of Major Rogers in the Great Lakes region in November, 1760, the British had sensed the need of some naval establishment on Lake Erie.[10] In July, 1760, Colonel Bouquet was building a blockhouse and establishing a military post at Presque Isle (modern Erie) with the aid of one hundred Virginians and one hundred and fifty Pennsylvania levies. Here he constructed a "flatt," which

---

[9] Stevens, *op. cit.,* pp. 152–53, gives a vivid account of these channels of trade and a colorful sketch of the *voyageurs.*

[10] For this information and much that follows I have relied upon the splendid article of H. R. Howland, "Navy Island and the First Successors to the *Griffin,*" *Buffalo Historical Society Publications,* VI; and also the valuable essay of M. M. Quaife, "The Royal Navy of the Upper Lakes," *Burton Historical Collection Leaflet,* II, no. 5. On August 13, 1761, Amherst wrote Pitt that two sloops armed with six four-pounders and one light swivel, and four four-pounders and six swivels have been built at Niagara, all properly manned and officered, under the command of Major Henry Gladwin, "whom I have sent with 300 of Gage's men to explore the Upper Lakes and the country surrounding them, to assist the commanding officers at Detroit in relieving all the outposts, to repair the same as far as may be necessary for insuring the possession of them, and for keeping the whole country in proper subjection to the King." Canadian Archives, C. O. 5, LXI, pt. i, 381–82.

was probably a large open scow provided with sails, and four bateaux. With great foresight he advised General Monckton on September 15 of the needs of the near future:[11]

A Vessel will be wanted next year I think the Timber should be cut and the Boards, planes, etc. be prepared at the Landing Place at Niagara so as to be finished early next Spring.

Again on January 14, 1761, Bouquet wrote Monckton inclosing the list of the naval stores needed for the " construction of a deck'd vessel on Lake Erie," and advising the General to purchase them from the shipbuilders at New York or at Philadelphia, if they could not be provided from Oswego.[12] Evidently Monckton was not interested, for in June, Bouquet again was calling that general's attention to the great advantage of a vessel on Lake Erie " to support the advanced posts." To this Monckton replied:

In regard to the vessel the General is not yet determined about it as by the act of the Officers that have been over the Lake the Shores they met with make it very dangerous navigation, tho' between Presqu' Isle and Niagara I believe it would do very well.[13]

But, apparently unknown to Monckton, General Amherst had already sent some ship carpenters with materials to construct two vessels at Niagara. Navy Island was chosen for the location of the shipyard,[14] and remained a principal center of the naval establishment on the Upper Lakes during the early days of the British régime. During 1771–1772, a second shipyard was located at Detroit, and it became the real center of the English naval establishment; especially was this true by reason of its military significance during the War of Independence.[15]

[11] Quoted in Howland, loc. cit., p. 20.
[12] Ibid.
[13] Quoted in ibid. Sterling wrote Duncan, July 8, 1761, that vessels on Lake Erie would need to be flat bottom " as the lake is very shallow." Sterling Letter Book. But by April 14, 1762, he had changed his mind and wrote that all vessels " ought to be made as sharp as any sea boat." Ibid.
[14] For the location of Navy Island, see the excellent map facing p. 260 of volume XXIII of the Ontario Historical Society Publications. On August 13, 1761, Amherst wrote Pitt that he had already built two sloops at Niagara, and was sending Gladwin with 300 men " to explore the Upper Lakes," and to help keep " the whole Country in proper subjection to the King." Canadian Archives, C. O. 5, LXI, pt. i, 381–82.
[15] Quaife, " The Royal Navy of the Upper Lakes." Considerable data on early shipbuilding and navigation are found in " The King's Shipyard," Burton Leaflet, II, no. 3.

From the Navy Island shipyard came all the ships which sailed the Upper Lakes during the early years of British power. Because of the part taken by them in the critical year of 1763, the first two ships built have a particular significance in the history of Michigan. Their story well describes the important work of the royal navy in maintaining British control over the Upper Country until 1796. Sir William Johnson on his way to an Indian council at Detroit in the fall of 1761, describes in his diary under date of July 26 a visit to Navy Island " whereon the vessel is building for exploring the lakes Huron and Michigan. . . . The Schooner building upon the island, was in such forwardness as to be ready to launch in about ten days." [16] Upon his return from Detroit he discovered that the schooner had been launched and was employed, under the command of Captain Robertson, in sounding the Niagara River near the outlet to Lake Erie.[17] Johnson, who dined on board, records that the boat carried ninety barrels of provisions, besides twenty-four barrels for Gage's sutler. This schooner, which was named the *Huron*, drew seven feet of water when loaded and was armed with six guns.[18]

Thus was built and put into service the first English vessel, and " the first decked sailing vessel to plow the waters of Lake Erie since the days of the *Griffin*." The second, a sloop named *Michigan,* was already laid down, but was not completed until sometime in 1762 because of sickness among the builders.[19] Both of these vessels were at Detroit when Pontiac began his famous siege, on the " change of moon in the month of May, 1763." [20]

From the beginning of the Pontiac War to the end, the *Huron* and the *Michigan* played a major rôle, possibly by their

[16] Stone, *Sir William Johnson,* II, 440; Sullivan (ed.), *The Papers of Sir William Johnson,* III, 512. Work had been temporarily stopped in order to construct a boat " pinnace fashion " for Major Gladwin.
[17] Stone, *op. cit.,* II, 440.
[18] Howland, *op. cit.,* p. 24.
[19] *Ibid.*
[20] Parkman, *The Conspiracy of Pontiac,* I, chaps. XII–XV. See Quaife, *loc. cit.,* and Howland, *loc. cit.,* where Parkman's error about the names of these boats is cleared up.

aid saving Major Gladwin's garrison from a gruesome massacre such as was enacted at the other western posts. The first attack of the savages fell upon a part of the small navy which was exploring Lake St. Clair and the St. Clair River. In early May of 1763, Captain Robertson and a small party set out from Detroit in canoes to chart the rivers and lakes to the north. Four days later, the party was surprised by the Indians and all of its members were either killed or captured.[21] Among the slain were Captain Robertson and Sir Robert Davers. Three days after this unfortunate affair Pontiac resolutely began his siege of Detroit, and the great Indian War of 1763 was on in earnest.[22]

Major Gladwin, commandant at Detroit, having been warned of Pontiac's plans,[23] stationed the *Huron* and the *Michigan* immediately in front of the fort, in such a position that the guns of one vessel could command the western flank of the fort and those of the other the eastern. From early daylight of May 10, from behind houses and fences, the Indians maintained an " incessant " fire for several hours on the two small vessels, for they were of the opinion that they " could eaisily get the Fort " if they could sink the vessels.[24] The vessels had a crew of six or seven men each; the *Michigan* was commanded by Nicolas Newman, and the *Huron* by Sergeant Miller of the Royal Americans. Until the end of the siege, these vessels were a continuous source of worry to the Indians and a veritable " tower of strength " to the valiant defenders of the post. By repeated night attacks and the use of fire rafts

[21] An excellent description of this attack, written by one of the captives, John Rutherford, is printed in *The Transactions of the Canadian Institute* (Toronto, 1893), III, 229–51. A copy of the original is in the Canadian Archives at Ottawa.

[22] Parkman, *loc. cit.*, is the classic account of this great Indian War. A more recent description is found in Wrong, *Canada and the American Revolution*, chap. IV.

[23] Humphrey, " The Identity of Gladwin's Informant," gives an exhaustive and scholarly account of this episode. Bassett to Haldimand, August 29, 1773, *Mich. Hist. Colls.*, XIX, 311. General Gage ordered other ships built for Gladwin, for he well realized the need of keeping open the communications with Detroit. Gage to Gladwin, April 23, 1764, Gage MSS.

[24] Quaife, " The Royal Navy," p. 54; John Porteous, " Journal of the Siege." MS. in the Burton Historical Collection.

the followers of Pontiac endeavored to destroy the small navy, but to no avail.

On the thirteenth of August, 1763, both ships weighed anchor, and sailed from Niagara to bring much needed supplies and reinforcements to the beleaguered garrison.[25] The *Huron* on the night of September 3, returning with provisions, entered the Detroit River, and anchored about nine miles below the fort. During the night, the tiny vessel and crew of ten men were attacked by 350 Indians in their canoes. After the death of the captain and two men, with four more seriously wounded, the mate ordered the ship blown up rather than allow it to be captured. This so frightened the savages they escaped precipitately into their canoes before the order was put into effect, and did not dare to renew the attack. The schooner reached port safely the following day. At the end of the siege the valiant vessel disappears from the pages of history. Small, built of unseasoned timber, and sailing uncharted seas, she probably went to an early, watery grave.[26]

The sloop *Michigan* was even less fortunate than the *Huron*. Sailing from Niagara toward the end of August, 1763, with eighteen officers and men, provisions, and supplies, she sprang a leak when only one day out.[27] After a valiant fight at the pumps, the boat was run on a sandbank and left to the fury of the surf. This loss embarrassed Gladwin, for late in November he wrote, " We had only provisions from hand to mouth." Thus it would appear that both vessels came to an early end, but not before they had demonstrated the real need of more vessels of the same type for the British army and traders at the western posts.[28]

[25] Because of the lack of just such assistance, Lieutenant Abraham Cuyler and his forces (nearly one hundred strong), in open boats, were cut to pieces at Point Pelée. Parkman, *Conspiracy of Pontiac*, I, 275–77.

[26] La Salle's *Griffin* was lost on her maiden voyage.

[27] John Montresor describes the wreck of the *Michigan* in an entry of August 28 in his " Journal." " Journal of John Montresor's Expedition to Detroit in 1763," *Transactions of the Royal Society of Canada* (Toronto, 1928), third series, XXII. Rutherford has left a graphic account of the foundering of the *Michigan*. See *Canadian Institute Transactions*, III, 247–48.

[28] Gladwin to ————, January 9, 1764, Gage MSS. The shipyard at Navy Island was a busy place during the next eighteen months. Howland, *op. cit.*, pp. 30–31.

The problem of reoccupying the destroyed posts, and conquering much of the Indian country, still remained at the close of 1763. Ships to take the place of the *Huron* and the *Michigan*, as well as two others, were begun, and through the special interest of Gage the work was speeded up with such vigor that the summer of 1764 saw the four vessels in service for Lake Erie and the Upper Country. They were the sloop *Royal Charlotte*, and the schooners *Boston, Victory*, and *Gladwin*.[29] No more vessels were built at Navy Island until 1772, by which time a shipyard had been established at Detroit, where the later ships were constructed. In 1768 Carver described the *Gladwin* as a vessel of eighty tons,[30] and possibly the other boats were of similar size. In the official " Return " of the vessels upon the Lakes from 1759 to 1778, the *Gladwin* is listed as carrying 8 swivels, and the *Boston*, the *Victory*, and the *Royal Charlotte*, six, eight, and ten, respectively.[31] It was the work of these ships to keep communications open and to transport military supplies and the merchants' goods and furs throughout the region of the Upper Lakes (except Lake Superior), an area a thousand miles in extent. The *Boston* was burned sometime prior to November 13, 1768.[32] The *Gladwin* was still in service during the summer of 1770, for General Gage suggested to General Haldimand " breaking " the *Gladwin* and the *Royal Charlotte* because of their " bad state " and using the materials for the building of a new vessel.[33] According to the " Return," however, both vessels " remained in service until decayed." [34]

The first ships to be built at the Detroit yard were the schooners, *Hope*, of sixty tons, and the *Angelica*, of fifty tons,

[29] Quaife, " Royal Navy," p. 55; Howland, *op. cit.*, pp. 31–32. On April 23, 1764, Gage wrote Gladwin: " By the latest Accounts from Niagara, the building of the Vessells went on very expeditiously, and there is room to believe that some of them will be afloat by the time this letter gets to Detroit." Gage MSS.
[30] Carver, *Travels*, p. 150.
[31] *Wis. Hist. Colls.*, XI, 198–200.
[32] Canadian Archives, *Report for 1885*, p. 168.
[33] *Ibid.*, B, XIX, 127. Carver states that the *Gladwin* was lost on Lake Erie due to the obstinacy of her commander in putting to sea without sufficient ballast. Carver, *op. cit.*, p. 155.
[34] Howland, *op. cit.*, p. 33; *Wis. Hist. Colls.*, XI, 198–200.

each armed with four swivels; these boats were constructed in the spring of 1771.[35] General Gage ordered Alexander Grant, better known as Commodore Grant, to build them, and wrote Captain James Stephenson, commandant at Detroit, to " assist Grant and give him such helps as your garrison affords, whenever he demands it." [36] The General was disturbed lest the merchants use all the cedar and the artificers to build their own vessels; so he directed Stephenson not to suffer " Mr. Grant's artificers or Sailors to be taken away from him," and further, " to reserve the cedar and suffer no person to cut it, but when it is used in the King's Service." [37] Apparently Gage learned there was cedar in plenty, for he later had no objection to the merchants cutting as much as they wanted, and advised the commandant not to " obstruct them in that or any other business not detrimental to the Service." [38]

In 1772 the schooners *Gage* and *Dunmore* were constructed. They were much larger than any built to date, being 120 and 90 tons, respectively, and carrying twelve and ten guns.[39] A smaller vessel, the sloop *Felicity* of 30 tons, was launched in 1775; the schooner *Faith*, of 30 tons, and the sloop *Archangel*, of 15 tons, were built in 1774.[40] By 1778, two more ships, the *Wyandot* and *Ottawa*, were under construction at Detroit, as well as four large scows and one gunboat. These vessels comprised the " royal navy of the Upper Lakes."[41]

[35] Canadian Archives, Q, XI, 226; *Wis. Hist. Colls.*, XI, 200.

[36] Gage to Stephenson, April 8, 1768, *Mich. Hist. Colls.*, XX, 303. This date has obviously been incorrectly printed, and should be 1771. Gage also ordered Captain John Browne to aid Grant in reaching Detroit. Gage to Browne, April 8, 1771, Canadian Archives, B, XVIII, 134.

[37] Gage to Stephenson, April 8, 1768 (1771), *Mich. Hist. Colls.*, XX, 303.

[38] *Ibid.* In a postscript, September 10, 1772, Bassett wrote: " The woods are I believe as fine as any in the world, very fine oak for ship building. We had two fine Vessels finished this Summer for the Service of the Crown, and the Merchants . . . have three others for the Fur Trade." Canadian Archives, Dartmouth Transcripts, 1765–1775, pp. 295–96.

[39] *Wis. Hist. Colls.*, XI, 200. In the Canadian Archives, Q, XI, 226, the armament is given as sixteen and twelve guns, respectively. Spencer mentioned the *Chippewa, Ottawa, Dunmore* " an old vessel of six guns," and the *Felicity* anchored in the river at Detroit in the spring of 1793. " Oliver Spencer's Narrative."

[40] Canadian Archives, Q, XI, 226.

[41] *Ibid.*, LVI, pt. ii, 553. The records list " a new ship built at Detroit in 1782," but give no name. *Ibid.* Other ships, the *Welcome* and the *Adventure*, were built sometime before 1780.

These ships provided the main channels of communication and transportation between the western posts and the East during the critical years of the War of Independence.[42] It is possible that without them the British would not have retained the Old Northwest during the war and the western posts until 1796. The significance of this force was clearly shown when Hamilton led his expedition against Vincennes in 1778. Captain Grant conveyed Hamilton's small army and supplies as far as the Maumee Rapids. The *Archangel* carried fourteen tons of provisions,[43] and fifteen large pirogues, capable of carrying 1,800 to 3,000 pounds each, were also employed.[44] Hamilton's campaign ended in disaster, and thus the British at Detroit were kept in constant dread of Clark's marching northward; so Grant ordered all the boats to return as soon as possible to defend that place.[45]

In 1780, the English planned an intensive campaign against St. Louis and the Illinois villages. In all the operations, which utterly failed, the navy played a significant part. Ships were dispatched to Chicago to bring back the prisoners whom the forces were expected to capture, and other boats were sent to the present site of Milwaukee with provisions. One unit of the army, meeting defeat at St. Louis, retreated up the

[42] Hamilton in 1777 gave orders for a dispatch boat of fifteen tons to be built at once "for carrying intelligence and conveying Powder, Provisions etc." Hamilton to Germain, June 17, 1777, *ibid.*, Q, XIV, 81. He found the King's vessels in the best of repair, and had the timber cut for a new one, but discovered naval stores and iron were lacking to ' equip the boat. This was possibly either the sloop *Wyandot* or *Ottawa*, as they were finished in 1778. Hamilton to Carleton, May 11, 1777, *ibid.*, Q, XIII, 275. For an interesting account of the coming and going of many vessels at Detroit, see *Mich. Hist. Colls.*, XVII, 642 ff.

[43] *Ibid.*, IX, 493.

[44] Hamilton to Haldimand, September 22, 1778, *ibid.*, 477. A different account is given in *ibid.*, 409. In a number of letters Hamilton expressed his absolute dependence upon the navy to bring "Intelligence, orders, & Instructions." Hamilton to Carleton, August 11, 1778, *ibid.*, 461; same to Cramahé, August 12, 1778, *ibid.*, 462.

[45] *Ibid.*, 390-92; X, 310, 342; XIX, 366; *Wis. Hist. Colls.*, XXIII, 56, 88; XXIV, 111-14. Again, in 1781, when Clark threatened Detroit, the *Faith* and the *Adventure* were stationed in the Maumee for defensive purposes. Grant to Powell, March 18, 1781, *Mich. Hist. Colls.*, XIX, 601; XX, 55. For Clark's plans against Detroit, see *Wis. Hist. Colls.*, XXIII; XXIV, introduction; and J. A. James, *The Life of George Rogers Clark* (Chicago, 1928), chap. XI.

Illinois River, and was brought back from Chicago to Michilimackinac by the navy.[46]

The commanders at Michilimackinac, believing they were
in an exposed place far removed from the other posts, constantly urged their superior officers to send a vessel to their
fort.[47] De Peyster wrote Haldimand July, 1779:

It would be necessary for the good of the Service (If your Excellency thought proper) to order a vessel to ply constantly twixt
the two places. In the situation we are at present. The Indians
are in constant alarm, and are often much persuaded Detroit is
taken that they are ready to leave their habitations. . . . The
commanding officer at Detroit gives me all the intelligence he
receives. But to hear often that all is well would be most essential
service in the management of the Indians.[48]

Governor Sinclair asked to be removed from Michilimackinac,
unless more attention was given to it "as to proper armed
vessels, Materials and men." [49] Never fully realizing the vast
area to which the royal navy had to transport supplies, he
requested an armed vessel from Detroit to " remain in the
French River for a few weeks every spring," as it would tend
" much to the security of the goods coming up the Ottawa
River," he explained.[50] Apparently puffed up with his own
importance and believing De Peyster was being especially
favored, Sinclair protested to Haldimand. That General replied: " after having perused with attention his [De Peyster's] Letters to which you refer me, I protest I cannot see
the smallest reason to interpret them in the lights you have
conceived. From the Distribution he gives you of the shipping,
it would appear that he had it not in his Power to assist you
sooner." [51] Nevertheless, the same day Haldimand ordered two
vessels, the *Hope* and *Welcome*, to be stationed at Michilimackinac, " to be entirely dependent upon that Post " for

---

[46] Sinclair to Haldimand, July 8, 1780, *Mich. Hist. Colls.*, IX, 558–60; Sinclair to Bolton, June 4, 1780, *ibid.*, XIX, 529; *Wis. Hist. Colls.*, XI, 152–55.
[47] Sinclair to Haldimand, May 29, 1780, *Mich. Hist. Colls.*, IX, 553.
[48] De Peyster to Haldimand, July 21, 1779, *ibid.*, 391.
[49] Sinclair to Haldimand, May 29, 1780, *ibid.*, 553.
[50] Same to same, undated, *ibid.*, 564.
[51] Haldimand to Sinclair, August 10, 1780, *ibid.*, 565.

supplying it with provisions and other wants from Detroit.[52]
To this order, Grant in high dudgeon replied to Bolton at
Niagara:

I can stake my veracity and twenty-one years knowledge of the
Lakes to his Excellency, That the Sloop *Welcome* answers all the
end of a vessel of War at Mackina, as the Great Fleet of England
would particularly as the Channel is open for all our Vessels to
run there, whenever there is occasion.[53]

In an attempt to keep complete control of the navigation
of the lakes during the war, orders were issued to allow no
vessels (except those of the Indians) " to pass upon the lakes
without proper passports." [54] No permits to build ships " of
greater dimensions than a common boat," unless for the King's
service, were to be granted.[55] In 1777, Carleton forbade any
vessels to navigate the lakes, unless completely manned and
armed, " and in the King's Service." [56] Because of this order,
very much in the nature of a rebuke, the naval officers at
Detroit, and Governor Hamilton, prepared a report comment-
ing on the naval establishment and offering recommendations
for its improvement.[57]

These officials advised the enclosing of the shipyard at Detroit, the building of barracks for the officers and men, and
the constructing of a store house and a rigging loft.[58] Fearful
lest the rates of pay recommended would be considered unusually high, they justified themselves by " the remoteness

[52] Same to same, August 10, 1780, *ibid.*, 567.
[53] Grant to Bolton, undated, *ibid.*, XIX, 556.
[54] Foy to Hamilton, undated, *ibid.*, IX, 345.
[55] *Ibid.*
[56] Carleton to Bolton, September 24, 1777, *ibid.*, X, 280. This same order
was sent by Haldimand. Haldimand to Bolton, September 24, 1777, Canadian
Archives, B, XL, 28. It caused considerable hardship and met with protests
from the merchants. " Corn in all probability will be as hard to be got as
Rum," wrote Askin in 1778, " how to get it here now the Vessels are stopt, the
King's Vessell will come as usual perhaps, but besides Kings Stores, she has to
carry for so many persons, that each can have very little on Board." Askin to
McGill, Frobisher, Patterson, etc., April 28, 1778, *Askin Papers*, I, 74.
[57] *Wis. Hist. Colls.*, XI, 185–202. There are many papers printed here
dealing with the pay of officers and crews, and of the carpenters, store-keepers,
and others. *Mich. Hist. Colls.*, X, 281, gives Carleton's orders for the pay of
the men on His Majesty's ships.
[58] *Wis. Hist. Colls.*, XI, 185–202.

of situation, [and] the excessive prices of commodities." [59] For, they explained, a pair of shoes cost twelve shillings sterling; coarse stockings, six shillings; " check linnen," three shillings and six pence sterling a yard, and " other things proportionally dear." [60]

In July, 1778, two sets of orders and regulations for the naval establishment on the lakes were published.[61] By them, Samuel Graves was to be in full command on all the lakes, which were divided into three districts, with a naval officer under Graves' command over each. The officers of controller, paymaster, and commissioner were created, with definite rules for their work. The Upper Lakes made up the third district, with Detroit as the base of operations. This plan shows that the naval forces on the Upper Lakes were to be closely connected with those on the other lakes. The scheme also provided that the naval service was under the command of the " Eldest Land Officer serving in the same District." [62] It further stated:

that no land Officer is to interfere with the Interior discipline of the Seamen or in any of the Minutia belonging to the Naval Department, nor shall any Naval Officer interfere in any respect with the interior regulations of the Land Service.[63]

Nevertheless, a number of altercations occurred between the land and naval officers.[64]

There were many vessels owned by the traders and the merchants, the number increasing toward the close of the

[59] *Ibid.*, 186.
[60] *Ibid.*
[61] *Ibid.*, 193-97.
[62] *Ibid.*, 195. This was to avoid conflicts which had been common in the past.
[63] *Ibid.*
[64] Notable among these were the ones between Sinclair and Harrow, and Sinclair and McKay, the skipper of the *Felicity*. Sinclair to De Peyster, July 30, 1780, *Mich. Hist. Colls.*, IX, 600; Harrow to Grant, August 21, 1780, *ibid.*, 606. The logbook of the *Welcome*, commanded by Captain Harrow, is in the Burton Historical Collection. McKay wrote to Grant from Michilimackinac: " If I do not geet Relieved Verrey Soon I shall be obliged to leave the Vessel upon the Governor's hands, . . . there is such troubles heir, In one shape and another which I shall not mention that I cannot Tell What to Do." McKay to Grant, July 29, 1780, *ibid.*, 606.

British régime. John Askin of Detroit, in 1775, owned the *Archangel*,[65] named after his daughter, and the schooners *Hope* and *Faith*, while the sloops *Hope* and *Angelica* were owned by Commodore Grant.[66]

In an inventory of his estate in 1776, Askin records the sloop *Welcome*, valued at £ 700, and the schooner *De Peyster*, valued at £ 200.[67] During the war these vessels were taken into the King's service. In 1777, a return shows the vessels *Caldwell* (Lake Ontario), *Hope*, *Faith*, and *Angelica*, all owned by Grant as " employed by the Crown." [68] This was the general policy of the government during the war.

After the war was over, there were a number of vessels built at Detroit.[69] Haldimand gave the merchants permission to construct a boat in 1784 for use on Lake Superior, and ordered Governor Hay to render every aid and assistance in forwarding provisions and stores for the builders.[70] The schooner *Weazel* was built in 1786 at Detroit; and the sloop *Sagina* in 1787; and the *Esperance* in 1788.[71] There seem to be no records of vessels built thereafter. Possibly most of the officials were well aware of the insecurity of English control of the northwest posts, and did not wish to invest too heavily. Again, this may be explained by the fact that the large fur trading companies began to enter the field about this time, thus relieving the government of direct responsibility.[72]

[65] Canadian Archives, Q, XI, 226.

[66] *Ibid.* The schooner *Hope* was of sixty tons capacity and the sloop *Hope* of fifty. The sloop *Felicity* was owned at this time by Simon McTavish and George McBeath, fur traders. In 1776, the *Faith* was employed in carrying wood to the garrison. See "State of the Naval Force on Lake Erie and the Garrison at Detroit," MS. in Clements Library.

[67] Canadian Archives, Askin Papers, Inventory of December 31, 1776. The Inventory for 1779 does not list these boats, but speaks of a "Keel boat and small skiff" worth £ 64. *Ibid.*

[68] *Wis. Hist. Colls.*, XI, 185. Part of the log of the sloop *Felicity* for 1779 is published in *ibid.*, 203–212.

[69] See *Askin Papers*, I, 448–53, for an account of the hiring of a sailor, and the articles of partnership to build a ship.

[70] Haldimand to Hay, November 10, 1784, Canadian Archives, B, LXIV, 405.

[71] *Mich. Hist. Colls.*, XII, 5. After 1782 four large vessels, besides bateaux, were built at Detroit. None is named. They may be the ones mentioned above.

[72] Canadian Archives, Q, LVI, pt. ii, 553; Stevens, *Northwest Fur Trade*, chap. IV.

The upkeep of the naval establishment on the Upper Lakes was a large expense. As early as 1766 Grant estimated the expense of the navy at £ 5,318 N. Y. C.[73] The pay of the senior commanding officer was fifteen shillings a day which was reduced to ten shillings after the war.[74] The masters received ten shillings, and the lieutenants in command of a vessel six, while the lower ranks were paid in corresponding scale.[75] In the "Return" for 1778, the officers included the pay of eight servants, which amounted to £ 242/13/4 for the year.[76] This was "not allowed according to the Establishment" and was deducted. There were, besides, shipwrights, joiners, blacksmiths, sawyers, blockmakers, inspectors, clerks, carpenters, and "Labourers cutting firewood" in the navy muster roll, receiving from £ 100 per year for storekeepers and clerks, to four shillings a day for a sawyer.[77] In 1779 the entire naval establishment cost £ 10,047/10/4.[78] The average vessel's crew consisted of a captain, a mate, a midshipman, a boatswain, a carpenter, a cook, and ten seamen, and cost in times of peace £ 581/18/6 sterling.[79]

The officials found many serious problems in maintaining the naval establishment and in transporting the goods to and from the posts. One was that of desertion. Commodore Grant found that five privates of the 5th Regiment deserted his ship, the *Snow*, at Niagara, just before he left for Detroit, and as a result he was delayed for some time.[80] These men were serving

---

[73] Shelburne Papers, LVII, 85. Inclosed in Gage's letter of October 11, 1766, to Shelburne. For another copy see *ibid.*, L, 303.

[74] Canadian Archives, Q, LVI, pt. ii, 539, 557. There were 125 officers and men in the Lake Erie division, of whom twenty-nine belonged to the civil department, costing £ 4,281/1/8 per year. *Ibid.*, 549.

[75] *Mich. Hist. Colls.*, XIX, 333–34. For wages paid bateau men in 1768, see *Journal of John Lees*, p. 43.

[76] *Ibid.*, p. 368. In *Wis. Hist. Colls.*, XI, 202, the amount is given as £ 243/13/4.

[77] *Mich. Hist. Colls.*, XIX, 344. There were at one time in Detroit ten shipwrights, one joiner, two blacksmiths, two sawyers, and one blockmaker, who were supposed to keep the vessels in repair, also to repair and caulk the bateaux. Canadian Archives, Q, LVI, pt. ii, 554.

[78] *Wis. Hist. Colls.*, XI, 201.

[79] Shelburne Papers, XLVIII, 245.

[80] Grant to Askin, August 12, 1792, Canadian Archives, Askin Papers, XXVII.

as marines. They were later captured by some Indians and returned to Grant by a unit from the 26th Regiment. These deserters, upon examination, declared that they were drunk when they left and that later " coming to " they started back to their boats when the Indians captured them.[81] The record does not reveal what punishment the men received.

A more serious difficulty, and one which neither the engineers of that day nor this have ever completely solved, was the building of the vessels to withstand the destructive storms for which the Great Lakes (particularly Lake Erie) are noted. In 1768 a crew was sent from the Detroit navy yard to save the cargo, mast, and upper works of a schooner driven ashore in a " violent storm," not far below the Detroit River, near Sandusky.[82] This boat, probably the *Victory* (for the " Return " of 1768 fails to mention the vessel), though the records leave one in the dark as to her actual fate,[83] was used to transport provisions from Fort Erie to the garrisons at Detroit and at Michilimackinac. Commodore Grant lost a vessel on Lake Erie near Sandusky in 1771, with a cargo of pelts worth £ 5,000 sterling.[84] This accident was explained by the fact that the navigators were unskilful or the vessel too flat for the lakes.[85] The ship *Snow* sank in 1780 with forty seamen, all her officers, and thirty men of the 34th Regiment. This was a great loss, explained Haldimand to Lord Germain, for

[81] *Ibid.* See " Information Against Deserters from Naval Service," *Askin Papers*, I, 383–84.

[82] Gage to the Earl of Hillsborough, January 5, 1769, Canadian Archives, Dartmouth Transcripts, 1765–1775, pp. 162–63. Printed in Carter, *Gage's Correspondence*, I, 210.

[83] Canadian Archives, *Report for 1884*, p. 169. An account of an experience on board the *Felicity* during a storm on Lake Erie in 1793 is found in " Oliver Spencer's Narrative."

[84] Brehm to Edgar, July 4, 1771, Edgar MSS.

[85] Apparently flat-bottomed boats continued to be built for in December, 1788, Mann did not deem it advisable to continue the practice. *Mich. Hist. Colls.*, XII, 37. Governor Turnbull gave a different version of the disaster. He claimed that seventeen passengers perished, and the furs were valued at £ 2,500. He wrote about building two new ships at Detroit for the Crown. These were probably the *Gage* and *Dunmore*. Turnbull to the Governor of Quebec, 1771, June 12, Canadian Archives, S, Internal Correspondence of Quebec, 1771–1776.

these men were badly needed at the posts.[86] Another record mentions the sinking of the *Ottawa* in 1793, at the King's wharf in Detroit. Commodore Grant was so angry at Lieutenant David Cowan, the captain, that he treated him " in a very blackguard way," one observer thought.[87] Grant called the captain a " Rascal " and threatened him with his horsewhip, then sent him, under guard, to his room and ordered a court of inquiry. Later the vessel was floated to the very great " satisfaction of all Cowan's friends." [88] These losses and the use made of the other boats, at the close of the war in " Transporting the disbanded and discharged Troops," [89] brought a petition from the merchants of Detroit praying to be allowed to navigate the " three Small Shallops " to Niagara with the furs.[90] Grant favored this petition and advised that the two small sloops be so employed.[91] He was of the opinion this could be done without detriment to " His Majesty's Service " and added, " the necessity is the greater as the *Gage* and *Felicity* are employed in transporting the troops." [92]

During the next few years, until 1796, the navy was used mainly in transporting troops, supplies, and furs from east to west and *vice versa*.

The reduction of the naval department at the end of the war to two vessels on Lake Erie, caused the merchants of Detroit to build several small vessels, " presuming that in time of Peace there could not be any impediment to the free navigation of their own vessels." [93] In expectation of great pros-

<hr>

[86] Haldimand to Germain, November 20, 1780, *ibid.*, B, LV, 18. In 1775 the *Chippewa* sank in Lake Erie, and Caldwell ordered the goods destroyed which had been brought to shore to prevent them from falling into American hands. Hamilton to Haldimand, undated, *Mich. Hist. Colls.*, IX, 467. Another ship, the *Santeaux*, sank in 1776 near Presqu' Isle. *Ibid.*, XIX, 319.

[87] Smith to McKee, October 6, 1793, Canadian Archives, Claus Papers, VI, 32; Duggan to McKee, October 8, 1793, *ibid.*, 41.

[88] Smith to McKee, October 6, 1793, *ibid.*, 32.

[89] Grant to ———, July 15, 1784, *Mich. Hist. Colls.*, XI, 424–25.

[90] " Petition " of Detroit Merchants to Hay, July 15, 1784, *ibid.*, 424; " Petition " to the Honorable Governor and Council of Quebec, July 16, 1784, *ibid.*, 459–61.

[91] *Ibid.*, 424–25. Grant explains that one sloop " has been permitted to sail for Fort Erie already by Captain Bird."

[92] *Ibid.*, 425.

[93] *Ibid.*, XX, 242.

perity, following the somewhat lean years of the war, the Montreal merchants, in 1784, sent the usual annual supply of goods, amounting to approximately £ 40,000, earlier than usual to Carleton Island.[94] Here the goods still remained in August, 1784, when the merchants memorialized Haldimand that a third vessel be employed upon Lake Erie and another upon Lake Ontario, " and that Liberty be given small vessels of private property on Erie to navigate without hindrance." [95] They were expecting fully 4,000 packs of furs in the shipment from Detroit, and were decidedly of the opinion the ships in service could not begin to care for their needs.[96] Haldimand ordered another vessel to be put into use on each lake, and advised Governor Hay at Detroit that in the future there would be no occasion for permission to be given private vessels to navigate Lake Erie.[97] " You will therefore upon receipt of this," he commanded, " withdraw such Permission, and adhere strictly to the orders formerly given by Sir Guy Carleton and myself upon that subject." [98] Later, in October, Haldimand gave certain merchants permission to build a small vessel at Detroit " to be employed on Lake Superior for the purpose of transporting merchandize or provisions over that Lake to the Grand Portage." [99]

Because of fear lest goods be smuggled, and lest the Americans get a firm hold on the fur trade, no additional boats were placed at the service of the merchants.[100] This brought a

[94] *Ibid.*, a " memorial " dated August 4, 1785, signed by twenty-one of the leading Montreal merchants.
[95] *Ibid.*
[96] *Ibid.*
[97] As early as June, 1778, private vessels had largely been taken over for the use of the army and navy. Askin to McGill and Frobisher, June 30, 1778, *Askin Papers*, I, 155; Askin to the Northwest Company, July 2, 1778, *ibid.*, 160.
[98] Haldimand to Hay, August 31, 1784, *Mich. Hist. Colls.*, XX, 250.
[99] Mathews to Frobisher, October 11, 1784, *ibid.*, 267. Haldimand refused the Company's request to an exclusive right to the trade of the Northwest, but ordered Governor Hay to render " every service consistent with the Service " in forwarding provisions in the King's vessels to Michilimackinac. *Ibid.*
[100] Haldimand recommended to Lord Sydney on March 16, 1785, that only the King's vessels navigate the Lakes, because the large number of rivers going into the Great Lakes made smuggling easy. Haldimand to Sydney, March 16, 1785, Canadian Archives, Q, XXV, 329. Goods were smuggled into the United States by Lake Champlain. *Mich. Hist. Colls.*, XX, 279.

spirited protest to the Governor and Council of Quebec from the Detroit merchants, who had suffered such losses as to have reason " to apprehend the total Ruin of their affairs, by which not only the Merchants in Canada," they declared, " but also those in England, to whom from this Country there are immense Sums still due, will be materially injured if not altogether ruined." [101] Because of goods detained at the Niagara Portage, the merchants were paying an " annual Interest of upwards of Three Thousand seven Hundred pounds Sterling." [102] From delays, difficulties, consequent losses, arising from " notorious and unparalleled Thefts " the petitioners were of the opinion the trade would soon be ruined or fall into the hands of the Spaniards.[103] Governor Hay sent his protest to Haldimand also. He was convinced that if the government did not allow more vessels to navigate the Great Lakes, or permit the merchants to sail their own, the trade of Detroit would suffer materially, " and probably cause the fall of some of the first houses concerned in supplying the merchandise of this place [Detroit], if not totally prevent Great Britain from reaping the benefits heretofore arising from the Sale of a great quantity of her Manufactures." [104]

All these complaints and petitions fell upon deaf ears, for the Quebec Council continued to oppose the use of private vessels and strongly recommended to Governor Hamilton [105]

[101] " Petition " of July 16, 1785, ibid., XI, 459–60.

[102] Ibid. " This as is obviously known proceeds from the want of sufficient number of King's vessels to transport the goods destin'd for this country, or a permission to Merchants vessels to carry their own property," they further added.

[103] Ibid. One thousand packs did go to New Orleans in 1784, they claimed, and upwards of fifty small boat loads, destined for the Indian trade, were, because of their late departure, frozen up " before they reached the places of their Destination." Canadian Archives, Q, XXV, 128–30. McGill added his sentiments in a like manner. McGill to ————, August 1, 1785, Mich. Hist. Colls., XI, 461–65. McGill wrote to Askin, April 12, 1786, that it was generally thought that Carleton would allow the sailing of private vessels, but advised him to wait until he heard further from him. Askin Papers, I, 236; and again on December 20, 1786, ibid., 278.

[104] Hay to Hamilton, July 16, 1785, Canadian Archives, XXV, 132. On July 16, 1785, several Detroit merchants requested that at least the Gage, which was not in use, even in the King's service, be put at their disposal. Mich. Hist. Colls., XI, 460.

[105] Haldimand had been succeeded by Hamilton, in November, 1784.

that the whole matter be placed in the hands of Lieutenant Colonel Barry St. Leger.[106] This Hamilton did, sending with the minutes of the Council the memorials of the merchants, and requested that all the aid possible be given the merchants in the transport of their goods.[107] St. Leger informed the merchants, July 25, 1785, that no exertion would be wanting on his part to aid them, since he was very anxious to promote the trade; [108] he explained that all the obstructions and impediments were temporary only, and therefore did not justify any deviation from the permanent regulation.[109] In a letter to Lord Sydney he said that he had relaxed the regulations so far as to allow private bateaux and canoes to be employed, but no ships. These regulations were General Haldimand's, he added, and needed no change at present, since they were only temporary.[110]

This small change brought little or no relief, and James McGill [111] of Montreal wrote Hamilton that he gave up all hopes of succor this season (1785), even though 120 bateaux had been sent up since spring. In despair he exclaimed:

Judge what must be the feeling of those who were largely concerned in that business. I wish we could exchange Situations for a time with such persons as ever opposed to the sailings of private Vessels on the Lakes, they would be clamorous enough. I have done everything in my power to Obtain the redress necessary.[112]

William Robertson of Detroit [113] summed up the fur traders' and merchants' grievances, after the war, before the Quebec Council in 1788.[114] He said in part that the merchants were decidedly of the impression that, when the government prohibited the sailing of private vessels, a sufficient number of the King's ships would be available for carrying merchandise.

106 "Minutes" of Council of State, July 21, 1785, Canadian Archives, Q, XXV, 94–103. St. Leger was in charge of all troops.
107 Hamilton to St. Leger, July 21, 1785, ibid., 104.
108 St. Leger to the merchants, July 25, 1785, ibid., 159.
109 Ibid.
110 St. Leger to Sydney, July 25, 1785, ibid., 156.
111 For a sketch of the founder of McGill University, see Askin Papers, I, 73.
112 McGill to Hamilton, August 8, 1785, Canadian Archives, Q, XXV, 118.
113 For a sketch of Robertson see Askin Papers, I, 208.
114 Canadian Archives, Minutes of the Privy Council of Quebec, October 8, 1788, H, pt. iv, 613–17.

General Haldimand, with no previous notice to the merchants, in the summer of 1784 ordered the reduction of the naval establishment. The news reached Detroit the first of August and Jehu Hay stopped all outgoing vessels, had them unloaded and unrigged; then he discharged the crews. This in spite of the fact that, daily, goods were arriving at Carleton Island and Niagara for the western posts, resulting in confusion, crowding, and damage. Then the government ordered that preference in moving the goods should be given public stores and the Indian presents. This caused consternation among the traders, and they sent petitions, memorials, and letters besieging the Governor and Council for relief. As a result of these, the Governor ordered the ships to make ready to sail again, but this was most difficult, since there were no crews. Nevertheless, some men were brought together, and a few trips were made before the winter of 1784 arrived. Contrary to regulations, the goods were not shipped in rotation, for when forty bateau loads of goods arrived, belonging to some disbanded officers and to others who had "sufficient interest to procure them," they were sent up before some goods which "had lain fifteen months on the communication." Some of the latter even remained the second winter, while the owners were paying interest on their cost and charges of six per cent for carrying, besides storage for two years.

In the spring of 1785, Robertson further declared, the public stores and Indian presents were sent up; then followed the exchange of garrisons with baggage and stores. August arrived, and when more petitions were made the government did allow thirty-seven bateau loads to come to Detroit by Lake Erie, while twenty-two private vessels and small craft "ventured across the Lake." In addition, after repeated requests, the *Gage* was sent, and made one trip late in November, carrying twenty-seven bateau loads. For this voyage, the merchants had to give double allowance of pay and provisions to the crew, in order to "induce them to act with celerity." In addition, they paid the King at the rate of fifteen shillings a barrel of bulk freight.[115] Thus, explained Robertson, were brought ruin to the merchants and the loss of the fur trade to England. The government made promises to take all goods in rotation; instead, whenever public stores arrived, the merchandise of the traders was unloaded and then reloaded, some of it three or four times, and then detained in "miserable stores" for from twelve months to two years. All this led to vigorous protests from the merchants to the paying of the freight rates.

Finally the slow wheels of the government moved, and an ordinance was passed on May 8, 1788, which made the following provisions: [116]

1. Any *bona fide* British subject who has a pass may navigate a vessel.
2. Vessels must be under ninety tons.
3. Ships must be built and landed in His Majesty's dominions.
4. Crews and officers are to be British subjects.

Another ordinance was passed in October providing for superintendents of inland navigation at Detroit and Michilimackinac, with full instructions for them.[117] These regulations solved many of the navigation problems and the difficulties of transportation, and remained in force until the evacuation of Detroit in July, 1796.

[115] This was the usual charge for barrel freight.
For freight on the *Sagina*, Detroit, 1789.

July 5, one bbl.	15s
July 29, 40 13/15 bbl.	£ 30–13s
Sept. 10, one bbl.	15s
	£ 32– 3s

Angus McIntosh MSS., *passim*. In 1795 McIntosh paid Captain Mills £ 5–12 for passage from Fort Erie to Detroit. *Ibid*. For freight charges between Michilimackinac and the Grand Portage in 1778, see *Askin Papers*, I, 119. On page 101 there is mention of Captain Robertson's coming to Detroit from Niagara in three days.

[116] Canadian Archives, Q, XXXVIII, 280–88. In accord with this ordinance, Askin wrote that he and two associates were building "a fine Vessel fit for the Mackinac business." Askin to William Dickson, January 26, 1793, *Askin Papers*, I, 460.

[117] October, 1788, Canadian Archives, Q, XXXVIII, 288 ff. An account of the work of the Superintendent of Navigation at Detroit is found in *Askin Papers*, I, 483.

Thus the curtains were drawn on the first period of Great Britain's naval supremacy on the Upper Lakes. These were halcyon years in that it was the peculiar good fortune of the navy not to have been challenged by a civilized power. Nevertheless, it was this small fleet which kept Gladwin in touch with the outside world and brought the necessary supplies and reinforcements of men to his beleaguered garrison. Again, during the War for American Independence the British authority in the West must have collapsed entirely without the significant aid of the navy, and in times of peace it was practically the only means of communication and transportation between the several western posts and the East.

The historian can record no battles fought or victories won during the years 1760–1796, aside from the abortive attempts of some of Pontiac's men on the Detroit River in the summer of 1763. Possibly that explains why most writers have neglected or totally disregarded the significance of this small but important fleet. However, this period did demonstrate beyond a doubt the need of a naval establishment to maintain British control in the Old Northwest.

CHAPTER VIII

MICHIGAN AND THE AMERICAN
WAR OF INDEPENDENCE

One of the causes for the War of Independence as stated in the Declaration of Independence was that Great Britain had " abolished the free system of English laws in a neighbouring province, establishing therein an arbitrary government, and enlarging its boundaries so as to render it at once an example and fit instrument for introducing the same arbitrary rule into these colonies." [1] The act hereby designated was the Quebec Act of 1774, and the part to which the signers particularly objected was the inclusion of the region north of the Ohio within the new territory of Quebec. Within this area lay Michigan. Dr. Alvord has shown [2] that out of Shelburne's attempts to place an army on the frontier to protect the inhabitants, arose the vexatious problem of taxation — one of the immediate causes which rent the empire of George III asunder.

The beginning of the struggle of the Americans to gain their place as an independent nation had no immediate effect in the West. The frontier people but slowly grasped the meaning of the eastern struggle. There was very little the western folk could do to help the patriot cause, and perhaps they would even have preferred to remain distant spectators of the war. The leaders of the rebellion gave the West scanty attention. Congress concentrated its armies, its energy, and supplies upon the coast region, and left the West to care for itself. But in this connection it must not be understood that the colonies gave up their claims to the West. No patriot ever entertained

[1] Original draft of the Declaration of Independence is in the Library of Congress. Printed in MacDonald, *Documentary Source Book*, p. 193.
[2] Alvord, *Mississippi Valley in British Politics*, I, 241.

such an idea. All felt it was their destiny to spread across the illimitable and virgin West toward the setting sun.

The British were not willing to leave the West alone. They saw the great advantage to be gained by early using the Indians. Gage wrote Dartmouth in September, 1775, that Lord Dunmore had sent John Connolly to Boston " to impart a Project of raising " the people of Detroit and other settlers of the West to make a diversion upon the frontiers of Pennsylvania and Virginia.[3] Supplies were to be sent up the Mississippi and Ohio, and Gage planned, with the aid of Dunmore, to cut the colonies in two and restrict the war to New England. This plan failed, and late in December Connolly wrote Captain Lernoult at Detroit that he should be ready for an attack in the spring. He advised the Captain, if he judged it expedient, to evacuate Detroit and to move down the Mississippi through the Gulf and up the Atlantic to join Dunmore at Norfolk.[4] Lernoult was not the man to give up without a fight and so Detroit was not vacated.

During the war, Detroit was the western center from which radiated the British attacks to the east, south, and west. From it went war parties to the settlements of the Ohio, the Illinois, far into Kentucky and Pennsylvania, and even to St. Louis. The great Indian councils were held within the shadow of the Fort.[5] Every tribe that could be flattered, cajoled, or bought, received rum and presents largely from Detroit. It was the great war emporium of the West.

The garrison at Detroit contained one hundred and twenty soldiers under the command of Captain Lernoult when the war broke out.[6] The fort was protected by a stockade about

[3] Gage to Dartmouth, September 20, 1775, Carter, *Gage's Correspondence*, I, 415; Canadian Archives, C. O. 5, XCII, 37. The story of John Connolly is given in Thwaites and Kellogg, *Revolution on the Upper Ohio*, pp. 35 ff. It does not directly concern Michigan. See John Connolly, *Narrative of Transactions, Imprisonment and Suffering of John Connolly* (London, 1783).

[4] Connolly to Lernoult, December 16, 1775, *American Archives* (4th Ser.), IV, 618.

[5] *Mich. Hist. Colls.*, X, 268, 269, 500, 538, 542, 567, 576, 587. To a lesser degree this was also true of Michilimackinac.

[6] Unsigned letter, April 2, 1776, Thwaites and Kellogg, *Revolution on the Upper Ohio*, p. 147.

nine feet high made of pickets. There was a militia made up of three hundred and fifty French and English, mostly French under their own officers. Two armed schooners and three sloops manned by thirty " seamen and servants " under the command of Captain Alexander Grant were on the river commanding the fort.[7]

On November 9, 1775, Henry Hamilton arrived at Detroit as the new lieutenant governor and superintendent, " By the grace of King George the Third and the favor of the Earl of Dartmouth." [8] His journey was a hazardous one, for General Montgomery's army patrolled the waters and paths leading to Montreal. Hamilton, disguised as a Canadian, passed through these rather ineffectual American forces. After four days in a canoe, and " unprovided with everything," [9] Hamilton reached a place of safety, threw off his disguise, and travelled the remaining distance to Detroit as befitted an officer of George the Third. When spring arrived, he became enthusiastic over the beauty of the region around his new home.[10]

Hamilton found his time very much engrossed by holding Indian councils, sending agents out among the tribes to incite the natives, and caring for his routine work as post commander.[11] With presents, threats, and flattery he stirred up the Indians to let loose their fury upon the unprotected settlements of the frontier. Thus was inaugurated the Indian War in the West.[12] Fighting was almost continuous. In every corner of the wilderness the barbarous and bloody scenes of another Pontiac Rebellion broke out anew with redoubled fury.

Soon after Hamilton became governor at Detroit, he heard rumors that the Virginians were tampering with the Indians

[7] Ibid., pp. 148–50. There seems to be conflicting evidence here for Hamilton described the stockade as fifteen feet high and with a protected ditch. Hamilton to Dartmouth, August 29 and September 2, 1776, Mich. Hist. Colls., X, 265; James, George Rogers Clark, 30–31.
[8] Mich. Hist. Colls., X, 265, 268–69. Lord Harcourt had introduced Hamilton to Dartmouth, Harcourt to Dartmouth, March 15, 1775, Canadian Archives, Dartmouth Transcripts, II, pt. ii, 457.
[9] Mich. Hist. Colls., X, 267.
[10] Ibid., 266.
[11] Ibid., 268–70.
[12] Russell, " The Indian Policy of Henry Hamilton," 30 ff.

nearby.[13] Capturing some of them who were holding a meeting, he cut their belts, tore their messages, letters, and speeches in the presence of the assembled Indians. Thus with high-handed methods he restrained the red men. He wrote that they should " hold themselves in readiness next Spring to cooperate with His Majesty's Forces." Hamilton much feared the savages would fall in small parties upon the scattered settlers on the Ohio — " a deplorable sort of war," he said, " but which the arrogance, disloyalty, and imprudence of the Virginians has justly drawn down upon them." [14]

In August, 1776, William Wilson, a trader, Captain White Eyes, a Delaware Chief, and an Indian named Montour, " educated at Williamsburg, but a savage," had the " insolence " to appear at Detroit with a " letter, a string, and a Belt " from an agent of Virginia who was "soliciting " the Indians to go to a council at Pittsburgh.[15] Hamilton had a meeting with them and asked to see the messages they had. The Governor was considerably angered by the affair; so in high dudgeon he tore up the speech and cut the belt to pieces which he " contemptuously strewed " about the Council House.[16] Declaring that the Virginians were " enemies and traitors " to the King, he told the Indians he would suffer his right hand to be cut off before he would take " one of them by the hand." White Eyes was commanded to leave Detroit before sunset " as he regarded his head," while Wilson was ordered to depart at once.[17] The Governor gave them a canoe, blankets, shirts, and provisions for ten days, and, as Wilson says, " protected them because they came in the capacity of messengers." [18] Wilson informed the American Commissioners of Indian Affairs that Hamilton impressed upon him that all the Indian Nations were strong in their allegiance to the King, and that he [Hamilton] would be glad if all the people would

[13] *Mich. Hist. Colls.*, X, 268.
[14] *Ibid.*
[15] *Ibid.*, 269; " Report " of Wilson, September 26, 1776, *American Archives* (5th Ser.), II, 514–18.
[16] *Ibid.*, 516.
[17] *Ibid.*, 517.
[18] *Ibid.*, 516.

" consider the dreadful consequences of going to war with so terrible an enemy, and accept the King's pardon while it could be obtained." [19] He also told Wilson that the King had sent over several armies of twenty thousand each to conquer the recalcitrant Colonials.[20] It does not appear from the record that Wilson was much impressed by this tale. Hamilton, in reporting the affair to Dartmouth, said that the Virginians brought a copy of the Pennsylvania *Gazette* of July 25, containing a declaration of the Colonies by which they entirely threw off all dependence upon the Mother Country.[21] In this curious way the independence of America became known in the British capital of Michigan!

The Americans realized the great importance of Detroit. They had hoped that Canada would unite with the Colonies and thus Detroit would fall into their hands. With the disastrous campaigns of Arnold and Montgomery, their hopes faded. Many plans were proposed to Congress to capture Detroit,[22] and as early as April 23, 1776, Congress resolved " that an Expedition against Detroit be undertaken." [23] Not until April 29 was a committee appointed to prepare a plan for the expedition and the estimate of the expense.[24] General Charles Lee urged that the expedition be immediately sent,[25] and although Congress knew that there appeared to be much dissatisfaction at Detroit,[26] they postponed all action until Washington arrived. Nothing at all was accomplished because of the lack of funds. Arthur St. Clair had also proposed a volunteer expedition against Detroit,[27] but neither Congress[28]

[19] *Ibid.*, 517.
[20] *Ibid.*
[21] Hamilton to Dartmouth, August 29 and September 2, 1776, *Mich. Hist. Colls.*, X, 269. Hamilton made a mistake of one day in the date of the *Gazette*, for it was published on the twenty-fourth. James, *Clark*, 45–46.
[22] W. C. Ford (ed.), *Journals of the Continental Congress from 1774–1789* (Washington, 1904–1908), IV, 268.
[23] *Ibid.*, 301.
[24] *Ibid.*, 318.
[25] *Ibid.*, 373.
[26] Thwaites and Kellogg, *Revolution on the Upper Ohio*, pp. 147–151; *American Archives* (5th Ser.), I, 36 ff.
[27] W. H. Smith, *The St. Clair Papers* (Cincinnati, 1882), I, 15.
[28] Hancock to Morris and Wilson, September 15, 1775, *American Archives* (4th Ser.), III, 717.

nor Washington [29] gave hearty approval, and the project was given up. Hamilton at Detroit was aware of the American plans, and, although he did not feel greatly alarmed, he worked hard to put the fort in a state of defense.[30] In the fall of 1776, councils with all the northwestern Indian tribes were held at Detroit.[31] Hamilton, carrying out his orders,[32] enlisted the savages to be ready in the spring. He plied the Indians with presents, with rum, speeches, and promises. Troops of white rangers, consisting of French, British, and Tories, were organized at Detroit. They acted as allies and leaders of the red men. Among the most outstanding of these leaders were Alexander McKee, Matthew Elliott, and Simon Girty.[33] Hamilton advised Germain that he would raise a company of Chasseurs " by gentle or other means " of the active and spirited young men of the best French families.[34]

All through the winter of 1776–1777, the Indians were making preparations to take the war path. Runners were dispatched through the leafless, frozen forests to stir up the farthest tribes. Once more the warriors, as in 1763, sang the war song and danced the war dance, all the time pounding the ground with their war clubs. Bodies were gaudily bedecked, weapons made ready, bone necklaces were put on, and when spring approached the braves were ready.[35]

Hamilton had been so successful in arousing the savages that in June, 1776, he informed Carleton that he had explained His Majesty's proclamation with the special grants promised [36] to the various Indian tribes. Shortly after, he announced that the Ottawa, Chippewa, Wyandot, Miami, Potawatomi,

[29] Washington to Schuyler, November 5, 1775, *ibid.*, 1368.
[30] *Mich. Hist. Colls.*, X, 265.
[31] For the many councils see *ibid.*, X, 268, 269; for all other councils see *ibid.*, IX, 442, 452, 482; X, 348, 420; XI, 465, 470, 490; XIII, 89 ff.
[32] Carleton to Hamilton, October 6, 1776, Canadian Archives, Q, XIII, 87; *Mich. Hist. Colls.*, IX, 344.
[33] C. W. Butterfield, *History of the Girtys* (Cincinnati, 1890), *passim.*
[34] Hamilton to Germain, June 23, 1777, Canadian Archives, Q, XIV, 84.
[35] Roosevelt, *Winning of the West*, II, chap. V; Moore, *Northwest Under Three Flags*, p. 180; James, *Clark*, chap. III.
[36] Hamilton to Carleton, June 16, 1777, Canadian Archives, Q, XIV, 26. He had also written in June that he could assemble 1,000 warriors in three weeks if Carleton desired. Same to same, June 15, 1777, *ibid.*, XIII, 342.

Shawnee, and Delaware had taken up the hatchet.[37] By July the Governor of Detroit and the Indian Superintendent, Jehu Hay, were of the opinion that in a few weeks over a thousand warriors would be scattered over the frontiers in small bands.[38] In September this number was increased to at least eleven hundred and fifty, of whom seven hundred received their equipment or at least their ammunition from Detroit.[39] This gave to the year 1777 the very sinister name of the " bloody year."

Many scalps were brought to Detroit in 1777 and 1778. Among the goods listed in 1778 were one hundred and fifty dozen scalping knives.[40] In June of 1778 Hamilton congratulated the assembled warriors upon having succeeded in almost all of their enterprises, and because they had taken a number of prisoners " and a far greater number of scalps." [41] September showed nine scalps brought in by the Chippewa,[42] and later the Indians brought in eighty-one more,[43] and in 1780, De Peyster wrote Haldimand that the Indians were daily bringing in scalps and prisoners, " having at present a great field to act upon." [44] Hamilton informed Carleton that early in 1778 the Indians had captured seventy-three prisoners and taken one hundred and twenty-nine scalps.[45] But he wrote that he presented a gift on " every proof of obedience they shew, in sparing the lives of such as are incapable of defending themselves." [46] Thus every means was employed " that Provi-

[37] Same to same, June 23, 1777, ibid., 79.
[38] Same to same, July 3, 1777, ibid., 42. July 27, Hamilton wrote Germain that only 319 had left Detroit and gone to war. Ibid., 72.
[39] Same to same, September 5, 1777, ibid., 225; James, Clark, chap. III.
[40] Mich. Hist. Colls., IX, 471. This is not unusual, as scalping knives formed a part of every frontiersman's equipment. See Russell, " Indian Policy of Henry Hamilton," and Roosevelt, Winning of the West, II, passim.
[41] Hamilton to Indians, June 15, 1778, Mich. Hist. Colls., IX, 445.
[42] Hamilton to Germain, September 5, 1777, Canadian Archives, Q, XIV, 225.
[43] Same to Haldimand, September 16, 1777, Mich. Hist. Colls., IX, 477.
[44] De Peyster to Haldimand, May 17, 1780, ibid., X, 396. For a discussion of the practice of scalping see Russell, " Indian Policy of Henry Hamilton."
[45] Hamilton to Carleton, 1778, ibid., IX, 431.
[46] Same to Haldimand, undated, ibid., 465. See especially A. M. Davis, " The Indians and the Border Warfare of the Revolution," in Justin Winsor, Narrative and Critical History of America, VI, 604 ff. This was Germain's orders of March 26, 1777. Mich. Hist. Colls., IX, 347.

dence " had put in " His Majesty's Hands, for crushing the Rebellion." [47]

There was a rumor spread throughout the frontier in August, 1777, that the British from Detroit, ten to sixteen thousand strong, were marching towards Pittsburgh.[48] George Morgan, the American Indian Commissioner at Pittsburgh, urgently advocated an attack upon Detroit.[49] He felt the French were sympathetic, and even Hamilton admitted that.[50] Morgan asserted that with the fall of Detroit the Indians would be compelled to enter into an alliance with the Americans.[51] But again Congress had no money and the plan went unfulfilled. An event of some significance did occur when General Edward Hand was sent to take command of Fort Pitt.[52] This looked as if Congress had determined upon a more aggressive western policy. Outside the scope of this study, but indirectly connected with it, were other events which occurred, such as the almost total extermination of the Kentucky settlements by the Indians, and the barbarous murder of Chief Cornstalk and three of his tribe.[53]

General Hand (later replaced by General Lachlan McIntosh) was interested in promoting plans to capture Detroit.[54] But very little was accomplished and throughout the war Detroit was not endangered from the east. These attempts, however, did cause a great amount of uneasiness among the British. In the early part of 1778, Captain Bird was sent from Detroit with a few English regulars to take the post at Sandusky. He carried along a large supply of presents, and was able to induce the Indians to assist him in laying siege to one

[47] R. G. Thwaites and L. P. Kellogg, *Frontier Defense on the Upper Ohio* (Madison, 1912), p. 38.

[48] Morgan to Board of War, July 17, 1778, *Wis. Hist. Colls.,* XXIII, 112–13.

[49] Hamilton to Carleton. undated, *Mich. Hist. Colls.,* IX, 431.

[50] *Wis. Hist. Colls.,* XXIII, 112–13.

[51] Thwaites and Kellogg, *Revolution on the Upper Ohio,* p. 256.

[52] *Ibid., Frontier Defense,* p. xii; Roosevelt, *Winning of the West,* II, 40–54.

[53] Thwaites and Kellogg, *loc. cit.,* introduction; *Wis. Hist. Colls.,* XXIII, 18–32. McIntosh was succeeded by Colonel Daniel Brodhead.

[54] For a full account of these attempts see Dr. Kellogg's scholarly account, in *Wis. Hist. Colls.,* XXIII, introduction; also *Ill. Hist. Colls.,* VIII, introduction.

of McIntosh's outlying posts.[55] The Indians later deserted, due no doubt to Clark's great victory at Vincennes, and the expedition came to naught.

An event of considerable interest occurred in April, 1778, when Charles Beaubien and Louis Lorimer returned to Detroit from an attack upon some Kentucky settlers.[56] They had been aided by the Shawnee Indians. With them were twenty-seven captives, including Daniel Boone. Hamilton wrote Carleton that the savages so completely surprised the Kentuckians that the captives were taken without "killing or losing a man"; but he was much chagrined because they were afraid to attack the fort.[57] "By Boone's account," said Hamilton, "the people of the frontier have been incessantly harrassed by parties of Indians they have not been able to sow grain and at Kentucke will not have a morsel of bread by the middle of June. They have no clothing, nor do they expect any relief from Congress."[58] No doubt their dilemma, Boone explained, will probably induce the settlers to trust the savages "who have shewn so much humanity to their prisoners" and come to Detroit before the winter.[59] Hamilton was still unaware of what metal the American frontiersman was made.

On June 14,[60] and 29,[61] Hamilton assembled all the braves of the Ottawa, Chippewa, Huron, Shawnee, Mohawk, Mingo, Miami, Delaware, and Potawatomi tribes at Detroit. The Governor of Detroit assisted by Captain Lernoult, Lieu-

[55] *Wis. Hist. Colls.*, XXIII, 25.
[56] Hamilton to Carleton, April 25, 1778, *Mich. Hist. Colls.*, IX, 435; Thwaites and Kellogg, *Frontier Defense*, p. 283.
[57] *Mich. Hist. Colls.*, IX, 435.
[58] *Ibid.*
[59] Hamilton treated Boone very kindly, as did all the people of Detroit. The Indians were greatly attached to Boone and refused a ransom of £ 100 offered by Hamilton. Boone was adopted by the Shawnee, and was a captive for five months. Later he escaped and warned the Kentucky settlements of a proposed attack by the Indians. Roosevelt, *Winning of the West*, II, 42–44; Constance L. Skinner, *Pioneers of the Old Southwest* (New Haven, 1920), p. 143–46; R. G. Thwaites, *Daniel Boone* (New York, 1903), pp. 149–58.
[60] *Mich. Hist. Colls.*, IX, 442 ff.
[61] *Ibid.*, 452 ff.

tenant Caldwell, the Indian agents, Hay, McKee, and Girty, and Captain Edward Abbott, former Governor of Vincennes, chanted the war song, danced the war dance, and gave the Indians large quantities of presents. Hamilton returned thanks to the Great Spirit, and congratulated the savages upon being so faithful to the King. He then gave them a large belt for having succeeded in almost all their enterprises. He spoke to them of their success in driving the rebels back to the coast into the hands of the King's troops, and also announced the recall of Carleton who was succeeded by Haldimand — " a brave officer, a wise man, and esteemed by all who know him." [62] Hamilton then removed the old French medals from the necks of the Indians and replaced them with the English, after which the war song was sung and they all danced the war dance. [63]

The Indians in the councils which followed replied to the English that the wiles of the Virginians and Spanish had not affected their loyalty, and they were pleased to wage war upon the Virginians. [64]

Scarcely had the Indians returned home when Hamilton received news by an " Express " from the Illinois that a party of rebels, about three hundred in number, had taken Philippe Rocheblave prisoner, put him in irons, and exacted from the inhabitants of Kaskaskia an oath of obedience to Congress. [65] The " Express " also stated that Gibault, " a French Priest, had his horse ready saddled " to go to Vincennes to receive the submission of the people there, and that the rebels were on their way to Cahokia. [66]

All was confusion at Detroit! Hamilton had proposed a campaign in January, 1778, against Fort Pitt, in order to fore-stall any American attack, [67] but General Carleton never favored the plan. The Detroit commandant was a man of

[62] *Ibid.*, 443–46.
[63] *Ibid.*, 451–52, 456.
[64] *Ibid.*, 453–57.
[65] Hamilton to Carleton, August 8, 1778, *ibid.*, 459; James, *Clark*, pp. 118–23.
[66] *Mich. Hist. Colls.*, IX, 459.
[67] Same to same, undated (probably January 15, 1778), *ibid.*, 431.

tremendous energy, and he at once began to make the best of a very bad situation. Realizing the necessity of holding the Wabash Indians loyal, he dispatched an agent to de Cèloron to hold these tribes firmly to England.[68] Nothing came of this effort, as one of Clark's lieutenants, Leonard Helm by name, arrived about the same time, and de Cèloron fled.[69] Hamilton summoned all the Indians to meet him at Detroit,[70] and in conference the commander found the red men very anxious to accompany him.[71] His pride was aroused by the rebels' insults. Haldimand was of the opinion that under proper leadership the Indians could clear the Illinois of the rebels; nevertheless, he did not direct Hamilton to undertake a regular expedition.[72] He only authorized him to employ the Wabash Indians to dislodge the Americans — but this information never reached Detroit.[73] All during September, 1778, everybody in Detroit worked unceasingly, mending boats, baking biscuits, and preparing ammunition and other stores.[74] Provisions of all kinds, and plenty of presents for the Indians, were forwarded in fifteen large bateaux and pirogues, each holding from eighteen hundred to three thousand pounds. On October 7 the expedition left Detroit under Hamilton's leadership, after having sung the war song [75] and received the blessing of Father Potier [76] upon condition that they continue " strictly adhering to their oath." The force consisted of thirty-six English regulars, under two lieutenants, forty-five Detroit volunteers (mostly French) under Captain Guillaume La Mothe; seventy-nine Detroit militia under a

[68] Same to same, August 8, 1778, *ibid.*, 459, 491.
[69] W. H. English, *Conquest of the Country Northwest of the Ohio, 1778–1783, and the Life of General George Rogers Clark* (Indianapolis, 1896), I, 427; James, *Clark*, p. 122; *Mich. Hist. Colls.*, IX, 486.
[70] " Council at Detroit," September 24, 1778, *ibid.*, 482 ff.
[71] Hamilton to Haldimand, October, 1778, *ibid.*, 487.
[72] C. W. Butterfield, *History of George Rogers Clark's Conquest of the Illinois and the Wabash Towns, 1778–1779* (Columbus, 1904), pp. 163–68.
[73] Haldimand to Hamilton, August 26, 1778, *Mich. Hist. Colls.*, IX, 402.
[74] Hamilton to Haldimand, September 22, 1778, *ibid.*, 477, 491. See Macomb Papers for the expenses of the expedition.
[75] *Mich. Hist. Colls.*, IX, 482, 492.
[76] *Ibid.*, 491. The priest Pierre Gibault at Kaskaskia was a staunch supporter of the Americans and Potier at Detroit was equally as staunch for the British.

major and two captains, seventeen members of the Indian Department, and sixty Indians, making a grand total of two hundred and forty-three men.[77]

The route followed was down the Detroit River to Lake Erie, on Lake Erie to the Maumee, up this river to its source, over a short portage to the Wabash, the " Petit Rivierre," and down the Wabash to Vincennes. The journey was about six hundred miles in length and took seventy-one days.[78] It had three main objects.[79] These were:

(1) To erect a fort at the junction of the Ohio and Mississippi in order to " bridle " American trade;

(2) To get control of the mouth of the Missouri with the hope of underselling the Spanish;

(3) To dislodge the rebels from the Illinois and regain the Mississippi trade; thus the expedition might contribute to the security of the Floridas.

Perhaps the expedition relieved Hamilton from trying circumstances at Detroit. It was at this time the grand jury at Montreal had prepared the presentment against him and Dejean.[80] During the journey the English were joined by large numbers of Indians.[81] Hamilton arrived within three miles of Vincennes before Captain Leonard Helm, who was in charge, knew of his approach. Consternation seized the French people and, with only one man to aid him, Helm surrendered the post in December, 1778.[82] The 621 inhabitants were summoned to the church and renewed their oath of alle-

[77] Ibid., 487, 492. Clark reported Hamilton's forces numbered 800. J. A. James, George Rogers Clark Papers (Springfield, 1912), I, 138; James, Clark, p. 132.
[78] Hamilton's Report, Mich. Hist. Colls., IX, 495; Ill. Hist. Colls., VIII, 181.
[79] Ibid., lxx; Hamilton to Haldimand, September 22, 1778, Mich. Hist. Colls., IX, 477–78; James, Clark, p. 132.
[80] Mich. Hist. Colls., X, 293, 304, 336.
[81] Ill. Hist. Colls., I, 220.
[82] Van Tyne, The American Revolution, chap. XV; Roosevelt, Winning of the West, II, chap. VII; Moore, Northwest Under Three Flags, chap. VII; Avery, History of U. S., VI, chap. VIII; R. G. Thwaites, How George Rogers Clark Won the Northwest (Chicago, 1903), p. 211; English, George Rogers Clark, I, chaps. VIII–XI; G. A. Hinsdale, The Old Northwest (New York, 1888), chaps. IX–X; R. L. Schuyler, The Transition in Illinois from the British to the American Government (New York, 1908), chap. V; James, Clark, chap. VII.

giance.[83] Hamilton kept a garrison of ninety, sending the Detroit militia home, while most of the Indians returned to their villages. But before the following February ended, Hamilton was in turn attacked and defeated by George Rogers Clark, a young Virginian, and a most able leader and a determined frontier fighter. Clark had carried out a daring winter march from Kaskaskia of over 180 miles, " one of the most heroic and dramatic undertakings of the whole Revolution," according to Professor James. Hamilton, taken unawares, was forced to surrender at discretion, and then according to his account,[84] was treated with unusual harshness through long months of imprisonment. The truth was that, as the war continued, bitterness increased, and especially on the frontier, where the combatants were rangers, Indians, and backwoodsmen, the fighting became a series of savage reprisals.

When Hamilton began his elaborate plans and preparations for his Vincennes campaign, he sent word to De Peyster at Michilimackinac and to the commander at St. Joseph,[85] informing them of his plans, and asking for the co-operation of the Indians by " the way of the Illinois River." De Peyster had previously sent a " belt " to the Illinois tribes to encourage them against the Colonials, but he found the rebels too firmly fixed for his efforts to have any prospect of success.[86] He gave Hamilton his hearty support, and tried to convince the tribes over whom he had some influence that it was to their commercial advantage to aid the English.[87] Most of the Indians who frequented Michilimackinac had dispersed be-

[83] *Ill. Hist. Colls.,* VIII, lxxiii; James, *Clark,* p. 134; Hamilton to Shelburne, April 9, 1782, Shelburne Papers, LXVI, 177–99.

[84] *Mich. Hist. Colls.,* IX, 489–516, gives Hamilton's full account of his expedition against Vincennes and of his imprisonment. See also Canadian Archives, *Report for 1881–1884,* 24 ff. The action of the Virginia council is found in *The Remembrancer,* VIII, 337. Hamilton described his imprisonment in a long letter to Shelburne of April 8, 1782, Shelburne Papers, LXVI, 177–79. Haldimand protested to Washington, August 29, 1779, in no uncertain terms condemning the barbarous treatment of Hamilton by Virginia. He said he would retaliate if something was not done. *Ibid.,* Q, XVI, pt. ii, 371–73. Hamilton was released in October, 1780.

[85] Hamilton to Haldimand, September 16, 1778, *Ill. Hist. Colls.,* I, 364; *Mich. Hist. Colls.,* IX, 475.

[86] De Peyster to Haldimand, September 21, 1778, *ibid.,* 371–72.

[87] Same to same, *ibid.; Wis. Hist. Colls.,* XI, 117.

cause of the lateness of the season, and those who could be reached were far from showing any enthusiasm for the enterprise.[88] Nevertheless, De Peyster did all he could to aid Hamilton. He sent Langlade to stir up the Ottawa and Chippewa, and also Gautier to St. Joseph to encourage the Potawatomi.[89] He wrote Louis Chevalier, a trader at St. Joseph, to raise what Indians he could and to give Hamilton " every assistance in his power." [90] At the same time, he suggested to Haldimand that a body of Indians be sent " from Labay to the Prarie de chiern " and down the Mississippi River, early in the spring as the country was full of resources.[91] Gautier and Langlade were unsuccessful in their efforts, and so De Peyster sent the former back to his post on the Mississippi, and the latter to Green Bay.[92] They carried speeches and belts to " exhort the Indians to be ready in the Spring if called upon." [93] Thus in spite of De Peyster's sincere efforts to assist Hamilton, he was unsuccessful.

Hamilton sent word, from his post at Vincennes, during the winter of 1778–1779, to Langlade at Green Bay to come with all the Indians he could collect and assist him in an attack upon Kaskaskia.[94] Gautier was also advised to the same effect. He was to gather all the red men of the Upper Mississippi and descend to the rebel post, while Langlade was to come down Lake Michigan, and thence by the Illinois River. Thus with Hamilton coming from the east an attack would be made upon Kaskaskia from three directions. Gautier and Langlade found their earnest efforts to arouse the Indians

---

[88] Same to same, October 24, 1778, ibid., 119; Ill. Hist. Colls., I, 364; Mich. Hist. Colls., IX, 374.

[89] Same to same, October 27, 1778, ibid., 376–77; idem, May 29, 1779; ibid., XIX, 425.

[90] Same to same, October 24, 1778, ibid., IX, 375; XIX, 375–76.

[91] Ibid., IX, 375.

[92] Gautier, a nephew of Charles Langlade, did not reach St. Joseph until December, and he found Chevalier had already taken the few Indians which could be raised to Hamilton's aid. Langlade found the savages he went among so angry for not receiving previous notice that they declined to start until spring. De Peyster to Haldimand, January 29, 1779, ibid., 377–78; Gautier to De Peyster, April 19, 1779, ibid., XIX, 397–98.

[93] Ibid., IX, 378; Wis. Hist. Colls., XI, 122–23.

[94] De Peyster to Haldimand, May 13, 1779, Ill. Hist. Colls., I, 436–38.

met with much opposition from agents that Clark had sent into the region.[95] Some chiefs had already signed a treaty with Clark at Cahokia.[96] The Indians were naturally following the victorious side. Gautier and Langlade, with great patience, finally raised a small body of Indians, with whom they proceeded as far as Lake Michigan, where Milwaukee now stands. Here they received news of Hamilton's debacle and their forces melted away like " snow before a summer's sun." [97] The Indians had become so insolent that they mocked Gautier when he harangued them, and even forced him to release one hundred and twenty of his prisoners.[98]

Rumors reached De Peyster in the early spring that the Colonials were advancing against his post from Illinois coming by Lake Michigan. Frightened squaws reported that they had seen boats building near Milwaukee and Chicago, but later De Peyster informed Haldimand that these rumors were the inventions of " some evil-minded Indians." [99] At the same time it was thought that the Ottawa and Chippewa had accepted belts from the rebels to remain neutral in the event of an attack upon Michilimackinac.[100] De Peyster immediately began to put his post in a state of defense. The sand dunes on the west were levelled. Presents were sent to the Sioux and Winnebagoes to persuade them to oppose any movement of the " Virginians " up the Mississippi or Rock Rivers. Gautier with a group of faithful Indians was ordered to destroy the post at Peoria, where a number of traders who secretly favored

[95] Gautier to De Peyster, April 19, 1779, *Mich. Hist. Colls.*, XIX, 397–98; *Wis. Hist. Colls.*, XI, 126–27; M. M. Quaife, *Chicago and the Old Northwest, 1673–1835* (Chicago, 1913), and Louise P. Kellogg, in *Wis. Hist. Colls.*, XXIII, XXIV, introduction, give exhaustive accounts of De Peyster's work, upon which I relied. See also Dr. Kellogg's *British Régime in Wisconsin*, chap. X.

[96] *Ibid.*, XI, 130; XVIII, 384; *Ill. Hist. Colls.*, VIII, 246–55; De Peyster to Haldimand, June 27, 1779, *Mich. Hist. Colls.*, IX, 389.

[97] *Wis. Hist. Colls.*, XI, 128, 132, 134; De Peyster to Haldimand, May 13 and June 1, 1779, *Mich. Hist. Colls.*, IX, 381, 383; same to Campbell, May 13, 1779, *ibid.*, XIX, 411.

[98] Gautier to De Peyster, April 19, 1779, *ibid.*, 397.

[99] De Peyster to Haldimand, May 2 and May 13, 1779, *ibid.*, IX, 380; Canadian Archives, B, XCVI, pt. i, 32.

[100] *Ibid.; Mich. Hist. Colls.*, IX, 380.

the rebels had gathered.[101] De Peyster himself held a great
council with the Indians in the region of his post. His address
to them is a curious mixture of Indian terms and skilful ap-
peals to the fickle red men to maintain their English allegiance.[102] He then wrote Haldimand that he did not care how
soon Clark might arrive if he came by Lake Michigan, providing " the Indians prove staunch & above all that the Canadians do not follow the example of their brethren at the Illinois
who have joined the Rebels to a man."[103] De Peyster was well
aware that the fate of his post depended upon that of Detroit,
for if the latter fell his would have to be surrendered though
the rebels might " not send a man against it." [104]

Panic seized the inhabitants of Detroit when news arrived
about Hamilton's defeat.[105] Lernoult was greatly perturbed
by the coolness of his Indian allies and their widespread dissatisfaction. He was informed that all of the powerful tribes
of the Wabash region were either neutral or actively engaged
in the Colonial cause.[106] But most disconcerting to the Captain was the condition of the Wyandot, his nearest and most
powerful neighbors. It was reported that they were favorably
considering a belt forwarded to them by the Delaware to make

[101] De Peyster to Haldimand, June 27, 1779, *ibid.*, IX, 389. Gautier again
was unsuccessful. *Ibid.*, 395; Gautier to De Peyster, April 19, 1779, *ibid.*, XIX,
397–98; De Peyster to Campbell, May 13, 1779, *ibid.*, 411.

[102] " Speech " of July 4, 1779, *Wis. Hist. Colls.*, XVIII, 377–90. Also published in De Peyster, *Miscellanies.*

[103] De Peyster to Haldimand, May 13, 1779, *Mich. Hist. Colls.*, IX, 381.
Bennett of De Peyster's garrison was sent to watch the Potawatomi at St.
Joseph, and Langlade was to get all the English allies on the west of Lake
Michigan and then join Bennett at Chicago. Again these plans failed. Bennett's
Journal, *Wis. Hist. Colls.*, XVIII, 398–401; De Peyster to Haldimand, July 9,
1779, *Mich. Hist. Colls.*, IX, 390; De Peyster to Bolton, July 6, 1779, *ibid.*,
XIX, 448; Bennett to Lernoult, August 18, 1779, *ibid.*, 456. Copy of Bennett's
letter of August 9, 1779, *ibid.*, IX, 392–93; Bennett's Report, September 1,
1779, *ibid.*, 395.

[104] De Peyster to Brehm, June 20, 1779, *ibid.*, 387.

[105] James, *Clark*, pp. 134–46 gives a vivid picture of Clark's recapture of
Vincennes. Even before Hamilton's capture, the Detroit officials demanded
his return. Captain Lernoult wrote: " The loss of Governor Hamilton is a most
feeling one to me, I find the burden heavy without assistance, it requires I
confess superior abilities, & a better constitution. . . . I beg leave to report to
you the necessity of a reinforcement being sent as the consequences may be
fatal." Lernoult to Bolton, March 26, 1779, *Mich. Hist. Colls.*, IX, 430.

[106] McKee to Lernoult, May 26, 1779, *ibid.*, XIX, 423–24; Brehm to Haldimand, May 28, 1779, *ibid.*, IX, 411.

THE WAR OF INDEPENDENCE

peace with the Americans.[107] Later they did make a treaty with the Colonials, and thus helped the Americans in protecting the frontier.[108]

A great council was held at Detroit in June, 1779, of the Ottawa, Chippewa, and Potawatomi.[109] The English attempted to appease them and allay their suspicions, but to no avail. The Indians declared they were going to visit their " brothers, the Virginians, to make peace and receive that which is good." Then, according to the Indian story, Lernoult, in high dudgeon, flung defiance at them and their rebel allies.

Lernoult greatly strengthened the fort at Detroit and made ready to receive any American attack.[110] He utilized the Loyalists, who had escaped from Pittsburgh, to keep the tribes across the Ohio loyal. The services of McKee and Girty were enlisted and through their efforts the Indians again spread desolation throughout the Kentucky settlements.[111] But all of the English fears and preparations were in vain for the Americans were unable to carry out any concerted plan for an attack upon their posts. Thus the curtain fell on the year 1779, which ended the first phase of the war in Michigan. The greatest offensive operations planned by the English from Michigan during the war came to an inglorious end.

The year 1779 had closed most successfully for the Colonials in the West. Clark had driven out the British from their posts in Illinois and Indiana, and Hamilton and his forces had been captured and the leaders sent to Virginia.[112] Clark adopted a most unusual policy with Hamilton's men. He discharged

[107] Ibid., 411; Ill. Hist. Colls., VIII, 109.
[108] Wis. Hist. Colls., XXIII, 33.
[109] Ibid., 363.
[110] Bolton to Haldimand, February 12, 1779, Mich. Hist. Colls., XIX, 373; Bird to Powell, August 13, 1782, ibid., X, 626; Lyster wrote Moorehead, February 4, 1779: "We worked Every Day since it began but Christmas Day as no weather Ever hinders us let it be Ever so bad, Capn Lernoult and all the Officers work Constantly . . . the merchants and all the inhabitants in the sittlement work 3 Days out of Every nine." Ill. Hist. Colls., VIII, 101. Lernoult wrote Hamilton, February 9, 1779: "The Merchants lend a hand Willingly the Canadians pr force." Ibid., 109.
[111] Wis. Hist. Colls., XXIII, 384–85; Butterfield, History of the Girtys, chaps. XII, XIII.
[112] Ante, p. 197.

the French volunteers upon their taking the oath of neutrality instead of sending them to Virginia,[113] as they had been led to expect. Some of these joined Clark's army. Those who returned to Detroit were given boats, arms, and provisions. The boats were sold upon reaching their destination and the proceeds shared. This act of magnanimity was calculated to aid the American cause, and it did.[114] Clark assured the French that he would be in Detroit almost as soon as they, and he showed them a copy of the alliance between France and the United States. " I after this," he wrote, " had Spies constant to and from Detroit I learnt they answered every purpose that I could have wished for, by prejudiceing their friends in favor of America." [115] It was Clark's greatest desire to lead his men northward and capture Detroit. " I learn by your letter to Govr. Hamilton," he wrote Lernoult at Detroit, " that you were very busy making new works, I am glad to hear it, as it saves the Ammericans some expenses in building." [116]

The victory of Clark put the British in Michigan on the defensive for a while. Clark had completely won over the Indians in the region of the Wabash, Illinois, Rock, and Miami Rivers; [117] and thus the English had to spend even greater sums for presents to win back their former allies.[118]

Clark was fully cognizant of the importance of his victory and he at once began to plan for an attack upon Detroit. " This stroke," he wrote, " will nearly put an end to the Indian

[113] " Clark's Memoir, 1773-1779," *Ill. Hist. Colls.*, VIII, 291-92. See particularly the excellent introduction by James, lxxxviii ff.

[114] *Ibid.*, I, 436. For the most scholarly and exhaustive account of Clark's work, see James, *Clark,* chaps. IX-XII.

[115] Clark to Mason, November 19, 1779, *Ill. Hist. Colls.*, VIII, 146. Clark was informed that the French at Detroit celebrated Hamilton's defeat for three days. That the Americans would be successful was openly expressed; even the children drank to Clark's success. This is no doubt a colored statement. Helm to Clark, May 31, 1779, *ibid.*, 324. Clark also dealt diplomatically with the Indians, Clark to Mason, November 19, 1779, *ibid.*, 146-49.

[116] Clark to Lernoult, March 16, 1779, *ibid.*, 306-7; *Mich. Hist. Colls.*, X, 309.

[117] *Ill. Hist. Colls.*, VIII, 149. Clark, it is claimed, secured the neutrality of at least three to four thousand warriors. See *Collection of Virginia State Papers,* III, 501.

[118] Haldimand to Lernoult, July 23, 1779, *Mich. Hist. Colls.*, IX, 408. See also 411, 423, 634; X, 465.

War." [119] He counted upon aid from Kentucky,[120] from Virginia,[121] and from the French of the Illinois.[122] Jefferson also became greatly interested in an expedition to capture Detroit.[123] He urged Washington,[124] to whom Clark also appealed, to use every means at his disposal to aid Clark. But Clark was doomed to disappointment. Every attempt upon his part to collect men and supplies for so great a campaign came to naught.[125] " Never was a person more mortified than I was at this time, to see so fair an opportunity to push a victory; Detroit lost for want of a few men." [126] Thus Clark expressed the defeat of his plans.

The British in Detroit were well aware of Clark's program. They had hoped to recapture Vincennes but had to give up their plans, and they likewise did not succeed in their efforts directed against Fort Pitt.[127] They strengthened the fort, and urged Haldimand to send reinforcements, which he did.[128] Dissatisfaction was rife among the Indians and was rapidly becoming open.[129] The French were also alarmed over the report that France, Spain, and the Colonies had formed an alliance to drive out the English from America.[130] Expeditions were sent out from Michilimackinac [131] and Detroit to

[119] Clark to Harrison, March 10, 1779, *Ill. Hist. Colls.*, VIII, 305.
[120] Clark to Mason, November 19, 1779, *ibid.*, 150; " Clark's Memoir," *ibid.*, 300–301.
[121] Clark to Harrison, March 10, 1779, *ibid.*, 305.
[122] Bowman to Clark, June 3, 1779, *ibid.*, 327.
[123] Jefferson to Clark, December 25, 1780, Ford (ed.), *Writings of Jefferson*, II, 298, 345, 375; *Ill. Hist. Colls.*, VIII, 485 ff.
[124] *Ibid.*
[125] " Clark's Memoir, 1773–1779," *Ill. Hist. Colls.*, VIII, 300.
[126] Clark to Mason, November 19, 1779, *ibid.*, cix–cx. See James, " George Rogers Clark and Detroit," *Miss. Valley Hist. Soc. Proc., 1908–1910*, pp. 291–317, for a careful study of Clark's plans; James, *Clark*, pp. 171–72.
[127] *Ill. Hist. Colls.*, VIII, cx.
[128] Haldimand to Clinton, August 29, 1779, *Mich. Hist. Colls.*, XIX, 461.
[129] De Peyster to Haldimand, August 13, 1779, *ibid.*, IX, 392; Brehm to same, May 28, 1779, *ibid.*, 411; same to same wrote on July 5, 1779: " Fear acts stronger on them than all the arguments that can be made use of to convince them of the Enemy's ill designs against their Lands." *Ibid.*, 417. Only the Sioux and Menominee Indians remained true to the English. De Peyster to Haldimand, July 9, 1779, *ibid.*, 390.
[130] Brehm to Haldimand, May 28, 1779, *ibid.*, 411.
[131] *Ante*, pp. 198 ff.

keep the Indians loyal and to intercept any units of Clark's army which were out scouting.

The most important of these expeditions was the one sent out from Detroit by De Peyster [132] under the command of Captain Bird. Bird set out from Detroit in May of 1780 with one hundred and fifty whites, one thousand well-equipped Indians, and two pieces of light artillery. The expedition went up the Glaize and down the Great Miamis to the Ohio. It planned to attack Clark's post at the Falls.[133] Learning of Clark's receiving reinforcements,[134] Bird turned from his original plans and destroyed two small posts, and then laden with plunder and prisoners, he returned to Detroit.[135] Many Indians deserted Bird upon his retreat, because, it was claimed, of their fear of a large force of French at Vincennes.[136]

Again, late in the winter of 1780–1781, the British at Detroit were informed that Clark was approaching with an army of three thousand well-armed Americans and Creoles.[137] Consternation reigned supreme! Every effort was made to strengthen and complete the new fort. A ditch was dug around the fortifications, and a well sunk to a depth of sixty feet.[138] But again the expedition failed to materialize and although Congress, Washington,[139] Jefferson,[140] and Clark [141] bent every

[132] De Peyster went to Detroit in 1779. He was succeeded by Patrick Sinclair at Michilimackinac. Haldimand to De Peyster, August 29, 1779, *Mich. Hist. Colls.,* IX, 365.

[133] De Peyster to Bolton, March 10, 1780, *ibid.,* XIX, 501; same to same, June 8, 1780, *ibid.,* 532; same to Haldimand, May 17, 1780, *ibid.,* X, 395.

[134] Jefferson to Clark, January 29, 1780, *Ill. Hist. Colls.,* VIII, 387; Bird to De Peyster, June 3, 1780, *Mich. Hist. Colls.,* XIX, 527; same to same, July 24, 1780, *ibid.,* 545–46.

[135] De Peyster to Bolton, August 4, 1780, *ibid.,* 553.

[136] Haldimand to De Peyster, August 10, 1780, *ibid.,* X, 416; same to Bolton, August 10, 1780, *ibid.,* XIX, 558; James, *Clark,* p. 209.

[137] *Ill. Hist. Colls.,* VIII, 582; McKee to De Peyster, March 1, 1781, *Mich. Hist. Colls.,* XIX, 598; De Peyster to Powell, March 17, 1780, *ibid.,* 601. One rumor had it that in 1779 Clark had a force of 1,400 Bostonians and 600 French for an attack upon Detroit.

[138] *Ibid.,* X, 465, 478, 482.

[139] Washington to Brodhead, January 4, 1780, *Wis. Hist. Colls.,* XXIV, 123; *Ill. Hist. Colls.,* VIII, 535.

[140] Jefferson to Washington, February 10, 1780, *Wis. Hist. Colls.,* XXIV, 133, 311; Jefferson to Clark, December 25, 1780, *Ill. Hist. Colls.,* VIII, 485 ff.

[141] *Ibid.,* chap. XIII; James, *Clark,* chap. XI.

effort toward capturing Detroit, it was never seriously menaced during the war.

The closing years of the war brought forth a new problem for the English. Spain, never neutral, came into the struggle in 1779, and at once bent every effort to regain Florida and parts of the West.

As early as 1777 De Peyster warned Carleton that the Spanish were sending agents into the far north to gain trading advantages over the English " during our troubles." [142] Hamilton asserted that the Spanish reinforced New Orleans in 1777 and then began to make advances toward the French as far north as St. Joseph and Detroit.[143] He also outlined for Carleton the plans of an elaborate campaign against the Spaniards of the whole Mississippi Valley.[144] England had enough to occupy her attention, and so made every attempt to keep the Indians from knowing that the French and Spanish were friendly toward the Americans, and that later they even joined in the war.[145]

British officials early were well aware that the acts of Spain were far from neutral. The work of Bernardo de Galvez, Governor of New Orleans, in aiding Captain James Willing in 1778 to equip an expedition which was used against the English possessions in the Lower Mississippi, was well known in London.[146] The earlier accomplishment in 1776 of Lieutenant William Linn, who received nine to ten thousand pounds of powder from Governor Louis de Unzaga, nearly brought the two nations into war.[147] England was not anxious to bring Spain into the struggle, as that would probably mean that France would come to Spain's aid. Governor Carleton had

[142] De Peyster to Carleton, June 4, 1777, Canadian Archives, Q, XIII, 273; Mich. Hist. Colls., X, 275–76.
[143] Hamilton to Carleton, August 6, 1778, Canadian Archives, Q, XIII, 324; XIV, 89; Mich. Hist. Colls., IX, 458; Hamilton to Haldimand, undated, ibid., 465.
[144] Hamilton to Carleton, June 26, 1777, Canadian Archives, Q, XIV, 30–35.
[145] " Council," August 3, 1779, Mich. Hist. Colls., X, 349.
[146] Charles Gayarré, History of Louisiana (New York, 1854), III, 117.
[147] James, " The Significance of the Attack on St. Louis, 1780," Miss. Valley Hist. Assoc. Proc., II, 199 ff. James, Clark, pp. 91–94.

been informed, sometime in October of 1776, that the Colonials were in communication with the Spaniards.[148] Nevertheless, he advised Hamilton that every care should be taken to pursue a policy which would not have any tendency to create a breach between England and Spain.[149] " The Spanish side of the Mississippi," he wrote, " must be respected upon all occasions." Governor Hamilton wrote to General Haldimand in January, 1779, that he was personally convinced of the existence of a Spanish and a French war, yet he had no accounts by which he might venture to act on the offensive as he ardently desired.[150] Hamilton was positive that there would be little difficulty in pushing the Spanish entirely out of the Mississippi.[151] The Governor of Michigan also wrote to Galvez that he hoped the commerce in gunpowder with the Colonials would be prohibited.[152]

When Hamilton set out in the fall of 1778 to destroy Clark and his forces, one of his main objectives was to gain control of the mouth of the Missouri with the purpose of underselling the Spaniards and thus currying favor with the Indians.[153] Hamilton failed to win any of his objectives.[154] There was considerable fighting between the Spanish and British in west Florida, but that has no place in this study.

As soon as Governor Sinclair at Michilimackinac was aware of the actions of Spain, he dispatched a war party to enlist the services of the Sioux, " a warlike people undebauched," and under the " authority of a chief named Wabasha of very singular & uncommon abilities." [155] Wabasha could raise two

[148] Carleton to Hamilton, undated (probably October, 1776), *Mich. Hist. Colls.*, IX, 344.

[149] *Ibid.; Ill. Hist. Colls.*, VIII, cxxv.

[150] Hamilton to Haldimand, January 24–30, 1779, Canadian Archives, B, LXI, 302.

[151] *Ibid.*

[152] Hamilton to Galvez, February 13, 1779, Canadian Archives, *Report for 1882*, p. 25. At this time Captain Bloomer was stationed at Natchez to intercept supplies sent from New Orleans to the Colonials. *Ibid.*, p. 26.

[153] Hamilton to Haldimand, September 22, 1778, *Mich. Hist. Colls.*, IX, 478.

[154] *Ante*, p. 197.

[155] Sinclair to Brehm, February 15, 1780, *Mich. Hist. Colls.*, IX, 542; same to Haldimand, February 15, 1780, *ibid.*, 544.

hundred warriors with ease, warriors well-disciplined and attached to the British cause,[156] so Sinclair informed Haldimand. These Indians dwelt so far in the West that they were
not affected by Governor Hamilton's disaster; indeed, wrote
Sinclair: "many of them never heard of it." [157] Wabasha was
ordered to move with all haste to join General John Campbell
on the Lower Mississippi, harassing any Spanish or rebel
settlements on the way.[158] This campaign would not deserve
any place in this treatment were it not for a return attack by
the Spanish upon the small post of St. Joseph, a campaign of
less importance than the Wabasha expedition, but which, from
Spanish pretensions, as we shall see later, was made a matter
of great significance in Europe.

On March 10, 1780, Sinclair dispatched a band of seven
hundred and fifty men, including traders, servants, and Indians, to attack the Spanish at St. Louis and the rebels in the
Illinois country.[159] The Governor, believing the conquest of
the region to be an easy task, entrusted the command to a
trader, Captain Emanuel Hesse.[160] Captain Hesse assembled
his motley army at Prairie du Chien and began to intercept
boats ascending the river with provisions. Upon reaching the
lead mines, they captured seventeen Spanish and rebel prisoners and fifty tons of lead ore and large supplies of provisions.[161] The Indians were enthusiastic over the opportunity
to make war upon their ancient enemies, the Illinois. Traders
were enlisted by Sinclair's promise to give them the exclusive
trade of the Missouri for the following winter.[162]

Captain Hesse was to be assisted by three other units. Captain Langlade, "with a chosen Band of Indians and Canadians," was to assemble at Chicago and proceed down the

[156] Same to Brehm, February 15, 1780, *ibid.*, 542.
[157] *Ibid.*, 541.
[158] *Ibid.; Wis. Hist. Colls.*, XI, 144 *et seq.*
[159] Sinclair to Haldimand, February 17, 1780, *ibid.*, 151; *Mich. Hist. Colls.*,
IX, 546, 548.
[160] *Wis. Hist. Colls.*, XI, 151.
[161] Same to same, May 29, 1780, *ibid.; Mich. Hist. Colls.*, IX, 548.
[162] *Ibid.*, 549.

Illinois River.[163] Another party (Sinclair does not give the leader's name) was ordered to watch " the Plains between the Wabash and the Mississippi." [164] The third and by far the largest was the one sent by De Peyster, under Captain Bird's command, to " amuse the Rebels at the Rappids " [165] of the Ohio with the results noted above.[166]

St. Louis was warned of the enemy's approach and immediately made plans for defense.[167] The town was inadequately defended by only twenty-nine regulars and two hundred and eighty-one villagers.[168] The enemy expected to meet with little, if any, resistance, and were much surprised to find themselves repulsed and thrown back in confusion.[169] The attack was resumed, but the Sacs, who were under the leadership of Mons'r Calvé, and the Foxes falling back made the rest of the Indians suspicious of treachery; so they scattered over the country and destroyed crops " and inflicted . . . the most bitter torments which tyranny has invented " upon the " helpless country people," according to the Spanish account.[170] Sinclair, although not pleased with the outcome, felt that the expedition was not without some value.[171] Forty-three scalps, thirty-four prisoners, seventy persons killed, and several hundred cattle destroyed was his summary of results to Colonel Bolton.[172] Some of these prisoners were used in building the new fort at Michilimackinac.[173] The failure of the party was due, so Sinclair wrote, to:

(1) the " treachery of Mr. Calvé and the Sacs and Renards " and his partner Mons'r Ducharme;

(2) " the backwardness of the Canadians; " and

[163] *Ibid.*, 548.
[164] *Ibid.*
[165] *Mich. Hist. Colls.*, X, 395.
[166] *Ante*, p. 204.
[167] Louis Houck, *The Spanish Régime in Missouri* (Chicago, 1909), I, 167; James, *Clark*, pp. 202–207.
[168] *Missouri Historical Society Collections* (St. Louis, 1906), II, no. 6, p. 45.
[169] *Wis. Hist. Colls.*, XVIII, 407 ff.
[170] *Ibid.*, see also Houck, *loc. cit.*, I, 167; James, *Clark*, p. 206.
[171] Sinclair to Haldimand, July 8, 1780, *Wis. Hist. Colls.*, XI, 156; *Mich. Hist. Colls.*, IX, 559.
[172] *Ibid.*, 558–59.
[173] Moore, *The Northwest Under Three Flags*, p. 257.

(3) the lack of secrecy whereby the Spaniards received information of " the meditated attack." [174]

In addition to these, no doubt the most potent cause for the retreat of the Indians and British was the appearance of George Rogers Clark, who hurriedly left the Falls of the Ohio and came to the aid of the Spaniards when he learned of the English expedition.[175] Although Clark took no part in the fight at St. Louis, his presence at Cahokia across the river was no doubt a great factor in causing the English to abandon their scheme; and at once he sent a force under Colonel John Montgomery to pursue the defeated expedition.[176]

The English forces broke up into two units [177] upon retreating northward, one going up the Mississippi under the leadership of M. Joseph Calvé, who incurred Sinclair's displeasure by allowing several prisoners " to fall into the hands of the enemy"; [178] the other going directly across Illinois and northward to Mackinac.[179] The forces under Langlade, upon hearing of Colonel Montgomery's army approaching, beat a hasty retreat to Chicago.[180] Here the party was rescued from a group of Indians " in the Rebel Interest " by two vessels sent down Lake Michigan by Sinclair, who informed General Haldimand that five days after the vessels left Chicago two hundred Illinois cavalry arrived there.[181]

Sinclair was undaunted by the disasters which his first expedition experienced. Scarcely had the remnants returned when he began to lay more careful and elaborate plans for 1781.[182] He had Wabasha come to his post where his wants

[174] Sinclair to Haldimand, July 8, 1780, *Wis. Hist. Colls.*, XI, 154; *Mich. Hist. Colls.*, IX, 558–59; *Missouri Historical Collection*, II, 48.
[175] *Virginia State Papers*, III, 443. See James, "The Significance of the Attack on St. Louis, 1780," *Miss. Valley Hist. Assoc. Proc.*, II, 210–13.
[176] *Virginia State Papers*, III, 443; *Ill. Hist. Colls.*, II, 541; *Early Western Travels*, II, 185. Professor James believes that Clark's opportune appearance at Cahokia was the potent " cause for the precipitate retreat." James, *Clark*, pp. 206–207.
[177] Sinclair to Haldimand, July 8, 1780, *Mich. Hist. Colls.*, IX, 558.
[178] *Ibid.*
[179] *Missouri Hist. Colls.*, II, no. 6, p. 48.
[180] *Ibid.; Wis. Hist. Colls.*, XVIII, 411.
[181] Sinclair to Haldimand, July 8, 1780, *Mich. Hist. Colls.*, IX, 558. See *Ill. Hist. Colls.*, VIII, cxxvii–cxxxv, for an excellent account of this expedition.
[182] Sinclair to Haldimand, July 8, 1780, *Mich. Hist. Colls.*, IX, 559–60.

were well supplied.[183] " This did away," Sinclair explained to Haldimand, " with the reports of curriers (couriers) and the curiosity and suspicion they always excite in traversing such an extent of country." [184] This, the Governor thought, would give the secrecy which the expedition of 1780 entirely lacked and with the most disastrous results.[185] Sinclair wrote Haldimand that the Sioux chieftain would be in the field with one thousand braves, " without any mixture from neighboring tribes," by April next.[186] All of his efforts to maintain secrecy were of no avail. Francisco Cruzat, the new Governor at St. Louis, wrote in December of 1780 to Don Jose Galvez, Viceroy of Mexico, that the English were distributing " exorbitant amounts of merchandise . . . among the Indian tribes, in order to attract them to their side, inducing them, by deceitful and threatening words, to turn against us." [187] Cruzat claimed that Sinclair was planning to direct the expedition in order that the results would be more favorable than the former attack upon St. Louis.[188] In the same letter he writes that the great chief of the Sioux tribe is returning " from Michely Makinak, where he had gone, with a great quantity of merchandise of all sorts, not only to arouse his own tribe, but also those who are near him." [189] Measures were undertaken by the Spanish Governor to checkmate the designs of Sinclair, but just what they were the letter does not say.[190] Other affairs soon occupied Sinclair's attention; so the expedition did not materialize.

Just what affair diverted Sinclair's energies must remain a matter of conjecture. In the summer of 1780 a French officer, Augustin Mottin de la Balme, appeared among the Illinois and tried to arouse the inhabitants with the story that their

[183] *Ibid.* This letter is published in Houck, *The Spanish Régime in Missouri,* I, 176.
[184] *Mich. Hist. Colls.,* IX, 559.
[185] *Ibid.*
[186] Sinclair to Haldimand, July 8, 1780, *ibid.,* 559.
[187] *Wis. Hist. Colls.,* XVIII, 410.
[188] *Ibid.*
[189] *Ibid.,* 411.
[190] *Ibid.*

former King had sent him to assist them, and asked them to help him in an expedition against Detroit and thence into Canada.[191] Perhaps this was one of the plans Cruzat had in mind, to checkmate Sinclair.[192] La Balme's sudden presence in the West may be explained as a part of the plan of Washington, approved by Lafayette, and the French minister, Luzerne, to make an attempt from Detroit to arouse the Canadians to unite with the Americans and gain their independence.[193] The French, who at this time were having serious difficulties with the Americans, welcomed La Balme, " just as the Hebrews would receive the Mesiah," or as a Moses, " who would lead them out of captivity." [194]

This Frenchman collected about eighty French and Indians, and in October started for Detroit with the French colors flying.[195] He successfully attacked the small post of Miamitown (Fort Wayne), plundered a settlement, and then began to retreat because of weakened forces.[196] The Indians, however, rallying to the English support, in turn attacked the French and defeated them; about thirty were killed including La Balme.[197] All of his baggage, papers, and the French memorials were captured by the English, and today they form a part of the Canadian Archives. This unsuccessful and ephemeral expedition destroyed for a time the hope of the French for a restoration of the West to France.

On the other hand, Cruzat may have referred to the contemplated attack upon St. Joseph. This small post had had a checkered career during the War of Independence.[198] Be-

---

[191] La Balme to Luzerne, June 27, 1780, *Ill. Hist. Colls.*, V, 163–68; Canadian Archives, B, CLXXXIV, pt. ii, pp. 421, 442; James, *Clark*, pp. 213–15.

[192] *Ante*, p. 210.

[193] Sparks (ed.), *Washington's Letters*, VII, 44, 72; Calendar of La Balme's Expedition, Canadian Archives, *Report for 1888*, p. 856.

[194] " Address " of Colonel La Balme, September 17, 1780, *Ill. Hist. Colls.*, V, 181–92; Winston to Todd, October 17, 1780, *ibid.*, 196. See especially *ibid.*, II, lxxxix–xciv.

[195] " Petition of May 1, 1781," *ibid.*, 237.

[196] Canadian Archives, B, vol. 100, p. 486; James, *Clark*, p. 215; *Ill. Hist. Colls.*, V, 199–200.

[197] De Peyster to Powell, November 13, 1780, *Mich. Hist. Colls.*, XIX, 581; *Ill. Hist. Colls.*, V, 246.

[198] George Paré, "The St. Joseph Mission," *Miss. Valley Hist. Review*, XVII, June, 1930.

cause of its commercial advantages, the traders had built up a lucrative fur business here.[199] It had no regular garrison but was the rendezvous of the Potawatomi Indians. In June of 1780, the post contained a population of forty-eight French and halfbreeds.[200] Sinclair removed some of the inhabitants to Michilimackinac during the summer, so that in the fall of '80 St. Joseph contained a smaller number of people than in June.[201]

Before La Balme departed on his expedition to Detroit,[202] he sent Jean Baptiste Hamelin with a small force of seventeen men assisted by a number of Indians to capture and destroy St. Joseph.[203] The party was so planned as to arrive at St. Joseph early in December while the savages were absent hunting.[204] They succeeded in taking the fort, overpowered the few traders, seized their goods, and hastily retreated around Lake Michigan toward Chicago.[205] Lieutenant Louis De Quindre, who had been stationed by De Peyster at St. Joseph, was absent when the attack took place. Upon returning he assembled a party of Indians and pursued the "Robbers nearly all of whom he captured and killed." [206] This victory helped to restore English prestige with the Indians, which had been lost by Hamilton's defeat.

This attack upon St. Joseph and the forays against it would not deserve a place in our treatment if it were not for the importance of another assault against the post in 1781, the echoes of which were heard in far distant Europe. The Spanish, much incensed over the attack upon St. Louis, the Cahokians, eager for revenge for their earlier defeats, and the Indians, anxious for plunder, all joined in January of 1781 to capture the fort. The Spaniards were genuinely alarmed over

---

[199] *Mich. Hist. Colls.,* X, 367.
[200] *Ibid.,* XIII, 58–59.
[201] *Ibid.,* X, 435.
[202] *Ante,* pp. 210–11.
[203] *Missouri Historical Review* (Columbia, 1906–), II, 204.
[204] De Peyster to McKee, February 1, 1781, *Mich. Hist. Colls.,* X, 452.
[205] De Peyster to Haldimand, January 8, 1781, *ibid.,* X, 450 ff.; same to Powell, January 8, 1781, *ibid.,* XIX, 591–92; *Virginia State Papers,* I, 465.
[206] *Mich. Hist. Colls.,* X, 450–51; XIX, 591–92.

Sinclair's preparations for a new attack upon St. Louis,[207] and possibly affected by the example of Clark in his carrying the war into the enemies' country, determined to anticipate the English. The force consisted of sixty-five militia men and sixty Indians, under the command of Eugene Pouré, captain; Charles Tayon, ensign; and Louis Chevalier, interpreter.[208] The fatigues of the march of four hundred miles in the dead of winter were not exaggerated by Cruzat in his report that the forces " experienced all that can be imagined of cold, peril, and hunger." [209] The post was easily captured but very few details of the expedition were reported by the Spaniards, for at this time, St. Joseph contained no English and a few French. The booty was given to the Indians of the expedition and those of St. Joseph, who had remained neutral upon the promise of receiving half of the spoils.[210] Don Pouré " took possession, in the name of the King of that place and its dependencies, and of the river of the Illinois; in consequence whereof the standard of his majesty was there displayed during the whole time "— so reads the Spanish account.[211] During the occupation of the village, which lasted only twenty-four hours, the Spanish flag was kept flying.[212] Pouré delivered the English standard upon his return to St. Louis to Cruzat, the Spanish commander.[213] The day following his departure from St. Joseph a small English force under Lieutenant De Quindre arrived. As the Spanish had gotten so far away, he was unable to induce the Indians to go in pursuit of

[207] Cruzat to Galvez, December 2 and 19, 1780, *Wis. Hist. Colls.*, XVIII, 412–15; *Missouri Historical Review*, V, 223; Houck, *Spanish Régime*, I, 175–76; *Virginia State Papers*, I, 481. *Chicago Historical Society Collections* (Chicago, 1890–), IV, 341.

[208] Wharton, *Revolutionary Diplomatic Correspondence*, V, 363.

[209] *Missouri Historical Review*, V, 216.

[210] De Peyster to Powell, March 17, 1781, *Mich. Hist. Colls.*, XIX, 600; James, *Clark*, pp. 220–21.

[211] Wharton, *Revolutionary Diplomatic Correspondence*, V, 363.

[212] *Mo. Hist. Rev.*, V, 217; *Wis. Hist. Colls.*, XVIII, 430–32; Houck, *The Spanish Régime*, I, 207. For the English account see *Mich. Hist. Colls.*, X, 452–55; XIX, 600–601. The American account is in *Ill. Hist. Colls.*, II, 620; *Va. State Papers*, I, 465. See also F. J. Teggart, " The Capture of St. Joseph, Michigan, by the Spaniards in 1781," *Mo. Hist. Rev.*, V, 214–28; and C. W. Alvord, " The Conquest of St. Joseph, Michigan, by the Spaniards in 1781," *ibid.*, II, 195–210.

[213] Wharton, *Rev. Dip. Corres.*, V, 363.

them but the red men " insisted upon his conducting them to Detroit." [214] Thus Spain had possession of a small portion of Michigan during the War of Independence, a factor she did not forget at the peace parleys which followed.

The year 1781 brought another important expedition from Michigan. Alexander McKee set out from Detroit with a group of rangers and Indians to destroy the settlements of Kentucky. When the Indians learned that Clark was unlikely to disturb their villages, they refused to advance and dispersed into small bands.[215] Haldimand was greatly concerned over the failure of this force to destroy Clark. He fulminated against the savages, and deeply regretted the heavy expenses for clothing, feeding, and caring for such thankless allies.[216] Upon returning to Detroit, McKee advised De Peyster to remove the Moravian teachers from the banks of the Muskingum to Michigan.[217] De Peyster did so and they were given a small plot of ground near the present city of Mt. Clemens. Scarcely had they reached their new home when they heard of the terrible massacre by the frontiersmen of their brothers on the Muskingum.[218] This slaughter had a tremendous effect upon the frontiers. Once again the savages, aroused to fury, spread devastation through the West. The immediate result of the massacre was Colonel William Crawford's campaign against the Shawnee.[219]

Colonel Crawford, a close personal friend of Washington's, marched from Fort Pitt in May with 480 mounted men to put an end to the Indian atrocities. Setting out for the Wyandot and Shawnee towns on the Upper Sandusky, he was met near the Indian villages by a force of rangers, volunteers, and Lake

---

[214] *Mich. Hist. Colls.*, XIX, 600.

[215] Thompson to De Peyster, September 26, 1781, *ibid.*, X, 515–16.

[216] Haldimand to ———, November 1, 1781, *ibid.*, 534–35.

[217] The Moravians were not neutral. They gave the Americans considerable information, *ibid.*, 538–41.

[218] For the story of the massacre, see Roosevelt, *Winning of the West*, II, 189–217; Moore, *Northwest Under Three Flags*, pp. 262–67.

[219] C. W. Butterfield, *An Historical Account of the Expedition against Sandusky under Col. William Crawford in 1782* (Cincinnati, 1873); James, *Clark*, pp. 263–67; Moore, *Northwest Under Three Flags*, pp. 269–76. Spies reported Crawford's plans to Detroit before any campaign got under way.

Indians under Captain Caldwell from Detroit. The battle which began on June 4 lasted until dark, with little advantage to either side, notwithstanding the larger number of Colonials. The next day 140 Shawnee joined the British, and believing the enemy so superior to them, the Americans retreated in confusion. Discipline was thrown to the winds, and after the loss of 50, including Colonel Crawford, the Americans recrossed the Ohio River and continued without further difficulty. The British losses were small, and after the Indians had put the captives to death [220] with great cruelty, they retreated toward Detroit.

In retaliation, Clark planned another campaign against Detroit.[221] The British were greatly alarmed for they heard that he had four thousand men with him. About the same time they also learned that Cornwallis had been defeated and the Iroquois were inclined to make peace.[222] No help was forthcoming from Canada, for all the available troops were to be used to support General Henry Clinton at New York.[223] Haldimand ordered that "every precaution possible for the safety" of the fort at Detroit be made and to collect sufficient provisions to enable the men to withstand a formidable assault.[224] The forces at Detroit were so decimated by the war and sickness that De Peyster could not support the Indians further, and thus he was put on the defensive.[225] The Major was well aware that the way to Detroit was open and he passed a hectic winter waiting for Clark's attack. In November, 1782, Clark with an army of 1,050 mounted men set out from Kentucky to Chillicothe, the Shawnee stronghold. Warned of his approach the Indians fled. The Americans burned the villages, and destroyed large quantities of corn and other pro-

---

[220] For the story of the inhuman treatment of Colonel Crawford see Croghan to Davies, July 6, 1782, *Ill. Hist. Colls.*, XIX, 71–73.

[221] James, *Clark*, chap. XI.

[222] De Peyster to McKee, April 3, 1782, *Mich. Hist. Colls.*, X, 565; Haldimand to ———, April 21, 1782, *ibid.*, 566–67.

[223] *Ibid.*

[224] *Ibid.* The fort was strengthened and a gunboat was stationed at the mouth of the Miami. Bird to Powell, August 13, 1782, *ibid.*, 625–27.

[225] De Peyster to Maclean, November 21, 1782, *ibid.*, XI, 321; De Peyster to Haldimand, November 21, 1781, *ibid.*, 322.

visions.[226] Colonel Benjamin Logan with 150 men also captured the trading post of Miamitown, burning such stores as
they were unable to carry away. Vainly attempting for four
days to bring on a general engagement with the Indians, Clark
retreated to the mouth of the Licking, where his forces separated.[227] By this attack, Clark not only saved the frontier
inhabitants from the danger of attack, but he ruined the plans
of the British to unite the various Indian tribes. The Indians
were panic-stricken; their winter supplies were destroyed; and
because of the need of retrenchment the British officials cut
down the quantities of presents.[228] The Indians interpreted
this as a step toward their abandonment to the Americans.
With this victory for the Americans the war in the West came
to an end. The closing years were largely one continuous petty
fight carried on in the country between the Ohio and the
Great Lakes. Over this vast area bands of red men and
rangers from Michigan roamed, carrying on an increasing
war against the American frontier. In April, 1783, word was
received at Detroit by De Peyster that the cessation of hostilities had been ordered. He at once informed the Indians
of this fact and told them England intended to keep her promise of peace, and they must not continue their depredations.[229]
The proclamation of a general peace soon followed.

[226] *Virginia State Papers,* III, 383.

[227] I have relied upon the article of Professor James entitled: "To What
Extent was George Rogers Clark in Military Control of the Northwest at
the Close of the American Revolution," *Annual Report of the American Historical Association, 1917,* pp. 324–29.

[228] Haldimand to Townshend, November 9, 1782, *Mich. Hist. Colls.,* XI,
320–21.

[229] "Council at Detroit," July 30, 1783, *ibid.,* XX, 154; James, *Clark,* chap.
XII.

CHAPTER IX

MICHIGAN AND THE
TREATY OF PARIS

THE SOLDIER HAD FAILED to win large portions of the Old Northwest; would the diplomat succeed? The solution of this problem determined whether Michigan should remain within the British empire, or become a part of a new nation, the United States.

The surrender of Cornwallis at Yorktown in October, 1781, evoked a strong feeling in English official circles for peace with their recalcitrant colonies.[1] On March 20, 1782, Lord North, who had conducted the war in spite of intense criticism, resigned, and the King was forced to call in the Rockingham Whigs.[2] In this ministry, foreign affairs were under the direction of Charles James Fox, and Lord Shelburne was secretary for Home, Irish, and Colonial Affairs. It was most fortunate for the Americans that a man of Shelburne's understanding and appreciation came into power to exert the greatest influence upon the peace negotiations. Because of long experience with the Colonials,[3] Shelburne well realized how inevitable was the movement of the Americans westward, and thus was unwilling to prevent what he considered almost the " force of nature."

Long before Yorktown the Continental Congress had appointed John Adams as sole commissioner to discuss terms of peace with Great Britain. He was instructed to demand for the boundaries of the United States a line from " the south

[1] Grafton to Shelburne, November 14, 1781, Shelburne Papers, LXXII, 5.
[2] Fitzmaurice, *Life of Shelburne*, II, 87–91.
[3] *Ante*, chap. I; Alvord, *Mississippi Valley in British Politics*, I, chaps. IV–VI, XII; Fitzmaurice, *Shelburne*, I, chaps. IV, VIII.

end of Lake Nipissing; and thence straight to the source of the River Mississippi; west by a line to be drawn along the middle of the River Mississippi " from its source to the thirty-first parallel.[4] He was to act in accordance with the agreement of 1778, and not to treat with England without the co-operation of France.[5] Soon afterwards Congress gave new instructions which allowed more freedom to Adams.[6] These provided that if the English were unwilling to agree to the line drawn from Lake Nipissing that some other boundary should be drawn, but it was not to be south of latitude forty-five degrees. This would have meant the surrender of the upper portion of Michigan, Wisconsin, and Minnesota, with their valuable mineral deposits. Adams did not find relations very cordial with Vergennes,[7] then the European patron of America; so Congress, doubtless influenced by the French minister, annulled Adams' commission and issued another to him and to four others. The new members were Benjamin Franklin, John Jay, Henry Laurens, and Thomas Jefferson.[8]

When Spain joined France in 1779, the issues over boundaries immediately arose. Spain already held the right bank of the Mississippi River, and was anxious to get control of the trade of the entire valley. She was very unfriendly to the westward movement of the American frontiersmen as they were settling so close to her poorly fortified and garrisoned posts. Again, the very radical ideas of the Westerners would endanger the despotic sway Spain kept over her peoples.

[4] *Secret Journals of the Acts and Proceedings of Congress* (Boston, 1921), II.
[5] *Ibid.*, Jared Sparks, *Diplomatic Correspondence of the American Revolution* (Boston, 1829–1831), IV, 339 ff.
[6] *Ibid.*
[7] J. Durand, *New Materials of the History of the American Revolution* (New York, 1899), pp. 232, 233.
[8] Sparks, *Diplomatic Correspondence*, III, 220. The best accounts of the work of the American negotiators are: E. E. Hale and E. E. Hale, Jr., *Franklin in France*, 2 vols., (Boston, 1887–1888); Bernard Fäy, *Franklin, the Apostle of Modern Times* (Boston, 1929); Phillips Russell, *Benjamin Franklin* (New York, 1926); George Pellow, *John Jay* (Boston, 1890); Gilbert Chinard, *Honest John Adams* (Boston, 1933); James Truslow Adams, *The Adams Family* (New York, 1930); E. S. Corwin, *French Policy and the American Alliance* (Princeton, 1916); A. C. McLaughlin, *The Confederation and the Constitution* (New York, 1905); Frank Monaghan, *John Jay* (New York, 1935).

Spain gained West Florida by conquest, as we have seen, and also held the small post of St. Joseph for twenty-four hours.[9]

The incident of the ephemeral capture of this post became of great moment to the Spanish. Franklin wrote to Livingston on April 12, 1782: " I see by the newspapers that the Spaniards, having taken a little post called St. Joseph, pretend to have made a conquest of the Illinois country." [10] It was Franklin's idea that the Spanish were trying to keep the Americans between the Ocean and the Alleghenies.[11]

A similar view was taken by Jay. He also insisted that France and Spain were hostile to " the essential interests of America." He told Franklin: " We shall never, as long as I represent the United States, relinquish our claim to the Western Country and to the Mississippi." [12]

This gave Spain her claim to the region east of the Mississippi and Jay found it impossible to get her to give it up. The Count d'Aranda argued that the West had never belonged to the Colonies. He maintained that it had belonged to France previous to the Seven Years' War and that it remained a part of Great Britain after the cession in 1763, " until, by the conquest of West Florida, and certain posts on the Mississippi and Illinois, it became vested in Spain." [13] As Spain unfolded her policy, she proposed a " conciliatory line " which would have confined the United States east of the Alleghenies, and would have made the region south of the Ohio an Indian reserve over which she and America would have been joint guardians; while England would control the area north of the Ohio.[14]

It surely was not the plan of Congress to surrender its claims to the West. Jay's instructions of 1780 decisively stated that " the people inhabiting these states, while connected with Great Britain, and also since the Revolution, have settled

[9] *Ante,* pp. 212 ff.
[10] Sparks (ed.), *Franklin's Works,* IX, 206.
[11] Wharton, *Revolutionary Diplomatic Correspondence,* V, 300, 657.
[12] Monaghan, *John Jay,* p. 196.
[13] Wharton, *loc. cit.,* VI, 22; Sparks, *Diplomatic Correspondence,* VIII, 150 ff.
[14] *American State Papers, Foreign Relations* (Washington, 1832–), I, 572; Winsor, *Narrative and Critical History,* VII, 148.

themselves at diverse places to the westward near the Mississippi; are friendly to the Revolution, and being citizens of the United States and subject to the laws of those to which they respectively belong, Congress cannot assign them over as subjects to any other power." [15]

France had not come into the war as America's ally solely out of friendly motives.[16] One of her objects had been to regain European prestige and to bring about the humiliation of the nation that had destroyed her power by the Seven Years' War. She was not dominated by a desire to recover her lost territory. The independence of America, with boundaries limited on the west by the Appalachian mountains, would give her sufficient reward.

Why did France hope to " coffin up " the Americans between the mountains and the Atlantic Ocean? [17] Among her many objects was the desire to please Spain, her very close ally, in aiding her in the recovery of Gibraltar, Minorca, and East Florida; also, she was anxious to gain England's good will, so that the age-long fishing dispute might be settled without further delay.[18]

Spain and France acted in accord to limit the new Republic. They first tried to influence Congress,[19] as well as the Commissioners abroad.[20] These nations insisted that America had no claim to any area west of " the ancient English establishments." [21] Finally, exasperated because their arguments had small effect, Rayneval, Vergennes' secretary, threatened, Jay wrote to Livingston in 1782, " that in case we should not agree to divide with Spain in the manner proposed, that then this Court [France] would aid Spain in negotiating with Britain

[15] *Secret Journals of Congress*, III, 155.
[16] C. H. Van Tyne, *The Causes of the War of Independence, American Phase* (Boston, 1922), chap. XXI.
[17] C. F. Adams, *John Adams, Life and Works* (Boston, 1856), VII, 626–631; Winsor, *Narrative and Critical History*, VII, 148.
[18] Madison, *Works*, II, 467.
[19] George Bancroft, *History of the United States* (Boston, 1834–), X, 216.
[20] C. F. Adams, *loc. cit.*, I, 357, 370; III, 303, 357. Hale, *Franklin in France*, II, 143.
[21] Sparks, *Diplomatic Correspondence*, VIII, 158.

for the territory she wanted, and would agree that the residue should remain to Britain." [22]

The ministry of Great Britain did not seem so desirous of gaining the territory their ancient enemies were so anxious to grant them. Lord North had offered to return Canada to France, provided she would make a separate treaty,[23] but as we have seen, his ministry fell and men of broader views came into power. It is to them we must turn to find the amicable solution of the boundary question.

With the advent of the Rockingham Ministry, Franklin, the only member of the American commission in France, wrote to Shelburne expressing his earnest desire for peace.[24] Thus they renewed the conversations of former years as to the best means of promoting the welfare of humankind.[25] An understanding was reached by these letters concerning the western problems even before Jay or Adams arrived. Shelburne attached very great importance to these unofficial negotiations, and explained to Richard Oswald, his representative in Paris, that if these preliminary plans failed, the war would have to be carried on vigorously, as the British people on the whole were not at all reconciled to the independence of the Colonies.[26] It became Shelburne's plan to stir up difficulties between the Colonies, France, and Spain wherever their interests conflicted.[27] At any rate, if the United States were to be independent, Shelburne was convinced that it should be free from all nations, or at least it should not be the protegé of England's arch enemy, France.[28]

Franklin gave Oswald his ideas in April, 1782, as to what would bring about reconciliation. He advised that Canada

[22] P. H. Johnston (ed.), *Correspondence and Public Papers of John Jay* (New York, 1891), II, 398–99. See especially the very able study of Jay's work in Monaghan's excellent biography of John Jay.

[23] Adams, *John Adams*, 357.

[24] Franklin to Shelburne, March 22, 1782; Sparks, *Diplomatic Correspondence*, III, 377–78.

[25] *Ibid.*, 461; for the most exhaustive account of Lord Shelburne's work, see Fitzmaurice, *Life of Shelburne*, II, chaps. III-VII.

[26] Shelburne to Oswald, 1782, Bancroft MSS.

[27] Fitzmaurice, *loc. cit.*, II, 126, 132, 135, 170, 191, 206.

[28] *Ibid.*

and Nova Scotia be ceded to the United States, as their retention would constantly cause friction between the new nations.[29] Oswald returned to England, but soon came back and presented Franklin with the Cabinet's absolute refusal to cede Canada.[30] Oswald seemed to have been somewhat under the domination of Franklin, for later he told him he agreed concerning Canada and had even urged the same on Rockingham, Shelburne, and Fox.[31] Thus Franklin continued to hope for the cession of Canada.

Congress early concerned itself with its title to the western lands, for in 1779 it insisted that the states had succeeded to all claims which they had had as colonies, or that, when the King of Great Britain ceased to be King of the Colonies, all lands which he held as ruler passed to the United States as a whole.[32] This would show that the Colonies were not at all affected by the Proclamation of 1763, which was an attempt to keep them temporarily east of the Alleghenies.[33] Many Americans felt that their claims would be greatly strengthened if they actually held the West. Jefferson was of this opinion, and had expressed the view that Clark's victory would have a great influence on the establishment of the western boundary.[34] No doubt the same idea was held by Congress when it proposed several expeditions to capture Detroit.[35]

Livingston, the foreign secretary of Congress, writing to Franklin in January, 1782, on his ideas concerning the West, said: " Our western and northwestern extent will probably be contested with some warmth, and the reasoning on that subject be deduced from general principles, and from proclamations and treaties with Indians. . . . I believe it will appear, that our extension to the Mississippi is founded in justice; and our claims are at least such as the events of the war give us

[29] Franklin to Shelburne, April 18. 1782, *ibid.*, 122; *Works*, VIII, 465.
[30] Fitzmaurice, *Life of Shelburne*, II, 128.
[31] *Ibid.*, 140.
[32] *Secret Journals of Congress*, III, 170, 198.
[33] *Ante*, pp. 48 ff.
[34] P. L. Ford (ed.), *The Writings of Thomas Jefferson* (New York, 1892–), II, 345 ff.
[35] *Ante*, p. 204.

right to insist upon." [36] To clinch his argument, Livingston spoke of the actual settlement which had been made in the trans-montane region by people who claimed allegiance to the United States. It would be unjust to abandon them, the secretary averred.

Lord Shelburne raised few, if any, real objections to the demands that the Americans made about following the Great Lakes as a boundary. The British seemed to prefer to lay more stress upon the subject of the loyalists, the payment of debts, and the fisheries.[37] There gradually developed an idea that the boundaries would be easily adjusted when weightier matters were cared for. Possibly Shelburne was greatly impressed by Franklin's arguments that there would always be very grave danger along a boundary where were gathered together, " the most disorderly of the people, who being far removed from the eye and control of their respective governments, are most bold in committing offenses against neighbors, and for ever occasioning complaints and furnishing matter for fresh differences between their states." [38]

The situation facing the American commissioners was serious. The Treaty of 1778 bound the Americans to make no peace independent of France, and Congress had emphatically ordered the commissioners not to conclude any arrangements with the English without the approval of the French Government.[39] Spain had come into the war to regain her lost territory, and also to keep the Americans in check. It naturally would be more difficult to govern her colonies in an autocratic way if she allowed a democratic nation to arise on their eastern boundary.[40] These hostile plans of Spain were finally defeated by Jay, who, becoming convinced that Spain and America could never agree on the Mississippi boundary question [41] and that France was abetting Spain, sent an agent to Shelburne

[36] Sparks, *Diplomatic Correspondence*, III, 269.
[37] Fitzmaurice, *Shelburne*, II, 128, 137, 170, 173.
[38] *Ibid.*, 122; Sparks, *loc. cit.*, III, 388.
[39] *Secret Journals of Congress*, II, 446.
[40] *Ante*, p. 205.
[41] Jay, *Correspondence and Papers*, II, 395 ff.; Monaghan, *John Jay*, chap. X.

saying that he would open separate negotiations with England.[42]

This was what Shelburne had hoped would come to pass: altercations between America, Spain, and France. Oswald received new instructions, and at once negotiations were begun without the knowledge of Vergennes.[43]

After much deliberation and discussion a provisional treaty was signed at Paris on November 30, 1782.[44] By this treaty the area of Michigan was secured by the United States, as was all the West, from the Alleghenies to the Mississippi, and from the Great Lakes to the thirty-first parallel.[45] This territory was really not ceded to America, but was recognized as included within her boundaries. In order to placate France, these provisional articles were " to be inserted in and to constitute the Treaty of Paris," but the treaty was not to be concluded until England and France had made peace.[46] On December 5, George III announced from the throne to Parliament that a provisional treaty had been made with the American commissioners.[47] " Religion, Language, Interest, Affections, may, and I hope," said the King, " will yet prove a bond of permanent union between the two countries; to this end neither attention nor disposition on my part shall be wanting." [48]

As soon as the fur traders in Canada and Michigan were aware that the Northwest posts were to be ceded to the Americans, a storm of indignation arose. They petitioned Haldimand, who in turn presented their demands to Shelburne.[49] The merchants asked especially that if the posts

[42] Fitzmaurice, loc. cit., II, 173, 174, 176; Sparks, Diplomatic Correspondence, VIII, 165.
[43] Wharton, Revolutionary Diplomatic Correspondence, V, 748; Fitzmaurice, loc. cit., II, 183, 205.
[44] Wharton, loc. cit., VI, 96 ff.; Fitzmaurice, loc. cit., II, 206.
[45] MacDonald, Documents, pp. 205–206. Jefferson never left the United States, and Laurens arrived only in time to sign the treaty. See Annual Register for 1783, p. 339.
[46] Fitzmaurice, loc. cit., II, 206.
[47] Parliamentary History of England, XXIII, 206.
[48] Ibid.; Fitzmaurice, loc. cit., II, 209–210.
[49] Shelburne Papers, LXXII, 455, 459, 463.

were to be surrendered, three years be allowed in which they could withdraw their valuable effects, and also permit the inhabitants of Detroit to remove across into British territory. They demanded free and equal navigation of the lakes and rivers. Haldimand had ordered all work on the forts to cease before the treaty was signed.[50] De Peyster, as soon as he was aware that the war was over, made every effort to restrain the Indians,[51] and especially ordered McKee to use all his energy to end further depredations.[52] After the treaty was signed, Haldimand was never reconciled to the boundary provisions. He felt they meant a distinct check upon commerce,[53] and when the territory was given up, the Indians could not be held in leash.[54]

The British ministry had little hope or desire to overcome the boundary claims of the Americans. The following reasons have been suggested for England's yielding so much territory with so little apparent opposition.

(1) They knew the British had no real claim upon it.

(2) Experience had shown that it could be held, if at all, only at a tremendous expense.

(3) They preferred the United States rather than Spain as a neighbor.

(4) They had the hope of building up a strong friendly commercial nation in America.

(5) Some of them did not appreciate the value of what they were yielding.

(6) They (the English commissioners) were anxious to hasten the negotiations in order that the completed treaty might be presented at the approaching meeting of Parliament,

---

[50] Haldimand to Maclean, April 26, 1783, *Mich. Hist. Colls.*, XI, 361.
[51] De Peyster to McKee, May 6, 1783, *ibid.*, 363; De Peyster to ————, June 5, 1783, *ibid.*, 367; De Peyster in Indian Council, June 28, 1783, *ibid.*, 371.
[52] De Peyster to McKee, May 6, 1783, *ibid.*, 363–64. Canadian Archives, Claus Papers, III, 217.
[53] *Ibid.*, *Report for 1885*, p. 350.
[54] *Ibid.*, 347. Haldimand was definitely opposed to the immediate surrender of the Northwest posts. Haldimand to ————, November 14, 1784, *Mich. Hist. Colls.*, XX, 269; *post*, pp. 239–40.

for the national expectation of peace must be satisfied, if the ministry was to be sustained.[55]

Why England yielded so much territory to America has long been a puzzling problem. Did the claims based upon colonial charters have any great influence? Perhaps no more than mere theoretical claims usually do. Surely such rights would not explain why the British ministry abandoned an area which had been won from France at a tremendous cost in 1763, and in 1783 was still largely in its control.

Again, did the success of Clark mean much? John Fiske has made a great conscious empire-builder of this frontier leader.[56] Miss Rowland claims that Clark's victory was of tremendous importance for the American claims to the Northwest.[57] Van Tyne makes the assertion that the posts of Vincennes, Cahokia, and Kaskaskia " were sufficient to insure the American hold upon the Northwest, until, in the peace negotiations of 1782, the military prowess of Clark was followed by the diplomatic triumph of Jay. . . . Few events have had a vaster influence upon the future of the nation than this expedition of Clark." Professor James maintains that Shelburne had been moved by Franklin's appeal for generosity which would regain the love of the Americans.[58] But if this were the case, surely frequent mention would be made in the documents concerning the peace negotiations. There is no mention of Clark's work anywhere, although Franklin had been informed of the capture of Vincennes and Clark's other work in July of 1779.[59] Perhaps Franklin, Jay, and Adams intentionally avoided the subject of Clark's success, for his work had ended in failure by 1782, as the Virginia government in

---

[55] These deductions are taken from Annah May Soule's article " The International Boundary Line of Michigan," *Mich. Hist. Colls.*, XXVI, 608. See Fitzmaurice, *Shelburne*, II, 169, 220 for Shelburne's ideas.

[56] John Fiske, *Critical Period in American History* (Boston, 1888), p. 18.

[57] K. M. Rowland, *Life of George Mason* (New York, 1892), I, 365.

[58] Van Tyne, *The American Revolution*, p. 284. See the summary of these and other viewpoints in James, *Clark*, pp. 283–87. Temple Bodley, " The National Significance of George Rogers Clark," *Miss. Valley Hist. Rev.*, XI, 165 ff., makes Clark a second Washington.

[59] Petre Sargé to Franklin, July 6, 1779, *Miss. Valley Hist. Rev.*, XXI, 376–78.

the West had utterly collapsed.[60] In fact the control of the West by the Americans amounted to very little in 1782.

It was Shelburne's plan to make an early peace with the Americans, as England was also at war with France, Holland, and Spain. The victory of Rodney at St. Eustatius and the repulse of the Spanish and French forces at Gibraltar naturally made England realize she could take care of the European situation. Shelburne was desirous to break up the French-American alliance,[61] and he had always been greatly interested in America. He was no doubt very anxious to concede much for the sake of peace with the Americans.

But more conclusive reasons for the surrender of the Northwest may be seen in the attitude taken by England toward the fur trade. This trade was the leading reason why she wanted the West. She had failed in her attempt at monopolization of the pelts, as we have shown.[62] Her chief motive in holding the area had failed! When in February, 1783, the Lords asserted that the region given to America had lost the fur trade to England, Shelburne replied that the trade was not lost but only divided.[63] He further stated that the annual imports to Great Britain from Canada, were about £ 50,000, and for this small sum it had cost the Mother Country at least £ 800,000.[64] If the " entire fur trade sunk into the sea," said Shelburne, " where is the detriment to this country? Is £ 50,000 a year imported in that article any object for Great Britain to continue a war of which the people of England by their representatives have declared their abhorrence? " Other cabinet members agreed with Shelburne.[65] Here, it would

---

[60] *Ill. Hist. Colls.*, II, introduction. Surely the American could scarcely argue the principle of *uti possidetis* as a claim for the West. This is Dr. Alvord's contention in " Virginia and the West," *Miss. Valley Hist. Rev.*, III, 34. Dr. Alvord was a firm believer that the cession was due to Shelburne's liberal principles. See especially, James, " To what extent was George Rogers Clark in Military Control of the Northwest," *American Historical Association Annual Report 1917*, pp. 313–29.

[61] *Ante*, p. 221.

[62] *Ante*, pp. 58 ff.

[63] *Parliamentary History of England*, XXIII, 377, 381; Fitzmaurice, *Shelburne*, II, 236.

[64] *Parliamentary History of England*, XXIII, 409.

[65] *Ibid.*, 465.

seem, was England's reason for giving up so large an area. It was unprofitable!

Perhaps the region gained was not as large as Franklin desired: it surely was more than the Americans expected, and far more than Europe ever dreamed of as possible. Vergennes, in expressing his very great amazement, wrote to Rayneval, his secretary, that the area won, the concessions regarding the loyalists and fisheries, " exceed all that I could have believed possible." [66] He felt that England had bought a peace rather than made one. Rayneval replied that to him the treaty seemed a dream. D'Aranda, in Paris, wrote to his master, the King of Spain:

"The Federal republic is born a pigmy. A day will come when it will be a giant, even a colossus, formidable to these countries. Liberty of conscience, the facility for establishing a new population on immense lands, as well as the advantage of the new government, will draw thither farmers and artisans from all nations. In a few years we shall watch with grief the tyrannical existence of this same colossus." [67]

In America the treaty was well received. Livingston said that the boundaries were more extensive than we had any right to expect.[68] Hamilton was of the impression that the treaty exceeded the expectations of the most sanguine.[69] " The treaty is everywhere universally applauded," a friend wrote Jay upon his return.[70] Well might America feel gratified, for only through French aid and Shelburne's great generosity did the states gain so much.

Shelburne himself took a very justifiable pride in the treaty. On March 5, 1797, after the Northwest posts had been surrendered, he wrote to Major William Jackson, an American friend:

"I cannot express to you the satisfaction I have felt in seeing the forts given up. I may tell you in confidence what may aston-

[66] John Jay, *Address on Treaty of 1783* (New York, 1888), p. 107.
[67] Printed in Moore, *Northwest Under Three Flags*, p. 290; Fiske, *The Critical Period*, p. 19.
[68] Sparks, *Diplomatic Correspondence*, X, 130.
[69] Jay, *Correspondence and Papers*, III, 46.
[70] *Ibid.*

ish you, as it did me, that up to the very last debate in the House of Lords, the Ministry did not appear to comprehend the policy upon which the boundary line was drawn, and persist in still considering it as a measure of necessity not of choice. However, it is indifferent who understands it. The deed is done; and a strong foundation laid for eternal amity between England and America. General Washington's conduct is above all praise. He has left a noble example to sovereigns and nations: present and to come." [71]

[71] Fitzmaurice, *Life of Shelburne*, II, 202, n. 2.

CHAPTER X

THE END OF THE RÉGIME

THE WAR FOR AMERICAN INDEPENDENCE came to its official close with the signing of the Treaty of Paris on September 3, 1783. This treaty stipulated that the boundary of the Old Northwest, between the United States and British North America, should follow generally the middle of the Great Lakes and their connecting rivers. Nevertheless, England continued to maintain sizable garrisons at Detroit and Michilimackinac and to hold a decided ascendancy over the Indians and the fur trade south of the Great Lakes until the Jay Treaty put an end to this *de facto* control in 1796. It is the purpose of this study to re-examine some of the developments in this area from 1783 to 1796 which finally culminated in the end of the British régime and the occupation of the posts by the Americans. No attempt has been made to be definitive, for the author fully realizes that the final word has not been written on this important phase of British-American relations. Rather it is the desire to synthesize the voluminous and scholarly work already done in the field, and to utilize those source materials which recently have come to light, or which have not been of special interest to other historians. But there has been another purpose, namely: to concentrate attention on a narrower field of Anglo-American history from 1783 to 1796, that region south of the Great Lakes known in history as the Old Northwest. It was in this very territory that Britain held the most strategic posts — most strategic from the political view as these gave her a commanding influence over the Indians, or a possible foothold for further expansion; and most strategic indeed from the economic standpoint, because they were the western emporiums of the fur trade. Again, it was in the Old Northwest where the forces developed " in the womb of time " which, to a large degree, forced England to finally acquiesce to the boundary agreed upon by the Treaty of Paris.

When the news was announced that the provisional peace had been signed, bringing the War for American Independence to an end, the post officials in the Old Northwest were greatly disturbed over the Indian situation which confronted them. Colonel De Peyster, commandant at Detroit, wrote:

We are all in expectation of news. Everything that is bad is spread through the Indian country — but as I have nothing more than the Kings Proclamation from Authority I evade answering Impertinent questions.

Heavens If goods do not arrive soon what will become of me — I have lost several stone wt. of flesh within these 20 days.[1]

He further complained that entire villages of Indians had journeyed to Detroit, " Impatient to know what is to become of them and their lands, and, to request a supply of goods so long promised them." [2] During a council he held with the Wabash, he complained they were very impertinent, " using expressions not proper to be committed to paper." Almost in desperation the Colonel exclaimed that he had written repeatedly representing his dilemma, and now hoped that orders were on the way directing him how to act, " in what, in all probability will be a most critical situation." [3]

Captain Robertson at Michilimackinac was not so much concerned about fresh supplies of goods, for he expected his

[1] De Peyster to Haldimand, June 18, 1783, British Museum, Add. MSS., 21,783, p. 318; De Peyster to Mathews, June 18, 1783, *Mich. Hist. Colls.,* XI, 369. General William Irvine had sent De Peyster some newspapers containing the " definite " treaty. *Ibid.,* 381. On June 18, 1783, De Peyster wrote: " I am still in hopes that notwithstanding it is reported we are to give up the Posts, we shall have it in our power to acquit ourselves honourably of our promises to the Indians, to whom much clothing is due—I am almost harassed out of all patience, but hitherto have kept from communicating the articles relative to the boundaries, the Indians nevertheless hear them from all quarters, and there are many Indians as well as whites amongst them that can read, and to whom even Lord Carlisle's speech is no secret." De Peyster to Maclean, *ibid.,* XX, 128.
[2] De Peyster to Haldimand, June 28, 1783, Add. MSS., 21,783, p. 320; *Mich. Hist. Colls.,* XI, 372. For a list of Indian presents, see *ibid.,* 382.
[3] De Peyster to Haldimand, June 28, 1783, Add. MSS., 21,783, p. 320.

post to be evacuated soon,[4] but seemed very uneasy that his bills were not paid.[5] In spite of exerting himself " to the utmost to decrease the Expenses in every Line," [6] Robertson was " much hurt & concerned " when the government did not honor his accounts.[7] He maintained that the post expenses were " fifty Thousand Pounds less than last year & much more work done than ever — hitherto partly to my Ruin as my pay goes faster than it comes." [8] This was often the experience of many a western official, confronted by most perplexing problems, and hundreds of miles away from the center of the government.[9]

Official intelligence of the Treaty of Paris via New York reached Quebec and the Governor, General Haldimand, on April 26, 1783. This was his first intimation of what the new boundary was to be, and it was a considerable shock. Much concerned about the Indians, he advised the western officials to avoid publishing the terms.[10] He ordered all labor upon fortifications to cease, and the transport of stores and provisions to be discontinued.[11] Haldimand sensed, as did the mer-

---

[4] Robertson to Claus, September 7, 1783, *Mich. Hist. Colls.*, XI, 383.

[5] Robertson to Mathews, April 20, 1783, *ibid.*, 358; same to same, June 27, 1783, *ibid.*, 369; same to Brehm, April 20, 1783, *ibid.*, 359.

[6] Same to Mathews, *ibid.*, 358.

[7] Same to Brehm, July 6, 1783, *ibid.*, 374; same to Mathews, August 9, 1783, *ibid.*, 379.

[8] Same to Brehm, July 6, 1783, *ibid.*, 374.

[9] On July 10, Robertson wrote Maclean: " I am sorry & ten times so that I ever came here, to be obliged to cringe & borrow Rum from Traders on account of Government, and they making a merit of giving it, is very distressing, and all that for a mere Bagatelle, however, it is my Lot to be here at this Juncture & no Friend to attempt to give me common assistance, to carry on the Service with the least Honour to Government or credit to myself—Now, Sir, if you cannot relieve my Distresses be pleased to represent them in a proper light." *Ibid.*, 375–76. Mathews informed Robertson July 22, 1784 (a year later), that his bills had been "duly honored." *Ibid.*, XX, 240.

[10] Canadian Archives, B, CIV, 407–9; Haldimand to Maclean, April 26, 1783; *Mich. Hist. Colls.*, XI, 361.

[11] *Ibid.* De Peyster informed Haldimand May 20, 1783, that he had ordered all work to "cease" at Detroit. *Ibid.*, 365. Major John (Jehu) Hay, De Peyster's successor at Detroit, must have failed to obey the above order for Haldimand wrote him, September 3, 1784, referring Hay to his former orders and said that any further expense incurred would be rejected save "such Repairs in Barracks as shall be indespensibly necessary for the Health and Comfort of the Troops." *Ibid.*, XX, 251. Haldimand had repeatedly asked Whitehall for instructions about the posts. Haldimand to Lord North, April 26, 1784, P. R. O., C. O. 42, XLVI, 261.

chants, the considerable loss to the fur trade by the surrender
of the western posts. Nevertheless, this was not his greatest
concern, as he often said, but what disturbed him most was
the reaction of the Indians. Just what would they do when
they understood that Britain had betrayed them by agreeing
to deliver their territories to their " implacable " enemies? He
therefore spent a great deal of energy in reconciling the Indians
with the victorious Americans. Fairly consistent efforts, directed from Quebec, were made to show the red men that it
was for their best interest to come to terms with their former
enemy. " It will be a difficult task," wrote the General, " after
what has happened to convince them of our good faith." He
complained to the Secretary for Home Affairs, Lord Sydney,
that the Americans " in the exultations of their present success," were making no attempts to conceal their designs
against the Indians.[12]

Soon after the information about the treaty had been received, the Governor was embarrassed by a visit from Joseph
Brant and another chief named John, who came as delegates
from the Six Nations. They had heard evil rumors and now
wished an explanation of the terms of the treaty. Haldimand
allayed the suspicions of his visitors with his usual astuteness,
and ordered Sir John Johnson to Niagara to pacify the fears
of the Indians, but his own mind was greatly troubled.[13] Possibly the horrors of the Pontiac War, only twenty years before, caused Haldimand to shudder, and made him fully conscious of the urgent need of satisfying the red men.

With this idea in mind he discussed with Brant and the
Indian agent Daniel Claus the expediency of settling the Indians, who were deprived of their lands by the Americans, on
the north side of Lake Ontario in the peninsula of southwest
Ontario.[14] This program was approved by Brant and some

[12] *Ibid.,* XLIV, 240. Thomas Townshend became Lord Sydney of Chislehurst
on March 6, 1783.
[13] Canadian Archives, Q, XXI, 220–21.
[14] Haldimand to Johnson, May 26, 1783, *Mich. Hist. Colls.,* XX, 123. North
had approved of this plan. North to Haldimand, August 8, 1783, Canadian
Archives, B, XLV, 115.

other leaders, but few Indians, in spite of their discontent, accepted the offer of the new lands. Every possible effort was now put forward to keep the tribes loyal to England, and especially to persuade them by increased presents [15] that Britain had not done what the suspicious red men thought she had done.[16] The union of the various tribes, developed during the War of Independence, was to be maintained. Brant was dispatched as a special agent of the Iroquois to the Creek and Cherokee tribes, while Alexander McKee among the Michigan tribes, and Simon Girty among the Ohio and Wabash Indians used their influence to uphold British ascendancy.[17] There is abundant evidence that throughout the years following the war the post officials and Indian agents pressed upon the untutored Indian minds the need of peace, and urged them to commit no depredations against the Americans.[18] But the crowning point in the practical argument from the viewpoint of the savage was the retention of the western posts.

Nevertheless, in spite of the Governor's endeavors the news of the treaty spread rapidly throughout the western country and the Indians by " entire villages " came clamoring to the posts begging for supplies.[19] This was exactly the state of affairs which Haldimand had foreseen when as early as May 7, 1783, he wrote Sydney:

My own anxiety at present arises from an apprehension of the effects which the Preliminaries will have upon the Minds of our Indian Allies, who will consider themselves abandoned to the resentment of an ungenerous and implacable Enemy; and who, in the exultation of their present Success, are at no pains to conceal their designs against them.[20]

[15] *Mich. Hist. Colls.*, XX, 124, 139, 177.
[16] Canadian Archives, Q, XXI, 220–21.
[17] *Ibid.*, 164, 174, 176, 179, 183; *Mich. Hist. Colls.*, XX, 164, 174–83.
[18] Canadian Archives, Q, XI, 367–71; XX, 154, 177; XXIV, 39; Add. MSS., 21,783, pp. 254, 261, 292, 311; P. R. O., C. O. 42, XLIV, 240; Canadian Archives, Claus Papers, III, 217; *ibid.*, *Report for 1885* (Ottawa, 1886), p. 347.
[19] Add. MSS., 21,783, p. 320; *Mich. Hist. Colls.*, XI, 372, 379, 407.
[20] P. R. O., C. O. 42, XLIV, 240. Robertson found the Indians "very anxious" about the treaty and hoped they would be "treated handsomely." Robertson to Brehm, July 6, 1783, *Mich. Hist. Colls.*, XI, 373–74. See also De Peyster's views, *ibid.*, 372, and those of McKee, *ibid.*, 385.

Haldimand had earlier advised De Peyster to inform the Indians that England could no longer assist them or " approve of their carrying war into the Enemy's country," but every possible aid would be given to " secure & defend their own against every Incursion of the Enemy." [21] De Peyster found that, in general, the Indians were " well disposed " to follow such instructions as they received from time to time. He was of the opinion that the Virginians would first break the truce,[22] and that all back settlers were " determined to exterminate the Indians." [23]

The Indians were very bitter over the treaty and informed the British that they were a free people, " subject to no power upon earth." They were allies of the King, but not his subjects, and therefore " he had no right whatever to grant away to the States of America, their rights or properties without a manifest breach of all Justice and Equity, and they would not submit to it." [24] No doubt the Indians looked upon England's conduct as " treacherous and cruel," as " scandalous & dishonorable," [25] and as " basely betraying " them without their consent; " an act," they claimed, " of cruelty and injustice that Christians *only* were capable of doing." [26] General Allan Maclean deeply pitied the Indians, and wrote Haldimand that should they commit outrages at giving up these posts, it would by no means surprise him.[27] Aside from assuring the Indians they would be cared for, and to cease making war [28] and to return to their hunting, the post officials did

[21] Haldimand to De Peyster, February 14, 1783, Add. MSS., 21,783, p. 292.

[22] De Peyster to Haldimand, May 3, 1783, *ibid.*, 311. This was in answer to Haldimand's orders of October 21, 1782, to restrain the Indians from every hostile act. *Ibid.*, 261.

[23] Same to same, November 21, 1782, *ibid.*, 274–75. De Peyster made an earnest effort to restrain the Indians but wrote that he was bound to support them in a defensive war which " will in spite of human prudence almost always terminate in an offensive one." Same to same, September 29, 1782, *ibid.*, 254.

[24] Maclean to Haldimand, May 18, 1783, *Mich. Hist. Colls.*, XX, 119.

[25] *Ibid.*, 118, 120. One Englishman wrote: " England had delivered up her innocent, valuable, and ancient Indian allies (no less than 24 different nations) to their most inveterate foes, who will soon exterminate the very race, although humanity shudders to the thought." P. R. O., Foreign Office V, vol. VII.

[26] *Mich. Hist. Colls.*, XX, 119.

[27] Maclean to Haldimand, May 18, 1783, *ibid.*, 121.

[28] *Ibid.*, XI, 370–71; XX, 117–21. The Indians were of the impression the

their utmost to prove to their former allies that England had not forsaken them.

There was good foundation for Haldimand's apprehensions. Captain Robertson had found it necessary to use the " well affected Traders " in mounting a guard to protect his post. He insisted that the Indians had not abandoned their scheme of attacking the fort. " However I will not be surprised by them," he wrote.[29] Brant was in high dudgeon, for he believed that England and the Five Nations were desirous of leaving the western Indians " in the lurch." In great umbrage, the Mohawk chief insisted that the English were " always too slow " offering " some excuse or other " for their delays. " You better say at once those goods [at Montreal] are not for the Indians, then you have a right to keep them where they are," he fumed.[30] De Peyster was alert and cautious, using all his influence to keep the red men peaceful. He pleaded with the Indians to surrender their prisoners and to end further atrocities on the frontiers.[31] He urgently requested his superiors for aid and orders, but in vain. At last, and in despair, he wrote McKee that the most they could do was to sit upon their " matts and smoke, or at most do no more than keep a lookout for our own Security."[32] Haldimand sent Johnson to hold a council with the Six Nations at Detroit, hoping to calm their

Americans desired peace, never entertaining " an Idea that the Americans looked upon them a conquered People." McKee to Johnson, June 2, 1785, P. R. O., C. O. 42, XLVIII, 137; Mich. Hist. Colls., XI, 458.

[29] Robertson to Mathews, August 26, 1784, Add. MSS., 21,758, p. 319. " The Traders do Duty every night in the Village," the Captain claimed. Later he wrote that some Chippewas came and abused him when he did not consent to their demands, calling him a liar and an imposter. The Indians insisted they had been encouraged to go to Canada and fight, losing their brothers and children, but now they were despised and allowed to starve. Same to same, September 7, 1784, ibid., p. 322. Robertson found the Ottawas hard to satisfy. " I am on my Guard," he wrote, " and uncompleated and ill provided as the Fort is, they must give me a hearty Beating before they succeed," in cutting off the fort. He knew the Indians were disgusted and in bad humor, so he warned the Detroit commander to be on his guard. Same to same, May 26, 1784, ibid., p. 280.

[30] P. R. O., C. O. 42, XLIX, 867–69.

[31] De Peyster to ———, June 5, 1783, Mich. Hist. Colls., XI, 367, 370–71; Canadian Archives, Claus Papers, III, 217. McKee also urged the Indians to make peace. Mich. Hist. Colls., XX, 177.

[32] De Peyster to McKee, ibid., XI, 364.

fears. Sir John held the conference on June 28, 1783, and addressing the braves, he said in part:

Although the King your Father has found it necessary . . . to conclude a long, bloody, expensive and unnatural war, by a Peace which seems to give you great uneasiness on account of the boundary Line agreed upon . . . you are not to believe, or even to think that by the Line . . . it was meant to deprive you of an extent of country, of which the right of Soil belongs to, and is in yourselves as Sole Proprietors. . . . Neither can I harbour an idea that the United States will act so unjustly or impolitically as to endeavour to deprive you of any part of your country under the pretext of having conquered it.[33]

But as time passed the Indians became more restless and the situation so serious that, in spite of former orders to observe the most rigid economy,[34] Sir Guy Carleton, now Lord Dorchester, who had succeeded Haldimand in 1786, ordered Johnson to meet the Indian deputies from the Upper Country and make every possible effort to placate them. "Actions will best express our good intentions," said Dorchester. "You will therefore send them away warmly clothed and bountifully supplied for their return."[35]

Thus it would seem that Britain's retention of the northwest posts in violation of the treaty can be explained, at least in the early days, in the desire to keep faith with her Indian friends. This is very clearly shown by a close examination of the documents. Nevertheless, many American historians have long insisted that Britain was simply desirous of holding on to the fur trade.[36] On the other hand, British authors have long defended the retention of the posts as a justifiable reprisal for American non-observance of the treaty, a *quid pro quo.*

[33] *Ibid.,* XX, 177.
[34] *Ibid.,* 251, 268; Canadian Archives, B, LXIV, 366-69. The expense was enormous and as Haldimand said "out of all proportion to what it was before the Rebellion." *Ibid.*
[35] Dorchester to Johnson, November 27, 1786, *ibid.,* B, LVII, 558; *Mich. Hist. Colls.,* XXIV, 40.
[36] This is the thesis of A. C. McLaughlin, "The Western Posts and British Debts," American Historical Association, *Report for 1894* (Washington, 1895). Stevens advances the idea that the failure to deliver the posts was a natural outgrowth of the incomplete nature of the treaty. Stevens, *Northwest Fur Trade,* chap. VII.

Naturally Haldimand had sensed the danger in the peace settlement to the fur trade, upon which so much of Canada's prosperity depended. It is useless to deny this fact. "The minds of the People," the Governor wrote, "are much alarmed at the Idea of abandoning the Posts in the Upper Country, which are no less necessary to their security than to their Commerce." [37] Earlier, he urged Townshend that "great care should be taken that "Niagara & Oswego should be annexed to Canada," for they were absolutely essential for securing the fur trade.[38] The Canadian fur merchants were "indignant at a lavish unnecessary concession, which induced the negotiators of the treaty with America to lay at her feet the most valuable branch of trade in this country." [39] Protests in the form of memorials literally swamped the British officials in Canada and at home.[40] The fur trade was of considerable value. In 1785, Lieutenant Governor Henry Hamilton was informed that the trade was estimated at £ 180,000 of which £ 100,000 came from territories under the jurisdiction of the United States.[41] This return shows a steady growth for in 1780 when the trade was disturbed by the war, the value of the returns from the Upper Country was estimated at about £ 150,000 of which one-third came from the Niagara and the Detroit areas,[42] and yet was the trade worth the great expense involved in retaining the posts and the possibility of war? Lord Shelburne certainly was not impressed with its great value and was of the opinion that its preservation was a great

[37] Haldimand to Townshend, May 7, 1783, P. R. O., C. O. 42, XLIV, 240.
[38] Same to same, October 25, 1782, *Mich. Hist. Colls.*, X, 668. Haldimand was hopeful that when peace did come the contending parties would retain what they possessed at the cessation of hostilities. Canadian Archives, Q, XX, 315. When three bateaux arrived at Niagara with passes from Governor George Clinton, Maclean refused to let them go "up the country" to trade. This seemed to be carrying out Haldimand's orders. Maclean to Haldimand, August 1, 1783, *Mich. Hist. Colls.*, XX, 158–59.
[39] Kingsford, *The History of Canada*, VII, 345.
[40] Canadian Archives, *Report for 1888*, p. 59; *ibid., Report for 1890*, p. 221; *ibid.,* Q, XX, 315; Shelburne Papers, LXXII, 455 ff.; Add. MSS., 21,885, p. 344.
[41] McGill to Hamilton, August 1, 1785, P. R. O., C. O. 42, XLVIII, 207–10; Canadian Archives, Q, XXV, 111 *et seq.*
[42] Grant to Haldimand, April 24, 1780, G. C. Davidson, *The Northwest Company* (Berkeley, 1918), appendix A; Stevens, *Northwest Fur Trade*, p. 106.

drain on the exchequer.[43] Lord Hawke asked Parliament whether a monopoly of the fur trade, which might cause another war, was worth alienating the good will of the Americans.[44] Gouveneur Morris held similar views and informed William Pitt that London would remain the center of the fur trade whoever carried it on in America.[45]

It was not until November, 1783, that Haldimand made up his mind that the posts should be retained, and even then it was not the value of the fur trade which brought this conclusion. It was something far more precious in his mind. It was human lives! In spite of the constant efforts the post officials and various Indian agents had made to establish amicable relations between the Americans and the Indians, outrages continued.[46] The Governor wrote Lord North on October 14:

> The Indians are still impatient for the communication of the conditions of the definitive treaty and of His Majesty's gracious intentions for their future welfare, which I promised them as soon as my dispatches should arrive. They have completed the general confederation from one extremity of North America to the other. They keep a watchful eye over the conduct of the Americans settled on the frontiers of this country. I hope the American States will exert themselves to prevent their subjects from making encroachments upon the Indian lands, to which some of them have had the impudence to assert a claim in consequence of the provisional treaty. In case things are carried to extremities, the Indians seem determined to defend themselves and to make the Americans feel the difference of a war carried on in their own manner from the late one, which was subject to restraints imposed upon it by His Majesty's officers.[47]

But a letter of November 27 shows Haldimand's final judgment. He said, in part, that the Indians:

> Entertain no idea (though the Americans have not been wanting to insinuate it) that the King either has ceded or had a right to cede their territories or hunting grounds to the United States of America. These people, My Lord, have as enlightened ideas of the nature and obligations of treaties as the most civilized nations have, and know that no infringement of the treaty in 1768 [Fort Stanwix] which

[43] *Parliamentary History of England*, XXIII, 409.
[44] *Ibid.*, 389.
[45] McLaughlin, " The Western Posts and British Debts."
[46] Winsor, *The Westward Movement*, pp. 243 ff.; James, *Clark*, pp. 342–58.
[47] Haldimand to North, October 14, 1783, Canadian Archives, Q, XXII, 5–6.

fixed the limits between their country and that of the different provinces in North America can be binding upon them without their
express concurrence and consent . . . In case things should proceed
to extremities, the event no doubt will be the destruction of the
Indians, but during the contest not only the Americans but perhaps
many of His Majesty's subjects will be exposed to great distresses.
To prevent such a disastrous event as an Indian war, is a consideration worthy the attention of both nations, and cannot be prevented
so effectually as by allowing the posts in the upper country to remain as they are for sometime.[48]

Thus not an argument is given for the fur trade, in the proposed retention of the upper posts. The Governor did make a
suggestion which later became an important part of England's
policy until the Jay Treaty in 1794. His own words best express it:

It would certainly be better for both nations and the most likely
means to prevent jealousies and quarrels that the intermediate
country between the limits assigned to Canada by the provisional
treaty and those established as formerly mentioned by that in the
year 1768 should be considered entirely as belonging to the Indians,
and that the subjects neither of Great Britain nor of the American
states should be allowed to settle within them, but that the subjects of each should have liberty to trade where they please.[49]

Another reason for Britain's refusal to surrender the posts
is one which does not lie so well marked on the surface. Did
not the sudden fall of the Shelburne Ministry, so friendly toward America, to be succeeded by the North-Fox combina-
tion which after a few months was followed by the Pitt Ministry, bring about a decided change in England's attitude
toward her former colonies? [49a] It was Lord Sydney, Secretary of State for Colonial Affairs in the Pitt Ministry, who replied to Haldimand's letters of the summer and autumn of
1783. Sydney commended the Governor for his work and
assured him that the ministry would never approve the sale
of military provisions and stores to the western posts, and

---

[48] Same to same, November 27, 1783, *ibid.*, XXIII, 46–47. This is the thesis
maintained by Professor Burt, *The Old Province of Quebec*, pp. 335–47.

[49] Canadian Archives, Q, XXII, 48.

[49a] Shelburne's Ministry fell in April, 1783, to be followed by the Fox-North
coalition (the Duke of Portland was the nominal Prime Minister), which in
turn was succeeded by that of Pitt in December, 1783.

also was of the opinion that these posts should be retained.[50] On the other hand, Britain was well aware of the impotency of the Confederation Congress, of the financial chaos and political disorders, and of the jealousy and quarreling in the newly established states. Not one of the European nations expected the American political experiment to succeed. The strategic importance of the frontier posts was well known in England and Canada, and surely in case of a war with America or with Spain, the British would be in a strong position. One may only conjecture, for naturally the records of the period are shrouded in mystery on this point, but did England also retain the posts with the hope that she might use them as a base of operations to win back her former colonies? To drive a wedge between the New England States and the others, or to " coffin up " the new nation between the Atlantic and the Appalachian Mountains, would be to her advantage. This would conform in general to eighteenth century British policy, and especially to the program followed after the downfall of Lord Shelburne.[51]

Whatever may have been England's various reasons for retaining the posts, a very satisfactory excuse soon arose when it became apparent that the feeble American Congress was unable to prevent the states from placing impediments in the way of the collection of British debts as stipulated by the treaty. Also, the states did not carry out the provisions of the treaty concerning the loyalists. These infractions were *ex post facto* excuses, but nevertheless strong ones.[52] Even had England promptly and entirely carried out the treaty, surely

[50] Sydney to Haldimand, April 8, 1784, Canadian Archives, Q, XXIII, 60–62.

[51] The British gave considerable aid and encouragement to the various separatist movements in Vermont, Kentucky, and Tennessee. S. F. Bemis, *Jay's Treaty* (New York, 1924), pp. 17–19. Johnson wrote Brant in 1787 that the American Union was falling to pieces (Shay's Rebellion), and that the eastern states were anxious to return to their former allegiance. Johnson to Brant, March 22, 1787, W. L. Stone, *The Life of Joseph Brant* (New York, 1838), II, 267–69.

[52] April 8, 1784, Lord Sydney wrote Haldimand as follows: " America has not on her part complied with even one article of the treaty." Canadian Archives, Q, XXIII, 62.

it may be questioned whether Congress would have been able to compel the states to fulfill their obligations. Very little time elapsed after ratification by America before vexatious state laws made collection of *bona fide* debts impossible. But one must remember there was no Supreme Court in existence to declare state laws violating a treaty unconstitutional. It is true both sides nullified provisions of the treaty. The American excuse may be explained by political impotency rather than an executive order to neglect the settlement of 1783. There was a sincere effort made by Congress to carry out its obligations until it was clearly evident that the posts were not to be vacated.

The Americans lost no time in their efforts to secure the possession of the posts which the treaty stipulated would come within their boundaries.[53] On May 1 of 1783, Congress directed the Secretary of War, Major General Benjamin Lincoln, to inform the Indian nations that the war had ceased, peace had been concluded, the posts would " speedily be evacuated," and that the United States would be " disposed to enter into friendly treaty with the different tribes." [54] Accordingly two days later Lincoln appointed Major Ephraim Douglass of Princeton, New Jersey, to carry out the instructions of Congress. Douglass, accompanied by Captain George McCully, immediately set out for Pittsburgh, and from there through the Indian country to Detroit.[55]

The commissioners arrived at Detroit July 4, where they were courteously received by Colonel De Peyster, to whom the message of General Lincoln was delivered.[56] De Peyster professed a desire to be helpful and bring about pacific relations with the Indians, but politely refused to allow any publication of the commissioners' instructions. His excuse was

[53] The posts of our immediate concern were Detroit and Michilimackinac. Others were Oswego, Fort Erie, Niagara, Oswegatchie, Point-au-Fer, and Dutchman's Point.

[54] Frank H. Severance, " The Niagara Peace Mission of Ephraim Douglass in 1783," *Buffalo Historical Society Publications* (Buffalo, 1914), XVIII, 115–42.

[55] P. R. O., C. O. 42, XLIV, 449–51.

[56] De Peyster to Maclean, July 7, 1783, *ibid.*, 439; *Mich. Hist. Colls.*, XX, 136–37.

that he had not had any orders to surrender the posts, and could not do so until authorized by his superiors.[57]

The following day, July 5, Douglass again requested permission to speak to the Indians, pledging his word " to confine himself to the offer of Peace or choice of War, and the Invitation to Treaty." But the commandant was not impressed, and sent McKee to inform the Americans that he desired they should depart as soon as possible for Niagara.[58]

Notwithstanding this refusal De Peyster invited Douglass to an Indian council on the 6th. There were assembled the chiefs of eleven tribes, but the American representative was not permitted to speak. De Peyster addressed the chiefs, advising them to live in peace with the Americans and giving notice he would not aid them against the people of the United States. The message from the Secretary of War was read, and with this Major Douglass had to be satisfied.

Frustrated in their efforts, the Americans left Detroit on the morning of July 7 for Niagara. De Peyster was considerably relieved when they departed. He wrote:

I have shewn them every civility consistent with my Duty, during their stay at this Place — and I have great reason . . . to be happy that they are embarked.

However great Enthusiasts (those Missionaries as they call themselves) may be, and however willing to risk martyrdom in the American cause, still it would bring an eternal slur upon me, should any drunken Indian, or any one whose suffering have been to great to have allowed him to listen to my Council, do them an ill turn. . . . Detroit is by no means a place for American Deputies to reside in until His Excellency's final orders are received.[59]

The peace embassy arrived in Niagara on the 11th. General Maclean graciously received them, but, as in Detroit, their efforts were futile and they left for home on the 16th. MacLean had never been kindly disposed toward the commissioners. He wrote De Peyster long before the Americans left for Niagara that:

[57] P. R. O., C. O. 42, XLIV, 437; Canadian Archives, Q, XXI, 347–49.
[58] Severance, " Peace Mission of Douglass," p. 126. Much of the correspondence of Douglass and Maclean is published by Severance in this article.
[59] De Peyster to Maclean, July 7, 1783, P. R. O., C. O. 42, XLIV, 439; Canadian Archives, Q, XXI, 350–51; Mich. Hist. Colls., XX, 138.

Ephraim is a suspicious name, I therefore am glad you have sent to bring him in to Detroit, for we really cannot be too much on our guard against these designing knaves, for I do not believe the world ever produced a more deceitful or dangerous set of men than the Americans: and now they are become such Arch-Politicians by eight years practice, that were old Matchioavell alive, he might go to school to the Americans to learn Politics more crooked than his own; we therefore cannot be too cautious.[60]

Contemporary with the peace mission of Douglass was the effort made by Baron Von Steuben who following orders from Washington set out for Canada to arrange with Haldimand for the transfer of all the American territory still in British possession. Steuben was instructed to proceed westward as far as Detroit to inspect the various posts which would soon be evacuated.[61] He arrived at Chambly on the 3rd of August and sent an aide-de-camp to Quebec giving notice of his mission.[62]

General Haldimand arranged for a meeting at Sorel on the 11th of August. The Baron began by stating that " every object of Dispute between Great Britain and the United States " had been settled by the peace lately proclaimed. Although not authorized to demand the posts " within the limits of the United States occupied by the British," yet he hoped there would be no objection to his visiting them, in order that he might " make such arrangement for the interest of the United States as may be necessary when they shall be delivered up." He further stated:

The United States of America wish to establish a perfect harmony with Great Britain by making good every engagement on her part & at the same time they have a right to expect that every promise which has been made on the part of Great Britain will be fulfilled.[63]

General Haldimand informed Von Steuben that although the United States might " consider the Provisional Treaty " as definitive, nevertheless, the sense he had of his own duty and the customs of war would not permit him to consider a

[60] Maclean to De Peyster, July 8, 1783, ibid., 139.
[61] Washington to Haldimand, July 12, 1783, ibid., 141; Washington to President of Congress, May 3, 1783, Ford, Writings of Washington, X, 239–40.
[62] Instructions to Steuben, July 12, 1783, ibid., 285–89; Steuben to Maclean, August 3, 1783, Mich. Hist. Colls., XX, 160–71; same to Haldimand, ibid.
[63] Same to same, August 11, 1783, ibid., 166–67.

cessation of hostilities in that light. He had received orders to discontinue hostile acts, which he had "punctually obeyed," and this he would continue to do. At such time as the ratification of peace was formally announced, he would carry out every order he might receive with "the utmost punctuality & despatch." Until that time he could not permit the Baron to continue his journey westward, nor could he negotiate with him further for the posts.[64] It seemed futile to continue their conversations, so Steuben soon set out for Philadelphia, but not until he wrote Haldimand a note of thanks for all the civilities heaped upon him by the General and his officers.[65]

Haldimand was justified in his position, for the definitive treaty had not been signed, and Steuben's mission was at least premature and as unfruitful as that of Douglass. Haldimand's actions were dictated by his sense of duty, for he had been informed " to do all in his power to conciliate the affections and confidence of the United States of America." [66] Then how may one explain his attitude toward Steuben? The explanation he gave is found in a letter to Lord North wherein he mentioned the recent visit and very candidly admitted that he was playing for time. He wrote:

Many bad and no good consequences might have arisen from such premature discussion. The longer the evacuation is delayed, the more time is given our traders to remove their merchandise, or to convert it into furs, and the greater opportunity is given to the officers under my command to reconcile the Indians to a measure for which they entertain the greatest abhorrence.[67]

No further efforts were made in 1783, but in May, 1784, Governor George Clinton of New York sent an embassy to obtain possession of Fort Niagara. This was no more success-

---

[64] Haldimand to Steuben, August 12, 1783, *ibid.*; P. R. O., C. O. 42, XLIV, 495. T. B. Wait, State Papers (Boston, 1814), I, 350 ff., contains all this correspondence; Canadian Archives, Q, XXI, 370, 388, 399, 402, 405.

[65] Steuben to Haldimand, August 17, 1783, *Mich. Hist. Colls.*, XX, 168. " The civilities and the politeness which I have received from these gentlemen from my entrance into Canada till my return to Crown Point will never be effaced from my memory," Steuben wrote.

[66] Canadian Archives, Q, XXI, 388.

[67] Haldimand to North, August 20, 1783, *ibid.*, 390.

ful than the earlier efforts.[68] The last American attempt to secure the posts was made in July of the same year when Secretary of War, General Henry Knox, sent Colonel William Hull; but again Haldimand pleaded his lack of instructions.[69] He declared to the Colonel that it was his private opinion that the posts ought not to be surrendered until the American states fulfilled the part of the treaty which concerned the loyalists. Haldimand felt that many of these had met " with the grossest ill treatment of every Kind, and for which they could not obtain the smallest redress." But Haldimand's real attitude was more clearly revealed in his correspondence with Lord North and Lord Sydney as has been shown.[70] After Hull's failure the army officials dropped the whole matter, allowing the diplomats to settle the controversy. For it was apparent that by 1784 no move would be taken by England to evacuate the posts except as a part of a general compact which would determine the future status of the Old Northwest. But a decade was to run its course before any agreement of the outstanding problems could be negotiated. Meanwhile the fur merchants, expecting that the posts would be held for an indefinite time, began once more the exploitation of the " rich commercial prize which the fortunes of war and a diplomacy of opportunism and delay had delivered into their hands."

Favor with the Indians had to be preserved and all discontent quieted if the fur trade was to be profitable. It was only natural for the Indians to turn to the British, their former allies, for aid and advice. It was a difficult position for the English to sympathize with the red men and at the same time

[68] Clinton to Haldimand, March 19, 1784, *Mich. Hist. Colls.*, XX, 215; Knox to Haldimand, June 13, 1784, *ibid.*, 230.

[69] Knox to Haldimand, June 13, 1784, Canadian Archives, Q, XXIII, 332; Hull to Haldimand, July 12, 1784, *Mich. Hist. Colls.*, XX, 238; Haldimand to Hull, July 13, 1784, *ibid.*; Haldimand to Knox, July 13, 1784, Canadian Archives, B, LXIV, 57; *ibid.*, Q, XXIII, 333–35.

[70] Haldimand to North, August 20, 1783, *ibid.*, B, LVI, 125; Haldimand to Townshend, May 7, 1783, P. R. O., C. O. 42, XLIV, 240. Townshend in a letter of April 8, 1784, expressed complete approval of Haldimand's actions. Townshend to Haldimand, April 8, 1784, Canadian Archives, B, XLV, 129.

to avoid any policy of open support. Brant journeyed to London during the winter of 1785–1786, in an effort to learn exactly what position His Majesty's government would take if any serious difficulties developed between his people and the Americans. But Lord Sydney gave Brant little encouragement, although he informed him that the King had the welfare of the Indians at heart.[71] On the other hand, Sydney instructed Lieutenant Governor Henry Hope of Quebec to give no open assistance to the savages, but not to abandon or estrange them, for the very peace and prosperity of the province demanded that.[72] One cannot doubt that the British desired peace between the Americans and Indians; indeed, the very life of the fur trade depended upon it. Lord Dorchester informed Sydney that he was of the opinion that the Americans would leave the English in control of the posts for the time being. In the meantime, they would locate along the line of communications in the Northwest in such a way as eventually to control the fur trade as well as to occupy the entire area when they deemed the time opportune.[73] During 1786 and 1787, when it seemed as if war would break out between the Indians and the Americans, the British felt that the friendship of the nations northwest of the Ohio should be maintained at all costs, for they might be needed to protect the forts. Even Sydney suggested that it might be necessary to give the savages ammunition with which to defend themselves.[74]

An important factor in strengthening British control over the Indians of the lake region had been the formation of the North West Fur Company in 1783.[75] Ever since the beginning of the British régime the French traders and *voyageurs* in the employ of the independent English and Scotch traders came

[71] Sydney to Brant, April 6, 1786, *ibid.*, Q, XXVI, pt. i, 80; Bemis, *Jay's Treaty*, p. 14. See Stone's *Life of Brant*, II, pp. 247–61, for the best account of Brant's trip to England and the receptions accorded him.

[72] Sydney to Hope, April 6, 1786, Canadian Archives, Q, XXVI, pt. i, 73.

[73] Dorchester to Sydney, June 13, 1787, *ibid.*, XXVIII, 16.

[74] Sydney to Dorchester, April 5, 1787, *ibid.*, Q, XXVII, pt. i, p. 44; same to same, September 4, 1787, *ibid.*, Q, XXVIII, 28.

[75] See especially Stevens, *The Northwest Fur Trade*, chaps. V and VI.

in the spring season to Detroit, Michilimackinac, St. Joseph, Green Bay, Sault Ste. Marie, and Grand Portage with their bateaux loaded with the furs purchased in trade with the Indians. To these same posts were carried up from Montreal, at the opening of the season, the woollen and cotton goods, trinkets, hardware, liquor, *et cetera* imported from London for the fur trade. Competition was keen between the independent traders, often causing open warfare which brought complete chaos to the trade.[76] There were twelve large operators in the Old Northwest at the close of 1782. The next year most of these pooled their business and formed a stock corporation, known as the North West Company. In 1787 the other independent traders joined this association.

Detroit and Michilimackinac were the headquarters for the trade between the Great Lakes and the Mississippi, as well as important bases for the trade at Grand Portage. The canoes from Montreal stopped at these posts to procure additional supplies or to change the nature of their cargoes, then consisting of one-third provisions and two-thirds merchandise. The vital importance of these posts is revealed by Frobisher who wrote: " Should the United States be put in possession of the Posts, their situation will be still more precarious, as the Americans will have it in their power to injure or Ruin every man from this part of the Province, who depends on receiving his Provisions from that Settlement." [77]

Meanwhile with the war between England and her former colonies brought to a close, American emigrants began settling across the Appalachian Mountains, especially the region northwest of the Ohio.[78] This disturbed and angered the Indians, and alarmed over the loss of their hunting grounds,

---

[76] Benjamin and Joseph Frobisher to Haldimand, October 4, 1787, Canadian Archives, Q, XXIV, pt. ii, 409; Johnson, *The Michigan Fur Trade*, pp. 87, 92–94; Stevens, *loc. cit.*, chap. V.

[77] Frobisher to Hamilton, May 2, 1785, Canadian Archives, Q, XXIV, pt. ii, 423. The area dependent upon Detroit included roughly the Maumee and Wabash Valleys, with that section of Illinois which was reached by way of the Wabash, and the region south of Lake Erie. The small posts at Saginaw and Sandusky also procured supplies from Detroit.

[78] Haldimand to Sydney, October 24, 1784, *ibid.*, B, LVIII, 14. Winsor, *Westward Movement*, p. 243. An excellent account of this migration is found in James, *Clark*, chap. XV.

they brought on a series of wars which greatly injured the fur trade. Although the savages were primarily fighting the Americans, nevertheless, the British suffered considerably, for in the minds of the Indians there was a deep anger against their former allies for having given their lands to their enemies. This all materially affected the fur trade, for the time of the Indians was taken away from hunting and trading, while many British traders were unable to avoid serious losses in the constant warfare. The trade of Detroit was at its lowest point in the years of 1785 and 1786. Alexander Henry comments on the conditions in a letter to William Edgar: " I don't either pitty the Indians nor blame the Americans, but I feel for you and my friends at Detroit, who has [sic] large connections in that country." [79] James McGill of Montreal expressed a very clear understanding of the problems confronting the Wabash traders, when he wrote:

We sincerely hope that the disturbance raised in the Indian Country by the Americans may be at an end, but we fear there will for many years to come be frequent interruptions to the quiet of the Indians which must constantly affect the Trade of your place, and we confess to you that with respect to the Wabash Trade we do not entertain favorable Sentiments were Peace even assured, the easy communication with new Orleans & the proximity to the Americans are strong temptations to people of loose Principles when in debt to defraud their Creditors, and if prudence would permitt that Trade being given up, at least as to giving Credit, perhaps the general Returns would not be much inferior to what they now are, or if they were, better prices might be obtained for Peltries.[80]

This was a prophecy which proved only too true. All attempts to maintain order were wasted although the officials made every effort.[81] The trade declined year after year,[82]

[79] Henry to Edgar, November 12, 1786, Edgar MSS.

[80] McGill to Askin, December 20, 1786, *Askin Papers*, I, 278.

[81] Dorchester to Johnson, November 27, 1786, *Mich. Hist. Colls.*, XXIV, 39. Dorchester advises Sir John to " mildly reproach them [Indians] for the Injuries and violence offered to our Traders . . . and represent to them the great want of understanding as well as injustice in thus ill treating inoffensive men who peaceably go among them, only to supply their wants."

[82] In 1789, the number of packs of furs which the Detroit area yielded was reported as 500 less than the year before. Canadian Archives, M, vol. 852 (no pagination). This situation did not improve. In 1784, the trade was estimated at £ 60,000, in 1790 at only £ 40,800. Stevens, *Northwest Fur Trade*, p. 109, n. 59.

and in 1790 the fur trade was seriously injured by General Josiah Harmar's invasion of the Miami country. As the Americans advanced westward the Indians retreated, burning their own homes, their corn, as well as that of the traders, and seized the traders' ammunition.[83]

The conditions in and about Detroit did not improve with the passing years. It was obvious that the fur trade in that area was doomed before the onrush of settlers. Hamilton had predicted such a situation as early as 1785. He wrote:

The Western Indians must in a very few Years have the Mississippi for their Eastern Boundary, in which case the Beaver, Deer, and Buffaloe skin trade will decline so fast that it will scarcely be an object worth attention throughout all that district which they now occupy. The active and avaricious Americans having driven the Indians and exhausted the hunting Country, will become planters.

They must force a trade for their Lumber, Maiz, Cotton and Tobaco. The vast range of natural meadows which fed numerous herds of Buffaloe, will furnish such an abundance of forage, that the raising herds of Cattle will be no expence, and demand few hands.[84]

By the summer of 1785 the Americans were still uncertain as to the real intentions of Great Britain. Since English officials persisted in their friendship toward the savages and their aid to the emigrants from the states, it was believed they had no intentions of surrendering the posts.[85] Indeed, General Haldimand had ordered that the posts were to be

[83] *Ibid.*, p. 108. Major John Smith writes: "Mr. Sharp states in a letter to Mr. Leith, that his houses, corn etc. were consumed in the general conflagration. That the Indians burned not only the houses of the traders, but even their own." Letter of Major Smith, October 16, 1790, *Mich. Hist. Colls.*, XXIV, 103; also 107; Smith to Le Maistre, October 20, 1790, *ibid.* Here Smith mentions the burning of the "Miamis Town."

[84] Hamilton to Sydney, April 7, 1785, Canadian Archives, Q, XXIV, pt. i, 247. Quoted in Stevens, *op. cit.*, p. 109. While the trade at Detroit was declining, that at Michilimackinac was in its heyday. See *ibid.*, pp. 109–19 for an excellent account of this trade.

[85] Johnston, *Correspondence and Public Papers of John Jay*, III, 214. Haldimand had given strict orders concerning all emigrants who proposed to settle in the neighborhood of Detroit. Haldimand to Hay, April 26, 1784, Canadian Archives, Claus Papers, IV, 21–22. All new settlers were required to take the following oath: "I .... do promise and declare that I will maintain and defend to the utmost of my Power the Authority of the King in His Parliament as the supreme Legislature of this Province." *Ibid.*

defended to the last, if the Americans made any attempt to take them.[86] The situation for the post commanders was most delicate. Strict orders had been issued by their superiors to limit expenses,[87] and at the same time they had to maintain their posts and keep the Indians satisfied. Expenses mounted higher and higher until Haldimand refused to sanction many bills presented to him.[88]

Nevertheless, expenses continued. Prices were high at the posts and repairs were essential for safety. Johnson forbade the Indian Department to purchase fresh meat " not only on account of the shameful price . . . but as an article totally unnecessary, particularly at this time." [89] He estimated the cost at three or four times the amount for which it could be sent down from Montreal, but added that McKee was doing his best to keep expenses down.[90] During the critical year of 1793 Colonel England at Detroit felt himself " very awkwardly circumstanced " about issuing provisions for the Indian Department. His " private opinion " was that McKee should have everything he demanded for the use of the people under his charge, for he felt the requests were made with discretion, but found that his powers were limited.[91] This refusal brought forth strong protests from Elliott and Selby of the Indian Department. Selby wrote:

> I never was so much astonished as to hear from Elliott that Colonel England would allow no more provision to be sent to the rapids untill he heard from the Gov'r — I conceive the Commanding officer wants no other authority than your requisition for whatever you may judge necessary for the Department. . . . I have enclosed my thoughts on the subject which I would not hesitate one moment in dispatching to the Governor, and in case of absolute necessity, I would order Provisions to be brought or borrowed

---

[86] Haldimand to De Peyster, October 15, 1784, *ibid.*, B, LXV, 52.

[87] Mathews to Robertson, August 12, 1784, *Mich. Hist. Colls.*, XX, 244. The order of April 26, 1783, read: " discontinue entirely every species of public works," while the entire expense of the Indian Department was to be controlled by Sir John Johnson.

[88] Haldimand to Hay, September 3, 1784, *ibid.*, 251; Haldimand to ————, November 14, 1784, *ibid.*, 268. In 1783 it cost £ 12,307/15/1½ to maintain the post of Detroit and £ 7,594/11/9¾ for Michilimackinac. *Ibid.*, 109.

[89] Johnson to Haldimand, November 17, 1783, *ibid.*, 200.

[90] Johnson to Mathews, September 23, 1784, *ibid.*, 259.

[91] England to McKee, May 21, 1793, *ibid.*, XII, 53.

that the public service might not suffer from the ignorance or folly of one of its officers.[92]

Rather strong language from an inferior officer, but Selby felt that the British control over the Indians was at stake. Prices were high in the back country. Flour cost £ 5 per hundred at Detroit in 1783. Other prices paid toward the close of the period were: corn at £ 1 per bushel, tobacco at 6/ per pound, cotton 2/2 [93] while salt which cost 2/6 at Montreal, and 15/ at Kingston, sold for 40/ per bushel at Detroit.[94]

Repairs were necessary at the posts as long as they were to be held. Robertson found that with the opening of spring in 1784, the wharf at Michilimackinac was broken to pieces, " so that no kind of Craft could be loaded or unloaded." He had it repaired, but " it was a very troublesome Jobe in very cold weather, & not a drop of Rum to give the workmen," he complained.[95] By August the picketing of the fort, the road to it, and the wharf seemed to require " repairing after every shower of Rain and Gust of Wind." [96] In 1792, Captain Gother Mann made a survey of the posts. He reported to Lord Dorchester that the cause for so many repairs at Michilimackinac was due to the fact that the works were " injudiciously designed " and were never half finished. " The only object," he wrote, " as to the Works, has been to keep the place in such a temporary state of repair and defense, as might make it looked to with some sort of respect by the Indians, and consequently give a proportional degree of safety and protection to the trade." [97] It was estimated that £ 367/17/3 would have to be spent to repair the " ruinous conditions " of the walls and the " perfectly rotten pickitting." [98] Colonel England grumbled that the platforms of the fort were " so decayed as to be rendered

[92] Selby to McKee, May 20, 1793, *ibid.*, 52; Elliott to McKee, May 20, 1793, *ibid.*

[93] *Ibid.*, XX, 170, 455; Canadian Archives, M, CVII, 192. For other prices see *Mich. Hist. Colls.*, XII, 87, 109, 182, 184, 192.

[94] Simcoe to Dundas, May 26, 1792. P. R. O., C. O. 42, vol. 316, p. 198.

[95] Robertson to Mathews, May 26, 1784, Add. MSS., 21,758, p. 280.

[96] Same to same, August 26, 1784, *ibid.*, p. 319. On September 7, he wrote that the wharf was again broken up by a gale of wind. *Ibid.*, p. 322.

[97] Mann's report to Dorchester, October 29, 1792, P. R. O., C. O. 42, vol. 88, p. 530.

[98] Canadian Archives, Q, LX, 222.

useless, and only two Gun Carriages in the Garrison fit for Service." [99] Other requests were made from time to time by the various officials connected with Michilimackinac,[100] but in May of 1793 it was reported that the post had been so long neglected and so completely decayed that " nothing short of an entire reestablishment on some new system can . . . answer any purpose." [101]

Detroit fared somewhat better than many other western posts. Some of the " picketing " was renewed, small repairs to the barracks were made, and a new provision store was built.[102] It was estimated in 1792 that it would cost £ 3,499/7/6 to repair properly the wharf and works, and to put up the necessary buildings.[103] This was prohibitive and only the essential repairs were sanctioned. Lord Dorchester had recommended to Henry Dundas, the Home Secretary, the precautions necessary for defense if the posts were to be held, for Canada was one to fourteen in population as compared with the United States, he wrote.[104] But England was engrossed in a war with France, and there was very little money to spend on forts which soon might be relinquished.

The situation in the western country had yearly become more alarming for the United States. The fertile lands were inviting increasing numbers of settlers, who were isolated from the eastern seaboard by the Appalachians. The Northwest was in the control of hostile Indian tribes who were naturally

[99] England to Le Maistre, July 17, 1792, *Mich. Hist. Colls.*, XXIII, 333.

[100] *Ibid.*, XXIV, 359, 428–30.

[101] Fisher to Clarke, May 3, 1793, *ibid.*, 534.

[102] *Ibid.*, XII, 57; XXIII, 336–38, 396–97; XXIV, 409, 533, 535; Canadian Archives, C, vol. 247, p. 229.

[103] *Ibid.*, Q, LX, 222. See also England to Le Maistre, May 1, 1795, *Mich. Hist. Colls.*, XXIII, 396.

[104] Dorchester to Dundas, October 25, 1793, *ibid.*, XXIV, 621–23. The problem of supplying the posts during the last years of the régime grew more difficult due largely to increased costs, the Indian wars, and lack of proper transportation facilities. Craigie to Clarke, August 2, 1792, P. R. O., C. O. 42, vol. 319, p. 88: same to same, October 27. 1792. *ibid.*, p. 94; same to Dorchester, July 19, 1794, *ibid.*, p. 154; Simcoe to Dorchester, December 10, 1794, *ibid.*, pp. 111–44; Cruikshank, *The Correspondence of Simcoe, etc.*, III, 205 ff. There was often an insufficiency of stores, " unserviceable," or destroyed with " filth & vermin." Sparkman to England, July 12, 1792, *Mich. Hist. Colls.*, XXIII, 332; England to Le Maistre, August 29, 1793. *Ibid.*, 335; Doyle to Le Maistre, July 15, 1795, *ibid.*, 339; " survey of barrack utensels," May 4, 1796, *ibid.*, 340–41.

desirous of carrying on a war against those who encroached upon their lands. These were indeed critical years for the young American republic. Alert to the need of peace with the Indians, agents of Congress were negotiating everywhere, and all the time, but in vain. At Fort Stanwix in 1784, at Fort McIntosh in 1785, at Fort Finney in 1786, and at Fort Harmar in 1789, earnest efforts were made to unravel the ugly problem, and to provide new boundaries which would make room for the white settlements beyond the old line.[105] These treaties were to become mere scraps of paper for the political union of the Indians was exceedingly loose and weaker than that of the Americans. Meanwhile the trickle of immigrants continued and was growing into an angry stream. Upon the establishment of the new national government in the spring of 1789, President Washington decided to end negotiations and to demonstrate the power of the new government by a vigorous military movement. Accordingly, General Harmar in 1790 was placed in command of a punitive expedition against the Miamis. The recruits were raw and Harmar was without the necessary experience, so the whole campaign " petered out." [106] But more energetic and elaborate preparations were undertaken the following spring to wipe out the disgrace of Harmar's failure. The command was given to Arthur St. Clair, Governor of the Northwest Territory.[107] Congress voted two thousand troops for six months, and two small regiments of regulars. The recruits were without discipline and shamefully inefficient, while supplies were shockingly inadequate. St. Clair was ordered northward from Fort Washington (near the present Cincinnati) to the Indian villages on the Maumee River. Setting out on October 4, 1791, the army moved slowly through dense forests in favorable weather, but handicapped by discontent, desertion, and lack of discipline. On the night of November 3, the army camped on the eastern fork of the

[105] For these treaties and negotiations, see *American State Papers, Indian Affairs*, I, 5–6, 10–11; J. H. Perkins, *Annals of the West to 1845* (Cincinnati, 1846); Winsor, *Westward Movement;* Bemis, *Jay Treaty,* pp. 111–12.

[106] Roosevelt, *The Winning of the West,* III, 83–92.

[107] *American State Papers, Indian Affairs,* I, 137. The St. Clair papers, which were captured by the Indians and turned over to the British, are calendared in Canadian Archives, *Report for 1890.*

Wabash, some ninety miles north of Fort Washington. The next morning, the Indians burst unexpectedly upon the ill-equipped and poorly-led Americans and inflicted a second Braddock's disaster.[108] This crushing defeat crippled American military operations in the Old Northwest for about a year.[109]

Naturally the American officials sensed the possibility of St. Clair's expedition causing some tension among the British officials at Detroit. Knox instructed St. Clair that "every measure tending to any discussion or altercation must be prevented." He was simply to awe and curb the Indians.[110] In fact, some months later this same advice was given when the Secretary of War stated:

We must by all means avoid involving the United States with Great Britain, until events arise of the quality & magnitude as to impress the people of the United States and the world at last of the rank injustice and unfairness of their procedure. But a war with that power in the present state of affairs, would retard our power, growth and happyness beyond almost the power of calculation.[111]

St. Clair was meticulous in carrying out these orders, although he never got near enough the Maumee to cause the Detroit officials much alarm. He informed the officers at Detroit before he set out on his expedition that his efforts were solely directed toward the Indians and not at the British,[112] and this was Dorchester's impression.[113]

Nevertheless, in spite of these disastrous American cam-

[108] One of the most graphic accounts of St. Clair's campaign is found in Roosevelt, *Winning of the West*, III, chap. IV.

[109] The British account of St. Clair's defeat is found in P. R. O., C. O. 42, LXXII, 153–54; LXXXVIII, 348–49; LXXXIX, 381–85; Quebec *Gazette,* January 5, 1792; *Mich. Hist. Colls.,* XXIV, 159–65; Canadian Archives, *Report for 1890,* 320 ff. William May of Detroit claimed that the doctor in St. Clair's army was ordered to poison the liquor which would be left for the Indians, if St. Clair's men were defeated. But in the confusion and haste following the battle the doctor forgot to carry out his orders. *Mich. Hist. Colls.,* XXIV, 420–21.

[110] Knox to St. Clair, March 21, 1791, P. R. O., C. O. 42, XC, 359–60; *Mich. Hist. Colls.,* XXIV, 197.

[111] Same to same, July 14, 1791, P. R. O., C. O. 42, LXXXIX, 195–96; *Mich. Hist. Colls.,* XXIV, 288.

[112] St. Clair to Smith, September 19, 1790, Canadian Archives, Q, XLIX, 105–106; *Mich. Hist. Colls.,* XXIV, 99; Smith to St. Clair, October 14, 1790, *ibid.,* 102–103; Canadian Archives, Q, XLIX, 107–109.

[113] Dorchester to Lord Grenville, November 15, 1791, *ibid.,* LIV, pt. ii, 622 ff. This was not the impression of Simcoe who was made the first lieutenant governor of Upper Canada in 1791. He wrote Dundas that St. Clair had established "with a strong hand" a post in the vicinity of Detroit, "which both in manner

paigns, they were not without far-reaching results. Dorchester made even greater efforts to preserve Britain's neutrality and offered his good services to bring about peace. " We are at peace with the United States," he wrote, " and wish to remain so"; [114] and Brant was warned that Great Britain was anxious for the Indians to avoid hostilities.[115] In this respect, Dorchester was only carrying out the orders of his superiors.[116] He proposed a definite plan for settling the disputes, but to no avail.[117] Simcoe was of the impression that St. Clair's defeat would have beneficial results,[118] and he suggested a definite boundary between the Americans and Indians.[119]

But the most important result from the American standpoint was the effect upon the fur trade. These American campaigns resulted in considerable losses to the fur merchants in pelts, while the Indians, whenever they retreated, burned their villages, destroyed the traders' houses, seized their ammunition, and burned their corn.[120] The merchants at Detroit urged Dorchester to persuade the Indians to listen to terms of

& purpose according to European Politicks would be deemed a most dangerous aggression." Simcoe to Dundas, February 16, 1791, P. R. O., C. O. 42, CCCXVI, 79. This was typical of Simcoe's snap judgments, long before he knew anything about the Upper Country. As early as 1790, Dorchester had written to Grenville that he had given strict orders to the officers at Detroit against giving the Indians any aid. Dorchester to Grenville, November 20, 1790, Canadian Archives, Q, XLIX, 173. Sir John Johnson was reproved for not using every means to preserve peace. Motz to Johnson, September 27, 1790, *ibid.*, XLIV, pt. ii, 526–28.

[114] Dorchester to Gordon and Smith, January 20, 1791, P. R. O., C. O. 42, LXXIII, 109–10; same to Johnson, February 10, 1791, *ibid.*, 137–38; Le Maistre to Gordon, January 23, 1792, Canadian Archives, Claus Papers, IV, 1–2; Dorchester to Dundas, March 23, 1792, *Mich. Hist. Colls.*, XXIV, 386–89.

[115] Gordon to Brant, March 20, 1792, P. R. O., C. O. 42, XC, 324–25. Major John Smith at Detroit urged the Indians to make peace. *Mich. Hist. Colls.*, XXIV, 137–38.

[116] Grenville to Dorchester, October 20, 1789, P. R. O., C. O. 42, LXV, 358–59; same to same, March 7, 1791; *ibid.*, LXXIII, 30–31. Dundas to Dorchester, September 16, 1791, Canadian Archives, Q, LII, 206–207.

[117] Dorchester to Dundas, March 23, 1792, *Mich. Hist. Colls.*, XXIV, 386–89. For an excellent account of Dorchester's work see Bemis, *Jay's Treaty*, pp. 115 ff.

[118] Simcoe to Dundas, February 16, 1792, *Mich. Hist. Colls.*, XXIV, 377; P. R. O., C. O. 42, CCCXVI, 76–77.

[119] Simcoe to George Hammond, June 21, 1792, *ibid.*, CCCXVII, 26; *Mich. Hist. Colls.*, XXIV, 426.

[120] Smith to Le Maistre, October 20, 1790, *ibid.*, 107; Richardson to Porteous, April 23, 1790, Canadian Archives, M, vol. 852; Beaubien to Smith, February 18, 1792, P. R. O., C. O. 42, XC, 355; McKee to Johnson, September 19, 1790, Canadian Archives, Q, XLVI, pt. ii, 530–31.

peace, in order that the trade might be carried on "with safety."[121] Major John Smith at Detroit was of the opinion that the trade was greatly affected, not only by the wars, but also because the Indians were discontented for they believed that the English had deceived them.[122] Governor Simcoe maintained that the wars had ruined the trade of Detroit and even that of Michilimackinac was on the decline.[123] In 1793, the "returns" were "very bad" and some of the traders were threatened with ruin.[124] Meanwhile, political control over the Indians south of the Great Lakes was threatened by the American forces and by the increasing settlements. This had been clearly foreseen by Hamilton as early as 1785, as we have noted.[125]

In the fall of 1791, the British government sent George Hammond as their minister to the United States, for they realized the need of more direct negotiations. It was suggested that Hammond should propose the good offices of the British government to end the strife between the Indians and the Americans.[126] But these long drawn out negotiations have no part in our story.[127]

Fate was playing a major rôle in determining the future of the Northwest posts. The years from 1789 on were filled with international complications upon which England had to center all her energy. Again, the growing strength of the American national government under Washington's able guidance, and the westward movement of the Americans, all tended to make

[121] Northwest Traders to Dorchester, August 10, 1791, P. R. O., C. O. 42, LXXXIII, 411–13.
[122] Smith to Leith, February 14, 1792, *Mich. Hist. Colls.*, XXIV, 375–76.
[123] Simcoe to Dorchester, August 24, 1793, *ibid.*, 600. Simcoe had urged the entire fur trade be put in the hands of companies. Simcoe to ———, April 28, 1792, P. R. O., C. O. 42, CCCXVI, 157–58.
[124] Richardson to Porteous, August 15, 1793, Canadian Archives, M, vol. 852, p. 57.
[125] Hamilton to Sydney, April 7, 1785, *ibid.*, Q, XXIV, pt. i, 247. Quoted, *ante*, p. 250.
[126] Bemis, *Jay's Treaty*, pp. 92, 94, 115.
[127] The official correspondence dealing with these negotiations will be found in P. R. O., C. O. 42, vols. 72, 89, 90, 316, 318, 319; *ibid.*, F. O., IV, vols. 14, 15, 16; V, vol. 4; CXV, vol. 1; Canadian Archives, Q; *Mich. Hist. Colls.*, XXIV, 384, 424–26, 459–66.

the British more willing to begin conversations which led to the settling of the boundary dispute.

The first international complication was the Nootka Sound controversy between England and Spain, which for a time seemed to assume the proportions of a general European war.[128] Spain's surrender in this crisis put an end to England's anxiety as to the action America might take in case of a Spanish war.

Soon after this problem had been settled, England's attention and resources were taxed to the utmost for nearly twenty years by the great struggle with France, known in history as the French Revolution and Napoleonic Wars.[129] Therefore, from 1792 on, Britain's attitude toward America was more promising, until in 1794 negotiations were undertaken which finally culminated in the Jay Treaty.

But there were other factors which played a major rôle in this controversy. Among these was the gradual realization that the fur trade, at least that carried on south of the Great Lakes, was showing evidences of decline. The Indian wars were disastrous to the trade.[130] Many traders refused to continue their labors because the business was more and more uncertain and unsafe.[131] The trade of Michilimackinac suffered only slightly during this period from 1783 to 1796, because the traders extended their operations far to the west and northwest, holding the areas against all competitors. The close of the Revolution had ushered in a period of great competition which was ruinous. In order to survive the market which was glutted with goods, the merchants of Michilimackinac pooled their

[128] The best account for the relation of the United States to this controversy is W. R. Manning, "The Nootka Sound Controversy," *American Historical Association Annual Report, 1904* (Washington, 1905), pp. 279–479; and Bemis, *Jay's Treaty,* pp. 51–62.

[129] The effect of these wars has been ably handled by Professor Bemis, *ibid.,* chap. VII.

[130] *Mich. Hist. Colls.,* XXIV, 306; XXV, 29; *Wis. Hist. Colls.,* XII, 76–82; Todd to Askin, August 10, 1792, *Askin Papers,* I, 426.

[131] Governor Simcoe wrote in 1793 that the trade of Detroit was ruined by the wars. Simcoe to Hammond, August 24, 1793, *Mich. Hist. Colls.,* XXIV, 600. The whole problem of the collection of debts was also a factor. Todd and McGill to Askin, December 20, 1786, *Askin Papers,* I, 273–79; Dorchester to Sydney, October 14, 1788, *Canadian Archives, Q,* XXXVIII, 164.

interests in an organization called the General Store which lasted until 1787.[132] Similar problems faced the Detroit merchants, and this led to the formation of the Miami Company in 1786. But as the trade continued in a depressed condition, only large-scale enterprises could be even partially successful. As early as 1790 the name of but one trader appears in the returns, whose outfit was a single canoe.

The French Revolution had a decidedly injurious effect upon the fur market, almost causing a commercial panic. Furs fell rapidly in price and some of the merchants suffered a loss on the pelts already consigned to their London agents. This is well illustrated by William Robertson of Detroit who, while in London, wrote to John Askin that the war with France had brought about a " great fall of furs " and very likely " to produce a further depreciation of their value." [133] In 1793 John Richardson of Montreal summed up his feelings in the following words:

The Returns from the Indian Country are this year very bad, which with the great fall in prices at home, will go nigh to ruin every man concerned in the Trade. . . . May all the curses of Emaulphus fall upon these *Sans Culottes Villains of France*. The War injures this Country most seriously in every point of view.[134]

England's change of front may also be explained by the fact that there was a slow but steady appreciation that the government of Washington was rapidly bringing order out of chaos. This coupled with the very rapid settlement of the trans-montane areas made some of the British statesmen realize the hopelessness of holding on to the Northwest. As early as 1788, Dorchester marveled at the immigration into Kentucky. It exceeded the " bounds of credulity," he wrote, and they " travel in hordes," for inconveniences did not hold them back.[135] The flow of settlers kept up and in 1790 Dorchester was amazed that the Americans had been able to establish justice beyond

---

132 Stevens, *Northwest Fur Trade*, chap. V.
    133 Robertson to Askin, April 10, 1793, *Askin Papers*, I, 471. For the effect of the French Revolution on the price of furs, see Stevens, *loc. cit.*, pp. 149–50.
    134 Richardson to Porteous, August 15, 1793, Canadian Archives, M, vol. 852, p. 57.
    135 Dorchester's "Observations," October 14, 1788, *ibid.*, Q, XXXVIII, 152–53.

the Alleghenies. " Such an Exertion in a vast wilderness never was made before," he wrote. Kentucky had grown in twelve or thirteen years to 100,000 people. " The annual accession of people, beyond the Allegheny mountains is incredible," the Governor said.[186] These observations were only too true and were of importance, for as Dorchester explained to Dundas, the " kings Provinces as compared with the United States [in population] are as one to fourteen." [137] Could England overcome this handicap?

On the other hand the item of expense must also be taken into consideration, especially after the war with France began. Sydney was informed in 1787 that if England were determined to hold the posts a " considerable expense must be incurred to put the works in a proper state of defense & a considerable reinforcement should be sent."[138] Mann's inspection trip to Detroit and Michilimackinac we have mentioned, and his report only too well revealed the weakness of the posts against any enemy except the Indians.[139] The following year, in 1793, it was estimated it would cost £ 3,499/7/18½ for repairing the posts in Michigan, including a few small new buildings.[140] Year after year this same story had been repeated. Either some new building was required, or an old one was " rotten and insufficient," or the picketing was " daily tumbling down," or some ditching had to be done.[141] Bills increased yearly from over £ 20,000 (this includes the Indian Department) in 1783,[142] to such " prodigious " amounts by 1794 that the Governor was in despair and refused to sanction some.[143] It was

---

186 Dorchester to Grenville, May 27, 1790, ibid., XLIV, pt. i, 283.

137 Same to Dundas, October 25, 1793, ibid., LXVI, 217. For the movement of settlers into Kentucky see James, Clark, chap. XV; Winsor, Westward Movement, passim.

138 Same to Sydney, January 16, 1787, ibid., XXVII, pt. i, 35.

139 Ante, p. 252.

140 Canadian Archives, Q, LX, 222.

141 There are numerous records to this effect. Ibid., C, vol. 247, p. 229; Mich. Hist. Colls., XII, 57; XX, 109; XXIII, 336–38, 371–74, 377–87, 390–93, 396; XXIV, 359, 409, 533–35.

142 Ibid., XX, 109.

143 Dorchester to Simcoe, September 18, 1794, ibid., XXV, 35.

Colonel England's opinion, while he was stationed in Detroit, that in spite of all the expense the Indians could not be relied upon for any defense of the country.[144] It was Dorchester's belief that it would require some four or five thousand more men to protect Canada and the posts; and large amounts of naval stores, ten or twelve ships of 150 guns for the lake service, 700 to 800 seamen, several frigates, and 6,000 men and a naval squadron at Halifax.[145] Dorchester claimed Canada alone could withstand no contest with America, and certainly Nova Scotia and New Brunswick would be of no assistance.[146] All of this at a time when England's energy and resources were daily concentrated more and more on the French Revolution. An impossible demand, and British statesmen were not stupid.

But the most important factor which brought about the cession of the posts was the movement undertaken by the Americans culminating in the successful campaign of General Anthony Wayne. During the larger part of 1792 and 1793, Wayne was busy recruiting and drilling the American army.[147] In the meantime, the United States made a final effort to bring about a peaceful settlement with tribes north of the Ohio. Benjamin Lincoln, Timothy Pickering, and Beverley Randolph were appointed as commissioners and departed for the Northwest by way of Niagara in the spring of 1793.[148] They arrived at the mouth of the Detroit River the 21st of July, after having been delayed for weeks by Governor Simcoe. Colonel England refused to allow the Americans to proceed to Detroit, so they disembarked on the Canadian side and were entertained at the home of Captain Elliott. Meanwhile McKee and his staff were holding a general council with all the tribes at the Rapids of

[144] England to Simcoe, September 8, 1794, Canadian Archives, C, vol. 247, p. 229.
[145] Dorchester to Dundas, October 25, 1793, ibid., Q, LXVI, 217.
[146] Ibid., 217.
[147] Winsor, Westward Movement, p. 451; J. S. Bassett, The Federalist System (New York, 1906), p. 65.
[148] The Journal and the correspondence of the commissioners are published in American State Papers, Indian Affairs, I, 337–61. An excellent account is found in Bemis, Jay's Treaty, pp. 162 et seq.

the Maumee, for the purpose of uniting the Indians and to present unanimous terms to the Americans.[149] For two weeks the commissioners remained on the shore of Lake Erie, unable to get passage across to the mouth of the Maumee where they could confer with the Indians. Thwarted on every hand by Simcoe's men, the commissioners finally departed for home. It seemed that a renewal of the Indian war was inevitable.[150]

During the late fall and winter of 1793–1794, General Wayne began his march northward from the Ohio into the Indian territory, making his winter quarters on the site of St. Clair's disaster in 1791.[151] The English interpreted Wayne's movements as a direct menace to Detroit. Deserters from the American army fled to Detroit carrying stories of Wayne's plan to fortify the Maumee and from thence to push on to capture the post.[152] McKee urged Simcoe to fortify the old Miamis fort just below the Glaize.[153] Simcoe had long sensed the strategic value of this location and advised Dorchester that the place be garrisoned and considerably strengthened.[154] In February, 1794, Dorchester ordered Simcoe to occupy a position at the rapids of the Maumee with a garrison from Detroit.[155] Just a week earlier the Governor had entertained a delegation of Indians in Quebec. He told them that the Americans did not desire peace, that they refused the King's

---

[149] Stone, *Brant,* II, 236; Bemis, *loc. cit.,* pp. 166–68, describes McKee's efforts to unite the Indians. Brant claimed that it never was the intention to allow the commissioners to meet the Indians. Brant to Chew, March 25, 1794, *Mich. Hist. Colls.,* XX, 336. See also letter of United States commissioners to McKee, August 14, 1793, *ibid.,* 320; reply of the commissioners to the Indians, July 31, 1793, *ibid.,* XXIV, 579–85.

[150] Winsor, *Westward Movement,* pp. 446–51.

[151] For maps of the Miamis country and Wayne's march see *Mich. Hist. Colls.,* XX, facing 368, 369; *ibid.,* XXIV, facing 667. Much of the correspondence dealing with the British and Wayne's campaign is found in *ibid., passim,* and *ibid.,* XX, *passim.*

[152] Canadian Archives, Indian Papers, 1792–1796; 1792–1850; McKee's "Journal," September-December, 1793, *ibid.,* C, CCLXVII, 42; *Mich. Hist. Colls.,* XII, 104, 105–109. One deserter claimed that Wayne paid $40.00 for every Indian scalp, and offered $1,000.00 for the scalp of Simon Girty. McKee to ————, June 2, 1794, *ibid.,* XX, 357, 372.

[153] Cruikshank, *Simcoe;* Bemis, *Jay's Treaty,* p. 175.

[154] Simcoe to Dorchester, April 29, 1794, *Mich. Hist. Colls.,* XXIV, 658–59.

[155] Dorchester to Simcoe, February 17, 1794, *ibid.,* XXIV, 642–43; Canadian Archives, Q, LXVII, 97.

offer of mediation, and hinted that the British and Americans would soon be at war.[156] This address and the completion of the fort at the Miamis by Simcoe almost brought the two nations into war. Fortunately the British ministry disavowed Dorchester's address, sharply reprimanded him, and this eased the situation somewhat.[157]

By the end of April, 1794, Simcoe had finished the fortifying of the Miamis post and had also placed some guns on Turtle Island at the mouth of the Maumee. These precautions would hinder Wayne in any advance upon Detroit, or in establishing communications via Lake Erie with the American settlers at Presque Isle. Simcoe was of the impression that Wayne's advance upon Detroit would surround that post, severing its intercourse with the Indians, and possibly turn them against the British.[158] The fortifications at Miamis, the Lieutenant Governor believed, would make it possible to prevent Wayne's march northward or at least greatly delay him. While if Wayne should attempt to move around the fort to the northwest, Simcoe declared he would use the entire garrison from Detroit, if necessary, and make an effort to cut Wayne's long line of communications.[159]

But Wayne had no intentions of marching against Detroit. His real objective was to smash the Indians. In June, 1794, having been joined by some 1,600 mounted Kentucky militia, he began his march from Fort Greenville. Near the junction of the Glaize and Maumee, he built some defenses which he named Fort Defiance. Then proceeding down the Maumee, he found, on August 18, a group of some 1,300 Indians about two miles from the British fort. In an ambush of fallen trees,

---

[156] *Ibid.*, LXIV, 109. Text of the speech in *The Annual Register for 1794*.
[157] Dundas to Dorchester, January 8, 1794, P. R. O., C. O. 42, XCVIII, 4; same to same, July 5, 1794, Canadian Archives, Q, LXVII, 175; *Mich. Hist. Colls.*, XXIV, 680. Simcoe was not censured at this time apparently, but Whitehall did reprove him later for part of his program. ―――― to Simcoe, September 10, 1794, P. R. O., C. O. 42, CCCXVIII, 404.
[158] Simcoe to Dundas, February 28, 1794, *ibid.*, 113; *Mich. Hist. Colls.*, XXIV, 646; Canadian Archives, Q, CCLXXX, pt. i, 75. Simcoe had informed Dundas he would occupy Turtle Island. Simcoe to Dundas, June 21, 1794, P. R. O., C. O. 42, CCCXVIII, 256.
[159] Same to same, June 21, 1794, *ibid.*; *Mich. Hist. Colls.*, XXIV, 667–68.

through which had grown a new forest, a natural protection difficult to break through, the Indians attacked the Americans. Wayne's men behaved excellently, and by a rapid movement of cavalry outflanked the savages who retreated toward the fort where they expected to be received. But its gates were not opened to them, whereupon they disappeared into the forests. Thus occurred the battle of Fallen Timbers of August 20, as it was named, which soon brought a settlement to the Indian question that had embarrassed America since the Revolution.[160]

Meanwhile, as Wayne advanced, the English officers at Detroit and Michilimackinac were making earnest efforts to unite the Indians and to make more effective their resistance to the American forces. "We have done everything in our power to hurry on the Indians to the Rapids," wrote one Detroit official.[161] Detroit was almost stripped of ammunition, guns, and provisions by McKee, who begged headquarters for more supplies at once, " provided His Majesty's Posts are considered by His Excellency as objects of importance." [162] Simcoe held that war was " inevitable " and felt that Wayne must be driven back rapidly.[163] He also suggested attacking the United States in the west and on the seacoast, in order that it might be " effectually dismembered, and disabled from prosecuting those malignant & ambitious views," which in Simcoe's eyes were the foundation of America's policy.[164]

Surely a crisis was imminent. After his victory, General

[160] Roosevelt, *Winning of the West*, III, chap. V; Logan Esarey, *History of Indiana* (New York, 1922), I, chap. V. See especially McKee's account of the battle, McKee to Chew, August 27, 1794, *Mich. Hist. Colls.*, XX, 370–71. Duggan's letters, *ibid.*, XII, 121–23, give another sketch of the affair. See also *ibid.*, XXXI, 489, and XXXIV, 346–502 for Wayne's orderly books. The daily journal of Wayne's campaign by Lieutenant John Boyer is published in *ibid.*, 539–659. Other accounts are in Canadian Archives, C, vol. 247.

[161] Duggan to McKee, August 18, 1794, Canadian Archives, Indian Papers, 1792–1796; Doyle to Chew, June 9, 1794, *Mich. Hist. Colls.*, XII, 120.

[162] McKee to Chew, July 7, 1794, *ibid.*, XX, 364. McKee also complained about the " badness of the guns." Same to same, May 30, 1794, *ibid.*, 355.

[163] Simcoe to ———, August 8, 1794, Canadian Archives, M, CIX, 203; same to Dundas, August 5, 1794, *Mich. Hist. Colls.*, XXV, 2–4, gives similar views.

[164] Same to Dorchester, August 10, 1794, P. R. O., C. O. 42, CCCXVIII, 419.

Wayne remained in the vicinity destroying crops, huts, and other property of the Indians and the fur traders, within the very range of the guns of Fort Miamis. Inside the fort " torches hovered above the breeches of loaded cannon trained on the American cavalry," while outside the log walls were the American forces " flushed with their success and indignant at the recent encroachments of the British." [165] In this dramatic and tense setting only the coolness of the commanders " prevented a precipitation of hostilities that might have set the whole frontier afire," and, as Professor Bemis asserts, possibly " destroyed the last chance for peace " between England and America.[166] A war in 1794 would probably have been fatal to American nationality.

Major William Campbell, the English commander, sent a flag of truce to Wayne asking the American general in what light he was to view Wayne's approaches so near his own garrison.[167] Wayne replied that " without questioning the authority or propriety " of the interrogatory that his answer was the action of yesterday " against the heard of Savages in the vicinity of your Post." [168] To this Campbell sent back word that although he was anxious to avoid hostilities, any further insults " offered to the British Flag flying at this Fort, by approaching it within pistol shot " should cease or it was his " indispensable Duty " to King and Country to meet further advance by armed forces.[169] Wayne, expressing his surprise that England had built a fort within the " acknowledged limits of the United States," an act of " the highest aggression," requested Campbell to remove his forces to Detroit.[170] But the British leader flatly refused to do this, replying that he was under military orders, and that the " impropriety " of his

[165] Bemis, *op. cit.*, p. 180.
[166] *Ibid.*
[167] Campbell to Wayne, August 21, 1794, *Mich. Hist. Colls.*, XXV, 16.
[168] Wayne to Campbell, August 21, 1794, *ibid.*, 16–17.
[169] Campbell to Wayne, August 22, 1794, *ibid.*, 17–18. This correspondence is also found in P. R. O., F. O. 5, VII. Simcoe praised Campbell's firm stand very highly. Simcoe to Dundas, August 30, 1794, *ibid.*, *Mich. Hist. Colls.*, XXV, 23.
[170] Wayne to Campbell, August 22, 1794, *ibid.*, 18.

occupying the Miamis Fort should be " best left to the ambassadors of our different nations." [171] Fortunately Wayne was wise and did not attack Campbell. For three days more he remained along the banks of the Maumee, destroying Indian crops and stores, also the buildings of McKee, for whom he had a particular grudge.[172] This accomplished, the Americans withdrew to Fort Defiance, where they were in a position to check effectively any further depredations on the part of the Indians.[173]

During the days that Wayne was on the Maumee, the British in Detroit were passing many anxious hours. The news of the Indian defeat at Fallen Timbers brought consternation to the officers for they feared that Wayne would march upon their post. The fort was in no condition to withstand an army with guns and the militia could not be depended upon.[174] At the same time a fever was prevalent in the regular army, causing the death of six men of the 24th Regiment during the summer of 1794, while at one time 120 were on the sick list.[175] These disorders left the men in a " very low debilitated state," unfit for duty, and made it impossible to send any help to Major Campbell at Miamis.[176] The Indians would give no aid as they were " in much confusion " and angry for " not receiving any assistance from the English." [177] Possibly the best picture of the uncertainty at Detroit was conveyed by Duggan, the storekeeper of the Indian Department, who was mustered into the army. He wrote:

The Militia do duty here and I am just going the rounds, so shall leave this unfinished until my return. ½ after 12, I am just returned from my rounds, nothing extraordinary, all is well at present, God knows how long it will be so, as there are a great number of dis-

[171] Campbell to Wayne, August 22, 1794, *ibid.*, 19.
[172] Campbell to ———, August 22, 1794, *ibid.*, 20–21.
[173] The official correspondence of these incidents has been published in *American State Papers, Indian Affairs*, I, 490.
[174] Simcoe to Dundas, August 30, 1794, *Mich. Hist. Colls.*, XXV, 24. Colonel England said the Canadian militia "behaved in a very mutinous shameful manner, very little short of Rebellion." England to Simcoe, August 30, 1794. *Ibid.*, 26.
[175] Same to same, *ibid.*; England to Le Maistre, October 28, 1794, Canadian Archives, C, vol. 247, p. 311.
[176] *Ibid.*
[177] Brant to Chew, October 22, 1794, *ibid.*, p. 281.

affected persons here, it is reported the Americans have surrounded Fort Miamis and intend to attack it.[178]

Colonel England, the commander at Detroit, could not comprehend why Wayne did not march on Detroit instead of retreating. Especially " at a time that it wou'd appear," he wrote, " he had effectually accomplished his purpose by defeating the Indians perfectly and by having the whole Country at his Command." [179] The answer was that the United States never had any idea of using Wayne's army to attack the occupied posts, and the " excitable " Wayne did not dare, on his own responsibility, to commit himself to such a dangerous enterprise.[180]

While General Wayne was carrying on his successful campaign against the Indians of the Old Northwest, the American government had sent John Jay, in May of 1794, to London to carry on discussions leading to a settlement of the many disputes between the two countries. After several months of negotiations, on November 14, 1794, Jay affixed his signature to a treaty which has since borne his name,[181] a treaty in Admiral Mahan's words of " epochal significance."

Of most significance for the history of the Old Northwest was the settlement by this treaty of the long controversy over the boundaries. Article two stipulated that the evacuation of the frontier posts should take place on, or before, June 1, 1796, and that all settlers and traders residing within the jurisdiction of the posts should continue to enjoy the full rights of their property. Citizens living within the area of the United States might continue their British allegiance or become American subjects, one year being allowed for them to make a decision. Any person who had failed to make a declaration of

---

[178] Duggan to Chew, August 23, 1794, *ibid.*, p. 244; *Mich. Hist. Colls.*, XII, 123.

[179] England to Simcoe, August 30, 1794, *ibid.*, XXV, 25; Canadian Archives, Q, LXX, 39. It was Simcoe's idea that Wayne's forces were needed to crush the whiskey rebellion. Simcoe to Dundas, September 5, 1794, *ibid.*, 39; *Mich. Hist. Colls.*, XXV, 31.

[180] These negotiations are fully and ably discussed in Bemis, *Jay's Treaty*, chap. XII. See especially chap. XVIII in Monaghan's definitive biography, *John Jay*.

[181] The text of the treaty is published in MacDonald, *Documentary Source Book*, pp. 244–58.

intention at the end of the year was to be considered a citizen of the United States.

The withdrawal from the posts was not to disturb the "usual course of communication and commerce to the southward and eastward of the Lakes" between the Indian peoples and Canada. British subjects were to have the right to pass and repass freely over the boundaries with their goods and merchandise. In other words the treaty provided for "unlimited freedom of internal trade and communication between the two Canadas and the United States." [182]

On August 3, 1795, General Wayne concluded a treaty with the western Indian tribes, known as the Treaty of Greenville.[183] It ceded to the United States most of the area of the present state of Ohio, reserving to the savages a broad strip of land on the south shore of Lake Erie between the Cuyahoga and Maumee Rivers. This treaty was the forerunner of numerous other Indian cessions which, during the next fifteen years, yielded a large part of the Old Northwest to the United States. Article eight of the Treaty of Greenville provided that all persons trading with, or living among, the Indians must have licenses procured from the proper American officials. In the eyes of the British this provision was in direct violation of the Jay Treaty, which guaranteed free participation in the Indian trade to the citizens of both nations. Lord Grenville advised Phineas Bond, England's representative in America, to demand an explanation for this infraction of the treaty.[184] Dorchester was also advised to delay all plans for the withdrawal from the posts until the problem was satisfactorily adjusted.[185] This incident was settled, however, and an agreement was reached on May 4, 1796, which stated that no part of any subsequent treaty

---

[182] For certain defects in the Jay Treaty and for England's last effort to renew the Indian Barrier State, see Bemis, *loc. cit.*, pp. 258–71.

[183] *American State Papers, Indian Affairs,* I, 563.

[184] Grenville to Bond, January 18, 1796, Simcoe Papers, V, 5.

[185] Portland to Dorchester, January 15, 1796, P. R. O., C. O. 42, CV, 20–21. Dorchester had sent the treaty to Portland in a letter of October 26, 1795. *Ibid.,* CIV, 405–406.

should be interpreted as impairing the trading rights provided by the Jay Treaty.[186]

Dorchester had received orders in 1795 from Whitehall to make arrangements with the United States for the evacuation of the posts.[187] Britain was anxious for the entire matter to be settled amicably as was shown by the Duke of Portland's orders. He wrote Dorchester:

You are to be very careful [in carrying out the treaty] that all your communications on this subject, shall be couched in the most temperate and conciliatory terms, and that, in general, your conduct should be such as to manifest the most earnest desire, on His Majesty's part, to give the fullest effect, as well to the particular Stipulations of the Treaty as to its general spirit and principles, provided that on the part of the United States, the same good faith and liberality are shown.[188]

It was in this spirit that Dorchester carried out his part of the evacuation.

In order to protect England's western areas, new forts were erected to take the place of the old ones which were to be delivered to the Americans.[189] These usually were placed opposite or near the old posts, as the fort near Detroit was built a few miles down and across the river at Amherstburg.

General James Wilkinson, representing the United States, addressed a letter to Colonel England at Detroit on May 27, 1796, asking when it would be convenient for the British to withdraw their troops " from the Territory of the United States? "[190] To this request, the Colonel replied that he had not received final orders from Dorchester, but as soon as they arrived, and he did not believe they would be " unnecessarily delayed," he would immediately communicate them to Wilkinson.[191] On June 1, George Beckwith, the adjutant, sent orders to the post commanders to vacate their posts.[192] They

---

186 W. M. Malloy, *Treaties, Conventions, International Acts, Protocols and Agreements* (Washington, 1910), I, 607–609.
187 Portland to Dorchester, October 21, 1795. P. R. O., C. O. 42, CIV, 107.
188 Same to same, January 13, 1796, *ibid.*, CV, 24–25.
189 Dorchester to Portland, April 25, 1795, *Mich. Hist. Colls.*, XXV, 89.
190 Wilkinson to England, May 27, 1796, *ibid.*, XII, 210.
191 England to Wilkinson, June 10, 1796, *ibid.*, 220.
192 Beckwith to the Post Commanders, June 1, 1796, P. R. O., C. O. 42, CV, 571–72.

were to leave one captain, two subalterns, and fifteen men at Detroit; while one officer and twenty men were to remain at Michilimackinac, to act as a guard for the protection of the works and public buildings until the American troops arrived.

During the summer and fall of 1796, the principal posts were delivered to the United States forces.[193] This definitely ended the British régime in Michigan and the Northwest, and brought to a close the long diplomatic struggle which had been continuous since the negotiations preceding the Treaty of Paris of 1783. Timothy Pickering's summary of the delivery of the posts well described the situation. He wrote:

By this time all the British posts must have been delivered up to the troops of the United States, except perhaps the remote one of Michilimackinac. The deliveries, as far as we have rec'd intelligence, have been made in the most handsome manner, on the part of the British.[194]

All the records indicate that the British troops carried on " in the most handsome manner," and no unfortunate complications arose to mar the final American occupation.

We have herewith reviewed certain basic events and facts which effected the surrender of the posts by Great Britain in 1796. All of these tended to have more or less influence, but it is the opinion of the author that there were two movements of most significance. One was the irresistible movement of the peripatetic American into the trans-Allegheny West, and the other was the shifting of the major field of the fur trade farther into the Northwest, largely within British territory. The solution of the frontier problems in a peaceful manner was fortunate, as America's first President, Washington, so well visualized. War would have been tragic for the young nation just in its " swaddling clothes " with only a loose union and a mere shadow of government. On the other hand, peace was not unwelcome to England. The might of that great empire

---

[193] Detroit was surrendered by England to Colonel John Hamtramck in command of the Americans, on July 11, 1796. *Mich. Hist. Colls.*, XXV, *passim; Askin Papers*, II, 46–50. Michilimackinac was taken over in October. Wood, *Historic Mackinac*, I, *passim.*

[194] Pickering to King, August 8, 1796, Rufus King MSS., Henry Huntington Library.

was sorely tried during the years of the French Revolution and the long Napoleonic Wars. It was very expensive to maintain garrisons in the vast hinterland and to send great quantities of presents to the red population "whose appetite was almost as large as the area over which it roamed." History was made for the young republic in general, and for Michigan in particular, as well as for the British nation, by the peaceful solution to the "raw edge" which the frontier posts had caused.

Thus the curtains were finally drawn on the last act, the area known as the Old Northwest passed into history, and emerged soon as the states of Michigan, Ohio, Indiana, Illinois, and Wisconsin. Within a few short decades the fur trade was a thing of the romantic past. In its place today we find a great population deriving its livelihood from the fertile soil, the manufactures, the forests, the railroads, the mines, and the avenues of commerce.

BIBLIOGRAPHY

BIBLIOGRAPHY

I

Manuscript Sources

Askin, John. Books of Account, Detroit, 1780–1833; Letter Book at Michilimackinac, 1778; Diaries, 1790–1815; Letters and Documents, 1747–1845; Originals in the Burton Historical Collection, of the Detroit Public Library.[1] Many volumes are in the Canadian Archives.

Baby Manuscripts. This collection, which is in the Bibliothèque St. Sulpice, Montreal, contains a mass of material relating to the fur trade carried on at Michilimackinac. Transcripts are found in the Burton Hist. Coll.

British Museum, Additional Manuscripts.

21686   Journals of exploring expeditions, maps and plans, 1750–1780.

21756   Register of correspondence with the officers commanding at Michilimackinac, 1778, 1779; and at Niagara, 1777–1783.

21757 ⎫ Correspondence with officers commanding at Mich-
21758 ⎭ ilimackinac, 1778–1785.

21759   Letters and papers relating to the upper posts, 1778–1782.

21781   Register of correspondence with officers commanding at Detroit, 1776–1783.

21782 ⎫ Correspondence with Lt. Gov. Hamilton and papers
21783 ⎭ relating to Detroit, 1772–1784.

21801 ⎫ Letters from officers of the provincial navy, 1778–
21802 ⎭ 1784.

21803   Copies of letters to officers of the provincial navy, 1778–1784.

21804 ⎫
21805 ⎭ Miscellaneous papers covering the period 1775–1784.

21852   Returns of provisions and stores in the upper posts, 1778–1784.

21885   Miscellaneous papers, chiefly relating to Canada, 1777–1787.

[1] Hereinafter referred to as Burton Hist. Coll.

CAMPBELL, J. V. Manuscripts and papers. Originals in Burton Hist. Coll.

Canadian Archives. Transcripts of:

(1) Bouquet Papers; these consist of letter-books, disbursements accounts, warrants and regimental orders, etc. There are letters to Amherst, Gage, Stanwix, Monckton, St. Clair, Loudoun, Forbes, Washington, and other officers of lesser rank. Some of these are published in volume XIX of *Michigan Pioneer and Historical Collections*. They are calendared in the Canadian Archives, *Report,* 1889 (Ottawa, 1890).

(2) Correspondence of Pitt, First Earl of Chatham.

(3) Colonial Office Records, under the title of " Military Correspondence, Series America and West Indies." Here are also the " Board of Trade Papers." These are in Series C. O. 5, and C. O. 42.

(4) Dartmouth Papers. Several volumes of transcripts of the correspondence of the Earl of Dartmouth.

(5) Haldimand Collection, Series B. This series covers the years 1758–1785, and consists of correspondence with Gage, Amherst, Sir William Johnson, John Stuart, and the governors at the various western posts. Many of these letters are published in *Michigan Pioneer and Historical Collections*, IX, X, XI. They are calendared in the Canadian Archives, *Reports for 1884–1889.*

(6) Indian Papers; these consist of several bound volumes dealing with every phase of activity relating to the Indians and the British, particularly in the Northern Department.

(7) Internal Correspondence of Quebec. Miscellaneous papers known as Series C.

(8) Lansdowne Manuscripts. Transcript from the papers of Lord Shelburne. Known as the Shelburne Papers.

(9) Q Series. These are copies of Colonial Office Papers contained in C. O. 42.

Census of Detroit in 1765. MS. in the Library of Congress.

Claus Papers. Six volumes of the correspondence and accounts of the Indian agent, Daniel Claus, in Canadian Archives.

Detroit Notarial Records, 1754–1796. The records of the local courts. Volumes A, B, C are in the Register's Office, Wayne County Building, Detroit. Volume D is in the Canadian Archives at Ottawa. Copies are in the Burton Hist. Coll.

Detroit merchants' day books, ledgers, etc. MSS. in the Burton Hist. Coll.

DODGE, JOHN. Strength of the Fort and Vessels on Lake Erie and Ontario in 1777–1778. Published in volume XCIII, 1778, of the letters of Washington in the Library of Congress.

EDGAR, WILLIAM. Collection of papers containing material relative to the political, economic, and social life of Detroit and vicinity. These papers are in the private collection of Herman Edgar of New York City.

Gage Papers. These contain the correspondence to and from every important official in the Colonies up to 1776. This collection is in the William L. Clements Library, Ann Arbor, Michigan. Only the Gladwin and John Campbell papers were used in this study.

GAGE, THOMAS. Letter to Captain Stephenson, Military Commander at Detroit, relative to Detroit affairs. April 8, 1771. MS. in Burton Hist. Coll.

HAMBURGH, ————. Journal of Mr. Hamburgh, who travelled in this country (Detroit) in 1763. MS. in Library of Congress.

HARROW, ALEXANDER. Logbook of His Majesty's Armed Sloop *Welcome*, 1779–1781; also of the *Angelica, Dunmore*, and *General Gage*, 1781–1782. MS. in Burton Hist. Coll.

MACOMB, EDGAR, AND MACOMB. Books of Accounts and Financial Agents of the British Government, including the volunteers' account for the Vincennes and Kentucky Expeditions, Detroit, 1775–1782. MSS. in Burton Hist. Coll.

MCINTOSH, ANGUS. Papers relating to the fur trade and commercial life of the Old Northwest. MSS. in the private collection of Francis Davis of Windsor.

MAY, JAMES. Condensed Statement of his Reminiscences of Detroit, 1756–1829. MS. in Burton Hist. Coll.

Michigan Historical Society MSS. containing: " Protest Against Excessive Taxation," and " A Protest Against Repairing Fort Detroit." MSS. in Burton Hist. Coll.

Morgan Letter Books. Transcripts of the Correspondence of George Morgan in the Illinois State Historical Library, Springfield. The original MSS. are in the Carnegie Library, Pittsburgh.

Moran Papers. Accounts, seigniorial tax receipts — land transfers (Moran family) and militia returns, Detroit, 1747–1838. Journals of trading voyages, Schenectady to Detroit and Michilimackinac, 1762–1771. Indian Council at Detroit, 1762. MSS. in Burton Hist. Coll.

PORTEOUS, JOHN. Diary of Siege of Detroit in 1763. MS. in Burton Hist. Coll.

Registre de Sainte Anne, Detroit, February 2, 1704 to December 30, 1848. Copy in Burton Hist. Coll. The original is owned by the Church.

Register of Notaries, and Administration of Justice, District of Hesse. Several volumes containing material relating to the courts, wills, deeds, etc. MSS. in Canadian Archives.

RUTHERFORD, JOHN. "An Episode in the Pontiac War, 1763." Transcript in Canadian Archives. Published in *The Transactions of the Canadian Institute*, III. Toronto, 1893. The original cannot be located.

Sterling Letter Book. Letters to and from James Sterling. Copy in Burton Hist. Coll.

Shelburne Papers. A collection containing correspondence to and from a large number of important colonial officials. These papers are in the William L. Clements Library of the University of Michigan.

State of the Garrison at Detroit in October, 1776. MS. in Clements Library.

Washington Manuscripts. Papers of George Washington, in the Library of Congress.

WILLIAMS, THOMAS. Documents relating to the mercantile correspondence, inventories, and peltry returns, Detroit, 1771–1781. Books of account for general merchandise and Indian trade, Detroit, 1781–1786. MSS. in Burton Hist. Coll.

II
PUBLISHED SOURCES

ADAMS, C. F. *The Life and Works of John Adams,* 10 vols. Boston, 1856.

ALMON, JOHN. *The Remembrancer; or impartial repository of public events from 1775 to 1784,* 17 vols. London, 1775–1784.

American Antiquarian Society, *Transactions and Collections.* Worcester, 1820 to date.

American State Papers, Documents, Legislative and Executive of the Congress of the United States. Public Lands. Washington, 1832, vols. I–III.

Annual Register, or a review of the History, Politics and Literature, for the Years 1758–1776. Sixth Edition, London, 1810.

Archives of Maryland. The Proceedings and Acts of the General Assembly of Maryland. Baltimore, 1883 *et seq.*

BOSSU, M. *Travels throughout that Part of North America called Louisiana.* Translated from the French by J. R. Foster. London, 1771.

BOUQUET, HENRY. "Journal of Henry Bouquet," Francis Parkman, *Conspiracy of Pontiac,* II, Appendix D.

Buffalo Historical Society. *Publications.* Buffalo, 1879 *et seq.*

BURTON, C. M. *Manuscripts from the Burton Historical Collection.* Detroit, 1916.

BUTTERFIELD, C. W. *The Narrative of John Leith,* Cincinnati, 1883. *The Washington-Irvine Correspondence.* Madison, 1882.

BRYMNER, DOUGLAS. *Report on the Canadian Archives*, 19 vols. Ottawa, 1882–1902.

Calendar of the Virginia State Papers and Other Manuscripts. Arranged and edited by W. P. Palmer, 11 vols. Richmond, 1875–1893.

Canadian Constitutional Development shown by Selected Speeches and Despatches. Edited by H. E. Egerton and W. E. Grant. London, 1907.

CARTER, C. E. *The Correspondence of General Thomas Gage with the Secretaries of State 1763–1775.* New Haven, 1931.

CARVER, J. *Travels Through the Interior Parts of North America in the Years 1766, 1767 and 1768.* Third Edition. London, 1781.

CAVENDISH, SIR HENRY. *Debates of the House of Commons in 1774, on the bill for making more effectual provision for the government of the province of Quebec now first published by J. Wright with a map of Canada, copies from the second edition of Mitchell's map of North America, referred to in the Debates.* London, 1839.

CHALMERS, GEORGE. *A Collection of Treaties Between Great Britain and Other Powers.* London, 1790.

Chicago Historical Society *Collections*, Chicago, 1890 *et seq.*

CLARK, COL. GEORGE ROGERS. *Sketch of his Campaign in the Illinois in 1778–1779, with an Introduction by Hon. Henry Pirtle and an Appendix.* Cincinnati, 1869.

Collections of the Connecticut Historical Society. Hartford, 1860 *et seq.*

Collections of the Illinois State Historical Library. Springfield, 1904 *et seq.*

Collections of the Massachusetts Historical Society. Fifth Series. Boston, 1871 *et seq.*

Collections of the New York Historical Society. Publication Fund Series. New York, 1868 *et seq.*

Collections of the State Historical Society of Wisconsin. Madison, 1855 *et seq.*

Collections of the Virginia Historical Society. New Series, 11 vols. Richmond, 1882–1892.

CONNOLLY, JOHN. *Narrative of the Transactions, Imprisonment and Suffering of John Connolly, an American Loyalist and Lieutenant-Colonel in His Majesty's Service in Which Are Shown the Unjustifiable Proceedings of the Congress in his Treatment and Detention.* London, 1783.

CROGHAN, GEORGE. "Letters and Journals Relating to Tours into the Western Country, November 16, 1750–November, 1765," R. G. Thwaites, *Early Western Travels*, vol. I.

CRUIKSHANK, E. A. (ed.). *The Correspondence of Lieutenant Governor John Graves Simcoe, with Allied Documents Relative to His Administration of the Government of Upper Canada,* 4 vols. Toronto, 1923 *et seq.*

DE PEYSTER, A. S. *Miscellanies, by an Officer,* 1774–1813. Edited by J. W. De Peyster. New York, 1888.

Documents Illustrative of the Canadian Constitution. Edited by William Houston. Toronto, 1891.

DODGE, JOHN. *An Entertaining Narrative of the Cruel and Barbarous Treatment and Extreme Suffering of Mr. John Dodge During His Captivity of Many Months Among the British at Detroit.* Danvers, 1780.

FORCE, PETER. *American Archives.* Fourth Series, 6 vols. and Fifth Series, 3 vols. Washington, 1837–1853.

FORD, P. L. *The Writings of Thomas Jefferson,* 10 vols. New York, 1892–1899.

FRANKLIN, BENJAMIN. *Complete Works.* Compiled and edited by John Bigelow, 10 vols. New York and London, 1887–1888.

Writings. Collected and edited with a life and introduction by A. H. Smyth. New York, 1907, 10 vols.

Works. Edited by Jared Sparks, 10 vols. Boston, 1837–1844.

FRAZER, ALEXANDER. *Reports of the Bureau of Archives for the Province of Ontario.* Toronto, 1902 *et seq.*

GLADWIN, MAJOR HENRY. " Gladwin Manuscripts," in *Mich. Hist. Colls.,* XXVII.

GORRELL, JAMES. " Journal of Proceedings from October 14, 1761, to June, 1763." MS. in Canadian Archives, Indian Papers, October, 1763–May, 1768. Published in the *Wis. Hist. Colls.,* I, 24–48.

GRIGNON, A. " Seventy-Two Years Recollections of Wisconsin," *Wis. Hist. Colls.,* III, pp. 255 *et seq.*

HAMILTON, HENRY. " Journal of Captain Henry Hamilton from August 6, 1778, to June 16, 1779, on his Expedition from Detroit to Vincennes." Copy in the Harvard Library. *Mich. Hist. Colls.,* IX, 489 ff.

HAY, HENRY. " Journal from Detroit to the Miami River," *Wis. Hist. Soc. Proc.,* 1914. MS. in the Burton Hist. Coll.

HENRY, ALEXANDER. *Travels and Adventures in Canada and the Indian Territories.* New York, 1809.

HINMAN, R. R. *A Historical Collection from Official Records, Files, etc. of the Part Sustained by Connecticut during the War of the Revolution.* Hartford, 1842.

HOUCK, LOUIS. *The Spanish Régime in Missouri; a Collection of papers and documents relating to Upper Louisiana, principally within the present limits of Missouri, during the dominion of*

Spain, from the Archives of the Indes at Seville, etc., 2 vols. Chicago, 1909.

HOUGH, F. B. *Diary of the Siege of Detroit in the War with Pontiac; also a narrative of the principal events of the siege, by Major Rogers; a plan for conducting Indian affairs by Colonel Bradstreet; and other authentic documents never before printed.* Albany, 1860.

Indiana Historical Society *Publications*, Indianapolis, 1895 *et seq.*

JAMES, J. A. *George Rogers Clark Papers, 1771–1781. Ill. Hist. Colls.*, VIII. Springfield, 1912.

George Rogers Clark Papers, 1781–1784. Ill. Hist. Colls., XIX. Springfield, 1926.

JAY, JOHN. *Correspondence and Public Papers.* Edited by H. P. Johnston, 4 vols. New York, 1890, 1899.

JEFFERSON, THOMAS. *Writings.* Collected and edited by P. L. Ford, 10 vols. New York, 1892–1899.

JOHNSON, SIR WILLIAM. *The Papers of Sir William Johnson.* Edited by James Sullivan. Albany, 1921 *et seq.*

" Journal of a Voyage made by Mr. Hugh Heward to the Illinois Country," *Askin Papers*, I, 339–60.

Journals of the Continental Congress from 1774–1789. Edited by W. C. Ford, 12 vols. Washington, 1904–1908.

KELLOGG, LOUISE PHELPS. *Frontier Advance on the Upper Ohio, 1778–1779.* Madison, 1916.

Frontier Retreat on the Upper Ohio, 1779–1781. Madison, 1917.

French Régime in Wisconsin and the Northwest. Madison, 1925.

KENNEDY, W. P. M. *Documents of the Canadian Constitution, 1759–1915.* Toronto, 1918.

KNOX, WILLIAM. *The Justice and Policy of the late Act of Parliament for Making more Effectual Provision For Government of The Province of Quebec, asserted and proved; and the conduct of administration respecting the province stated and vindicated.* London, 1774.

LEES, JOHN. *Journal of J. L., of Quebec, Merchant.* Detroit, 1911. Burton, C. M., editor.

LINDLEY, JACOB. " Account of a Journey to attent the Indian Treaty, proposed to be held at Sandusky, in the year 1793; interspersed with various observations, remarks, and circumstances, that occurred on this interesting occasion." *Mich. Hist. Colls.*, XVII, 566 ff.

MACDONALD, WILLIAM. *Documentary Source Book of American History, 1606–1913.* New York, 1918.

" Mackinac Register, 1741–1821." MS. in the Church of Ste. Anne at Mackinac. Translation in *Wis. Hist. Colls.*, XVIII, XIX.

MADISON, JAMES. *The Writings of James Madison, Comprising His Public Papers and His Private Correspondence, and Numerous Letters and Documents, — now for the first time printed,* 9 vols. New York, 1900–1910. Edited by Gaillard Hunt.

MAY, JAMES. " Excerpts from His Note Book," R. E. Robert's *Sketches of the City of Detroit.*

Michigan Pioneer and Historical Collections. Lansing, 1877 *et seq.*

MITCHELL, JOHN. *The Contest in America Between Great Britain and France.* London, 1757.

The Present State of Great Britain and North America with Regard to Agriculture, Population, Trade, and Manufactures, impartially considered. London, 1767.

MONTRÉSOR, JOHN. " Journal of John Montrésor's Expedition to Detroit in 1763," *Transactions of the Royal Society of Canada,* Third Series, XXII, Toronto, 1928.

MOORE, JOSEPH. " Journal of a tour to Detroit, in order to attend a Treaty, proposed to be held with the Indians at Sandusky." *Mich. Hist. Colls.,* XVII.

MORISON, S. E. *Sources and Documents illustrating the American Revolution 1764–1788, and the formation of the Federal Constitution.* Oxford, 1923.

MORRIS, THOMAS. " Journal," Thwaites, *Early Western Travels,* I. Also printed in *The Magazine of Western History,* XIX, 171.

O'CALLAGHAN, E. B. *Documentary History of the State of New York,* 4 vols. Albany, 1849–1851.

Documents Relative to the Colonial History of the State of New York, 11 vols. Albany, 1856–1860.

Parliamentary History of England from the Earliest Period to the Year 1803. (Hansard) 36 vols. London, 1806–1820.

PECKHAM, H. H. *George Croghan's Journal of his Trip to Detroit in 1767.* Ann Arbor, 1939.

Pennsylvania Archives. Fourth Series, edited by G. E. Reed, 12 vols. Harrisburg, 1900–1902; Fifth Series, edited by T. L. Montgomery, 8 vols. Harrisburg, 1906.

Pennsylvania Colonial Records, Minutes of the Provincial Council of Pennsylvania, 16 vols. Harrisburg, 1838–1853.

PITTMAN, P. *Present State of the European Settlements on the Mississippi.* Edited by F. H. Hodder. Cleveland, 1906.

POND, SIR PETER. " Journal, 1740–1775." *Wis. Hist. Colls.,* XVIII, 314 ff.

Pontiac Conspiracy. " Journal ou relation d'une conspiration faite par les sauvages contre les anglois et du siege du fort du detroix mis par quatre nations differents Le Te May 1763." MS. in

Burton Hist. Coll. Printed and translated in *Mich. Hist. Colls.*, VIII, 266–339.

POWELL, ANNE. " Journal of a Tour from Montreal to Detroit, 1789," *Magazine of American History*, V, 1880; W. R. Riddell, *The Life of William Dummer Powell*, pp. 60–73. Lansing, 1924.

Publications of the Buffalo Historical Society. Buffalo, 1879 *et seq.*

QUAIFE, M. M. *The Capture of Old Vincennes.* Indianapolis, 1927. *The John Askin Papers, 1747–1795.* Detroit, 1928.

RANDOLPH, T. J. *Memoir, Correspondence and Miscellanies from the Papers of Thomas Jefferson.* Boston, 1830.

" Records of the Early Courts of Justice of Upper Canada," Ontario Archives, *Report for 1917.*

REYNOLDS, J. *My Own Times: Embracing also the History of My Life.* Belleville, 1855. Reprinted, Chicago, 1879.

ROGERS, ROBERT. *A Concise Account of North America.* London, 1765.

Ponteach, or, the Savages of America. Edited with biography of author by Allen Nevins. Chicago, 1914.

" Michilimackinac Journal." Edited by W. L. Clements, American Antiquarian Society, *Transactions* (New Series), XXVIII.

Journal of Major Robert Rogers. Edited by W. L. Clements. Worcester, 1918.

Secret Journals of the Acts and Proceedings of Congress, 4 vols. Boston, 1821.

SHARPE, H. " Correspondence," *Archives of Maryland*, VI, IX, XIV.

SHORTT, ADAM, and DOUGHTY, A. G. *Documents Relating to the Constitutional History of Canada, 1759–1791.* Ottawa, 1918, 2 vols.

SMITH, W. H. *The St. Clair Papers.* Cincinnati, 1882.

SPARKS, JARED. *The Diplomatic Correspondence of the American Revolution*, 12 vols. Boston, 1829–1831.

STEVENS, B. F. *Facsimiles of Manuscripts in European Archives Relating to America, 1773–1783*, 24 vols. London.

SWAN, CALEB. " Journal," *Magazine of American History*, XIX.

THWAITES, R. G. *Early Western Travels, 1748–1846.* Cleveland, 1904–1906.

Jesuit Relations and Allied Documents. Travels and Explorations of the Jesuit Missionaries in New France, 1616–1701, 73 vols. Cleveland, 1904.

(ed.), *A short Biography of John Leith, with an Account of his Life among the Indians.* Cleveland, 1904.

and LOUISE PHELPS KELLOGG (eds.), *Documentary History of Dunmore War.* Madison, 1905.

and KELLOGG (eds.), *The Revolution on the Upper Ohio, 1775–1777.* Madison, 1912.

VOLNEY, C. A. *A view of the Soil and Climate of the United States of America.* Philadelphia, 1804.

WALPOLE, HORACE. *Last Journals During the Reign of George III from 1771–1783.* Edited by A. F. Stuart, 2 vols. London, 1910.

WASHINGTON, GEORGE. *Writings.* Edited by W. C. Ford, 14 vols. New York and London, 1889–1893.

WELD, ISAAC. *Travels Through the States of North America During the Years of 1795, 1796, and 1797.* London, 1799.

WHARTON, F. *The Revolutionary Diplomatic Correspondence of the United States,* 6 vols. Washington, 1889.

III

SECONDARY MATERIAL

ALDEN, G. D. *New Governments West of the Alleghanies Before 1780. Bulletin* of the University of Wisconsin History Series, II, no. 1. Madison, 1897.

ALVORD, C. W. " Genesis of the Proclamation of 1763," *Mich. Hist. Colls.,* XXXVII.

    " The British Ministry and the Treaty of Fort Stanwix," *Wis. Hist. Soc. Proc., 1908.*

    " The Conquest of St. Joseph," *Mo. Hist. Rev.,* II, April, 1908.

    "Virginia and the West," *Miss. Valley Hist. Rev.,* III.

    and CARTER, C. E. *The Critical Period, 1763–1765,* X, *Ill. Hist. Colls.*

    The Illinois Country 1673–1818. Chicago, 1922.

    The New Régime, 1765–1767, XI, *Ill. Hist. Colls.*

    The Mississippi Valley in British Politics, 2 vols. Cleveland, 1917.

American Historical Association Annual Reports. Washington, 1890 *et seq.*

American Historical Review. New York, 1896 *et seq.*

AVERY, E. M. *A History of the United States and Its Peoples From Their Earliest Records to the Present Time,* 7 vols. Cleveland, 1904–1910.

BANCROFT, GEORGE. *History of the United States,* 10 vols. Boston, 1834–1874.

BARCE, ELINORE. *The Land of the Miamis.* (Indiana), 1922.

BEER, G. D. *British Colonial Policy, 1754–1765.* New York, 1907.

BEMIS, S. F. *Jay's Treaty.* New York, 1923.

BENTON, E. F. *The Wabash Trade Route in the Development of the Old Northwest.* Printed in Johns Hopkins University,

Studies in Historical and Political Sciences, XXI. Baltimore, 1903.

BOND, B. W. *The Civilization of the Old Northwest.* New York, 1934.

BOURINOT, SIR J. G. *Canada Under British Rule, 1760–1905.* Cambridge, 1909.

BRADLEY, A. J. *The Making of Canada.* New York, 1908.

BURNET, JACOB. *Notes on the Early Settlement of the Northwestern Territory.* Cincinnati, 1847.

BURPEE, L. J. " Highways of the Fur Trade," *Proceedings and Transactions of the Royal Society of Canada,* III, Third Series. Ottawa, Toronto, London, 1915.

BURT, A. L. *The Old Province of Quebec.* Toronto, 1933.

BURTON, C. M. " Amusements in Detroit in Colonial Days," *Mich. Hist. Colls.,* XXXVIII.
John Connolly, a Tory of the Revolution. Worcester, 1909.
The City of Detroit, Michigan, 1701–1922, 4 vols. Detroit, Chicago, 1922.
The Building of Detroit. Detroit, 1912.

BUTTERFIELD, C. W. *The History of the Girtys.* Cincinnati, 1890.
The History of George Rogers Clark's Conquest of the Illinois and the Wabash Towns, 1778–1779. Columbus, 1904.

CAMPBELL, J. V. *Political History of Michigan.* Detroit, 1876.

The Canadian Historical Review. Toronto, 1920 *et seq.*

The Canadian Law Times. Toronto, 1881 *et seq.*

The Canadian Magazine. Toronto, 1893 *et seq.*

CARTER, C. E. *Great Britain and the Illinois Country, 1763–1774.* Washington, 1910.

The Centennial Celebration of the Evacuation of Detroit by the British, 1896. Detroit, 1896.

CHANNING, E. *A History of the United States,* 7 vols. New York, 1905 *et seq.*

CHITTENDEN, H. M. *The American Fur Trade of the Far West,* 3 vols. New York, 1902.

COFFIN, VICTOR. *The Province of Quebec and the Early American Revolution. Bulletin* of the University of Wisconsin, Economics, Political Science and History Series, I. Madison, 1896.

CORWIN, E. S. *French Policy and the American Alliance.* Princeton, 1916.

COX, I. J. " The Indians as a Diplomatic Factor in the History of the Old Northwest," *Ohio Archaeological and Historical Quarterly,* XVIII.

COUPLAND, R. *The Quebec Act.* Oxford, 1925.

DAVIDSON, G. R. *The Northwest Company.* Berkeley, 1918.

DAVIS, A. M. " The Indians and the Border Warfare of the Revolution," Justin Winsor, *Narrative and Critical History of the United States,* VI.

DICKERSON, C. M. *American Colonial Government, 1696–1765.* Cleveland, 1912.

DURAND, J. *New Materials for the Study of American History.* New York, 1889.

ENGLISH, W. H. *The Conquest of the Country Northwest of the River Ohio, 1778–1783, and the Life of General George Rogers Clark.* Indianapolis and Kansas City, Mo., 1896.

FARMER, SILAS. *History of Detroit and Michigan.* Detroit, 1884.

FARRAND, M. "The Indian Boundary Line," *American Historical Review,* X.

FERNOW, B. *The Ohio Valley in Colonial Days.* Albany, 1890.

FISKE, J. *American Political Ideas, viewed from the standpoint of Universal History.* New York, 1885.
The Critical Period in American History. Boston and New York, 1888.
The American Revolution, 2 vols. Boston and New York, 1896.

FITZMAURICE, LORD. *Life of William, Earl of Shelburne,* 2 vols. London, 1912.

FULLER, G. N. *Economic and Social Beginnings of Michigan.* Lansing, 1916.
Historic Michigan, 3 vols. Lansing, 1928.

GAYARRÉ, CHARLES. *The History of Louisiana,* 4 vols. New York, 1854.

GREEN, ERNEST. "The Niagara Portage Road," *Ontario Hist. Soc. Pub.,* XXIII.

HALE, E. E. and E. E., JR. *Franklin in France,* 2 vols. Boston, 1887–1888.

HALSEY, F. W. *The Old New York Frontier.* New York, 1901.

Handbook of American Indians, North of Mexico, edited by F. W. Hodge, 2 vols. Washington, 1910.

HENDERSON, A. *The Conquest of the Old Southwest.* New York, 1920.

HILDRETH, R. *The History of the United States of America,* 6 vols. New York, 1880.

HILDRETH, S. P. *Biographical and Historical Memoirs of the Early Pioneer Settlers of Ohio, with Narratives of Incidents and Occurrences in 1775.* Cincinnati, 1852.

HINSDALE, B. A. *The Old Northwest, with a View of the Thirteen Colonies as Constituted by the Royal Charters.* New York, 1888.
"The Western Land Policy of the British Government from 1763 to 1775," *Ohio Archaeological and Historical Quarterly.*

Columbus, 1887.

HOSMER, J. K. *A Short History of the Mississippi Valley.* Boston and New York, 1901.

HOWLAND, HENRY R. "The Niagara Portage," *Buffalo Hist. Soc. Pub.,* VI.

"Navy Island and the First Successors to the *Griffin,*" *ibid.*

HUMPHREY, HELEN. "The Identity of Gladwin's Informant," *Mississippi Valley Historical Review,* XXI, September, 1934.

HUMPHREYS, R. A. "Lord Shelburne and the Proclamation of 1763," *English Historical Review,* XLIX, April, 1934.

"Lord Shelburne and British Colonial Policy, 1766–1768," *English Historical Review,* L, April, 1935.

and SCOTT, S. M. "Lord Northington and the Laws of Canada," *Canadian Historical Review,* XIV.

JAMES, J. A. "George Rogers Clark and Detroit, 1780–1781," *Mississippi Valley Historical Association Proceedings,* 1908–1910, III, 291.

"The Northwest After the Revolution, 1783–1786," *ibid.,* 1913–1914.

"The Revolution in the West, 1782," *ibid.,* 1912–1913.

"Significant Events During the Last Year of the Revolution in the West," *ibid.,* 1912–1913.

"The Significance of the Attack upon St. Louis, 1780," *ibid.,* 1908–9, II, 199.

"Some Phases of the History of the Northwest, 1783–1786," *ibid.,* 1913–1914.

"Indian Diplomacy and the Opening of the Revolution in the West," *Wis. Hist. Soc. Proc.,* 1909, pp. 125–143.

"To What Extent was George Rogers Clark in Military Control of the Northwest at the Close of the American Revolution," *Annual Report of the American Historical Association,* 1917.

The Life of George Rogers Clark. Chicago, 1928.

JENKS, W. L. *Patrick Sinclair.* Lansing, 1914.

JOHNSON, I. A. *The Michigan Fur Trade.* Lansing, 1919.

KELLOGG, LOUISE PHELPS. "A Footnote to the Quebec Act," *Canadian Historical Review,* XIII, Toronto, 1932.

The British Régime in Wisconsin and the Northwest. Madison, 1935.

KENNEDY, W. P. M. *The Constitution of Canada.* London, 1922.

KINGSFORD, W. *The History of Canada,* 10 vols. Toronto, 1887–1900.

LANMAN, J. H. *The History of Michigan, Civil and Topographical.* New York, 1839.

LECKY, W. E. H. *The History of England in the Eighteenth Century,* 8 vols. London, 1878–1890.

LUCAS, C. P. *A History of Canada, 1763–1812.* Oxford, 1909.

Magazine of Western History. Cleveland, 1883 *et seq.*

McARTHUR, DUNCAN. "The New Régime," *Canada and Its Provinces,* III, 21–49.

McCoy, D. "Old Fort St. Joseph," *Mich. Hist. Colls.,* XXXV.

McLAUGHLIN, A. C. *The Confederation and the Constitution* (American Nations Series), X. New York and London, 1905. "The Western Posts and British Debts," *Yale Review,* February, 1895; also printed in *American Historical Association Annual Report, 1894.*

MARTIN, CHESTER. *Empire and Commonwealth.* Oxford, 1929.

MARTIN, D. B. "The Fox River Valley in the Days of the Fur Trade," *Wis. Hist. Soc. Proc., 1899.* Madison, 1900.

Mississippi Valley Historical Review, Cedar Rapids, 1914 *et seq.*

Mississippi Valley Historical Society, *Proceedings,* Cedar Rapids, 1909 *et seq.*

Missouri Historical Review, Columbia, 1910 *et seq.*

MONAGHAN, FRANK. *John Jay.* New York, 1935.

MOORE, CHARLES. *The Northwest Under Three Flags, 1635–1796.* New York and London, 1900.

MORTON, R. K. *Robert R. Livingston — The Beginning of American Diplomacy.* Randolph-Macon College, J. P. Branch Historical Papers, III.

NOTESTEIN, W. "The Western Indians in the Revolution," *Ohio Archaeological and Historical Society, Publications,* XVI, 1907.

PACKARD, GEORGE. "The Administration of Justice in the Lake Michigan Wilderness," *Michigan Law Review,* XVII. Ann Arbor, 1919.

PARÉ, GEORGE. "The St. Joseph Mission," *Mississippi Valley Historical Review,* June, 1930.

PARKINS, A. E. *The Historical Geography of Detroit.* Lansing, 1918.

PARKMAN, FRANCIS. *Montcalm and Wolfe,* 2 vols. Boston, 1903. *The Conspiracy of Pontiac and the Indian War After the Conquest of Canada,* 2 vols. Boston, 1910.

PARTON, JAMES. *Life and Times of Benjamin Franklin,* 2 vols. New York, 1864.

PAXSON, F. L. *The History of the American Frontier, 1763–1893.* Boston and New York, 1924.

PHILLIPS, P. C. "American Opinions Regarding the West, 1778–1783," *Miss. Valley Assoc. Proc.,* VII, 1913–1914. *The West in the Diplomacy of the Revolution,* University of Illinois, *Studies in Social Sciences,* XI, no. 2, 3. Urbana, 1913.

POOLE, W. F. "The West, from the Treaty of Peace with France, 1763, to the Treaty of Peace with England, 1783," Justin Winsor, *Narrative and Critical History*, VI.

POTTER, W. W. "Michigan's First Justice of the Peace," *Michigan History Magazine*, VI. Lansing, 1922.

POUND, ARTHUR, and DAY, R. E. *Johnson of the Mohawks*. New York, 1930.

POWNALL, T. *Administration of the Colonies*. Second Edition. London, 1765.

Proceedings of the American Antiquarian Society. Worcester, 1882 *et seq.*

QUAIFE, M. M. *Chicago and the Old Northwest, 1673–1835*, Chicago, 1913.

"The Royal Navy of the Upper Lakes," *Burton Historical Collection Leaflet*, II, no. 5.

"John Askwith," *ibid.*, VII, no. 4.

"Detroit's First Election," *ibid.*, V, no. 2.

"Commodore Alexander Grant," *ibid.*, VI, no. 5.

Quebec *Gazette*. Quebec, 1760 *et seq.*

RANDALL, J. G. "Clark's Service of Supply," *Miss. Valley Hist. Rev.*, VIII.

REID, MARJORIE. "The Quebec Fur Traders and Western Policy, 1763–1774," *Canadian Hist. Rev.*, VI.

RIDDELL, W. R. "Marriage in Early Upper Canada," *Canadian Magazine*, LI, 384.

"Practice of the Court of Common Pleas for the District of Hesse," *Transactions of the Royal Society of Canada*, series 3, sec. ii.

"Some Marriages in Old Detroit," *Michigan History Magazine*, VI, no. 1.

"The Early Courts of the Province," *Canadian Law Times*, XXXV.

"The First Judge at Detroit and His Court," *Mich. State Bar Assoc.*, 1915. Lansing, 1915.

"The Law of Marriage in Upper Canada," *Canadian Historical Review*, September, 1921.

"William Osgoode — First Chief Justice of Upper Canada," *Canadian Law Times*, May, 1921.

"The Last Indian Council of the French at Detroit," *Transactions of the Royal Society of Canada*, series 3, XXV. Toronto, 1931.

Michigan Under British Rule, Law and Law Courts, 1760–1796. Lansing, 1926.

The Life of William Dummer Powell, First Judge at Detroit. Lansing, 1924.

ROOSEVELT, THEODORE. *The Winning of the West*, 4 vols. New York and London, 1889.

ROSALITA, SISTER MARY. *Education in Detroit Prior to 1850.* Lansing, 1928.

ROWLAND, K. M. *The Life of George Mason,* 2 vols. New York and London, 1892.

RUSSELL, NELSON VANCE. "The Indian Policy of Henry Hamilton," *Canadian Historical Review,* XI.
"The Battle of Bloody Run," *ibid.,* XII.

SCHUYLER, R. L. *The Transition in Illinois from the British to American Government.* New York, 1909.

SEVERANCE, F. H. *Old Trails on the Niagara Frontier.* Cleveland, 1903.
"The Peace Mission to Niagara of Ephraim Douglass in 1783," *Buffalo Hist. Soc. of Publications,* XVIII. Buffalo, 1914.

SHEA, J. G. *Life and Times of the Most Reverend John Carroll.* New York, 1888.

SHORTT, ADAM, and DOUGHTY, A. G. *Canada and its Provinces,* 21 vols. Toronto, 1914.

SMITH, W. *Historical Account of Bouquet's Expedition Against the Ohio Indians in 1764.* Cincinnati, 1904.

SOULE, A. M. "International Boundary of Michigan," *Mich. Hist. Colls.,* XXVI.

STARK, CALEB. *Memoir and official correspondence of General John Stark with notices of several other officers of the revolution. Also, a biography of Capt. Phinehas Stevens and of Col. Robert Rogers, with an account of his services in America during the "Seven Years' War."* Concord, 1860.

STEVENS, W. E. *The Northwest Fur Trade 1763–1800.* Urbana, 1928.
"The Organization of the British Fur Trade," *Miss. Valley Hist. Rev.,* September, 1916.
"The Fur Trade in Minnesota During the British Régime," Minnesota History Bulletin, X, no. 1.

STONE, W. L. *The Life of Joseph Brant,* 2 vols. New York, 1838.
The Life and Times of Sir William Johnson, 2 vols. Albany, 1865.

TEGGART, F. J. "The Capture of St. Joseph, Michigan, by the Spaniards in 1781," *Missouri Historical Review,* V.

THWAITES, R. G. "At the Meeting of the Trails: The Romance of a Parish Register," *Miss. Valley Hist. Assoc. Proc.,* VI.
Daniel Boone. New York, 1903.
How George Rogers Clark Won the Northwest and Other Essays in Western History. Chicago, 1904.

Transactions of the Colonial Society of Massachusetts. Boston, 1886 *et seq.*

TURNER, F. J. "The Character and Influence of the Indian Trade

in Wisconsin," *Wis. Hist. Soc. Proc., 1889.* Madison, 1889.
" The Policy of France Toward the Mississippi Valley in the
Period of Washington and Adams," *Am. Hist. Rev.,* X, no. 2.
January, 1905.
" Western State Making in the Revolutionary Era," *ibid.,* I.
VAN TYNE, C. H. *The American Revolution, 1776–1783,* vol. IX
(American Nation Series). New York and Boston, 1905.
The Causes of the War of Independence. Boston, 1922.
" Sovereignty in the American Revolution," *Am. Hist. Rev.,* X.
VOLWILER, A. T. *George Croghan and the Westward Movement,
1741–1783.* Cleveland, 1926.
WALKER, C. F. *The Northwest During the Revolution.* Madison,
1871.
WINSOR, JUSTIN. *Narrative and Critical History of America,* 8
vols. Boston and New York, 1888.
The Westward Movement. Boston and New York, 1897.
The Mississippi Basin. Boston and New York, 1895.
Wisconsin Historical Society Proceedings. Madison, 1874 *et seq.*
WOOD, E. O. *Historic Mackinac,* 2 vols. New York, 1918.
WRONG, G. M. *Washington and His Comrades in Arms,* vol. XII
(Chronicle of America Series). New Haven, 1921.
Canada and the American Revolution. New York, 1935.

BRITISH COMMANDING OFFICERS
AT DETROIT, 1760-1796[1]

1. Major Robert Rogers — 1760[2]
2. Major Donald Campbell — 1760–1763
3. Major Henry Gladwin — 1763 to August, 1764
4. Colonel John Bradstreet — 1764
5. Colonel John Campbell — 1765
6. Major Robert Bayard — 1766
7. Captain George Turnbull — 1767–1769
8. Major Thomas Bruce — June 2, 1770 to September
9. Captain James Stephenson — September, 1770 to June 8, 1772
10. Major George Etherington — 1772
11. Major Henry Bassett — 1772–1774
12. Major Richard B. Lernoult — 1774
13. Captain John Mompesson — 1775
14. Major Arent Schuyler De Peyster — 1776
15. Captain Hugh Lord — 1776
16. Captain James Stephenson — 1778, April
17. Major Richard B. Lernoult — December, 1778 to October, 1779
18. Major Arent Schuyler De Peyster — October, 1779 to June, 1784
19. Major William Ancrum — 1784
20. Lieutenant Thomas Bennett — 1786
21. Major John Wiseman — 1787
22. Major Robert Mathews — 1787
23. Major Patrick Murray — 1788
24. Major John Smith — 1790–1792
25. Colonel Richard England — 1791[3]
26. Colonel William Claus — 1792
27. Captain William Doyle — 1793
28. Colonel Richard England — March, 1793–1796.

[1] From the records available, it is impossible to determine the exact date when the commanding officers were at Detroit.

[2] Rogers took over the fort from the French in November, 1760, and expected to continue on to Michilimackinac, but was prevented by the ice in the lakes. *Ante*, p. 16.

[3] Colonel England was in command in 1791 during the temporary absence of Major Smith.

INDEX

INDEX